The Sacred in a Secular Age

The Sacred in a Secular Age

Toward Revision in the Scientific Study of Religion

Edited by

Phillip E. Hammond

SOCIETY FOR THE SCIENTIFIC STUDY OF RELIGION

UNIVERSITY OF CALIFORNIA PRESS
Berkeley   Los Angeles   London

University of California Press
Berkeley and Los Angeles, California

University of California Press, Ltd.
London, England

Copyright © 1985 by The Regents of the University of California

Library of Congress Cataloging in Publication Data

Main entry under title:

The Sacred in a secular age.

"A publication of the Society for the Scientific Study of Religion."
1. Religion—Addresses, essays, lectures.   I. Hammond, Phillip E.
II. Society for the Scientific Study of Religion.
BL50.S25   1985   306'.6   84–16470
ISBN 0–520–05342–7
ISBN 0–520–05343–5 (pbk.)

Printed in the United States of America

1 2 3 4 5 6 7 8 9

Contents

PART THREE
The Sacred in Traditional Forms

PART FOUR
Culture and the Sacred

PART FIVE
Private Life and the Sacred

PART SIX
The Sacred and the Exercise of Power

Introduction

Phillip E. Hammond

A linear image dominates Western thought about society. Even cyclical views are cast in spiral form, thus helping to maintain the notion that social life is systematically "coming from" somewhere and "going" elsewhere. Social science, born in nineteenth-century evolutionism, matured with this perspective almost exclusively, indeed contributing to it many of the master terms used in contemporary discourse about social change: *industrialization, modernization, rationalization, bureaucratization,* and *urbanization,* to name but a few. All imply one-directional processes.

In the social scientific study of religion this dominant linear image is expressed chiefly in the term *secularization,* the idea that society moves from some sacred condition to successively secular conditions in which the sacred evermore recedes. In fact, so much has the secularization thesis dominated the social scientific study of religious change that it is now conventional wisdom. Even today, scholars do not—and probably cannot—doubt the essential truth of the thesis. But increasingly they are coming to doubt its adequacy, and it is this adequacy we explore here.

Certainly, the authors of the essays of this volume assume that we live in a secular age and that somehow secularization brought it about. This assumption explains the prominent position given to the lead article by Bryan Wilson, which not only reminds us of the intellectual power of the secularization thesis but also prepares us to expect the thesis to endure the challenges it receives in all the other essays. Those challenges point up the need to specify the thesis if it is to be applied to the contemporary scene. Immediately following the Wilson essay, therefore, are stunning illustrations of this need—

1

three essays dealing with the anomalous appearance of "new" religious movements in a "secular" age.

So-called new religious movements are, however, only one—though no doubt the most colorful—example of the reemergent sacred in a secular age. The persistent, even resurgent, expression of conservative Protestantism in Europe and America is another, as is the undeniably religious element in the political situation found in Northern Ireland, Lebanon, Iran, India-Pakistan, Poland, and many places in Latin America. Religion is hardly moribund if these instances are taken seriously, but, to the degree they *are* taken seriously, they call for new thinking about the sacred. While we are therefore not yet ready to replace the secularization paradigm with some other master scheme, we are prepared to look at secularization and the sacred through new lenses. That, at least, is what the essays of this volume set out to do.

Only fifteen years ago I joined Charles Y. Glock in organizing the 20th Annual Program for the Society for the Scientific Study of Religion. Working with a theme that encouraged social scientists to "take stock" of the field, we commissioned a small group of distinguished scholars to write papers tracing the accumulative work by one or another of the founders of the scientific study of religion: Marx, James, Durkheim, Weber, Freud, Malinowski, and H. R. Niebuhr. In expanded form, these papers were then published under the title *Beyond the Classics?* (1973). Many persons, it is safe to say, were edified by those essays but, as Glock and I pointed out in the epilogue to that book, little or no evidence of accumulation appeared in them. The founders had identified the links connecting religion to culture, society, and personality, but subsequent investigators showed little in the way of systematic elaboration or development. Certainly they exhibited little skepticism toward the founders' formulations. It was as if those founders had said it all; by early in the twentieth century the social scientific study of religion had received the model bequeathed by these giants but had not gone importantly beyond it. As Glock and I explained then, little more than a decade ago, we added the question mark to the book's title as an admission that we were still in the grip of a model conceived fifty to a hundred years earlier.

That model, of course, is the secularization thesis whose adequacy we now question. What seemed then an entrenched conceptual scheme seems now to need considerable overhaul, a view only dimly perceived a mere decade ago. "All hope is not lost," Glock and I wrote, "our gloomy forecast [that a new paradigm is *not* just around the corner] could indeed be proven wrong by the events of the coming decade" (1973:415). We cited new nations, civil religion, and science as possible sources of new or renewed religious images. We mentioned Vatican Council reform, lay movements, urban sects, and "Oriental and other mystical bodies" as possible innovations on the organizational level. And we allowed that a new religious consciousness—new ways to *feel* religious—might be in the making.

Now, however, the kind of challenge that barely registered in *Beyond the Classics?* has, since publication of that book, come as an onslaught in the study of religion. From the psychology of affiliation to the sociology of complex organizations, from the study of power to the study of love, from cross-cultural investigations to the growing awareness of a world political economy, the scientific study of religion has been shaken to its roots by events of the last two decades, and published works—especially in the last ten years—reflect this turmoil. The sacred obviously is persisting, but the secularization thesis—as traditionally understood—is not sufficient to allow us to understand why.

We cannot blame the founders. A sensitive reading of them makes clear the distinction they drew between "sacred" and "religion," so that, if secularization meant the decline of religion, it did not necessarily mean as well the disappearance of the sacred. Simmel, for example, spoke of the experiences people encounter in a "certain inner mood" which

stir relations, meanings, sentiments, which of themselves are not yet religion, nor do their realities in any way conform to the religion of a differently attuned soul; but divested of this reality and forming in themselves a sphere of objectivity, they become "religion," which here means "the objectified world of faith." (1959:11)

Encounter with the sacred, or what Simmel calls "piety," is thus not necessarily religion but "religiosity in a quasi-fluid state . . ." (1959:24), that is, not yet "objectified." In a poetic passage from an otherwise opaque little book, Simmel tells us:

There exist souls whose very being and action are steeped in the characteristic gentleness, warmth and devotion of love, who yet never feel love for a particular individual. There exist evil hearts whose very thought and longing runs the whole gamut of a cruel and selfish mind, without actually crystalliz-ing into evil deeds. There live artistic natures whose functional capacity to visualize things, to experience life, and to form their impressions and feelings is of an absolute artistic quality, but who never produce a work of art. There live pious men who do not turn their piety toward any god, i.e., to that phenomenon which is the very object of piety; they are religious natures without a religion. (1959:24-25)

Lest this brief passage leave the impression that Simmel imagined a religious impulse to be somehow innate, it needs to be added that he found this impulse not intrinsic to the human organism but induced through the experience of social life. In this respect, of course, he resembles Durkheim, for whom religion is also a "social product," though perhaps seemingly an inevitable one.

But only "seemingly" is religion—as distinct from the sacred—inevitable for Durkheim also. It is our careless reading that suggests religion's inevitability; what is inevitable for this unsurpassed theorist is the division of the world into sacred and profane. What happens thereafter is by no means foreordained to become religion. Consider simply his famous definition:

A religion is a unified system of beliefs and practices relative to sacred things . . . which unite into one single moral community . . . all those who adhere to them. (1961:62)

At the very least one may ask of the sacred/profane distinction whether it (1) leads to, or is expressed in, *beliefs* and/or *practices*, and (2) if such beliefs and practices are *unified* or *systematized*, and (3) then result in *uniting* some group of people. It is fair to say that, for Durkheim, *religion* does not exist unless all those conditions are met, though of course the fundamental building block in all this—awareness of the sacred—is endemic to social life. The development of the sacred through these stages to become religion is, for Durkheim, what Simmel calls objectified faith.

The distinction quite apparent to theorists like Simmel and Durkheim, the distinction between the "sacred" and "religion," is thus one we have lost sight of. When, therefore, in a period of *religious* decline, the *sacred* seems remarkably alive, we are puzzled and unable to comprehend events surrounding us. Those events clearly reflect the sacred, but are they religious as well? The secularization thesis would declare them not fully religious, but challenges to that thesis announce them as unambiguously sacred. We forget that the sacred may be—but also may not be—surrounded by layers of social customs, institutions, and history.

This otherwise elusive nitpicking may be clarified by analogy. Nobody equates love with marriage. Love—whether a personality trait or socially induced (or, indeed, heaven-sent)—is routinely under-stood as a quality that *may* be reflected in the institution of marriage and child-production, but it may also be independent therefrom. Moreover, while marriage is ideally seen, under some cultural conditions, to combine love between two persons with sex, parenthood, economic cooperation, and social identity, the *institution* of marriage is regularly distinguished from love in the sense that persons are known to marry without love, just as love may exist in many forms outside of marriage. The fact that all known societies have marriage institutions, and the fact that love sometimes is characteristic of relationships within those institutions, do not lead us to mask the difference between love and marriage.

And yet we seem to have mistaken religion and the sacred. In any era, therefore, when religion, at least as commonly understood, is receding, vitality of the sacred may thus come as a surprise. The present era would seem to fit such a description, and we find ourselves unable to comprehend the sacred. The past accretions that transformed the sacred into religion—accretions which in many instances have been corroded by secularization—keep us from the refocusing necessary if we are to study the sacred in a secular age . . . unless we can revise our thinking about secularization.

These essays direct us toward such revision. No apology is required for the fact that this revised target is not reached here, for it is enough now to expose the inadequacies of what has been the entrenched secularization paradigm. Already mentioned in this Introduction are the challenges from the emergence of new religious movements, discussed in Part One, but great challenges come also from methodological reviews (Part Two), the study of the sacred in traditional forms (Part Three), cultural institutions (Part Four), private life (Part Five), and power (Part Six). Moreover, the discerning reader will get glimpses of a possibly unfolding new model in such essays as those by Mol (who suggests a dialectical relationship between secularization and renewal of the sacred), Stark (for whom the soil of secularization necessarily contains new sacred seeds), Wuthnow (who stresses boundary maintenance as generative of sacred distinctions), Capps (who sees the transformation of ego as still possible in a secular, narcissistic age), and Robertson (to whom a world political-economy reimposes, though on a global scale, the very conditions Durkheim argued underlie all sacred/profane dichotomies). All is not vague, in other words; progress is being made.

This volume has its origins in the deliberations of the 1981 Council Meeting of the Society for the Scientific Study of Religion. Its members asked me to explore the feasibility of a follow-up volume to *Beyond the Classics?*—a volume that would attempt, as *Beyond the Classics?* attempted, to assess the current status of our field. I was gratified to find an affirmative response to my initial inquiry to colleagues, and I was further gratified—after the Council authorized a go-ahead a year later—by the willingness of those colleagues to become authors, and then prompt deliverers, of manuscripts.

A confession is in order here, however; these collected essays do not consolidate the accomplishments of twenty years' scientific study of religion. *Beyond the Classics?* started out to do just that but then we recognized that the theories being discussed were not of the mid-twentieth century but of the late nineteenth century. It is true that by 1960 enormous technical advances gave those discussions greater sophistication: more up-to-date data and more involved conceptual schemes. But they were nonetheless addressing the same issues addressed by the founders.

This classical hold is now broken, and these essays represent the outpouring of research and theory that has followed. Findings may seem scattered, therefore, and theories fragmented, though this is only because the master schemes—the eventual replacements of the secularization model—have not yet come into focus. Obviously, the successor volume to this one is waiting to be born. And when it is, it will—to the degree we are successful here—be drawing upon the resources these essays have accumulated, if not consolidated. For from them *will* develop the clear images, incisive questions, and testable theories relating to the sacred in a secular age. These essays, in other words, direct us toward revision in the scientific study of religion.

REFERENCES

Durkheim, Emile
    1961   *The Elementary Forms of the Religious Life*. Trans. J. W. Swain. New York: Collier.
Glock, C. Y., and P. E. Hammond, eds.
    1973   *Beyond the Classics?* New York: Harper and Row.
Simmel, Georg
    1959   *Sociology of Religion*. Trans. C. Rosenthal. New York: Philosophical Library.

PART ONE

Relocating the Sacred:
Conceptual Issues

I

Secularization: The Inherited Model

Bryan Wilson

August Comte is not now much remembered, even by sociologists, whose discipline he both shaped and named. Sociologists of religion, however, have special reason to remember him, and with him his immediate precursor, Saint-Simon, since they defined the new science of society with specific reference to, and in direct contrast with, the previously existing body of social knowledge. Man, society, and the world were, hitherto, explained—in the Western tradition, but perhaps in all traditions—by reference to transcendent laws, states, or beings. As a methodology for interpreting society, sociology was, from its first enunciation, directly set over against theology. Quite explicitly, Comte indicated the contrast between theological and (social) scientific ways of knowing. Although he did not use the term, and his interests were certainly broader, Comte provided a comprehensive account—its many factual errors notwithstanding—of a process of secularization. Sociology's charter as a discipline implied from the outset that it was to be an empirical, man-centered, this-worldly, matter-of-fact explanation of human organization and development. The work of Comte's major successors, beginning from different starting points, using different terms, and within different frameworks of argument, reinforced this general orientation: Marx's emphasis on materialism; Weber's *Entzauberung;* Durkheim's pursuit of a rational ethic; Veblen's "matter-of-fact" thinking. Sociology documented a secularizing process.

The deep-laid ambiguity in sociology, and its central epistemological problem, is evident in the fact that sociology was not merely a
commentary on a process of secularization; it was also—as Comte
claimed it to be—a value-free, positivistic discipline, as objective and
neutral as the natural sciences. (Marx, too, saw his own system of
explanation as managing to transcend the riddle of the relativism
implicit in a sociology of knowledge; Marxism, although issuing from
the world view of the proletariat, would also be established as an
objective science.) Sociology began as a contradiction of theology,
rejecting theological explanations because they were conditioned by
the limited range of social experience of their proponents and by
evaluative and emotional impediments to proper cognitive understanding. There was, then, a commitment to ethically neutral and
objective procedures and, simultaneously, an explicit rejection of the
various assumptions embodied in the earlier way of interpreting the
world. Sociology was a new methodology to explain society. Understandably, its rejection of theological assumptions and assertions was
taken not merely as a transfer from one methodology and one
philosophy to another but as an onslaught against the theological,
and against the supernatural entities (beings, laws, events, places,
and actions) which religion projected as of real, determining importance in man's affairs.

The theological world view was committed not only to the proposition of a purportedly factual account of society, history, psychology,
and the future but also to the active and vigorous advocacy of that
world view and of certain epistemological and moral commitments
thought to be implicit within it. Given this confusion of fact and
value, it was thus not possible—at least at that time—for the theologically committed to see sociology merely as a change of perspective,
as an alternative set of assumptions about history and society. It was
seen as an assault on truth, as a heresy—it was seen, in short, as all
previous alternative (inevitably theological) systems of knowing had
been seen, as an evil conspiracy against the supernatural entities
which the theologian not only projected as causal agencies but
towards which he also sought to inspire universal devotion. The
theologians were caught in a system in which the world was not
merely factually known (insofar as their assumptions allowed it to be
accurately known) but in which it was also evaluatively interpreted.
In accord with their evaluative procedures, they had to categorize the
new method of knowing in terms of praise and blame; this was
their métier. Despite its formal espousal of ethical neutrality, then,
sociology was compromised by the animosity engendered among the

theologically minded by its very different explanation of society—and of religion. To the theologians, in the light of the prevailing conventional body of knowledge and "way of knowing," the radical methodological premises of sociology were incomprehensible.

The confrontation is here depicted schematically as a philosophic divergence, but historical evidence could be adduced to illustrate it, occluded as it was by the more dramatic challenge to the theocentric view of the world arising from the natural sciences. With sociology, the battle was, if at first more muted, eventually more disturbing for the supernaturalist *Weltanschauung*. The natural sciences touched only the facts of nature, and even though, in Christianity at least, these were purportedly set forth in ancient revelations couched in terms supposedly timelessly true, it was eventually easier for the entrenched intellectual establishment to abandon these so-called facts about nature than to admit the possibility of an alternative methodology for the interpretation of facts about society, man's history, and the meaning of morality.

With the decline of strong forms of theocentric or supernaturalist views of the world, the diametrically opposite approaches of these two intellectual systems have regularly been forgotten or ignored. But suspicion has remained, and it has been echoed in misunderstandings particularly on the subject of secularization. The discussion of secularization, although acknowledged in everyday terms by many clerics, is often seen as in itself an aggressive commentary on religion. Committed religionists still confuse the evaluative and the analytic; they regularly mistake "secularization"—the process occurring within the social structure—for "secularism"—the ideology of those who wish to promote the decline of religion and to hasten the process of secularization. Hence the frequent assumption that those who seek to describe a process of secularization must favour that process, and may well be advocating a Marxist organization of society. The secularization thesis, despite the hostility it provoked toward sociologists who, in some form or another, propounded it, can be set forth (and the sociological intention is to set it forth) in entirely neutral terms, as a description of a process that can be traced in the course of social development.

The inherited model of secularization has lacked formal specification. It has frequently been used in diverse ways, encompassing a very wide range of phenomena. It has been appropriately referred to as a multidimensional concept. In essence, it relates to a process of transfer of property, power, activities, and both manifest and latent functions, from institutions with a supernaturalist frame of reference to (often new) institutions operating according to empirical, rational, pragmatic criteria. That process can be demonstrated as having oc- curred extensively, if unevenly, over a long historical period, and to have done so notwithstanding the spasmodic countervailing occur- rence of resacralization in certain areas and instances of cultural re- vitalization exemplified in the emergence of charismatic leaders and prophets.

In particular, the secularization model has been taken as referring to the shift in the location of decision making in human groups from elites claiming special access to supernatural ordinances to elites legitimating their authority by reference to other bases of power. Political authority is, however, only the most conspicuous arena in which this transfer from agencies representing the supernatural has occurred. Perhaps more basic has been the transformation of work activities by the development of new economic techniques and proce- dures that are increasingly dictated by more and more rational appli- cation of scarce resources and which, in consequence, more regularly ignore or abrogate rules of sacrality. To contrast North American Indian attitudes to the soil and agriculture with those of white men, or medieval codes of moral economic behavior with those of sub- sequent times, illustrates the steady transcendence of rational methods. Consequent on changes such as these, the reward struc- tures of society change in commensurate ways, with diminished rewards and status accorded to those who manipulate supernatural "explanations" and legitimations, and increased rewards to those whose work is directed to materialistic, empirically validated produc- tivity. Human ecology and population distribution, following changes in economic technique and (to some extent) political organization, have further secularizing implications. Religion had its basis in the local social group and in the solemnization and sacralization of inter- personal relationships. New methods of social organization and economic activity permitted, and at times necessitated, a new distri- bution of wealth and of people, as the surplus productivity of the countryside facilitated consumption in cities, the growth of tertiary industry, and perhaps now—with the growth of entertainment—one might say in quaternary industry.

The increasing awareness that rules were not absolute and heaven- sent but were amenable to changing need, and that even the most sacred norms of society could be renegotiated, altered, and perhaps even superseded, challenged assumptions about the will of higher beings in favour of the more conscious purposes of man himself. The shift, which might be most dramatically documented in the area of law, led to the steady modification of those absolute decrees and transcendent social norms in which individual well-being was always sacrificed to community cohesion. The steady accumulation of empirical knowledge, the increasing application of logic, and the rational coordination of human purposes established an alternative vision and interpretation of life. Steadily, the good of man displaced what was once seen as the "will of providence" (or such other supernatural categories) and, in such areas as health, the dispositions of the supernatural were no longer regarded as adequate explanation for man's experience. Sanitation, diet, and experimental pharmacology displaced prayer, supplication, and resignation as the appropriate responses to disease and death. Man ceased to be solely at the disposition of the gods. Change in the character of knowledge implied change in the method of its transmission, and the consequent amendment of the institutions concerned with the socialization and education of the young. And, finally, the shifting awareness of man's potential—and thus his freedom—diminished the sense of the need for responsibility and, indeed, responsiveness toward superhuman agencies. Man acquired greater control of wide areas of his own experience; mankind attained a sense of self-determination, and employed new criteria of human happiness—the latter particularly in the use of leisure time.

All of the foregoing processes have been documented, in varying terms, by sociologists, whether they explicitly recognized them as aspects of secularization or not. Most conspicuously in Weber's documentation of the processes of rationalization, the political and economic changes are discussed, while Marx sets forth the economic causes of changes in social stratification. Toennies's analysis of basic transformations in social organization, following from changing distributive and ecological patterns of human population, has strong implications for man's conception of the sacred. Durkheim documented the difference between retributive and restitutive justice, even though he only gradually perceived the implications for the character of moral norms, and even though the consequential shift in the basis of social cohesion was more radical than he recognized. Comte had already indicated the methodology of the natural sciences as the model for a new methodology in interpreting society. Hobhouse, among others, saw the possibilities for the growth of self-determining societies, and Freud provided a mode of analysis which related man's irrational psychology to his supernaturalist predispositions and which promised new conceptions of moral judgment and individual responsibility.

The shift from primary preoccupation with the superempirical to the empirical; from transcendent entities to naturalism; from other-worldly goals to this-worldly possibilities; from an orientation to the past as a determining power in life to increasing preoccupation with a planned and determined future; from speculative and "revealed" knowledge to practical concerns, and from dogmas to falsifiable propositions; from the acceptance of the incidental, spasmodic, random, and charismatic manifestations of the divine to the systematic, structured, planned, and routinized management of the human—all of these are implicit in the model of secularization which, in various strands, constitute the inheritance not only of the sociology of religion but of sociology per se.

This is not to say that the concept of secularization embraces all aspects of social change, of course, but rather to say that in the long-run course of such change, secularization has been a significant element. Since sacrality powerfully influenced so many of man's concerns in traditional society, the shift from the traditional to the innovatory affects conceptions of the sacred in all these departments. Nor is this to say that the sacred always gives way in equal measure as change occurs. The model does not specify the pace or the details of each aspect of the process. In institutions that remain locally organized—for example in the family, which is highly localized even in the more attenuated, more volatile, and increasingly mobile form that it has acquired—conceptions of the sacred may endure more easily than in politics. Similarly, education, which resists "massification," may for some time persist as a better vehicle for supernaturalism than, say, the economy. Nor does the model predicate the disappearance of religiosity, nor even of organized religion; it merely indicates the decline in the significance of religion in the operation of the social system, its diminished significance in social consciousness, and its reduced command over the resources (time, energy, skill, intellect, imagination, and accumulated wealth) of mankind.

An alternative way of formulating the implications of the secularizing process to the one already given is to indicate the loss of functionality of religion, in the process of the structural differentiation of society. There is no need here to set forth in these, somewhat different, terms the points already made with respect to various social institutions. All that need be said is that—whereas legitimate authority once depended on religious sanctions; whereas social control once relied heavily on religiously defined rewards and punishments; whereas social policies, conspicuously including warfare, at one time needed supernatural endorsement, or at least the endorsement of those who were recognized as the agents of the supernatural; and whereas revealed faith once specified the boundaries of true learning—now, all of these functions have been superseded. Authority is now established by constitutions. Social control is increasingly a matter for law rather than for a consensual moral code, and law becomes increasingly technical and decreasingly moral (even theologians now draw a sharp line between sin and crime), while effective sanctions are physical and fiscal rather than threats or blandishments about the afterlife. Social policies increasingly require the approval of an electorate, which endorses a manifesto. Revelation is a distrusted source of knowledge, and the methodology of modern learning puts a premium on doubt rather than on faith, on critical scepticism rather than on unquestioning belief. The erstwhile functions of religion have been superseded, and this constitutes a process of the secularization of society. Religion has lost its presidency over other institutions.

It is sometimes argued—and particularly so by Christian apologists—that this diminution of the role of religion is an evidence not of secularization but of religion's having been purged of extraneous social involvements which were, at best, a distraction from religion's true purpose and, at worst, a corruption of the spirit by the world. This argument, however, is in itself inconsequential for the secularization thesis. It is not the sociologist's concern to decide whether religion is purer now, in a secularized world where it has diminished power, than it was in a sacralized world, where it (or its agents) exerted considerable influence. It suffices to say that the influence of religion has declined. The argument is also heavily predicated on the specifically Christian case; its exponents, when they say "religion," clearly allude only to "Christianity," and their spectrum for secularization in all probability extends no further back than, perhaps, the age of faith of Innocent III. They forget that religion, in the wide sense, was more pervasive in society before it acquired its roles in the increasingly differentiated political, juridical, economical, educational, and status systems of the Middle Ages, and that this pervasive influence was "what religion was for"—this was its utility for man, and the reason for which he subscribed to it, long before its incorporation into the rules, roles, and procedures of medieval society.

It would follow from such an argument that, for those who espouse it, secularization is seen as in itself a not undesirable phenomenon—a purification agency for religion. That case could be made out, of course, only after a precise specification has been given of what a religion "should be like," and that is not a sociological concern. The process of secularization, however, may be seen as extending over the very long term—evident, according to Max Weber, particularly in Judaism in its elimination of the diverse, localized, immanentist magical cults of Palestine. To the extent that they disciplined, unified, and systematized conceptions of the supernatural, other major religions were also agencies of secularization, reducing, regulating, and circumscribing the operation of the sacred. But none of them—even the rigorous monotheism of Islam notwithstanding—has been so radically effective in this process as Judaism and Christianity (especially in its Protestant form), and some of them have not even been exclusivistic, but have tolerated, accommodated, or incorporated alien indigenous manifestations of magic and local religious cults.

It is not, however, to be assumed that the secularization thesis is merely a commentary specifically on Christian history. The model is intended to have general validity. Were it to be stated in sufficiently abstract terms, there would be no reason why it should not be applied in any context. In practice, because we are dealing with "historical individuals" on a grand scale, because of the uneven pace of economic and social development of different cultures, and because of the fullest availability of documentation in the Western case, secularization is sometimes discussed as if it were specific to Christianity. There is reason for this, since there are distinct differences among religions. Certain characteristics, embraced more fully or explicitly in some traditions than in others, directly favor the process of secularization. Exclusivity has already been mentioned. Commitment to intellectual coherence and formal logic—both agencies of secularization—are also more markedly evident in the case of Christianity than in other world religions. Christianity has influenced social development, but it has also been receptive to change in economy and polity that have made Christianity an obvious religious locus of secularizing dispositions. As the degree of technical, economic, and political changes occurring in Western societies is experienced elsewhere and comes to characterize other cultures, we can expect to see a recession of the influence of religion there, even though indigenous religious traditions may themselves have been less directly responsible for encouraging or accommodating social change than Christianity has been. The course of social change generally has been toward the diminution of religious influence on social organization. These trends occurred earlier, more extensively, and more pervasively, in the West than elsewhere and were first adumbrated within existing religious traditions among dominant intellectual elites who, historically, were necessarily religious or religiously informed elites. The source of change must now differ from one context to another because of the multiplicity and increased intensity of influences operative in societies in Asia, Africa, Latin America, and Oceania, including, specifically, influences from the West.

It may also be asked whether, given the very long term over which the inherited model posits the process of secularization as taking place, there may not also have been occasions, or even epochs, of "resacralization," which would account for the slowness of the process of secularization. Certainly, it is an open question whether secularization is reversible. It would be difficult to demonstrate that any such reversals have ever occurred. Mere processes of religious change, however, such as occurred as Christianity was transplanted throughout Europe, are not, in a sociological view, a resacralization; indeed, given the exclusivity that Christianity embraced from its origins, and the rationalizing disposition that Christianity eventually acquired, this diffusion of Christian faith may be said to have been the beginning of a secularization process that disciplined and partially absorbed and partially evacuated the religiosity of indigenous populations, eventually virtually eradicating its earlier manifestations. The process, nearly complete in Europe, continues, perhaps at a different pace, in Latin America and the Christianized parts of Africa.

At a less than societal level, periodic reform and revivalism might also appear to be reversals of the process of secularization. Closer examination of such relatively sudden upsurges in religious activity, however, are interpreted according to the secularization thesis as revealing the long-term effect of revitalization movements—not so much a restoration of the past as an accommodation of the pressing claims of the present. The Reformation is readily interpreted as a movement of secularization reducing the institutional power of religion and circumscribing the sacerdotalism and sacramentalism of the past. Processes of laicization accompanied subsequent revivalism, from Methodism to Pentecostalism, and even though the intensified religious commitment amounted to a resocialization of hitherto unaccommodated social groups, inducing work commitment and reinforcing social control, they nonetheless did not bring concepts of the sacred back to a central place in the social system. After a time, their effects weakened, the religiosity waned, even when new standards of duty and decency were disseminated. Once again, the magical and the emotional elements receded, and what was left—for as long as it lasted—was an ethical deposit. These inchoate moral dispositions, which were once religiously charged, were, for the remainder of their existence, effectively secularized. The new movements came to impose their own discipline which, in the Christian case, was eventually valuable as a social attribute facilitating the operation of a social system that functions without recourse to concepts of the supernatural.

The secularization process is recognized in the inherited model as being slow because religious dispositions are deep-laid in man's essential irrationality, which resists the rationalization of the external social order. The fears, hopes, fantasies, the search for meaning and wish fulfillment, and the encapsulation of these tendencies in folklore and local custom have provided religion with source materials. Local groups, and their ethnic, national, and class extensions, have had their identities sanctified and have acquired transcendent legitimation from religious formulations. At least for some, purpose, meaning, and motivation continue today to be enhanced by religious legitimations, and to be reinforced by religious supplication. Traditionally, religion supplied total and final explanations, not so much for intellectual and technical as for emotional and moral problems. It is the increasing dominance of the intellectual, scientific, technical, and practical over the emotional and the moral which is the basic premise of the inherited model of secularization. The secularization thesis acknowledges the unevenness of the decline in the significance of religion, and recognizes that this decline presents problems for the socializing and motivating of men, and the diffusion of dispositions conducive to public order.

Religious institutions are also slow to succumb entirely to the rationalizing tendencies of contemporary social systems, even though there is a process of internal secularization in religious institutions. These institutions fulfill other functions, some of which are quite specific to particular societies in particular historical periods, besides their functions in maintaining conceptions of the supernatural and stimulating the service and worship of it, and these other functions facilitate their endurance. The rhetoric (sometimes including liturgies) of past religion persists in these institutions, even though it is not always entertained with due intellectual seriousness. Even in the very attenuated religiosity of contemporary "liberal" churches, there is thus still reference to ultimate values, and still the canvas of religiously inspired moral dispositions and emotional orientations. Religion still facilitates communal expression, particularly when there is moral crisis, and no other agency claims the transcendent legitimacy which religious institutions still claim. More regularly, religion still provides occasions and opportunities for the private expression of emotions and aspirations, providing a language in terms of which individuals may choose to interpret their human experience. The secularization of the social system does not at once displace these attributes of religiosity; the native dispositions of man himself resist, in various aspects of experience, the rationalization that increasingly characterizes social systems.

Basically, the inherited model of secularization is concerned with the operation of the social system. It is the *system* that becomes secularized. Conceptions of the supernatural may not disappear, either as rhetorical public expressions or as private predilections, but they cease to be the determinants of social action. The system no longer functions, even notionally, to fulfill the will of God. Neither institutions nor individuals operate primarily to attain supernatural ends. As Comte predicted, and in ways that Max Weber indicated, rational planning and the deployment of new technology invoke as their justification the goal of human well-being, not the greater glory of God. Human consciousness is itself depicted as changing in response to the increasingly rational patterns of social organization and the imposition on man of increasingly abstract patterns of role playing. Men learn to regulate their behavior to conform to the rational premises built into the social order; action must be calculated, systematic, regulated, and routinized. In their private lives, men do not abandon their evaluative, emotional dispositions, and they may continue to resort to the supernatural for private gratification, but such dispositions are allowed to affect the public sphere to only a limited and decreasing extent. In his public roles, irrational man even contributes to the increasingly rational character of external order in an environment that is increasingly man-made. The secularization thesis implies the privatization of religion; its continuing operation in the public domain becomes confined to a lingering rhetorical invocation in support of conventional morality and human decency and dignity—as a cry of despair in the face of moral panic.

Various aspects of religious behavior may, at least for some time, remain independent of the major processes of secularization of the social system. Thus, although religious observance ceases to be obligatory (itself an evidence of the increasing secularity of society), it continues as a much commended voluntaristic exercise. Even so, churchgoing and other patterns of religious observance are activities that carry many extrareligious connotations: they express cultural conservatism, conventionality, attachment to custom, and claims to social status, according to the specific historical and psychological features of each society. Even apparent manifestations of religiosity are, then, not always what they seem. And despite some persistence of religious observance, there are intrinsic changes in religious ideology and procedures, mostly in a secularizing direction. The inherited model of secularization does not predict the eventual total eclipse of all religion, however. In this private sphere, religion often continues, and even acquires new forms of expression, many of them much less related to other aspects of culture than were the religions of the past. (This lack of relation is also an evidence of the inconsequentiality of religion for the social system.) Yet, the very rationalization of society's operation and its dessicating effect on everyday life may provide their own inducement for individuals privately to take up the vestiges of ancient myths and arcane lore and ceremonies, in the search for authentic fantasy, power, possibilities of manipulation, and alternative sources of private gratification. In this sense, religion remains an alternative culture, observed as unthreatening to the modern social system, in much the same way that entertainment is seen as unthreatening. It offers another world to explore as an escape from the rigors of technological order and the ennui that is the incidental by-product of an increasingly programmed world.

II

Utopian Communities: Theoretical Issues

William Sims Bainbridge

The proliferation of utopian communal groups arising out of the 1960s raises once again the question of the role religion might play in the creation and survival of such groups. A common view, although not one held by me, is that the society at large is becoming progressively more secular. If so, how is one to understand those contemporary intentional communities that are based in strong religious faith? And what are the prospects for success of utopian experiments that ignore religion in favor of secular socialist doctrines? If religion is essential for the survival of voluntary communism, then the theory that secularism is slowly vanquishing religion would predict the death of utopia as well as the decline of the churches. If religion strengthens utopian experiments, however, and the secularization thesis is incorrect, then the future will see many long-lived new religious communes (Bainbridge and Stark 1979; Stark and Bainbridge 1980).

From time immemorial, religious millenarian movements have believed that only divine intervention could create an ideal communal society in which brotherhood and equality would replace selfishness and stratification as the principles of organization. Many of the most successful utopian communes established in America possessed strong religious ideologies, and, to their members, community was a gift from God. Over a century and a half ago, two spokesmen for the Shakers wrote, "It is certain that nothing short of Divine Wisdom could ever have devised a system of equalization, so just and equitable, and yet so contrary to the partial, aspiring and selfish nature of man" (Green and Wells 1823:62).

Social scientists might deny the necessity of actual divine guidance, but many are convinced that strong, shared religious faith is especially favorable to success of communal experiments. Speaking both as a serious sociologist and as the founder of Oneida, John Humphrey Noyes wrote, "Judging from all our experience and observation, we should say that the two most essential requisites for the formation of successful Communities, are *religious principle* and *previous acquaintance* of the members" (Noyes 1870:57). Charles Nordhoff noted that the well-established communes he visited in the 1870s "have as their bond of union some form of religious belief," but he was not prepared to accept the view "that a commune can not exist long without some fanatical religious thought as its cementing force." He thus amended the proposition to state, "a commune to exist harmoniously, must be composed of persons who are of one mind upon some question which to them shall appear so important as to take the place of a religion, if it is not essentially religious; though it need not be fanatically held" (Nordhoff 1875:387).

Religion transcends the mundane concerns of ordinary life and thus supports the transcendent goals of utopianism, offering both general and specific compensators in promise of a sublime future. It can thus support self-sacrifice and altruism essential to communal society. The hope it offers can preserve members' commitment during rough times that might bring a secular experimental community to ruin. Furthermore, religion may regulate community leadership, placing a higher power over the potential tyranny of the founder or governing board. Parsons (1964:342) called religion one of the *evolutionary universals* required by every successful society to embody regulatory cultural traditions, and utopias by definition seek to be autonomous societies. Of course, one may impose communism by force with a police state, but religion may achieve as much by encouraging voluntary submission to a higher ideal. Not only are there many theoretical grounds for believing that religion is nearly essential for voluntary communism but empirical research appears to support the proposition as well (e.g., Stephan and Stephan 1973).

Unfortunately, the scientific status of this theory is much more uncertain than sociologists of religion generally assume, and several theoretical and methodological problems plague the best-known research studies. This essay will consider the key methodological issues, many of which reflect problems in theory which are too often neglected. The root difficulty proves to be of great subtlety yet vast importance. Social scientists have not yet established a firm conceptual basis for deciding what it means for a macrosocial entity to exist. We do not know what we are saying when we assert that a particular society exists—whether as a utopian community or as an ordinary social unit. As a corollary, we are uncertain how to determine when a macrosocial unit comes into existence, changes from one type of being to another, or goes out of existence. All these uncertainties undercut the value of quantitative research in which the unit of analysis is the utopian community.

There is always a need for good qualitative studies of particular communal experiments, whether histories (Carden 1969; Barthel 1984) or ethnographies (Zablocki 1971; Bainbridge 1978). But social scientists, as authors of such books, may not be superior to journalists (Nordhoff 1875; Wolfe 1968; Houriet 1971) or to members of the communes themselves (Noyes 1937; Kinkade 1973; Knight 1977). Occasional qualitative studies of utopian thought are also in order (Manuel and Manuel 1979), and sometimes it is even possible to use quantitative techniques to chart the structure of utopian ideologies (Rokeach et al. 1970; Bainbridge 1982*b*).

The main use of qualitative research on intentional communities, and of most quantitative research on utopian ideologies is, however, to suggest interesting images and ideas to the reader. Such literature is seldom capable of testing behavioral hypotheses, but it can propose them and render their possible human consequences vivid through illustrative detail. Also, it may give aesthetic pleasure and stimulate a range of emotional reactions. These are the functions served by all great literature, fiction as well as social history. Qualitative studies may therefore rank not among modern works of social science but among the utopian novels that continue to be published at a great rate (e.g., Skinner 1948; Heinlein 1961, 1966; Hogan 1982).

The possibility of using the community as the unit of analysis for quantitative research was most forcefully demonstrated by Rosabeth Kanter's (1972) study of thirty nineteenth-century American utopian experiments. This extremely ambitious and influential project sought to test six parallel hypotheses about the factors that promote communal success. The six concerned "commitment mechanisms," that is, sets of norms and values which the founders of an intentional community might establish as its principles, and which various traditions in social theory say would tend to strengthen the bond holding the individual member to the community and subjugating his private interest to the public good. Each of the six commitment mechanisms was operationalized through a number of indicators. For example, the commitment mechanism of *investment* was measured by such facts as whether nonresident members were permitted, whether newcomers had to sign their property over to the commune upon admission, and whether defectors had their property returned to them. To the extent that a community had such norms, it was said to make use of the investment commitment mechanism, and systematic search through the historical records permitted Kanter to compare the successful communes with the unsuccessful ones in this respect. Success was simply operationalized as longevity, a commune being counted as successful if it lasted twenty-five years or more.

The commitment mechanism of *transcendence* was presented in religious terms, but Kanter downplayed religion in her theoretical analysis. Although admitting that "all of the nine successful communities that I studied began with some kind of religious base," she countered that "this was also true of a large number of the unsuccessful communities" (Kanter 1972:136). Perhaps Kanter de-emphasized religion because a main purpose of her study was to determine how one could design successful modern utopias, and she and her commune-building associates personally disliked the demands of faith, ritual, and asceticism which a religion would place on them. The fact is that religion was associated with longevity even among Kanter's twenty-one "unsuccessful" cases. According to her own figures, the main lifetime of the nine successful religious communes was 74.3 years. Although the six unsuccessful religious communities lasted on average only 7.3 years, this was substantially longer than the 4.7-year mean life of the fifteen secular communities.

In a study of greater breadth but less depth, Karen Stephan and G. Edward Stephan (1973) compared the life spans of 143 American communes founded between 1776 and 1900, 71 of them religious. Although only 17 percent of the secular examples lasted ten years, fully 63 percent of the religious ones achieved this level of success. No secular commune reached its fortieth birthday, but 25 (35 percent) of the religious communities were still going after four decades. Although religion alone could not ensure success, apparently a commune had to be religious if it wanted to last for any significant period of time. Secular humanist communal experiments, lacking religious commitment, should thus be doomed to failure.

But both of these research projects were based on the assumption that communes actually exist as macrosocial entities, with definite properties such as life span, which can be measured. Although this seems a natural extension of traditional sociological thought (cf. Durkheim 1915), it is highly questionable. An alternate social-scientific approach, called *methodological individualism*, holds that the ultimate constituents of the social world are individual persons. In this view, all large-scale social phenomena can be reduced to the consequences of individual behavior, and attempts to create or discover social facts that transcend the individual are at best precarious and at worst fallacious.

Writing from this perspective, George Homans has criticized the sociological habit of speaking of societies as if they were definite, living creatures like human beings: "Beyond certain narrow limits of internal change a mouse body will simply die: it certainly cannot change into a hippopotamus. It is surprisingly hard to specify what constitutes the death of a society: the Assyrian empire is gone, but there are people, I hear, that still call themselves Assyrians. The organic analogy fails all along the line" (Homans 1967:88). Kanter implicity acknowledged this problem when she decided not to include Icaria among her thirty cases because she could not decide what its life span had been. One might guess the commune existed from the Icarians' departure from France in 1848, or their arrival at the abandoned Mormon buildings at Nauvoo in 1850, to their leader's death in 1856. But a branch of the movement carried on the communal experiment in Iowa until 1878. Since Icaria was a secular utopia, the difficulty of deciding its life span omits an important potential counterexample.

The ambiguity of birth and death of communes is illustrated by several of the thirteen contemporary utopias studied by Hugh Gardner (1978) who used Kanter's methods. One of the "communes" began as a pair of nuclear families who decided to pool their resources under the name Guild of Colorado, and Gardner could not decide whether it should be counted as dead or alive when it was reduced to only one couple and their children. A much more famous instance of ambiguity was Drop City, established in Colorado in 1965 according to radical anarchist principles. The population was extremely fluid, and the idealistic original inhabitants were long gone when, in 1973, they succeeded in selling the property out from under the last set of wanderers who had dropped in to live there for a while. But in 1968, eight of the original Drop City founders established Libre, with somewhat higher standards for admission. Although the land and buildings at Libre were owned by the group as a corporation, there was little sharing of resources, and the place appears little different from many another residential subdivision or artists' colony. Did Drop City die when the founders abandoned it or when the land was sold? Or is Libre a continuation of Drop City merely moved to a new site?

Three of Gardner's cases were religious: The Lama Foundation, Ananda Cooperative Village, and Maharaj Ashram. The first two of these met Gardner's criterion of success, lasting through 1973, but the last was pronounced dead in 1971. Thus the success rate for the religious communes was 67 percent, compared with 33 percent for the nine secular ones. Of course, the number of cases is so small that this apparent superiority of religion means nothing. Maharaj Ashram's life span cannot really be determined. It was a branch of Yogi Bhajan's 3HO (Healthy-Happy-Holy) movement, established when a young man bought twelve acres of land intending to create his own commune. When he sold the land again two years later, most members stayed in 3HO, merely moving to a new location. Did the community move with them or die with the landowner's private dream?

Several of Kanter's nineteenth-century communes also are of uncertain life span. For example, she says the Oberlin commune died in 1841, yet the college it founded has preserved strong communal features right up to the present day. This confusion becomes especially important when we realize that the list of communities from which she selected her thirty was hardly a complete tally. To be noticed by historians, a religious commune had to be fairly successful, although great publicity was often given to even the mere possibility that some new secular socialist community might be founded. Even the most ephemeral Owenist or Fourierist utopia was well advertised by the cultural movement that inspired it. But many a small communal sect may have flared briefly in the American hinterland without catching the eye of a scholar.

Kanter's practice of dating the birth of a commune from its formal establishment on American soil gives an extremely unfair advantage to religious communities. Five of her nine successful experiments were German-immigrant colonies. The Inspirationists of Amana began assembling in 1825, after more than a century of building congregations, and thus were already well established when their vanguard sailed to America in 1842. The Harmonists of Economy began to congregate in Wüertemberg in 1787, came to the United States in 1805, and planted their colony in its final location in 1825. The Separatists of Zoar also first assembled in Wüertemberg a generation before their arrival in America in 1817. Although the Germans at Aurora-Bethel did not come together until already in the United States, many of them were defected Harmonists who had some right to claim Aurora-Bethel was really the Harmony they wished to build.

Neglect of these theoretical-methodological problems is surprising because Noyes gave such emphasis to preexisting social bonds among members as a factor in success. If one thinks long on the issue, one might decide that the German religious groups were not "real utopias" founded according to an experimental plan, but rather natural social communities for which random cultural drift under the influence of sectarian religion happened to result in a communal phase. Neither the Inspirationists nor the Separatists intended to create communes, but fell into this economic arrangement because of the difficulties of the colonization enterprise. Thousands of boatloads of Germans and other Europeans voyaged to the United States as intact communities. One would imagine that these numerous transplanted villages varied normally along the dimensions of degree of economic sharing and intensity of religious sectarianism. The immigrant "utopias" thus might be reconceived as the few cases bound to fall in the tails of both distributions simultaneously. Or perhaps their religiosity was nothing more than a mere marker of cultural traditionalism rendered powerful by their social cohesion. They have no special claim to the status of "intentional community," since many an ordinary American town was the intended product of idealist visions.

The fact is that the standard list of American communes grew haphazardly, increasing every time any serious writer proposed a case, and never being purged of even the most controversial examples. I have serious doubts about the twin villages of Aurora and Bethel, despite the sweeping claims of utopianism asserted by their founder. Some residents of these villages denied being members, and often sections of "communal" land were registered in the names of individuals. If Harmony was an attempt to create an ideal society, why was it celibate and so reluctant to award formal membership even to a large portion of those who came to live within its community? If a society makes no provision for its own survival, it can hardly be an example to the world of how humans should live. The original manuscript enumeration schedules, filled out by County Assistant Marshal William Kerr when he visited Harmony to count heads for the 1870 U.S. census, lists the names of 225 residents, only 75 (33 percent) of whom are described as "members" of the society. Eighteen people, including a wealthy retired couple and the railroad agent's family, have no connection to the society, and the remaining 132 (59 percent) of the town's citizens are either "working for the society" or "bound to the society."

The longest-lived of the nineteenth-century religious communities was that of the Shakers, yet there is serious question whether it should be included in the list at all. A millenarian group expecting the end of the world, its members did not set out to create enduring communities according to any plan. Although they gradually developed various rhetorics to explain what they were doing, and why their society was superior to ordinary secular society, only selective reading of the historical record can make them out to be utopians. If one has to typify the Shakers, one could justly say they were a Protestant monastic order providing refuge and otherworldly compensation almost identical to that afforded by Catholic monastic orders. Far from attracting recruits seeking an ideal, communist style of life, the Shakers in their best time absorbed persons and families so aroused by one or another of the great American religious awakenings that they wished to turn away from the world. At other times, the Shakers were a refuge for persons suffering family dislocation and poverty in an age when the secular alternative would have been the poorhouse. Analysis of the census records for all twenty-one Shaker communities in 1850 and 1860 reveals that fully 68 percent of the 1,636 new "recruits" were children, while a substantial minority of the adult newcomers were single parents.

Kanter includes one Catholic group among her nine successful communes, St. Nazianz in Wisconsin, which identified itself to census takers variously as "Christian Brothers," a "Catholic Association," a "nunnery," and a "monastery." Undoubtedly, St. Nazianz was not a run-of-the-mill Catholic order, but one wonders with what right we count the Protestant monasteries/nunneries of the Shakers and ignore the numerous ordinary Catholic establishments. Della Fave and Hillery (1980) have shown that it is quite feasible to study status equality in a Trappist monastery, although one might deny that monastic orders are true experimental intentional communities designed as utopian models for the society of the future. If so, however, we should then have to drop the Shakers from our list, along with the German immigrants (including St. Nazianz). This leaves Kanter with only three successful communities: Snowhill, Jerusalem, and Oneida.

Certainly there is every reason to count Oneida as a real utopian community. It experimented not only with communism but also with a form of group marriage as an alternative to the conventional family. How long it lasted is open to question, since it began organizing a few years before moving to Oneida and took several years to unravel completely, but Kanter's estimate of thirty-three years is a reasonable minimum. For present purposes, however, Oneida presents some problems of classification. If we merely want to distinguish communities with a strong religious base from those lacking one, then it was religious. But if our two categories are *religious* and *modern-socialist*, then it qualifies as both or either. If our unit of analysis is the commune, then a single indisputable case offers nothing for quantitative analysis.

One might want to count Oneida not as one case but as two, noting that a branch colony in Wallingford, Connecticut, lasted thirty years, but both were run by the same leader who frequently traveled back and forth. If Oneida-Wallingford is best considered a single case, what about Aurora and Bethel, with two thousand miles between them and separate administrative structures? While Kanter counts each of these examples as a single case, Stephan and Stephan count Aurora-Bethel as two and get three cases out of Oneida by adding the original experiment in Putney, Vermont. And where Kanter counts the Shakers as a single case, the Stephans tally twenty-one Shaker settlements. Both studies consider each Owenist and Fourierist commune as a separate case, these two movements accounting for seven of Kanter's unsuccessful twenty-one communities.

The above litany of problems and ambiguities might provoke either of two opposite reactions in the reader. Some may want to forge bravely forward along the line projected by Kanter, hoping that the conceptual and methodological problems are not devastating and that (somehow) the truth will come out in the wash. Others will see little prospect for solid quantitative research in this area, given the horrendous difficulties. But a third alternative, both optimistic and realistic, presents itself. We can search for ways to operationalize our theories so that the commune is no longer the unit of analysis but instead count less ambiguous entities, such as individual human beings.

This is the approach taken by Benjamin Zablocki (1980), in his quantitative study of 120 contemporary communes. Since all were in existence during Zablocki's research, he was able to obtain questionnaires from hundreds of individual members, create membership censuses, and even observe recruitment and defection through follow-up surveys. In an interesting parallel analysis he not only looked at the factors that appeared to favor longevity of communes but also examined how these same factors influenced individual commitment. He made a serious if imperfect attempt to sample the entire nation's population of communes, and avoided some of the problems listed above by focusing on cases that were presumed to be fresh experiments, rather than on imported immigrant communities.

Zablocki (1980:151) reports that religious communes did show greater capacity to survive than secular ones, but his quantitative analysis is far from conclusive. He realized that serious problems might be caused by selection effects, so he focused on the "zero-year" cohort of twenty-nine communes that had been located right at the moment of birth (Zablocki 1980:148). Of the twenty-nine, eight were religious and twenty-one secular. Two of the communities were lost track of over the four years, and recalculation of the points on Zablocki's graph of longevity (1980:151) convinces me that both of them were religious. His analysis notes that "for the first two years of communal life, religious communes disintegrate at an even faster rate than secular communes" (1980:150) but, after that, the religious appear more stable. Stephan and Stephan noticed no such crossover effect in the first four years of nineteenth-century communes (Stephan and Stephan 1973:94), and Zablocki's percentage differences are miniscule. It appears that two out of six religious communities (33 percent) and five out of twenty-one secular communities (24 percent) survived four years. But if one more religious, or two fewer secular, communes had died, the superiority of religion would have vanished. Furthermore, it seems likely that the two lost communes that died were really religious ones, reducing the survival rate for their type to 25 percent. Thus Zablocki's relatively careful modern study does not support the traditional theory at all.

Much of Zablocki's book is a methodologically individualist analysis of opinion data, sociograms, and facts about the fates of individual persons. But a pair of provocative logarithmic graphs shows the incidence and prevalence of communitarian experiments from 1790 to 1980 (Zablocki 1980:32,34). It seems that communism has expanded greatly with the advance of secularism. Apparently there were 40 or 50 communes in 1850 but over 10,000 in 1980. One might wish he had corrected for population growth, giving rates per million of about 2 and 44. If we estimate rates of commune membership per million, using average commune sizes suggested by Zablocki (1980:43), we get something like 150 for 1850 and 1,100 for 1980, a much narrower difference (1 to 7) than that implied by absolute numbers of communes (1 to 220). Translating Zablocki's counts into rates, we find the number of communes per million population was about 3 in 1800, 2 in 1850, 0.75 in 1900, and 0.25 in 1950—hardly an increasing trend. The great leap which accounts for the present large number of communes came in the 1960s.

But is not this comparing apples with oranges? Or, considering how modest most contemporary communes are compared with the classical experiments, grapes with grapefruit? Some modern "anarchist" communes are little more than hippie crash pads, and should be compared, in the words of Rodney Stark, with the hobo jungles of the past, not with the intentional communities. Today, small groups of roommates may find some special honor in calling themselves "utopias." Can we really compare such casual associations with the heavy-investment agricultural colonies of the nineteenth century? Some modern communes owe their communism merely to the fact that public welfare supports the members equally. And, of course, the lists of communes for all years are highly incomplete, the error varying in unknown ways over the decades.

Again, the question of what constitutes a macrosocial unit intrudes. In his highly accurate 1874 census of the Shaker communities, Nordhoff (1875:256) lists eighteen societies, but these are subdivided into fifty-eight families averaging forty-two members each. Which is the unit, the society or the family? Nordhoff (1875:117) said, "each 'family' is practically, and for all pecuniary ends, a distinct commune," but in the Pleasant Hill colony, three of the five families had their property in common (Nordhoff 1875:211). Families had their own territories and living facilities within the societies. Sometimes they differed to some extent even in doctrine, as when the North family at Mount Lebanon practiced vegetarianism, while the others did not (White and Taylor 1905:216). For my research in the old census records (Bainbridge 1982a), I found it convenient to treat as separate each Shaker establishment officially listed as being in a different town. Thus the Poland Hill "Gathering Family" was studied separately from the Sabbathday Lake community, a mile distant, to which the Shakers felt it belonged.

There might be several ways of quantifying degree of separation between subunits of a large communal movement, following, for example, the standard techniques for charting the sociometric structure of networks of individuals (Homans 1950:64–74). In my recent work using the nineteenth-century census manuscripts, I have tracked all 3,842 Shakers of 1850 to see how many remained in 1860. Although fully 1,866 appeared again in the 1860 records, only 81 had switched colonies. This transfer rate of only 4.3 percent represents a high degree of separation. The total number of Shakers who remained from the 1850 populations of Poland and Sabbathday Lake was 43, while just 5 persons switched between them, a transfer rate of 11.6 percent, indicating a degree of isolation that could be compared with those between other pairs of colonies. I am sure that the surviving records of several nineteenth-century communities could provide many theoretically relevant measures in which the unit of analysis was the individual person or behavior, and official documents like the old censuses permit calculation of such important indicators of success as rates of defection. But the fact that the social scientist cannot collect entirely new data limits the value of historical cases for testing major theories.

An important field for contemporary research is the communal experiments of Israel. Recently, Aryei Fishman (1982, 1983*b*, 1983*c*) published a number of historical and theoretical studies of the role of religion in creating and sustaining the kibbutz. In his most recent article (1983*a*) he compares the success of thirteen religious communal farms with eighty-three secular ones. All ninety-six are successful in the sense of surviving until the present day, but the religious communities appear to have an economic advantage in terms of per capita income, savings, and net worth. The existence of religious communes, established simultaneously with secular ones in a modern nation, affords a marvelous opportunity for future sociological research, in which all kinds of data can be collected, following the canons of good scientific methodology rather than the caprices of historical preservation.

This essay has underscored the serious theoretical and methodological problems that vitiate much of the previous research relevant to the question of whether religion contributes significantly to the success of utopian, communal experiments. Of course, some would say that utopia is impossible, so that no factor, however innately potent, could give life to such chimeras. And others, committed to analysis solely at the level of entire communities, might despair of ever achieving adequate rigor in quantitative research. But with care in methodology, many problems may be overcome (Ember 1971). Opportunities clearly exist for analysis at the level of individual persons and actions, and an eclectic combination of approaches can provide greater validity than any one taken alone.

Even in research that uses the individuals as the ultimate unit of analysis it is possible to chart the shape and flow of larger social forces. Sociometric study of interaction networks is quite feasible in modern communes, as Zablocki has shown, and we can always hope that innovative use of historical data may permit this kind of analysis, bridging the gap between person and group for old communities as well. Rates, such as comparative defection statistics for various communities or proportions of the general population participating in social experiments, aggregate individual-level data into group data. Perhaps the most important future quantification work will be the development of reliable, valid measures of utopianism itself, permitting us to state in a "utopianism quotient" the extent to which a group, person, or behavior should be regarded as transcending the ordinary rules of life to establish a new ideal.

The question of the role of religion in promoting the perfect society remains open. The limitations of existing research do not permit us to conclude the issue either way. Of course, if no terrestrial utopia is actually possible, then religion at least postulates utopia in Heaven above. Whether or not the classical writers on American communes were right in saying religion gives strength to heavens on earth, we do not know. The converse of this question is whether contemporary utopianism will give strength to religion, for if only religious utopias succeed, natural selection will favor the sacred at the expense of the secular. One might argue that utopianism, whatever symbols of transcendence are used in its ideology, is by its very nature the close kin of religion because both seek a realm of perfection far above the limitations of mundane existence. Outside the narrow boundaries of formally established intentional communities, American culture has always had vague but often powerful utopian qualities, for in a sense the entire society, like that of Israel, intends to achieve ideals other peoples only dream of. The unanswered question of the link between utopianism and the sacred thus becomes a mystery about the soul of a supposedly secular age.

REFERENCES

Bainbridge, William Sims
  1978   *Satan's Power*. Berkeley, Los Angeles, London: University of California Press.
  1982a   "Shaker Demographics 1840–1900: An Example of the Use of U.S. Census Enumeration Schedules," *Journal for the Scientific Study of Religion* 21:352–365.
  1982b   "Women in Science Fiction," *Sex Roles* 8:1081–1093.
Bainbridge, William Sims, and Rodney Stark
  1979   "Cult Formation: Three Compatible Models," *Sociological Analysis* 40:285–295.
Barthel, Diane L.
  1984   *Amana: From Pietist Sect to American Community*. Lincoln: University of Nebraska Press.
Carden, Maren Lockwood
  1969   *Oneida: Utopian Community to Modern Corporation*. Baltimore: Johns Hopkins Press.

Della Fave, L. Richard, and George A. Hillery
  1980   "Status Inequality in a Religious Community," *Social Forces* 59:62–84.
Durkheim, Emile
  1915   *The Elementary Forms of the Religious Life*. London: Allen and Unwin.
Ember, Melvin
  1971   "An Empirical Test of Galton's Problem," *Ethnology* 10:98–106.
Fishman, Aryei
  1982   "'Torah and Labor': The Radicalization of Religion within a National Framework," *Studies in Zionism* 6:255–271.
  1983*a*   "Judaism and Modernization: The Case of the Religious Kibbutzim," *Social Forces* 62:9–31.
  1983*b*   "Moses Hess on Judaism and Its Aptness for a Socialist Civilization," *The Journal of Religion* 63:143–158.
  1983*c*   "The Religious Kibbutz: Religion, Nationalism and Socialism in a Communal Framework." In Ernest Krausz and David Glanz, eds., *The Sociology of the Kibbutz*. New Brunswick, N.J.: Transaction. Pp. 115–123.
Gardner, Hugh
  1978   *The Children of Prosperity*. New York: St. Martin's.
Green, Calvin, and Seth Y. Wells
  1823   *A Summary View of the Millennial Church, or United Society of Believers*. Albany, N.Y.: Packard and Van Benthuysen.
Heinlein, Robert A.
  1961   *Stranger in a Strange Land*. New York: Putnam.
  1966   *The Moon Is a Harsh Mistress*. New York: Putnam.
Hogan, James P.
  1982   *Voyage from Yesteryear*. New York: Ballantine.
Homans, George C.
  1950   *The Human Group*. New York: Harcourt, Brace and World.
  1967   *The Nature of Social Science*. New York: Harcourt, Brace and World.
Houriet, Robert
  1971   *Getting Back Together*. New York: Avon.
Kanter, Rosabeth Moss
  1972   *Commitment and Community*. Cambridge: Harvard University Press.
Kinkade, Kathleen
  1973   *A Walden Two Experiment*. New York: William Morrow.
Knight, Damon
  1977   *The Futurians*. New York: John Day.
Manuel, Frank E., and Fritzie P. Manuel
  1979   *Utopian Thought in the Western World*. Cambridge: Harvard University Press.

Nordhoff, Charles
  1875   *The Communistic Societies of the United States.* London: John Murray.
Noyes, John Humphrey
  1870   *History of American Socialisms.* Philadelphia: Lippincott.
Noyes, Pierrepont
  1937   *My Father's House.* New York: Farrar and Rinehart.
Parsons, Talcott
  1964   "Evolutionary Universals in Society," *American Sociological Review* 29:339–357.
Rokeach, Milton, Robert Homant, and Louis Penner
  1970   "A Value Analysis of the Disputed Federalist Papers," *Journal of Personality and Social Psychology* 16:245–250.
Skinner, B. F.
  1948   *Walden Two.* New York: Macmillan.
Stark, Rodney, and William Sims Bainbridge
  1980   "Secularization, Revival, and Cult Formation," *The Annual Review of the Social Sciences of Religion* 4:85–119.
Stephan, Karen H., and G. Edward Stephan
  1973   "Religion and the Survival of Utopian Communities," *Journal for the Scientific Study of Religion* 12:89–100.
White, Anna, and Leila S. Taylor
  1905   *Shakerism, Its Meaning and Message.* Columbus, Ohio: Heer.
Wolfe, Tom
  1968   *The Electric Kool-Aid Acid Test.* New York: Bantam.
Zablocki, Benjamin
  1971   *The Joyful Community.* Baltimore: Penguin.
  1980   *Alienation and Charisma.* New York: Free Press.

III

New Religious Movements: Yet Another Great Awakening?

Eileen Barker

Perhaps the safest generalization to have emerged from (or, at least, to have been thoroughly reinforced by) the latest wave of new religious movements is that, where people's beliefs are concerned, to generalize is a very tricky business. The new religions have been seen as the final flurry or last whimper of religiosity in an increasingly rational and secular age; they have been dismissed as a symptom of vulgar, superstitious superficiality in an already demystified age; and they have been heralded as the vanguard of a new religious revival— the dawn of a new religious consciousness.

A large, some might say disproportionate, number of sociologists has been attracted to the study of the movements.[1] A special Center for the Study of New Religious Movements has operated under the directorship of Jacob Needleman at the Graduate Theological Union in Berkeley since 1977; a Study Centre for New Religious Movements in Primal Societies is directed by Harold Turner in Birmingham, England. Individual movements have provided comparatively circumscribed areas of research for monographs or Ph.D. theses; they have also been used as a laboratory for examining a number of more general areas, such as socialization, power, control, institutionalization, social change, the relationship between the individual and society, and the reaction of society to new groups in its midst.

To what extent can research tell us whether the new religions are a sign that secularization is being stopped in its tracks, slowed down, helped along—or what? Can we assume that the movements meet universal needs (wants, desires, hopes) which are experienced by individuals and/or societies and which secular society does not meet?

Or should we assume that the movements cope with problems which the secular society has actually created, but has not yet learned to satisfy? Alternatively, is it possible that the movements are not so much reacting to society as reflecting, in miniature, its prevailing trends? Or, as a further possibility, can we assume that the membership of the movements is primarily the consequence of brainwashing, mind-control, or "thought reform," and that it has, therefore, *nothing* much to do with what is going on in society—except, perhaps, that it illustrates we live in a society that has developed and disseminated these sophisticated techniques?

Sociologists of religion can recognize in the new religions both responses to *and* reflections of many of the processes that are referred to in the classical theories of secularization. They can, for example, observe the seekers after spiritual development and/or transcendental goals, following the charismatic leader who promises to remystify their lives and to give them something better than the iron cage of rational, bureaucratic society; but one can also observe the growth of bureaucracies, the routinization of office as the leaders die—and antinomianism turns to anomie. But, before addressing ourselves further to the question of just what the movements may signify, let us first survey briefly what is known about the movements and how they have been approached by sociologists of religion.

WHAT IS A NEW RELIGIOUS MOVEMENT?

The danger of placing a large number of movements under a single, umbrella term lies in the assumption that movements thus designated must share certain characteristics. It is arguably the case that the only characteristic these movements share is to have been referred to at some time as new religious movements. To provide an initial orientation, however, one might say that the groups which are currently referred to as new religious movements have, in most cases, appeared since the Second World War, and, had they appeared earlier, nearly all of them would have been classified as either a cult or a sect.

HOW NEW ARE THEY?

The names of the movements are, of course, new, and so are the faces of the founders or leaders who may be seen by their followers as a god (Meher Baba), as the Messiah (Sun Myung Moon), as a prophet (Moses David Berg), as a religious philosopher (L. Ron Hubbard), as a guru (A. C. Bhaktivedanta Swami Prabhupāda), as a Spiritual Master, a Teacher, an Enlightened One, an inspired father figure . . . or any combination of these roles. Some of the movements employ the material trappings of modern society—an obvious example of "new technology" is to be found in the use by Scientology and its "substudy," Dianetics, of the E-meter;[2] some employ the concepts of modern psychoanalytic theory; several employ sophisticated marketing techniques; and nearly all employ the rhetoric of science to justify their beliefs and practices (Barker 1981).

Little that is new is created out of nothing, however. Most of the basic ingredients of the movements can be found to have existed in much earlier times. It is the idiosyncratic *structures* of both the belief systems and the practices which we are unlikely to have seen before. It is, in other words, the particular combinations of items that are selected, and the rhetoric in which they are packaged, rather than the items themselves, which provide the novelty.

HOW RELIGIOUS ARE THEY?

Sociologists are well acquainted with debates on what "really" constitutes a religion. Insisting on belief in a god has always ruled out Buddhism; with the new religions it would also exclude the whole gamut of groups that cater for the seekers after spiritual fulfillment, and which are collectively referred to as the Human Potential movement (Stone 1976). Resorting to functional definitions can, however, open the door not only to the Human Potential Movement but also to Marxism, nationalism, and any other ideology, however "secular" it may appear by other criteria. This is not to suggest that the term *religious* is otiose. Carelessly used it can ossify our perceptions and prevent us from seeing processes that are taking place in a changing society; when carefully used, however, it can alert us to all manner of questions which we might not otherwise have considered. Fascinating parallels have been found between eighteenth-century pietism and modern encounter groups (Oden 1972); it has been suggested that the California "fun movement" would, in a less secular milieu, be seen as an outbreak of religious ecstasy (Burfoot 1984); and small political movements have been usefully analyzed as though they were religious sects (O'Toole 1977).

But while it is both possible and helpful for the sociologist to keep his taxonomic options open, definitions can be of considerable moment for the movements themselves, and thus, indirectly, for drawing the boundaries between the sacred and the profane within modern society. It may not be insignificant that a movement's concern in this question often arises for secular reasons: the Church of Scientology on the one hand has enlisted academic support for its claim to be a bona fide religion and, as such, entitled to tax exemption; on the other hand, Transcendental Meditation (the Science of Creative Intelligence) lost a case in New Jersey in which it was trying to prove that it was *not* a religion—in order that its meditation techniques could be taught in the public schools without violating the First Amendment (Scott 1978:5,6). Furthermore, many of the more established religions have been affected by the mushrooming of the new movements, partly because newcomers classified as religions have a claim on the privileges and limited resources which the established churches have enjoyed in the past. At the same time, legislation curtailing the new movements' activities in certain areas (economic, political, recruitment, civil liberties) threatens the older religions' right to perform similar, if not identical, activities.

DEMOGRAPHIC DISTRIBUTION

It is important to stress that the actual spread of the movements is not necessarily correlated with their visibility. No one knows exactly how many new religions there are and, of course, even an approximate number will depend on the definition employed. It is, however, probably safe to say that the figure of three thousand movements would be a conservative estimate for the West (including Australia and New Zealand). It is even more difficult to establish the number of new religions in Africa and Asia and, in particular, the subcontinent of India.[3]

But, despite the fact that the number of actual movements is undoubtedly very high, membership of the various groups would seem, in the vast majority of cases, to be very small. Again, accurate statistics, even in the West, are hard to come by, since both the movements and their opponents tend to exaggerate membership, sometimes by factors of ten or more. In certain areas (most obviously in California), a considerable proportion of the U.S. population may have had transitory flirtations with several movements (Wuthnow

1976, 1978), but the number of full-time followers devoting their whole lives to a new religion has tended to remain far lower, and there is a far higher turnover rate than reports by the media would suggest—the number of full-time Moonies in the West, for instance, has never risen to ten thousand at any one time (although as many as forty thousand could have joined and then left during the seventies), and it is unlikely that many of the other movements have more full-time followers—some having only a score or less.

Not only is there an unfortunate paucity of information about numbers and membership of the new religions, there is also very little information about their geographical distribution. All five continents have given rise to indigenous new religions, but they also play host to many other groups, many of the most "mobile" groups having originated either in California or in the East and then traveled to the rest of the world. To complicate matters even further, although it would appear many of the new religions have their roots firmly planted in the East, frequently features that had themselves been imported from the West at an earlier date are the features selected for reimportation—especially to the West Coast of America, whence they will travel, with further accretions, to the East Coast and to Europe and the rest of the world (Hardy 1983).

The composition of the membership varies according to the type of movement—it even varies for the same movement at various times and in various locations. It is, however, clear that the current wave of movements in the West does not rely primarily on the oppressed for its membership. Although there were poor blacks who followed Jim Jones,[4] and other groups like the Rastafarians have a strong appeal among working-class blacks in both Britain and the West Indies (Cashmore 1979), one of the most prominent features of the movements is the disproportionate numbers of materially advantaged, middle-class followers whom they attract. Not surprisingly, those who are to become *full-time* members tend to be young (in their early twenties) and without any strong ties, although there are numerous examples of couples and many older people who have forsaken their former life-styles and life-chances to follow their new leader.

THE DIVERSITY

The rapid upsurge in international travel and communication during the second half of the century has turned the world not so much into a vast melting pot, within which diversity disappears, as into an enormous *smorgasbord* from which all manner of eclectic or syncretistic diversity may be selected.

One way of ordering the diversity of movements is to classify them according to the traditions with which they appear most closely affiliated (despite the fact that the more orthodox proponents of these beliefs will often produce vehement denials of the newcomers' authenticity). Hindu-based religions include the Hare Krishna, Ananda Marga, Sai Baba, Meher Baba, Divine Light Mission, Brahma Kumaris, and the disciples of Bhagwan Rajneesh. From the Buddhist tradition come various Zen groups and many of the movements from Japan, the largest being the Sokka Gakkai (Nichiren Shoshu) and Rissho Koisei-kai. Christian-based movements include the Children of God (now called the Family of Love) and the Way International (both offshoots of the Jesus Movement, which has itself been referred to as a new religious movement), and movements like the Unification Church which, although based on the Bible, has a theology within which scholars have detected the influences of the Eastern traditions of Taoism, Confucianism, and Buddhism, as well as spiritualism.[5]

A number of movements, such as the Emin, Eckankar, and White Eagle, can be classified as belonging to the esoteric tradition. Numerous occult, pagan, magic, and witchcraft movements are known to exist (Melton 1982; Holzer 1972, 1974; Lynch 1979) but, like the tribal and folk-based new religions that have emerged around the world, especially in Africa and Latin America, these have received comparatively little attention *as* new religious movements from sociologists of religion. Although the groups that can be loosely labeled the Human Potential Movement (e.g., Rebirthing, Primal Therapy, Arica, Silva Mind Control, and various gestalt and encounter groups) would seem to belong to the more secular end of the belief spectrum, many of them use (and transform) techniques (such as meditation and chanting) borrowed from Hindu and Buddhist traditions. Some of the new religions are so idiosyncratic that they would appear to defy any classification—although perhaps the Japanese group that venerated Thomas Edison as a subordinate deity (Arai 1972:99) could share a slot with the two thousand Kennedy Worshippers who believe JFK to be a god (Melton 1978:476).

Another way of classifying the movements is according to the degree of commitment given by the members. At one extreme, there is the demand for total involvement and obedience, with members residing in isolated community, devoting their whole lives to the movement. Jonestown was a tragic example of this. At the other extreme, members may have attended a weekend course (of, say, est), and then had no further contact with other "graduates." Movements frequently have two or more tiers of membership, however, with a hard core of full-time devotees (similar to nuns or monks in their level of commitment), and a wider, less involved "congregation" expressing sympathy or interest, or "clients" attending courses or meetings.

So far as practices are concerned, the diversity is, again, enormous. Some movements perform intricate, esoteric rituals; others have practically no rites at all. Sexual practices range from celibacy to sex-magic, wild orgies, and "love-ins." Some of the movements withdraw completely from the social life of the societies within which they are found; others play a very active role, the Sokka Gakkai, for example, having originated it own political party in Japan. And political positions range from the revolutionary socialism of the Children of God and the People's Temple to the vehemently anticommunist stance of the Unification Church.

RESEARCH

As already indicated, very limited mapping of the basic statistics (numbers of movements, density per population, number of members, turnover rates) of the new religious movements has occurred, although there are some notable exceptions for certain geographical areas (Wuthnow 1978; Bird and Reimer 1982). Furthermore, the coverage of the movements' beliefs and practices is by no means uniform. Some have been researched in detail, others not all.[6] Apart from their intrinsic interest, the new religions have provided useful material for research into processes and institutions that are not confined to the movements themselves.[7]

The methods employed have varied from researcher to researcher, and have included participant observation (both covert and open), questionnaire, and interview; and the ever-rising number of defectors has provided an invaluable, but not always reliable (Solomon 1981), source of information. Although some excellent work has been done by individuals, the research tends to be disappointingly disparate, with variations in concepts (e.g., class) and analytical tools (e.g., questionnaire design) only rarely allowing direct comparisons to be made. One of the most serious problems (which also affects other areas of the sociology of religion) is the lack of enough basic information about the populations from which the members are drawn (i.e., nonmembers) for the researcher to be able to assess just how far the characteristics, and indeed the beliefs and practices, of the new religious movements are *peculiar to* the new religious movements. The majority of the studies have not employed a control group, and all too often researchers (like the media who, more understandably, are after a good story) assume, without any empirical foundation, that the characteristics they uncover are typical of the movement and atypical of nonmembers.

Some attempts have been made to remind us of what all sociologists know in theory, but are apt to forget in practice: that there have been previous waves of new religious movements (e.g., Pritchard 1976), or that what might seem exotic or bizarre in one context is, or has been, unremarkable elsewhere (e.g., Werblowsky 1982). Some interesting comparisons have been drawn among movements in various countries (e.g., Wilson 1976), and Wuthnow (1980) has alerted us to the possibility of finding explanations for the rise of new religious movements by looking at what is happening *among* rather than *within* societies. Generally speaking, however, there has been a regrettable paucity of historical and cross-cultural comparisons in the literature.[8]

A further difficulty, which is inherent in the newness of the movements, is that changes in practices, membership, and even beliefs tend to occur rather rapidly. Few studies have been longitudinal (but see Lofland 1977), making it difficult to tell how far results of research carried out at different periods or locations might differ because the movement changed, or because the researchers came to different conclusions about the same phenomena.

EXPLANATIONS

As I indicated at the beginning of this chapter, diverse explanations have been offered as to why the new religions have emerged and what their significance is for the rest of society. One does, indeed, begin to suspect there might be a bit of "overkill" in the explanations for, although most people are likely to begin by thinking that the rise of the movements was a sufficiently strange phenomenon to need an explanation, they might be forgiven, after having read the literature, for wondering why there remain any people who are *not* now members of the new religions.

One cannot hope to do much more than indicate very briefly some of the more convincing theories that have been put forward. For those who see the new religions as a response to secularization, one of the more popular starting points is Weber's concept of rationalization—an increasing preoccupation with causal efficiency and utilitarianism, which results in the "disenchantment" of the world. Wallis (1978, 1982b) argues that rationalization results in the de-institutionalization of identity and the attenuation of community; "world-rejecting movements" (the Children of God, Hare Krishna) react to society, offering salvation in community as an alternative to the loneliness and impersonality of the outside world; "world-affirming movements" (Scientology, est) accept, and offer ways of coping with, the values and demands of modern society.

Robbins and Anthony (1982) see the movements as in part a response to the uncertainties of a relativism resulting from the disintegration of a traditional biblical morality which clearly proscribed "bad" actions (see also Bellah 1976). They argue that not only does one have difficulty in knowing what is right, one can also conclude that, because of environmental and genetic influences, one may not be able to do what is right (see also Glock 1976). Dualistic movements (e.g., the Unification Church) react to this relativism by offering a new moral absolutism with clear-cut definitions of good and bad; monistic movements (e.g., Meher Baba) deal with the problem by defining morality as instrumental and switching the emphasis of goodness to subjective, inner consciousness.

I have argued (1984) that a movement like the Unification Church can call upon support from idealistic youth who, although they react against the material values of secular society, have nonetheless imbibed a rational outlook, and thus respond to the combination of a transcendental goal (restoring the Kingdom of Heaven on earth), and calculable, qualifiable, secular means (making money and recruiting new members). Robbins et al. (1976) make a case for the Unification Church as "the last civil religion," but this does not help us understand why the movement has a roughly proportional membership (about 0.001 percent of the total population) in other countries such as Britain. Wilson, a veteran advocate of the secularization thesis, sees the general trend as being one of differentiation in which religion plays a decreasing role in society—many of the functions it fulfilled in the past being taken over by other agencies—but he considers civil religion a dubious alternative focus for the value consensus traditionally supplied by religion (1978). Something which most of the new movements do is to offer their followers a surer, more immediate promise of salvation than the often stagnant, institutionalized religions in a rapidly changing social environment (1976, 1982). Wilson (1978) has also argued that the new religions are more likely to point to needs and desires (such as for identity, commitment, and loyalty) than they are actually to meet these needs for more than a very small proportion of society.

Stark and Bainbridge (1979,1980, 1981*a*, 1981*b*) believe that secularization is a self-limiting process in that it stimulates new religious reactions; sects (by which they mean schisms) cluster where the conventional churches are stronger, whereas cults (i.e., innovations) are more successful in places where conventional churches are weaker. Their calculations suggest that, contrary to conventional wisdom, many distinctly American cults and sects fare better in more secularized Europe than in their homeland (Stark, forthcoming).

Theories that suggest that secular society does not adequately fulfill all the functions of a religious society point not only to the more obviously religious needs (respected means of salvation, permission to talk about religious experiences, the sense of the Holy, reverence) but also to more secular-sounding needs (provision of community, identity, belonging, stability, a sense of wholeness, someone in control, order, meaning, direction, hope, unambiguous moral standards, etc.). Then there are the theories that see the new religions providing instrumental means for achieving the material goals of modern secular society (Harris 1981; Wallis 1978). Other theories suggest a basic change in the nature of man—possibly an evolutionary leap that is biological in its nature and which is responsible for a new religious consciousness (see Roszak 1975). Alternatively, it has been suggested that the secular society has socialized its population into excessive individualism, shallow quests, receptivity to "psychobabble" (Rosen 1978), or what Lasch (1979) has called the "Culture of Narcissism" (see also Kuner 1984) and, thus, that "the new religions mirror the concern with self" (Johnson 1981:65). Brainwashing theories are liable to receive what support they have from psychologists, psychiatrists, the media, and anticultists (e.g., Conway and Siegelman 1978; Clark 1978; Lifton 1961; Singer 1981) but tend, so far as most movements are concerned, to be rejected by sociologists (Barker 1984; Bromley and Richardson, forthcoming; Richardson 1980; Robbins and Anthony 1981; Wallis 1982*b*).

CONCLUDING REMARKS

There can be no doubt that, during the last couple of decades, the sacred has appeared in many new forms—but many of the new forms are not unambiguously sacred. One might as well say that the secular has appeared in many new forms, some of which are not unambiguously profane. The central thrust of this chapter has been to point to diversity—to the diversity of the movements, their beliefs and practices, their membership; to the small numbers of people involved in large numbers of movements which have high turnover rates.

It would appear that within the modern, differentiated, pluralistic[9] societies of the West (in contrast both to earlier societies and to theocratic or totalitarian societies of the left or right), supermarket/ smorgasbord metaphors have a particular pertinence. Millions of individuals share certain cultural orientations, but as novelty and individualism are among the more accepted of these values, it is perhaps not surprising that these individuals should pursue different world views, different meanings, and different life-styles. This is not to suggest that the various pursuits are not socially constructed, or that social forces do not influence people as much as they always have— quite the contrary; organized spontaneity and mass individualism are prominent features of the new religious movements; and among the alternatives offered are those which offer no alternative.

Although the new religions are undoubtedly meeting some needs, various movements (and even the same movement) can meet various needs for various people. Although the movements undoubtedly mirror aspects of society, not one society but many different subcultures and substructures are reflected; although social persuasion is undoubtedly applied in many instances, the techniques that are employed have a highly differential efficacy;[10] although there is undoubtedly a considerable degree of contingency in who happens to join a particular movement, and although there is undoubtedly a high level of plasticity or suggestibility in the human condition, it does not follow that "anything goes"—those who become "Moonies" are not likely to have become Premies, and members of neither group are very likely to have done an est course.

Unlike economists, sociologists of religion tend not to rely too heavily on a heuristic of rational man maximizing profit, but this does not mean that they cannot find a *situational* logic to explain the membership of the divers movements. There are movements which people with particular sets of experiences would *not* join; there are some boundaries which socialization *prevents* most people from crossing. In a context in which there is obviously a considerable amount of experimentation occurring, the fact of experimentation is itself obviously one that needs exploring (Wuthnow 1978). But something sometimes forgotten in the enthusiastic search for the "true" meaning of the new religions is that not only is the smorgasbord not confined to goods or cuisine of any one tradition but a lot of other tables are laden with other kinds of (more obviously secular) options. One can also experiment with politics, sport, drugs, the arts, relationships, matchbox collecting, do-it-yourself, or switching from one TV channel to another.

Given this diversity, generalizing from one movement—or even from a few movements—to The Movement is a risky business, and given the *lack* of success most of the movements have enjoyed, to generalize from The Movement to Society is even more risky. Studies of new religious movements have, nonetheless, given us a wealth of clues and have sensitized us to many questions that might otherwise have passed unasked. Sociologists of religion should expend as much energy in checking the failures of the movements during the next ten years as they did in charting successes over the past decade. We may then get a clearer idea of whether the new religions portend yet another great awakening or whether, as I have come to suspect, they represent simply a highly publicized collection of options selected from the enormous variety already available in modern societies, which celebrate neither belief nor ideology under any single canopy.

NOTES

1. In this chapter, reference is mainly to the work carried out on the movements which either originated or found a home in North America and Europe, but there has been a considerable amount of study of the new religious movements in Japan where the "Rush Hour of the Gods" occurred at a slightly earlier date (McFarland 1967; Arai 1972; Earhart 1970, 1982; Offner and Straelen 1963; Thomsen 1963). There also exist numerous studies on new religions in Africa (Barrett 1968; Jules-Rosette, ed., 1979; Turner 1974, 1977, 1979); and other parts of the world (Hesselgrave, ed., 1978; Turner 1978a, 1978b); and special subgrouping such as black movements in the Americas and Caribbean (Simpson 1978); see also note 4 below.

2. "The Hubbard Electrometer is a religious artifact used in the Church confessional" (Hubbard 1956:2).

3. There is by now quite a large collection of directories and bibliographies of research into the new movements, some of which are arranged according to geographical area. Although these do not always give much in the way of statistical detail, they do provide a helpful point from which the investigator can begin his investigations. See, for example, for North America: Melton

1977, 1978, 1982; *New Consciousness Source Book: Spiritual Community Guide, no. 5* (Berkeley, CA: Spiritual Community/NAM, Box 1067). For Europe: Annett 1976; Mildenberger 1979; the Q Directory, Occult, Pagan and New Age (London: Pallas Aquariana Ltd. [published biannually]); Wilson, forthcoming. For India: Murray 1980. For Africa: Turner 1977, 1979. For Japan: Hori, ed., 1972. Worldwide: Adams 1982; Khalsa, ed., 1981; Werbner, ed., 1977. The best source for further bibliographies and directories is *New Titles*, distributed monthly by the Center for the Study of New Religious Movements at the Graduate Theological Union Library (2400 Ridge Road, Berkeley, Calif.). See also Choquette, forthcoming.

Short notes on several of the new religions can be found in Annett 1976; Melton and Moore 1982 (Appendix A); Melton 1977, 1978; and Barker, ed., 1982 (Glossary).

4. It is interesting to note that the People's Temple was not generally regarded as a new religious movement until after the mass suicide in Guyana in 1978.

5. The extent to which purity of origins is "negotiable" is nicely illustrated by the existence of an Islamic version of the Unificationist theology, the *Divine Principle*.

6. It is, of course, impossible to list all the movements that have been the object of sociological research but the better-known movements include: the Hare Krishna/ISKCON (Judah 1974; Daner 1976; Rochford, forthcoming); The Children of God/Family of Love (Wallis 1979, 1982a); The Divine Light Mission (Downton 1979); Scientology (Wallis 1976); the Unification Church (Lofland 1977; Bromley and Shupe 1979; Barker 1984); Meher Baba (Robbins and Anthony 1972); Synanon (Ofshe 1980); the Sokka Gakkai/Nichiren Shoshu (Murata 1969; Snow 1976); est and Zen Buddhism (Tipton 1982); the Ananda Cooperative Village (Nordquist 1978); The Process/Foundation (Bainbridge 1978); The Jesus Movement (Richardson et al. 1979).

Books in which several movements are examined include Cox 1977; Ellwood 1973, 1979; Hill 1980; Melton and Moore 1982; Needleman 1970; Shupe 1981; Wallis 1979; Wilson 1982; Wuthnow 1976, 1978.

Useful collections of papers on various movements are to be found in Anthony et al., eds., forthcoming; Barker, ed., 1982, 1984; Biezais, ed., 1975; Glock and Bellah, eds., 1976; Holm, ed., 1981; Kehrer, ed., 1981; Kehrer, ed., 1981; Needleman and Baker, eds., 1978; Richardson, ed., 1978; Robbins and Anthony, eds., 1981; Stark, ed., forthcoming; Wallis, ed., 1975; Wilson, ed., 1981; Zaretsky and Leone, eds., 1974. See also the special issues of *Social Compass* (vol. 30, no. 1, 1983); and, for a general overview, see the entries on new religious movements in the Encyclopedia of Religion (Eliade et al., forthcoming).

7. Particular attention has been paid to conversion (Rambo 1982; Lofland and Stark 1965; Richardson, ed., 1978; Snow and Machalek 1982; Lofland and Skonovd 1981). Other areas include finances (Richardson 1982); legislation (Shepherd 1981); the family (Kaslow and Sussman, eds., 1982); James, ed.,

1983; and a special issue of *Marriage and Family Review* (vol. 4. nos. 3–4, 1982). For essays placing the new religions in a wider social perspective, see Barker, ed., 1982; Glock and Wuthnow 1979; Robbins 1981; Stark, ed., forthcoming.

8. There have, however, been some excellent comparisons of societal reactions to the movements, the anticult movement on occasion being of as much, if not more, sociological interest than the movements themselves (see next chapter).

9. Wuthnow (1978) suspects *populist* might be a more accurate adjective.

10. About nine out of every ten of those who go to a Unification Workshop (where the so-called brainwashing is reputed to occur) do *not* end up becoming members; the majority of those who do become "Moonies" leave, of their own free will, within two years (Barker 1983, 1984, and forthcoming).

REFERENCES

Adams, Robert
　1982　*The New Times Network: Groups and Centres for Personal Growth.* London, Boston, Melbourne, and Henley: Routledge and Kegan Paul.

Annett, Stephen
　1976　*The Many Ways of Being: A Guide to Spiritual Groups and Growth Centres in Britain.* London: Abacus.

Anthony, Dick, and Thomas Robbins
　1982　"Contemporary Religious Ferment and Moral Ambiguity." *In* Barker, ed., 1982.

Anthony, Dick, Jacob Needleman, and Thomas Robbins, eds.
　　　Conversion, Coercion and Commitment in New Religious Movements. New York: Crossroads. Forthcoming.

Arai, Ken
　1972　"New Religious Movements." *In* Hori, ed., 1972.

Bainbridge, William Sims
　1978　*Stans's Power: A Deviant Psychotherapy Cult.* Berkeley, Los Angeles, London: University of California Press.

Barker, Eileen
　1981　"Science as Theology: The Theological Functioning of Western Science." *In* A. R. Peacocke, ed., *The Sciences and Theology in the Twentieth Century.* London: Oriel Press; Indiana: University of Notre Dame Press.
　1984　"The Ones Who Got Away." *In* Barker, ed., 1984. Also *in* Stark, ed. Forthcoming.
　1984　*Moonies.* 2 vols. Oxford: Blackwell.
　　　"Resistible Coercion." *In* Anthony et al., eds.

Barker, Eileen, ed.
   1982   *New Religious Movements: A Perspective for Understanding Society:*
             New York and Toronto: Edwin Mellen Press.
   1984   *Of Gods and Men: New Religious Movements in the West.* Atlanta:
             Mercer University Press.
Barrett, David B.
   1968   *Schism and Renewal in Africa: An Analysis of Six Thousand Contempo-
             rary Religious Movements.* New York: Oxford University Press.
Bellah, Robert
   1976   "The New Religious Consciousness and the Crisis of Modernity."
             In Glock and Bellah, eds., 1976.
Biezais, Haralds, ed.
   1975   *New Religions.* Stockholm: Almqvist and Wiksell International.
Bird, Frederick, and Bill Reimer
   1982   "Participation Rates in New Religious Movements," *Journal for the
             Scientific Study of Religion,* vol. 21, no. 1 (March); also in Barker,
             ed., 1984.
Bromley, David, and Anson D. Shupe, Jr.
   1979   *"Moonies" in America: Cult, Church and Crusade.* Beverly Hills and
             London: Sage.
Bromley, David, and James Richardson, eds.
             The Brainwashing/Deprogramming Debate. New York: Edwin Mellen
             Press. Forthcoming.
   1981   *Strange Gods.* Boston: Beacon Press.
Burfoot, Jean
   1984   "The Fun-Seeking Movement in California." *In* Barker, ed., 1984.
Cashmore, Ernest
   1979   *Rastaman: The Rastafarian Movement in England.* London: George
             Allen and Unwin.
Choquette, Diane
             New Religious Movements: A Bibliography. New York and London:
             Greenwood Press. Forthcoming.
Clark, John G., Jr.
   1978   "Problems in Referral of Cult Members," *Journal of the National
             Association of Private Psychiatric Hospitals,* vol. 9, no. 4.
Conway, Flo, and Jim Siegelman
   1978   *Snapping.* Philadelphia: J. B. Lippincott.
Cox, Harvey
   1977   *Turning East.* New York: Simon and Schuster.
Daner, Francine
   1976   *The American Children of Krsna: A Study of the Hare Krsna Movement.*
             New York: Holt, Rinehart and Winston.
Downton, James V., Jr.
   1979   *Sacred Journeys: The Conversion of Young Americans to Divine Light*

Mission. New York: Columbia University Press.
Earhart, H. Byron
1970   *The New Religions of Japan.* Tokyo: Sophia University Press.
1982   *Japanese Religion: University and Diversity.* Belmont, Calif.: Wadsworth Publishing.
Eliade, Mircea, et al., eds.
        The Encyclopedia of Religion. New York: Free Press. Forthcoming.
Ellwood, Robert S., Jr.
1973   *Religious and Spiritual Groups in Modern America.* Englewood Cliffs, N.J.: Prentice-Hall.
1979   *Alternative Altars: Unconventional and Eastern Spirituality in America.* Chicago: University of Chicago Press.
Glock, Charles
1976   "Consciousness Among Contemporary Youth." *In* Glock and Bellah, eds., 1976.
Glock, Charles Y., and Robert Bellah, eds.
1976   *The New Religious Consciousness.* Berkeley, Los Angeles, London: University of California Press.
Glock, Charles Y., and Robert Wuthnow
1979   "Departures from Conventional Religion: The Nominally Religious, the Non Religious, and the Alternatively Religious." *In* Wuthnow, ed., *The Religious Dimension: New Directions in the Quantitative Study of Religion.* New York: Academic Press.
Hardy, Fred
1983   "How 'Indian' Are the New 'Indian' Religious Movements?" Paper given at the "Development and Impact of New Religious Movements" Conference at King's College, London, 18–19 April.
Harris, Marvin
1981   *America Now.* New York: Simon and Schuster.
Hesselgrave, David J., ed.
1978   *Dynamic Religious Movements.* Grand Rapids, Mich.: Barker Book House.
Hill, Daniel G.
1980   *Study of Mind Development Groups, Sects and Cults in Ontario.* Report to the Ontario Government, June.
Holm, Nils G., ed.
1981   *Aktuella religiösa rörelser i Finland: Ajankohtaisia uskonnollisia liikkeitä Suomessa.* Åbo: Research Institute of the Åbo Akademi Foundation.
Holzer, Hans
1972   *The New Pagans.* Garden City, N.Y.: Doubleday.
1974   *The Dictionary of the Occult.* New York: Henry Regnery.
Hori, Ichiro, ed.
1972   *Japanese Religion: A Survey by the Agency for Cultural Affairs.* Tokyo,

New York, and San Francisco: Kodansha International.

Hubbard, L. Ron
1956   *Scientology: The Fundamentals of Thought.* Los Angeles: The Church
          of Scientology of California Publications.

James, Gene, ed.
1983   *The Family and Unification Thought: A Comparative Study.* New York:
          Rose of Sharon Press.

Johnson, Benton
1981   "A Sociological Perspective on The New Religions." *In* Robbins
          and Anthony, eds., 1981.

Judah, J. Stillson
1974   *Hare Krishna and the Counterculture.* New York: John Wiley.

Jules-Rosette, Bennetta, ed.
1979   *The New Religions of Africa.* Norwood, N.J.: Ablex Publishing.

Kaslow, Florence W., and Marvin B. Sussman, eds.
1982   *Cults and the Family.* New York: Haworth Press.

Kehrer, Gunter, ed.
1981   *Das Entstehen einer neuen Religion: Das Beispiel der Ver-
          einigungskirche.* Munich: Kösel.

Khalsa, Parmatma Sing, ed.
1981   *A Pilgrim's Guide to Planet Earth.* San Rafael, Calif.: Spiritual Com-
          munity Publications; London: Wildwood House.

Kuner, Wolfgang
1984   "New Religious Movements and Mental Health." *In* Barker, ed.,
          1984.

Lasch, Christopher
1979   *The Culture of Narcissism.* New York: W. W. Norton; London:
          Shere Books, 1980.

Lifton, Robert Jay
1961   *Thought Reform and the Psychology of Totalism: A Study of "Brainwash-
          ing" in China.* New York: W. W. Norton.

Lofland, John
1977   *Doomsday Cult: A Study of Conversion, Proselytization, and Main-
          tenance of Faith* (enlarged edition). New York: Irvington (original
          edition 1966).

Lofland, John, and Rodney Stark
1965   "Becoming a World-Saver: A Theory Conversion to a Deviant
          Perspective," *American Sociological Review* 30:862–875.

Lofland, John, and Norman Skonovd
1981   "Conversion Motifs," *Journal for the Scientific Study of Religion,* vol.
          20, no. 4 (December). Also, in an enlarged version, *in* Barker,
          ed., 1984.

Lynch, Frederick R.
1979   "'Occult Establishment' or 'Deviant Religion'? The Rise and Fall

of a Modern Church of Magic," *Journal for the Scientific Study of Religion*, vol. 18, no. 3 (September).

McFarland, H. Neill
1967   *The Rush-Hour of the Gods*. New York: Macmillan.

Melton, J. Gordon
1977   *A Directory of Religious Bodies in the United States*. New York and London: Garland Publishing, Inc.
1978   *The Encyclopedia of American Religions*. Wilmington, N.C.: Consortium Books.
1982   *Magic, Witchcraft, and Paganism in America. A Bibliography:* New York and London: Garland Publishing, Inc.

Melton, J. Gordon, and Robert L. Moore
1982   *The Cult Experience: Responding to the New Religious Pluralism*. New York: The Pilgrim Press.

Mildenberger, Michael
1979   *Die Religiose Revolte: Jugend zwischen Flucht und Aufbruch*. Frankfurt am Main: Fisher Taschenbuch Verlag.

Murata, Kiyoaki
1969   *Japan's New Buddhism*. New York: Walker/Westerhill.

Murray, Muz
1980   *Seeking the Master: A Guide to the Ashrams of India*. Jersey, Channel Islands: Neville Spearman.

Needleman, Jacob
1970   *The New Religions*. New York: Dutton (original edition 1970).

Needleman, Jacob, and George Baker, eds.
1978   *Understanding the New Religions*. New York: Seabury Press.

Nordquist, Ted. A.
1978   *Ananda Cooperative Village: A Study in the Beliefs, Values, and Attitudes of a New Age Religious Community*. Monograph Series from the Religions, Historiska Institutionen, Uppsala Universitet, 16.

Oden, Thomas C.
1972   *The Intensive Group Experience: The New Pietism*. Philadelphia: Westminster Press.

Offner, Clark, and Henricus Straelen
1963   *Modern Japanese Religions, with Special Emphasis upon Their Doctrines of Healing*. New York: Twayne; Tokyo: Rupert Endesle; Leiden: E. S. Brill.

Ofshe, Richard
1980   "The Social Development of the Synanon Cult: The Managerial Strategy of Organizational Transformation," *Sociological Analysis*, vol. 41, no. 2.

O'Toole, Roger
1977   *The Precipitous Path: Studies in Political Sects*. Toronto: Peter Martin Associates Ltd.

Pritchard, Linda K.
1976   "Religious Change in Nineteenth-Century America." *In* Glock
        and Bellah, eds., 1976.
Rambo, Lewis R.
1982   "Current Research on Religious Conversion," *Religious Studies
        Review,* vol. 8 (April).
Richardson, James T.
1980   "People's Temple and Jonestown: A Corrective Comparison and
        Critique," *Journal for the Scientific Study of Religion,* vol. 19, no. 3
        (September).
1982   "Financing the New Religions: Comparative and Theoretical Con-
        siderations," *Journal for the Scientific Study of Religion,* vol. 11, no.
        3 (September).
Richardson, James T., ed.
1978   *Conversion Careers: In and Out of the New Religions.* Beverly Hills
        and London: Sage. First published as *Conversion and Commitment
        in Contemporary Religion,* a special issue of *American Behaviourist
        Scientist,* vol. 20, no. 6 (July/August 1977).
Richardson, James T., M. H. Harder, and R. Simmonds
1979   *Organized Miracles: A Sociological Study of the Jesus Movement Or-
        ganization.* New Brunswick, N.J.: Transaction Books.
Robbins, Thomas
1981   "Church, State and Cult," *Sociological Analysis,* vol. 42, no. 3.
Robbins, Thomas, and Dick Anthony
1972   "Getting Straight with the Meher Baba: A Study of Mysticism,
        Drug-Rehabilitation and Post-Adolescent Role Conflict," *Journal
        for the Scientific Study of Religion,* vol. 11, no. 3 (September).
Robbins, Thomas, and Dick Anthony, eds.
1981   *In Gods We Trust: Patterns in American Religious Pluralism.* New
        Brunswick, N.J.: Transaction Books.
Robbins, Thomas, Dick Anthony, Madeline Doucas, and Thomas E. Curtis
1976   "The Last Civil Religion: Reverend Moon and the Unification
        Church," *Sociological Analysis,* vol. 37, no. 2.
Rochford, Burke
1985   *Hare Krishna!* New Brunswick, N.J.: Rutgers University Press.
        Forthcoming.
Rosen, R. D.
1978   *Psychobabble: Fast Talk and Quick Cure in the Era of Feeling.* New
        York: Atheneum; London: Wildwood House (1978).
Roszak, Theodore
1975   *The Unfinished Animal: The Aquarian Frontier and the Evolution of
        Consciousness.* New York: Harper Colophon; London: Faber
        (1976).
Scott, R. D.
1978   *Transcendental Misconceptions.* San Diego: Beta Books.

Shepherd, William C.
1981   "The Prosecutor's Reach: Legal Issues Stemming from the New
        Religious Movements." Paper presented to a conference on New
        Religious Movements, organized by the New Religious Move-
        ments Program, Graduate Theological Union, Berkeley, Calif.
        (June).
Shupe, Anson D., Jr.
1981   *Six Perspectives on New Religions*. New York: Edwin Mellen Press.
Simpson, George Eaton
1978   *Black Religions in the New World*. New York: Columbia University
        Press.
Singer, Margaret Thaler
1981   Evidence given in the High Court of Justice, Queen's Bench
        Division in the case of *Orme* vs. Associated Newspapers Group
        Ltd., 9–10 March.
Snow, David
1976   "The Nichiren Shoshu Movements in America: A Sociological
        Examination of Its Value Orientation, Recruitment Efforts and
        Speed." Ph.D. dissertation. University of California, Los Angeles.
Snow, David A., and Richard Machalek
1982   "On the Presumed Fragility of Unconventional Beliefs," *Journal
        for the Scientific Study of Religion*, vol. 21, no. 1 (March).
Solomon, Trudy
1981   "Integrating the Moonie Experience: A Survey of Ex-Members of
        the Unification Church." *In* Robbins and Anthony, eds., 1981.
Stark, Rodney, ed.
        Religious Movements: Genesis, Exodus and Numbers. New York: Rose
        of Sharon Press. Forthcoming.
Stark, Rodney, William Sims Bainbridge, and Daniel Boyle
1979   "Cults of America: A Reconnaisance in Space and Time." *Sociolog-
        ical Analysis*, vol. 40.
Stark, Rodney, and William Sims Bainbridge
1980   "Towards a Theory of Religion: Religious Commitment," *Journal
        for the Scientific Study of Religion*, vol. 19, no. 2 (June).
1981a   "Secularization and Cult Formation in the Jazz Age," *Journal for
        the Scientific Study of Religion*, vol. 20, no. 4 (December).
1981b   "American Born Sects: Initial Findings," *Journal for the Scientific
        Study of Religion*, vol. 20, no. 2 (June).
Stone, Donald
1976   "The Human Potential Movement." *In* Glock and Stark, eds.,
        1976.
Thomsen, Harvey
1963   *The New Religions in Japan*. Rutland, Vt.: Charles E. Tuttle.
Tipton, Steven
1982   *Getting Saved from the Sixties: Moral Meaning in Conversion and*

Cultural Change. Berkeley, Los Angeles, London: University of
California Press.

Turner, Harold
1974   "Tribal Religious Movements—New." In 1974 edition of *Ency-
        clopedia Britannica*, vol. 18.
1977   *Bibliography of New Religious Movements in Primal Societies. Vol. I:
        Black Africa.* Boston: G. K. Hall.
1978a   *Bibliography of New Religious Movements in Primal Societies. Vol. II:
        North America.* Boston: G. K. Hall.
1978b   "Old and New Religions in Melanesia," *Point*, no. 2.
1979   *Religious Innovation in Africa: Collected Essays on New Religious Move-
        ments.* Boston: G. K. Hall.

Wallis, Roy
1976   *The Road to Total Freedom: A Sociological Analysis of Scientology.*
        London: Heinemann.
1978   "The Rebirth of the Gods?" *In* New Lecture Series, no. 108,
        Queen's University, Belfast.
1979   *Salvation and Protest: Studies of Social and Religious Movements.* Lon-
        don: Frances Pinter.
1982a   "Yesterday's Children: Cultural and Structural Change in a New
        Religious Movement." *In* Wilson, ed., 1981.
1982b   "The New Religions as Social Indicators." *In* Barker, ed., 1982.

Wallis, Roy, ed.
1975   *Sectarianism: Analyses of Religious and Non-Religious Sects.* London:
        Peter Owen.

Werblowsky, Zwi
1982   "Religions New and Not So New: Fragments of an Agenda." *In*
        Barker, ed., 1982.

Werbner, Richard
1977   *Regional Cults.* London, New York, San Francisco: Academic
        Press.

Wilson, Bryan R.
1976   *Contemporary Transformations of Religion.* Oxford: Oxford Univer-
        sity Press.
1978   "The New Religions: Some Preliminary Considerations." In the
        *Proceedings of Tokyo Meeting of the International Conference on Sociol-
        ogy of Religion*, published by the Organizing Committee, Dept. of
        Religious Studies, University of Tokyo, Japan. Also *in* Barker,
        ed., 1982.
1982   *Religion in Sociological Perspective.* Oxford and New York: Oxford
        University Press.
        The Dictionary of Minority Religious Movements. Harmondsworth:
        Penguin. Forthcoming.

Wilson, Bryan R., ed.
1981   *The Social Impact of New Religious Movements.* New York: Rose of
        Sharon Press.

Wuthnow, Robert
  1976   *The Consciousness Reformation.* Berkeley, Los Angeles, London:
           University of California Press.
  1978   *Experimentation in American Religion: The New Mysticisms and Their
           Implications for the Churches.* Berkeley, Los Angeles, London: Uni-
           versity of California Press.
  1980   "World Order and Religious Movements." *In* Albert Bergesen,
           ed., *Studies in the Modern World-System.* New York: Academic
           Press. Also in Barker, ed., 1982.
Zaretsky, Irving I., and Mark P. Leone, eds.
  1974   *Religious Movements in Contemporary America.* Princeton, N.J.:
           Princeton University Press.

IV

Social Responses to Cults

Anson Shupe and David G. Bromley

The term *secularization* has been used in at least two analytically distinct ways: replacement of religious faith with faith in scientific principles, and increasing differentiation between the religious and secular spheres of life. Secularization in both senses clearly has been one of the major trends in modern history, but there is a real danger in extrapolating too much from this conclusion. The secularization hypothesis is premised on long-term, post factum observation rather than on theoretically based prediction. Perhaps the relatively linear pattern observed through the present will continue, or perhaps a longer-term cyclical pattern will emerge. The recent upsurge of new religions and the rapid growth of conservative groups in American society do not undermine the prediction of continuing secularization any more than the historical evidence up to the present confirms it.

Social science lacks the capacity to forecast the ultimate course of secularization. Instead we would argue that the most important issue on the sociological agenda should be investigating the process by which transcendent symbol systems are created and sustained. Nothing in the secularization hypothesis would lead to the conclusion that there is a net decline in transcendent (i.e., beyond the limits of possible experience) symbolic systems and their accompanying institutional forms. Indeed, everything we know about human relationships indicates that such symbols are necessary to the sustenance of the most important forms of human interaction. Although legitimating symbol systems have become differentiated along with institutions, all this means is that legitimation is now more institution-specific and not that there is less net use of transcendent symbol systems to legitimate specific spheres of social activity.

If we assume that the creation and maintenance of transcendent symbolic systems is a relative constant in social life, then what the contemporary social order offers is the opportunity to explore the role of these symbolic systems in a highly differentiated social context. It is particularly intriguing to explore the development of new religious (i.e., "cultic") forms since these constitute one of the responses to the rapid social change and anomie associated with differentiated social systems. In this chapter we shall discuss the *counter response* to new religious forms as a relatively neglected area of social research which, we hope, will broaden our understanding of both the role of the sacred in a secular society and the developmental process which new religious groups typically follow.

SYMBOL SYSTEMS AND CONFLICT

Invariably the creation of new sacred forms precipitates conflict because transcendent symbols are used to organize the mundane interactions that constitute the basic fiber of the social order. New symbolic and organizational systems offer new premises for social order. Confronted by a threat to legitimating symbols and behavioral systems, those elements of the established social order which are directly threatened reflexively initiate countermeasures to combat this threat. This reaction process results in the formation of religious countermovements. We contend that the study of religious countermovements in the context of secularized societies will yield a greater understanding of both secularization and the creation of the sacred. In our view, the current reaction to new religious groups reveals the perennial hostility to new forms of the sacred. In this particular case the forces of opposition happen to be largely secular.

Considerable research has been carried out on the formation and development of new religious groups. In contrast, research on religious countermovements is sketchy at best (Ben-Yehuda 1980; Goldstein 1978). Although historical accounts of the development of numerous religious groups make reference to organized opposition, there has been relatively little systematic study of it, particularly of opposition as an integral part of the process of the development of new religious groups. As a result, characteristic features and processes that accompany the development of many, if not most, religious groups have been treated as idiosyncratic. In recent years the need for an interactive model of the creation of the sacred has become more apparent, especially as the older deprivational approach (which ignores basic organizational issues and has not received impressive support from empirical research) and the classic church-sect model (which overemphasizes internal organizational factors in development) have fallen into disfavor among scholars.

The study of new religious movements and religious countermovements offers the beginnings of a useful corrective to these traditional approaches. Recent work, particularly what has grown out of the study of the controversy surrounding contemporary new religious movements, suggests a number of preliminary statements concerning religious countermovements. The illustrations presented in this chapter will be drawn primarily from the contemporary situation, although historical examples will be incorporated for comparative purposes. The preliminary statement presented here needs to be examined in light of historical as well as additional contemporary evidence; however, none of the limited findings available on earlier new religious groups and countermovements (Davis 1960; Robbins and Anthony 1979; Shupe and Bromley 1980*b*) appears to be inconsistent with current research findings.

THE EMERGENCE OF RELIGIOUS
COUNTERMOVEMENTS

Social movements are forces for change and, therefore, challenge to some degree established social beliefs and practices. By definition, countermovements arise as oppositional forces in response to strains created by efforts to produce change. The nucleus of such movements is therefore composed of those groups most directly affected by that change. The modern anticult movement, in the United States, Japan, and Europe, was formed by family members of converts to new religious groups (Shupe and Bromley 1980*a*, 1979; Beckford 1979, n.d.). Parents who had reared their children to achieve success in a secular society found the fact that their grown children would willingly abandon bright personal futures for a communal, religious life and/or the improbable goal of creating a utopian social order unacceptable, and often incomprehensible. Soon after such new religions as the Hare Krishnas, the Divine Light Mission, and the Unification Church began conducting intensive recruitment campaigns, family members began banding together in order to recover their errant offspring.

The established churches at congregational and denominational levels also often opposed the new religious groups. Mainstream denominations have largely accommodated themselves to the secular order and hence view the new religions as a threat to the delicate sacred-secular balance they have struggled so hard to achieve. Fundamentalist churches, which already regulate members' lives on the basis of Christian theology, have been threatened by new groups that offer different paths to salvation, different means by which to achieve spiritual experiences, and different voices of spiritual authority. Opposition by the churches is in many ways more easily organized since the contemporary new religious movements constitute merely the latest wave of newcomers to challenge orthodoxy.

In a larger sense, the conflict between new religious movements and the anticult movement constitutes a struggle between the sacred and the secular and, in a very real way, a struggle of a differentiated society against itself. The same differentiation and rationalization of the social order that produced extreme moral relativism and a pervasive sense of lack of community also yielded the fervent attempts to create religious meaning systems that would reinstitute a moral, integrated social order. Many of the new religions have appropriated to themselves the public role of restoring and defending a morally integrated social order, which is evidenced not just by their frequent microlevel projects, such as communal living, but sometimes by a deliberate attempt to try to bridge or blend separate societal institutions, such as science and religion. A classic example is the much publicized Unification Church. In turn, the anticult movement has appropriated the role of proxy defender of the secular order and has received the tacit and sometimes formal support of major institutions. The new religions and their youthful adherents make relatively easy targets since they are divided among themselves and lack any meaningful power base, but the campaign against "cults" addresses the symptoms rather than the source of social malaise. The anticult movement has gone to great lengths to deny that it is anti-religious, insisting that it merely opposes "pseudo-religions" (e.g., Rudin and Rudin 1980). However, in spite of such disclaimers, the vehement rejection of the new religious movements indicates the real limits for "legitimate" religion in a secular society.

THE ORGANIZATION OF COUNTERMOVEMENTS

Religious countermovements are organized for opposition, and therein lies both their strength and their weakness. On the one hand, it is always easier to unite in opposition to a common enemy than to cooperate in the achievement of positive goals. Thus the anticult movement consists of the unlikely coalition of moderate mainstream denominations, more radical elements among the fundamentalist Christian churches, middle-class parents, Jewish community groups, and the entrepreneur/mercenary deprogrammers. Despite the fact that each of these components of the coalition opposes new religious groups for different reasons, they avoid open criticism of one another.

On the other hand, strains do develop among these groups despite their common opposition to "cults." Parents (and deprogrammers as their agents), for example, are most concerned about the communally organized groups that take youth out of conventional life-styles. Jewish groups are opposed to any religious movements that pros- elytize Jewish youth, while fundamentalist Christian groups focus on new religions that challenge orthodox Christian theology (and simul- taneously often sponsor groups that proselytize Jewish youth). Par- ents of converts who turn to forcible abduction and deprogramming alarm fundamentalists and other sectarians who worry about the extension of such repressive tactics to themselves. At the same time that major parentally based anticult groups have sought to convince legislators that new religious groups are fraudulent and undeserving of the legal protections accorded legitimate groups (as they have done twice in public hearings held before federal officials [see CEFM 1976; Vol. I; AFF 1979]), fundamentalist Christian groups such as the Spiritual Counterfeits Project led a successful court fight to have Transcendental Meditation declared a religious organization so that its meditation techniques could not be taught in public schools. When most anticultists rail against cults they rarely mention the Jews for Jesus, an evangelical sect which many Jewish groups regard as the most pernicious cult of all. Such differences make apparent the patch- work quality of the coalition.

The organizational structures of religious countermovements are determined by their specific objectives, but they are also significantly influenced by the nature of the new religious groups they are combat- ing and by the legal and constitutional protections accorded to reli- gious organizations. The anticult campaign has been complicated (more than it would care to admit) by the diversity of its target groups. New religious movements differ substantially in theology, recruitment, and socialization practices. This heterogeneity has made it difficult both to develop effective substantive countermeasures and to make a convincing case that there is in fact a "cult problem" (Shupe and Bromley 1980a). Constitutional safeguards also have presented a major obstacle to anticult efforts to curb new religious groups. Although a number of powerful groups have expressed sympathy and support, particularly for the plight of parents whose adult children have joined new religions, there has been great official reluctance to overturn civil liberty guarantees simply in order to address their grievances. This combination of differences within the anticult movement, diversity among the new religious groups, and limitations on the tactics that can be used without provoking a counterreaction, reveal the real constraints on such countermovements.

One of the most intriguing and unexplored aspects of religious countermovements is the recurrence of certain key roles that predictably emerge. Certainly the most visible of these is the role of apostate; that is, defectors from the target group(s) who have converted to the countermovement (e.g., Edwards 1979; Martin 1979; Wood and Vitek 1979; Underwood and Underwood 1979). For most members of the public, knowledge of new religious groups remains indirect. They frequently learn about these groups only through media presentations. The media in turn rely heavily on apostate accounts since these humanize the face of evil, provide first-person accounts that verify the subversion claims of the countermovement, and reaffirm the moral superiority of conventional social values. Many of these accounts have a transparently vindictive or embellished "tall tale" quality about them (Bromley, Shupe, and Ventimiglia 1983), and countermovements have even been known to fabricate the credentials of apostates in order to provide such testimony (as in the nineteenth century's anti-Catholic and anti-Mormon movements when sham nuns and bogus "former" priests wrote tracts in abundance [see Billington 1974, 1952; Davis 1960]). The massive amount of literature and publicity attributable to these individuals is convincing evidence of their strategic importance.

Other generic features are prominent when direct action against the target group or its members is central to the countermovement strategy. One of the most common of these entails identifying and labeling individuals whose personal autonomy has been subverted by the new religious group. For instance, there is a remarkably consistent tendency to try to identify physical and mental characteristics presumably associated with any form of "possession" (Shupe and Bromley 1980b). These "stigmata" are used to identify individuals who require some type of processing in order to return them to a state of normalcy. Of course, the necessity of such processing results in specific ritualistic ceremonies, such as the traditional exorcism rituals of many religious traditions and the more recent deprogramming process, through which the individual is believed to be cleansed of subversive influences. It is this presumption of "possession" that creates the striking parallels between rituals such as exorcism and deprogramming. These stigmata and rituals can quickly evolve within a countermovement's folklore. If the countermovement is successful in gaining sufficient leverage over the target group (e.g., if police agents are either supportive or at least sympathetic and refrain from interfering during the "cleansing" ritual), some entrepreneurs may eventually attempt to institutionalize their activities and carve out quasi-legitimate careers. Witch-prickers and witch-hunters associated with various witch crazes throughout history (see Haining 1974) and contemporary deprogrammers exemplify both the profit and the peril of such ersatz careers. By and large, these occupations have been tenuous at best since they require a tremendous amount of unilateral power, continuing public hysteria, and a judiciousness in picking targets that is unlikely in emotionally charged conflicts.

COUNTERMOVEMENT IDEOLOGY

More predictable than the organizational structures of religious countermovements are their ideological structures. The terms in which the target groups are portrayed vary with the kind and degree of social control the countermovement seeks to exert: the greater the degree of control sought, the more extreme the imagery used to describe the group(s) and individual members. In general, countermovements seek a high degree of control when the threat to their constituent elements is great. Yet the degree of threat to other groups in the society which might be mobilized as allies is often minimal. It is imperative, therefore, that the countermovement couch its attack in terms of a broad defense of civic values. Target groups are thus typically portrayed as clear and present threats to the very survival of society. There have been predictions, for example, that unless cults are controlled by the federal government, America will witness a string of Jonestown-style mass suicides inspired by desperate gurus. It has even been suggested that cult mind-control techniques might be used on guards at military and nuclear installations. These accusations are not radically different from once-heard claims that Irish-Catholic immigrants were part of a papal conspiracy to take over the U.S. government by way of pro-Vatican voting blocs (Morse 1968), or that Joseph Smith intended to overthrow the state government of Illinois with his Mormon militia.

Where the blame is placed varies. Group leaders may be blamed, and followers regarded as innocent dupes (as in the case of Mormon women involved in polygamous marriages, Catholic girls who entered convents, and "Moonies" who raise funds for Sun Myung Moon's Unification Church). Or individual members may bear the brunt of the sanctions (as was the case during European witch crazes, when witch covens were fabricated to create the possibility of alleging participation in conspiracy). This highly rhetorical attack is effective since the changes in the social order envisioned by new religious groups often yield life-styles so at variance with those of conventional society that most individuals find them difficult to comprehend and often fundamentally threatening. For example, in the current cult controversy, the specter of hordes of robotlike youths doing the bidding of manipulative gurus has produced a fear similar to that produced by the belief that an obedient army of Jesuits was doing the bidding of a tyrannical Pope in nineteenth-century America. The various components of this ideology are frequently united in a conspiracy theory in which power and wealth constitute the motive, unscrupulous leaders are the architects of the plot, and unusual powers and manipulative tactics explain the participation of apparently innocent individuals in a sinister organization.

In the contemporary cult controversy, brainwashing is the basic explanation of how cults are able to gain and hold members. What is intriguing about this explanation is both the implicit positioning of the sacred and the secular and the effectiveness with which this metaphor serves the countermovement's purpose. The anti-cult movement has faced two problems in attempting to legitimate forcing adherents of new religious groups to renounce their affiliations. Both have contributed to the adoption of the brainwashing metaphor. First, in a highly differentiated society lacking a moral consensus and prizing individuality, allegations of serious damage to individuals are required to legitimate physical control over others' life-style preferences. Second, religious choices are regarded as matters of individual faith and, as such, immune from public or private interference. Brainwashing, then, constitutes a secular equivalent to spirit possession: the individual is rendered helpless against intrusive forces which, in this case, are scientifically grounded rather than religiously based.

The brainwashing argument thus removes the controversy from the religious sphere and, instead, purports that brainwashing compromises individual integrity seriously enough to warrant taking custody of the "victim." By treating changes in belief and life-style associated with membership in new religious groups as the products of secular forces, the boundaries of legitimate religion are redrawn in a manner consistent with secular interests.

The brainwashing metaphor also supports anticult interests in several other ways: (1) the concept has a certain public credibility as a result of its use in the Korean War POW literature (Lifton 1961, 1961; Schein, Schneier, and Backer 1961; Hunter 1953); (2) brainwashing permits lumping together many diverse and misunderstood recruitment and socialization techniques (ranging from chanting to "auditing" to meditation) under a common concept; (3) brainwashing implies neither mental illness in the conventional sense nor the usual stigma for participating in a deviant group. Individuals are thus free to reassume in rapid fashion conventional roles once the effects of mind control have been removed.

MOVEMENT-COUNTERMOVEMENT SYMBIOSIS

Ironically, movement and countermovement exist in a symbiotic relationship. Each in some respect needs the other despite their rhetoric and mutual antipathy. Despite their rejection of established churches in particular and conventional society in general, new religious groups nonetheless rely upon establishment values and life-styles to leverage their charges of corruption and moral decay. Members of these movements typically are most animated when they describe the difference between their former and present lives, and when they recount the persecution that they, as a group, experienced. In-group solidarity is enhanced by persecution itself, by the fact that the social order engaging in persecution is considered to be morally inferior, and by the fact that persecution continues even after its true face has been revealed. Individuals who have experienced persecution become "cultic" heroes, and apocryphal tales of their courage and endurance strengthen group loyalty. Currently, deprogramming serves precisely this function for new religious groups (Barker 1983). It is relatively easy for group leaders to depict deprogrammers as satanic agents, and to use repression to confirm their predictions that the group's spiritual truths will be rejected. Persecution can also exacerbate the conflict. Movements on the defensive become more likely to isolate themselves, ignore societal norms, lash out against apostates, draw up enemies lists, and even engage in violence as a result of "deviance amplification."

If the religious groups need the countermovement, the reverse is at least as true. Countermovements are by definition oppositional and hence require an opponent. Once established, therefore, countermovements are heavily dependent upon violations by the target movements if they are to sustain their campaigns. As a result, countermovements typically inflate the size, growth, and power of new religious movements. They increase the number of groups defined as subversive (i.e., cults), and they search for apostates with ever more sensational evidence to reveal (Shupe and Bromley 1980a:113). They use such measures to produce real or imagined evidence as they seek to have their own identifications and processing procedures accorded long-term legitimacy by other agencies of social control. Religious countermovements that span several decades, like fundamentalist coalitions, which have opposed Mormonism and Jehovah's Witnesses, frequently use new "cults" to revive interest in their campaigns. New groups are seen as evidence of continuing satanic intrusion in the world. There is a danger, of course, that such "hyping" will cause a countermovement campaign to collapse under the weight of its own contradictions. The course of anticommunist and anti-Catholic crusades suggests that the most likely prognosis is for the "scare" period to pass and the countermovement to linger on in relative obscurity, unless there is a renewal of tensions that once again make the group, or some new replacement, an inviting target.

THE IMPACT OF RELIGIOUS COUNTERMOVEMENTS

It is difficult to quantify the impact of religious countermovements on emerging religious groups. Although one can count the number of persons killed in anti-Catholic riots or the number of "Moonies" and Hare Krishnas forcibly deprogrammed, such figures do not represent the true measure of countermovement effectiveness or ineffectiveness. On the one hand, with the exception of anti-Mormon federal legislation that eventually disenfranchised that church's corporate structure in the late nineteenth century, religious countermovements have not been very successful at gaining passage of the repressive legislation they have sought, at mobilizing sufficient organizational resources to constitute a viable political force, or at capturing the limelight for long periods of time (Billington 1952; Kinzer 1964). On the other hand, they *have* been quite successful in rallying the public support for key institutions and in creating general fear and suspicion. In many ways this public discrediting has had the most profound consequences for new religious groups. The results have been problems in raising funds, recruiting new members, gaining favorable media coverage, securing the cooperation of public officials in purchasing property, establishing churches or starting businesses, holding public office, or finding a forum for conveying their theological messages. The results of official and unofficial fear and mistrust have usually outlived the religious countermovements as well as the practices that spawned the initial reactions.

Many of the current mechanisms of repression—creation of fear among the public by subversion mythology and apostate confirmations, investigations by governmental agencies, restrictive legislation and discriminatory application of rules and procedures, rejection by established churches—are remarkably similar to those employed in earlier conflicts. However, there are differences as well. In the contemporary conflict there has been less physical violence than was seen in reactions to earlier new religious groups, although coercive deprogrammings in many cases have involved tacitly sanctioned kidnapping. There have been no lynchings, few shootings, no castration. Likewise, the state has been more cautious about becoming involved, no doubt as a result of the constitutional precedents and the legacy of repression that modern eyes regard as overreaction.

New mechanisms of repression are, however, available which, even if less violent, are hardly less subtle. First, there is the enormous power of the printed and electronic media to create and disseminate imagery that is widely accepted without any direct, confirming experience on the part of the audience. The fierce competition for superior ratings and the strongly secular orientation of many media influentials have combined to produce a decidedly hostile and sensationalistic coverage of new religious groups. Second, there has been a tendency to "medicalize" deviance, which has permitted relatively severe sanctions, defined as "treatments," to be imposed on members of deviant groups (Robbins 1979). Indeed, the anticult movement has attempted to herald deprogramming as a "new mental health therapy" (Conway and Siegelman 1978) despite the legion of untrained practitioners associated with it, the forcible abductions, and the extensive use of theological refutations. The practice's many notable failures and obvious potential for preposterous application (e.g., in cases where persons are not associated with any religious group at all but are simply nonconformist, such as atheists or lesbians) are typically dismissed as irrelevant to the otherwise pressing need for deprogramming. Third, mirroring a more general social trend, extensive use has been made of civil suits by anticult groups. These suits have had the effect of seriously draining movement resources, forcing a defensive posture, and displacing energy that would otherwise be directed toward movement goals.

CONCLUSIONS

In this chapter we have argued that it is problematic whether the hypothesis that secularization is an enduring and irreversible process can be confirmed or disconfirmed, or that transcendent symbols and their accompanying organizational forms are less significant socially than they have been historically. It is nevertheless clear that there is more social differentiation now than at any previous time in history, and this situation allows us the opportunity to study the relationship between sacred and secular in a new context.

In exploring the sacred-secular relationship, particularly in a secular society, it is imperative that the social reaction to new religious forms be part of the agenda. Using data primarily from the contemporary cult controversy (but indicating some historical parallels), we have argued that an organized reaction to new religious movements is predictable, as are at least certain elements of its ideology and organization. In fact, there is a symbiotic relationship between movement and countermovement (which in the current controversy translates into sacred and secular) that shapes the form and direction of new religious groups. These statements constitute only the most preliminary basis for an understanding of the interactional relationship between the sacred and secular. Unlike many subjects in the sociology of religion and other topics analyzed in this volume, the systematic study of countermovements has had little precedent and is only just now beginning. A great deal more historical and comparative research is necessary if this perspective is to be developed further.

REFERENCES

AFF (American Family Foundation)
  1979   Transcript of Proceedings, Information Meeting on the Cult
           Phenomenon in the United States. Washington. D.C. Lexington,
           Mass.: American Family Foundation, Inc.
Barker, Eileen
  1983   "With Enemies Like That: Some Functions of Deprogramming
           as an Aid to Sectarian Membership." In David G. Bromley and
           James T. Richardson, eds., *The Brainwashing/Deprogramming Con-
           troversy.* New York: Edwin Mellen Press.
Beckford, James A.
  1979   "Politics and the Anti-Cult Movement," *Annual Review of the Social
           Sciences of Religion* 3:169–190.
  n.d.   "Cults, Controversy and Control: A Comparative Analysis of the
           Problems Posed by New Religious Movements in the Federal
           Republic of Germany and France." Durham, England: University
           of Durham.
Ben-Yehuda, Nachman
  1980   "The European Witch Craze of the 14th to 17th Centuries," *Amer-
           ican Journal of Sociology* 86 (July):1–31.
Billington, Roy A.
  1974   *The Origins of Nativism in the United States, 1800–1844.* New York:
           Arno Press.
  1952   *The Protestant Crusade, 1800–1860: A Study of the Origins of American
           Nativism.* Glouster, Mass.: Feter Smith.
Bromley, David G., Anson D. Shupe, Jr., and Joseph M. Ventimiglia
  1983   "The Role of Anecdotal Atrocities in the Social Construction of
           Evil." In David G. Bromley and James T. Richardson, eds.,
           The Brainwashing/Deprogramming Controversy. New York: Edwin
           Mellen Press.
CEFM (National Ad Hoc Committee Engaged in Freeing Minds)
  1976   *A Special Report. The Unification Church: Its Activities and Practices.*
           vols. 1 and 2. Arlington, Tex.: National Ad Hoc Committee: A
           Day of Affirmation and Protest.
Conway, Flo, and Jim Siegelman
  1978   *Snapping: America's Epidemic of Sudden Personality Change.* New
           York: Lippincott.
Davis, David Brion
  1960   "Some Themes of Counter-Subversion: An Analysis of Anti-
           Masonic, Anti-Catholic, and Anti-Mormon Literature," *The Mis-
           sissippi Valley Historical Review* 47 (September):205–224.
Edwards, Christopher
  1979   *Crazy for God.* Englewood Cliffs, N.J.: Prentice-Hall.

Goldstein, Robert J.
  1978   *Political Repression in Modern America.* Cambridge, Mass.:
          Schenkman Publishing Co., and Two Continents Publishing
          Group Ltd.
Haining, Peter, ed.
  1974   *The Witchcraft Papers: Contemporary Records of the Witchcraft Hysteria
          in Exxex, 1560–1700.* Secaucus, N.J.: University Books.
Hunter, Edward
  1962   *Brainwashing: From Pavlov to Powers.* New York: The Bookmailer.
  1953   *Brainwashing in Red China: The Calculated Destruction of Men's
          Minds.* New York: Vanguard.
Kinzer, Donald L.
  1964   *An Episode in Anti-Catholicism: The American Protective Association.*
          Seattle: University of Washington Press.
Lifton, Robert J.
  1961   *Chinese Thought Reform and the Psychology of Totalism.* New York:
          W. W. Norton.
Martin, Rachael
  1979   *Escape.* Denver: Accent Books.
Morse, Samuel F. B.
  1968   "The Dangers of Foreign Immigration." In *The Annals of America.*
          Vol. 6, *1833–1840, The Challenge of a Continent.* Chicago: William
          Benton. Pp. 158–163.
Robbins, Thomas
  1979   "Cults and the Therapeutic State," *Social Policy* 10 (May-June):
          42–46.
Robbins, Thomas, and Dick Anthony
  1979   "Cults, Brainwashing, and Counter-Subversion," *The Annals of
          the American Academy of Political and Social Science* 446 (Novem-
          ber):78–90.
Rudin, James, and Marcia Rudin
  1980   *Prison or Paradise? The New Religious Cults.* Philadelphia: Fortress
          Press.
Schein, Edgar H., Inge Schneier, and Curtis H. Backer
  1961   *Coercive Persuasion.* New York: W. W. Norton.
Shupe, Anson D., Jr., and David G. Bromley
  1980a   *The New Vigilantes: Deprogrammers. Anti-Cultists and the New Reli-
          gions.* Beverly Hills, Calif.: Sage.
  1980b   "Witches, Moonies and Accusations of Evil." In Thomas Robbins
          and Dick Anthony, eds., *In Gods We Trust.* New Brunswick, N.J.:
          Transaction Press.
  1979   "The Moonies and the Anti-Cultists: Movement and Counter-
          movement in Conflict," *Sociological Analysis* 40 (Winter):325–334.
Spiritual Counterfeits Project
  1978   *TM in Court.* Berkeley, Calif. Spiritual Counterfeits Project.

Underwood, Barbara, and Betty Underwood
  1979   *Hostage to Heaven*. New York: Clarkson N. Potter.
Wood, Allen T., and J. Vitek
  1979   *Moonstruck*. New York: Morrow.

PART TWO

Relocating the Sacred:
Methodological Issues

V

The Study of Social Change in Religion

Wade Clark Roof

Contemporary sociology of religion is frustrated in its efforts to study religious change in the modern world. It is difficult enough simply to document religious change, let alone interpret it. Virtually everyone admits that change has occurred in the twentieth century, yet few agree on the specific patterns or their implications. There is even little agreement among sociologists themselves, those who should presumably "know" best. As Jay Demerath (1968:349) says: "Ask [sociologists] any question and our response is likely to be a contemplative silence, a scholarly scowl, and finally a long list of methodological conundrums leading to that ultimate conclusion: 'It all depends.'"

The frustration is deeply rooted in the epistemological groundings of the discipline. Lacking is any consensus on a proper methodology or on a general data base for the field, and this is especially significant when it comes to the analysis of religious change. Here the "epistemic gap" between theory and data is most apparent, as a result of two quite divergent developments in recent times. On the one hand, the empirical base for the study of religious change has improved considerably in the past two decades. There is no question that, as a result of improved methods of sampling and data collection and analysis, considerably more is known today than even ten or fifteen years ago about church-oriented religion and its social characteristics. Not only is more known but we are also more confident about what we know. Increasingly the availability of national survey data makes it possible to describe the traditional religious parameters of the contemporary United States, and of many other modern societies, with remarkable precision and accuracy. General population data have helped to free the discipline from its long-standing captivity to church samples and denominational statistics, and thereby enhance the validity and reliability of its generalizations. Especially since the fifties, a large body of representative data on religious belief and behavior has accumulated, making it far more possible to draw sound inferences about religious trends (see Carroll and Roozen 1973; Davis 1978). In this respect it might be said that the data and analyses have never been better.

On the other hand, however, many of the new and exciting theoretical insights about modern religion have come from intellectual traditions not commonly associated with survey research. Especially phenomenology and symbolic anthropology have given the field fresh perspectives on the larger issues of religious symbolism, the relation of meaning to symbols, and the way in which "symbolic universes" convey religious realities to individuals and collectivities. The result is that we have a better understanding of contemporary religion and culture, changing religious forms in relation to modernity, and the plurality of meaning systems in contemporary society. Contemporary sociologists have come to recognize that religion in the modern world is diffused throughout the culture and no longer contained by formal institutions; they also recognize that many of the data obtained in conventional survey research fail to capture these important religious themes. The religious impulses most important in personal and social experience are often beyond the grasp of institutional indicators and standard survey items. Even with the best of sampling and survey techniques, it is not easy to obtain estimates of subtle religious and cultural trends that run deeper than those which are visibly manifest; operationally, approaches and procedures for examining cultural symbol systems and value-commitments are rudimentary at best.

The situation that exists, then, is a field characterized by a fundamental gap between its emerging theory and its most reliable data base. The best data tend to be limited to traditional religious patterns and tell us very little about the broader religious and cultural trends of modern society; and the theoretical perspectives that shed the greatest light on the trends are linked to very few hard data. The gap is serious, if for no other reason than that it leads to a good deal of conceptual confusion in matters of epistemology and methodology. The gap would be even more serious, however, were there not some signs of an emerging rapprochement between theorists and empirical researchers. Indeed, I shall argue that the situation is one that generates creative intellectual exchange and new insights about contemporary religious change. Much of the currently exciting research in the field is concerned with linking these newer theoretical approaches to empirical research, and thereby developing a firmer epistemological base for the field.

In this chapter I shall briefly examine three strands of current research focusing on: historical patterns of religious change, the secular context of religious belief, and varieties of meaning systems in modern society. The first involves macroreligious trends; the second, traditional church-oriented beliefs; and the third, broad reality structures. All three lines of research reflect recent efforts to link survey data with insights obtained from theoretical traditions emphasizing cultural themes and orientations. The topics are deserving of far more attention than can be given to them here, but in the space possible I hope to review some of the conceptual and methodological problems as well as the promises they hold for a better understanding of contemporary religious change.

PATTERNS OF RELIGIOUS CHANGE

Whatever else may be said about the 1960s and 1970s, events of the time raised some fundamental questions about the relation of religion and secularity in the modern age. Two religious developments elicited special attention: the rise of countercultural religions and the resurgence of evangelical Protestantism. Both gave evidence that religion, including "old-time" fundamentalist religion, was hardly dead and challenged any simple assumption about the inevitable decline of religion in the modern, secular world. The "secularization paradigm," which had held sway throughout most of this century and was highly influential among intellectuals, came under increasing criticism: it was too sweeping and too deterministic. Not that secularization was not a reality or force to be reckoned with, but it was becoming evident that modernity was not as antagonistic to religion as had once been thought. Secularization was neither as pervasive nor as irreversible as perhaps the early theorists had presumed; modernization entailed no obvious or necessary decline of religious belief and practice in contemporary society. The modern world was judged, almost intuitively, to be a complex phenomenon, consisting of religious and antireligious forces; to characterize it purely as either the secular city or a sacral culture was misleading.

There was more than intuition, however, to challenge any simple demise-of-religion thesis. Religious change itself surfaced as a topic

of inquiry, and with the improved trend data available, various researchers set out to examine empirically the patterns of religious
continuity and change. Both the temper of the times and the quality
of the research coincided to mark the efforts as worthy of serious
attention. Evidence bearing on the religious situation in the modern
period was much in demand.

One important research concern focused on the growth of conservative religion and its corollary, the decline of the liberal church. Kelly
(1977) led the way in charting the patterns of membership change for
various religious bodies. Several years later, in a Lilly-funded project
on "Church Growth and Decline," researchers explored in detail denominational and national religious trends from 1950 to the present
(Hoge and Roozen 1979). This project amassed a huge body of information on religious as well as cultural trends for the modern period.
Much that was important was uncovered here, but perhaps most
significant was the evidence documenting the decline of the liberal
mainstream churches. These churches flourished in the postwar years
when religion and the culture were well integrated but, about 1965,
institutional trends began to change. Data from many sources confirmed the turnaround in trends: denominational membership, Sun-
day School enrollments, church attendance, financial contributions,
and attitudes toward religious authority, the importance of religion,
and personal freedom. In a remarkable display of empirical consistency, the indicators pointed to what Martin Marty described as a
"seismic shift" in the religious landscape: the continuing and impressive growth of the conservative churches and the virtual demise
of the liberal religious establishment. The diverging denominational
patterns were symptomatic of a deeper, more basic polarization in
the culture. Values and attitudes generally were undergoing broad
shifts, with implications for the relation of the churches to the culture.

Themes of discontinuity and transition were echoed in other research quarters as well. At about the same time the "Church Growth
and Decline" project was getting under way, Robert Wuthnow published his provocative essay, "Recent Patterns of Secularization: A
Problem of Generations?" (1976). Here he looked at the widespread
religious changes in the context of the cultural ferment characterizing
the late sixties and early seventies. Documented was a general religious growth during the fifties followed by a general decline or substantially slower growth during the sixties and early seventies. As
with the denominational growth and decline trends, the data underscored a major discontinuity, or fluctuation, in institutional religious
commitment in the recent period. The fluctuation was interpreted by

Wuthnow as a generational phenomenon, resulting from the attempts of countercultural youth to differentiate themselves symbolically from other age strata. A decline in traditional religious commitment coincided, he argued, with the emergence of this self-conscious and disaffected generation.

These studies demonstrate rather conclusively the importance of distinct, and sometimes sudden and precipitous, shifts in patterns of institutional religiosity. Though there is some dispute about the nonlinearity of the data patterns (see Rigney et al. 1978, for a response to Wuthnow), the research offers empirical confirmation in the modern period for major transitions of the sort historians describe for the Great Awakening of the early eighteenth century, or the "religious depression" of the 1930s. From the erratic character of these patterns, it is clear that recent religious trends cannot be understood fully by theories of secularization which link religious decline to relatively continuous processes such as industrial expansion, urbanization, or the diffusion of scientific knowledge. Required are explanatory paradigms that allow for the shifts and irregularities that actually occur over the historical course.

With trend data increasingly available, it should be possible for researchers to specify more exactly the course of historical religious changes. Of course, even the better data that exist are far from complete, and qualitative religious changes of the sort described here are not fully captured by empirical indexes; yet the data available allow for far more longitudinal analysis than ever before. Simple linear conceptualizations must give way to more complex models of religious change, involving nonlinear, or a combination of linear and nonlinear, components. Both the magnitude and the temporal phasing of trends can be profiled with greater exactness, establishing periods of continuity and discontinuity. Better models will not only describe religious "fluctuations" and "eras" more accurately but will also yield the information necessary for determining how best to represent the long-term changes theoretically: whether as pendulum-type "cycles" or as brief religious reactions to the dominant secular trend.

In interpreting patterns of change, there is, of course, no substitute for an informed and creative sociological imagination. Once the data patterns are established, it is necessary to explain why they occur. For this, a sensitivity to historical and symbolic changes in the way in which religion is experienced is crucial. As the modern period has shown, religious shifts closely follow cultural shifts, with the greatest religious discontinuities occurring in times when there are sharp breaks in cultural perceptions and experiences. This suggests the importance of cultural and symbolic modes of interpretation for religious change. Hence, in future analyses of religious trends, we can expect more attention to be given to such considerations as *time periods* (e.g., "generations" or "cultural epochs"), *events* (e.g., Vatican II, the Great Depression, or the Vietnam War), *leaders* (e.g., Pope John XXIII, Martin Luther King, Jr., or Lech Walesa), and *pronouncements* (e.g., Harry Emerson Fosdick's rousing sermon in 1922, "Shall the Fundamentalists Win?" or the papal encyclical of Paul VI, *Humanae Vitae*, reaffirming traditional proscriptions against birth control). In combination—that is, with better trend data and symbolic interpretation—we are likely to have more reliable, culturally based explanations for religious change; also we are likely to have better, historically informed interpretations of the patterns of continuity and change.

TRADITIONAL BELIEF IN CONTEMPORARY SOCIETY

Of the many aspects of contemporary religion for study, few are as baffling as the changes in religious belief. The lack of historical data makes it virtually impossible to draw conclusions about how beliefs have changed since the turn of the century. Describing belief today is hard enough. The difficulties of measurement in this highly subtle and subjective realm are widely acknowledged. Consequently, there are few valid and reliable indexes of general religious belief, and even fewer that tap the specific beliefs of particular religious traditions. Yet because belief is so central a component of faith, it cannot be easily avoided or dismissed. Either implicitly or explicitly, the topic crops up almost inevitably in discussions on religion, and especially in the context of secular change.

Despite problems of measurement, questions on traditional religious belief are standard fare in survey research. The approach is generally to focus rather narrowly on the basic tenets of the historic Judeo-Christian heritage. Two beliefs have received most attention in the polls: belief in God and belief in life after death. Both beliefs are measured by very general questions that presuppose a traditional religious affirmation. And both questions have long been asked by the pollsters, thereby providing us with trend data on American belief over the past forty years.

This accumulated body of information has led to some new insights into the place of traditional belief in modern culture. It is known, for example, that between 95 and 98 percent of Americans consistently report belief in God, the figures varying little from year to year; the normative expectations are such that few Americans, apparently, will deny a belief in God. With respect to belief in life after death, the proportions have declined slightly from 77 percent in 1944 to 70 percent in the late seventies; but more importantly, there have been some further shifts that are discernible by survey techniques (see Nelsen 1981). The research shows that whereas the belief has declined only slightly, disbelief has increased more significantly than perhaps would be expected. The number of those openly rejecting belief in life after death appears to be growing while the number of those who are uncertain about the doctrine is shrinking—which suggests that disbelievers in America increasingly find it easier to express disbelief. If this is the case, we have evidence here describing an important change in the willingness of Americans to admit religious doubt or disbelief about basic religious doctrines (also see Hertel and Nelsen 1974).

It is also fair to say, however, that such studies have not advanced our understanding of religious change as much as we might have expected. The problem is partly lack of variation in the expressed beliefs and lack of comparable data on other beliefs, but more fundamentally it is one of conceptualization. Typically the measures focus upon the traditional beliefs as they have been handed down in creedal and doctrinal statements. Often quite literal and fundamentalist formulations of belief are taken as the norm against which to examine their acceptance or not. Substance of belief is assumed to be constant and the most important aspect, and hence the concern as usually stated is with the "extent" of orthodox belief rather than with the "nature" of what is believed. Lacking is concern with the qualitative aspects of belief, such as its content, its saliency, its urgency, or its centrality in a total religious system. The fact that the meanings of belief may vary independently of their formal properties is left unexplored.

This is a serious shortcoming when it comes to the conceptualization of religion and secularity. Given the focus on the "extent" of orthodox belief, the lack of belief in a narrow substantive sense tends to be construed as evidence of secularity. That is to say, traditional religious belief is often construed in a rather simple, "zero-sum" relationship with secularism: as religious belief goes down, secularism goes up, or vice versa. Implicitly in this calculation is the assumption that secularism is antithetical to religion, that the two are locked into a relationship in which a gain for one must result in a loss for the other. Obviously this is a very simplistic conceptualization and fails to reflect the subtler facets of religious and secular change, yet it is not uncommon in empirical studies.

Such conceptualization flies in the face of many of the provocative theoretical views on religion and secularity in American society. To cite an example from the past, Will Herberg (1960) envisioned a situation in the fifties in which the country was *simultaneously* becoming more religious and more secular. He described a nation in which the houses of worship were filled and religious indentification was at an all-time polling high, but the religious beliefs of Americans had eroded and had become more a celebration of the "American Way of Life" than of the historic Judeo-Christian faith. Important qualitative changes in belief were associated with changes in religious behavior— in a direction hardly in keeping with the alleged "religious revival" of the time. Or to take a more current example, consider the evangelical movement so prominent in American religious life today. The resurgence of evangelical Protestantism currently rests upon a complex synthesis of religious and secular elements. Viewed broadly from a sociology of knowledge perspective, this religiocultural form represents more than simply a traditional religious reaffirmation; it entails an accommodation to modernity as reflected in somewhat more domesticated belief and more rational cognitive styles, setting today's evangelicals off from their earlier counterparts. Through "cognitive bargaining," or the process of selective accommodation to the structural and symbolic forces of modernity, the evangelical belief system is shaped to meet the contemporary situation (see Hunter 1983). What both examples illustrate is that religion and secularism relate to each other in complex and subtle fashion, and that in order to understand belief systems and their dynamics in modern society they must be viewed in a broad social context.

It is quite clear that new approaches to the study of religious belief are called for which will encompass the qualitative aspects of belief and pose the relation of religion and secularity in a more insightful way. *Operative* versus *formal* types of belief emerges as an important distinction, helpful for analyzing how beliefs are appropriated in a given cultural context. Whereas formal beliefs refer to official doctrines and creeds, operative beliefs are the meanings associated with these doctrines and creeds in a particular circumstance. Operative beliefs are thus "filtered" through life-experiences and are associated with the myths, images, norms, and values that make up a way of life. From this vantage point, any simple distinction between religion and secularity breaks down, since the meanings associated with religious faith are generated out of social experience. Far from existing in a secular or cultural vacuum, operative beliefs are plausible insofar as they relate the historic affirmations of faith to a particular life-situation.

Empirical research is moving in several directions that promise to yield greater insight into traditional religious belief in its secular context. One is the focus on "images" of God. Broughton (1975) and, more recently, Piazza and Glock (1979) have shown that Americans vary considerably in how they imagine God—in traditional and non-traditional ways. Contrasting images of deity are found within all the major religious bodies in contemporary America; the evidence indicates that the types of images are socially distributed along predictable lines and are related to personal and social attitudes. Further research along this line will fill a conspicuous gap in our understanding of the content of contemporary religious belief. No doubt it will show that the content varies in response to types of social experience, extent of traditional religious socialization, and exposure to secular values.

Another line of research concerned with traditional belief systems in contemporary society is patterned largely after the analysis of political belief systems, a focus of study that has long attracted empirical researchers (Converse 1964). Belief systems vary in their degrees of consistency, constraint, cognitive complexity, and strength—all important characteristics in examining traditional religion in the modern setting. Research has demonstrated variation in belief systems by education and breadth of perspective: the broader the cognitive orientation, the greater the belief consistency and ethical constraint (Gabennesch 1972; Roof 1978). Variation of this kind helps to account for the wide discrepancies between the laity and the clergy, internal tensions and conflicts, and "private" versus "public" forms of religiosity within the churches. More than just explorations into belief system dynamics, such research also contributes to our understanding of the social bases of traditional religion in contemporary society. Studies of the "social construction of religious reality" underscore the fact that church-oriented beliefs and practices are not uniformly distributed in the society, but vary according to such factors as ethnic group, regional enclaves, family and kin networks, and the local community. The meanings and plausibilities of traditional faiths depend greatly in a secularized culture on the social location of the believer and extent of network attachments and group support.

Finally, "biographical"analysis is an undeveloped, but resourceful, means of studying religious change. According to the "Unchurched American" study, for example, 46 percent of Americans drop out of active religious participation for a period of two years or more at some time during their lifetimes (Roozen, 1980). A large proportion of these return to active participation, thus suggesting that there is no rigid religious or cultural boundary between the "churched" and the "unchurched" in the United States. With so many people moving in and out of the churches over the course of their life spans, there is need for intensive inquiry into individual life histories and the events surrounding individual decisions to drop out of, or return to, the churches. Although the "Unchurched American" study (Princeton Religion Research Center 1978) uncovered a great deal of survey information on the factors involved in religious disengagement, a more thorough reconstruction of life-cycle developments and experiences should help to sort out the many links between changing religious beliefs and changing institutional ties. Despite its limitations as a research methodology, biographical analysis can reveal important insights into the interrelation of religious and secular themes, and especially as these interact with age and gender experiences; indeed, it may be the only way to explore the subtle shifts of religious meaning and belonging as they relate to personal identities and distinctive experiences.

VARIETIES OF MEANING SYSTEMS

Still another approach to the study of religious change is that of alternative meaning systems. The focus upon meaning systems arises out of the phenomenological analysis of religion and is concerned with the meanings associated with cultural symbols. In modern society various forms of symbolism are presumed to exist: traditional and nontraditional, theistic and nontheistic. The approach is to look at the "symbolic universes" that convey meaning and order to reality, and to explore the similarities and differences in the many systems that exist in modern society. Quests for meaning are taken as universal life-experiences, recognizing that these quests may be fulfilled by various kinds of reality structures—religious or not.

The attraction of this approach is that it treats as worthy of investigation the larger question of reality construction and is concerned not simply with traditional religious meaning systems. For the sociology of religion, this is a welcome expansion of intellectual horizons that shifts attention from its long-standing preoccupation with "church religion" and places religious study in a larger framework. The recent infusion of ideas and insights from phenomenology and symbolic anthropology has had considerable theoretical influence in the sociology of religion. Peter Berger, Thomas Luckmann, Jurgen Habermas, Clifford Geertz, and Claude Lévi-Strauss, have all played an important part in shaping the discipline's intellectual parameters in recent times. Largely as a result of the new perspectives generated by these writers, the field has become more sensitive to the problematic aspects of traditional religion in modern culture and to the need for a broad approach to the study of religious and quasi-religious forms.

To what extent, however, have these ideas and insights inspired empirical study? Is there a developing link between such theory and research? Despite the difficulties of empirical research in this theoretical tradition, a burgeoning research agenda exists. Questions about the types of meaning systems and their distribution in modern society are increasingly defined as empirical issues for investigation, not as mere speculations. Yinger's research on "non-doctrinal religion" (1969) was an early attempt to identify and measure ultimate concerns independent of traditional belief. McCready and Greeley (1976) attempted to operationalize "the religious interpretative scheme" used by Americans in dealing with ultimate issues and were able to estimate how many people used the various schemes. Glock and Piazza's "Exploring Reality Structures" (1978) was a further attempt at probing several differing types of meaning systems, or ways of interpreting reality. The latter was particularly insightful in describing the plurality of meaning systems in contemporary America.

The most ambitious research of this kind, however, is Wuthnow's San Francisco study (1976), exploring what he regards as the most prominent symbolic frames in American culture. He postulates four major types of meaning systems distinguished from one another by what they identify as the primary force governing or interpreting life: theism, individualism, social science, mysticism. Symbolically they encompass quite differing notions of how and why the world is as it is, of the forces that operate in life, and the basis for imputing meaning to experience. The research examined the four meaning systems broadly, including the behavioral, value, and attitudinal correlates of each. On the basis of the findings, Wuthnow concludes that some fundamental shifts are occurring in the frames of reference by which people come to grips with their lives. Traditional theistic and individualistic conceptions, once fused into a single meaning system in

American culture, now appear to operate independently of one another. Moreover they both appear to be declining, whereas social-scientific and mystical modes of ordering reality are becoming more widespread. Having identified the dominant meaning systems (plus several mixed types), he goes on to examine the social contexts in which they are found in contemporary American life.

Quite clearly, the San Francisco study is of limited use for generalizing about American society, but the work is a major advance in that it combines a theoretical focus on symbolic frames of reference with survey research methods. This is not an easy accomplishment, given the inherent limitations of such theory in providing empirical directives. Yet it appears to be on the threshold of new ventures. Wuthnow's work will likely serve as a basis for further efforts of this kind. By incorporating empirical measures of meaning systems into national surveys and more sophisticated operational procedures, we can expect to learn a great deal more about alternative reality structures for the population as a whole. In this respect, Bibby's recent Canadian study (1983), exploring religious and humanist meaning systems in a national survey, is a welcome contribution to this line of research.

Already a number of conceptual issues have emerged which are likely to be the focus of attention and controversy in future research. One is the extent to which meaning systems are themselves identifiable in modern society. In a recent reanalysis of Wuthnow's data, Bainbridge and Stark (1981) report that they find empirical support for only one meaning system—theism. They argue that meaning systems are easier to sustain if based on supernatural beliefs and reinforced through tightly knit social relationships, thus accounting for traditional religion as a meaning system; however, with Wuthnow's more personal, more secular systems—individualism, social science, and mysticism—they note that these elements are lacking. Bainbridge and Stark raise important questions about the empirical basis of nontheistic meaning systems and whether it makes sense to treat these as similar to traditional religious approaches. The extent to which nonreligious symbols cluster as a coherent system of meaning, and are recognized as such empirically, is open for debate. The controversy encompasses epistemological as well as methodological issues (see Wuthnow 1981); its resolution will require both conceptual clarification and more empirical research.

Perhaps the most basic issue in this area is the extent to which integrated life-meaning systems actually exist. Philosophically we tend to assume that meaning systems bring about order and coherence, and thereby integrate personal life; types of meanings may vary but the need for meaning is taken for granted. It cannot be easily determined just how basic the search for meaning is, and it is conceivable that we may expect too much in the way of conscious and fully articulated meanings. In fact, Bibby's research (1983) casts doubt on the general assumption of integrated meaning systems. In his analysis of personal satisfaction derived from five spheres—work, family, friendships, leisure, and community—he found that significant numbers of Canadians fail to exhibit highly integrated lives; and, significantly, the lack of integration was not strongly associated with meaning system themes. These findings suggest that people's cognitive meanings in modern society are to a great extent fragmentary, and draw on mixed and syncretistic elements. Speaking of Canadians as an "unfocused majority," Bibby describes them as "people who hold bits and pieces of religious beliefs and humanist values, yet have unclear interpretations of their existence" (1983:118). Generally in this line of research it is unclear whether people in many instances lack an articulated meaning system, or if social science is as yet unable to measure such meanings successfully. With further advances in measurement techniques, and with ingenuity in research there will likely come a better understanding of these fundamental issues.

CONCLUSIONS

The research described in this brief chapter hardly exhausts the many empirical strands within the current sociology of religion. My intent was not to summarize the field as a whole but to point out some promising directions for its future. What is "promising" was defined from the standpoint of the emerging rapprochement between theory and research. While focusing primarily on issues that have already commanded attention, I have also speculated about leads that seem likely to provoke further study. My assumption is that significant developments are occurring in the field at present, and my purpose here has been to identify these as crucial issues for attention in future analysis of religious change.

Virtually everything today is converging in the direction of better analysis of religious trends: improved data, more sophisticated research methods, more insightful theoretical perspectives. And not least of all, contemporary society offers an unprecedented opportunity for the analysis of religious and cultural changes. For both the traditional and nontraditional religious realms, the situation today is one that invites inquiry into a rich and exciting field of study. The richness and excitement also hold great promise for the discipline. Better interpretations of religious change, both theoretically insightful and empirically based, can only lead to a more enriched and respected discipline. Indeed, the very future of the sociology of religion may depend on how well it grasps the breadth and depth of changes currently under way.

REFERENCES

Bainbridge, William Sims, and Rodney Stark
    1981   "The 'Consciousness Reformation' Reconsidered," *Journal for the Scientific Study of Religion* 20 (March):1–16.
Bibby, Reginald W.
    1983   "Searching for Invisible Threads: Meaning Systems in Contemporary Canada," *Journal for the Scientific Study of Religion* 22 (June): 101–119.
Broughton, Walter
    1975   "Theistic Conceptions in American Protestantism," *Journal for the Scientific Study of Religion* 14 (December):331–344.
Carroll, Jackson W., and David A Roozen
    1973   "National Sample Questions on Religion: An Inventory of Material Available from the Roper Public Opinion Research Center," *Journal for the Scientific Study of Religion* 12 (September):325–338.
Converse, Philip E.
    1964   "The Nature of Belief Systems in Mass Publics." *In* David E. Apter, ed., *Ideology and Discontent.* New York: Free Press. Pp. 206–261.
Davis, James A.
    1978   *General Social Surveys, 1972–1978: Cumulative Codebook.* Chicago: National Opinion Research Center.
Demerath, N. J. III
    1968   "Trends and Anti-Trends in Religious Change." *In* Eleanor B. Sheldon and Wilbert E. Moore, eds., *Indicators of Social Change.* New York: Russell Sage Foundation. Pp. 349–445.
Gabennesch, Howard
    1972   "Authoritarism as World View," *American Journal of Sociology* 77 (March):867–868.
Glock, Charles Y., and Thomas Piazza
    1978   "Exploring Reality Structures," *Society* 15:60–65.
Herberg, Will
    1960   *Protestant-Catholic-Jew.* Garden City: Doubleday.

Hertel, Bradley R., and Hart M. Nelsen
  1974   "Are We Entering a Post-Christian Era? Religious Belief and Attendance in America, 1957–1968," *Journal for the Scientific Study of Religion* 13 (December):409–419.
Hoge, Dean R., and David A. Roozen
  1979   *Understanding Church Growth and Decline: 1950–1978.* New York: Pilgrim Press.
Hunter, James Davidson
  1983   *American Evangelicalism: Conservative Religion and the Quandary of Modernity.* New Brunswick, N.J.: Rutgers University Press.
Kelley, Dean M.
  1977   *Why Conservative Churches Are Growing.* New York: Harper and Row.
McCready, William C., and Andrew M. Greeley
  1976   *The Ultimate Values of the American Population.* Beverly Hills: Sage.
Nelsen, Hart M.
  1981   "Life Without Afterlife: Toward Congruency of Belief across Generations," *Journal for the Scientific Study of Religion* 20 (June):109–118.
Piazza, Thomas, and Charles Y. Glock
  1979   "Images of God and Their Social Meanings." *In* Robert Wuthnow, ed., *The Religious Dimension: New Directions in Quantitative Research.* New York: Academic Press. Pp. 69–91.
Princeton Religion Research Center
  1978   *The Unchurched American.* Princeton: The Gallup Organization, Inc.
Rigney, Daniel, Richard Machalek, and Jerry D. Goodman
  1978   "Is Secularization a Discontinuous Process?" *Journal for the Scientific Study of Religion* 17 (December):381–387.
Roof, Wade Clark
  1978   *Community and Commitment: Religious Plausibility in a Liberal Protestant Church.* New York: Elsevier.
Roozen, David A.
  1980   "Church Dropouts: Changing Patterns of Disengagement and Re-Entry," *Review of Religious Research* 21 (Supplement):427–450.
Wuthnow, Robert
  1976   "Recent Patterns of Secularization: A Problem of Generations?" *American Sociological Review* 41 (October):850–67.
  1981   "Two Traditions of Religious Studies," *Journal for the Scientific Study of Religion* 20 (March):16–32.
Yinger, J. Milton
  1969   "A Structural Examination of Religion," *Journal for the Scientific Study of Religion* 8:88–99.

VI

New Perspectives from Cross-Cultural Studies

Hans Mol

Cross-cultural comparisons are the best possible means for puncturing theories of religion that have swollen prematurely. Explanations often have to be revised when a larger context is taken into account. Yet, astoundingly often, articles in reputable journals and books by well-known scholars are monuments of parochialism. (For early documentation of narrow American assumptions in explanatory schemes, see Mol, Hetherton, and Henty 1972:2–3.) Compulsion to publish, refereeing by colleagues of the same ilk, and the incapacity of scholars to keep up with publications in their specialty have done little to improve the situation since then.

Here is one example: Batson and Ventis (1982:40–43) review the (exclusively American) literature as to why race is a powerful predictor of religious experience in the United States, and why blacks are more religious than other races. Centrality of religion in the role definition of blacks (a tautology, if there ever was one!), plus minority oppression intensifying existential questions are their major explanations. In New Zealand, however, Maoris go to church less frequently than whites, even though the Maori wars in the nineteenth century and the present-day separateness of Maoris would lead one to expect them to be more religious than whites if the American argument were correct. It would seem that the availability of *various* means (religion being only one) for defending a subculture is a better frame of reference than a narrow deprivation theory for understanding the relation between race and religion. Unlike American blacks, perhaps, Maoris have other means than religion at their disposal for reinforcing racial integrity. This example of poor theory—resting on too parochial a data base—could be multiplied many times over.

More positively, then, I would state my main argument: Cross-cultural comparisons have directed at least some scholars (including myself) beyond the classics in the social scientific study of religion to more comprehensive models, which in turn has led to a rejection of secularization as an inexorable process. I want to lead up to this point by tracing the theoretical reformulations which cross-cultural data compelled me to make, especially the work sponsored by the research committee in the sociology of religion of the International Sociological Association in the 1970s. I want to apologize in advance for the somewhat autobiographical turn this chapter is thus going to take, but I can make the point best by using my own research problems as examples. Moreover, the procedure will show how the development of a comprehensive model of religion and society progressed precisely because of the ill fit of existing theories with cross-cultural and dia-chronic data. The procedure may also help meet the editor's request for maximum readability.

A Marxist interpretation of religion (that it preserves the power of the ruling classes) was taken for granted in the enlightened Dutch farming family in which I grew up during the Depression. Likewise the Weberian view of a fateful rationalization of magic and an inescap-able secularization of capitalistic society fitted well with the liberal rationalism of high school and university. But then in the spring of 1944 I found myself in the prison of Magdeburg (now East Germany) for subverting the German war machinery. At first there was not much reason to change my Marxist and Weberian views of religion: the prison chaplains began and ended their services with "Heil Hitler" and pliably prayed for Führer, fatherland, and victory. The German war effort was a grandiose example of successful, rational planning and efficient execution, and religion was seemingly irrelevant to what was going on.

Yet the old Lutheran guard in charge of the third floor of the prison where I was had strong millenarian convictions about the coming new age, and about heaven where the streets were paved with gold. There was also a dedicated communist and a Jehovah's Witness who proclaimed to all and sundry that Hitler was the anti-Christ. All three were held in as much respect by the assorted murderers, perverts, pickpockets, and political prisoners as the chaplains and other intellectuals (whose moral fiber proved to be remarkably fragile) were held in contempt. The guard, the communist, and the Jehovah's Witness appeared to be islands of religious integrity in a whirlpool of decadence, death (hundreds had died in the previous weeks in a typhus epidemic), and destruction. In an unobtrusive way they had become heroes of coping. On a much larger scale outside the prison walls, the efficient war machinery was driven by what can only be described as the religious fervor of nationalism. The reason my friends and I were inside was because we had made fun of ardent German patriotism and had countered the propaganda machine with news from the B.B.C. we had picked up on our clandestine radio receiver.

My point is that here was vibrant religion—on the level both of a prison subculture and of a nation—for which the interpretations of religion I had taken for granted gave no explanation. The Marxist view of religion as alienating individuals and reinforcing the ruling class was too narrow, and Max Weber's stress on methodical rationalization had to be complemented by an equal emphasis on nonrational commitment. ⟍ *charisma*

The historical data I unearthed for my Ph.D. dissertation in sociology at Columbia University at the end of the fifties similarly did not fit a Weberian frame of reference. In my thesis I tried to determine why in America the evangelical/pietist Dutch, German, and Scottish clergy in the first half of the eighteenth century succeeded in Americanizing their respective denominations while their orthodox counterparts failed to do so. Both doctrinal groups possessed what Max Weber and Talcott Parsons (1949:549) called the Archimedean point of the Protestant Ethic, which should have given them a reconstructing advantage in general, beyond the more particular capacity to reconstruct the economic order. (Robert K. Merton [1957:574 ff.], who was one of the supervisors of the thesis, had made a similar point for science.) Yet one group (the evangelicals) had been able to detach themselves from the units of social organization (family, community, nation) in Europe, whereas the other group (the orthodox) had not. The crucial intervening variable, I suggested (Mol 1968:69), was "the degree of commitment or surrender to this Archimedean point" which allowed for the relativizing of emotional attachments to previous patterns.

The implication of this point (worked out later in Mol 1974: 279 ff., and 1983:24 ff.) was that for a better-fitting social scientific theory of religion, transcendentalization (making order into an object so that mundane disorder and conflict can be relativized) had to be complemented by commitment (emotional attachment, which could also detach, change previous loyalties, and therefore "de-commit" as well as "commit").

My New Zealand research in the early sixties gave me more grounds to doubt the "inexorable secularization" thesis. In a research project dealing with the adjustment of Dutch immigrants to New Zealand society, I found that the least secularized religious organizations were the most viable and retained the best hold on their immigrant membership (Mol 1965:42). In another project, sponsored by the National Council of Churches in New Zealand, those religious organizations most in tune with secular society proved also to be least capable of integrating the Maoris (native Polynesians) and Pakehas (white settlers) into one worshipping community. In contrast, the anything-but-establishment Church of the Latter Day Saints mixed the races effortlessly, showing that the least secularized religious organizations were the most cohesive and could (and did) act independently of the secular culture (Mol 1966:60; also Mol 1982:53).

These findings suggested that, if the concept of secularization were to apply at all, one would have to distinguish between cultural and institutional secularization—between the decreasing influence of religious institutions (what Parsons [1963] called differentiation) and the tendency disposing religious institutions to become part of and like the world (Mol 1970:183). Since those churches and sects whose *institutional* secularization was minimal were also the fastest growing and most viable, I suggested that *cultural* secularization seemed to conjure up its own opposite (lessening secularization) in at least some Christian churches. This point was also taken up in my *Christianity in Chains* (1969). In that book I attacked the assumptions set forth in the prevailing church/society literature: that the social relevance of the Christian religion in Western society depended on its capacity to adjust to secular expectations. The book's thesis was that social relevance could result from an independent stance. As the book was published in Australia and my writing style in those days had not yet escaped a certain European heaviness, it was remaindered even before a similar thesis was developed by Dean Kelley in 1972.

What remained in my mind were two growing convictions: The first was that a comprehensive social scientific theory of religion must start from a perspective in which not just society and individuals but also numerous other units of social organizations (family, tribe, community, class, clan, neighborhood, sects, and other corporate organizations) are seen as both cooperating and contending. The second conviction is actually best stated in a much neglected book (Fallding 1974:210):

. . . secularization is the analytical process that has sacralization for the complementary synthesizing process. They make a dialectic. Secularization, through the operation of reason, breaks down; sacralization, through the operation of faith, builds up.

In the beginning of the 1970s an international body of sociologists of religion, most of whom met at the world congresses of the International Sociological Association, cooperated in producing *Western Religion* (Mol, Hetherton, and Henty 1972). This book provided an overview of data collected on religious beliefs, practices, and their correlations with sex, residence, occupation, education, political affiliation, and so forth, for approximately thirty Western countries. In the Introduction, we attempted to use the data on church attendance for an appraisal of the secularization thesis. Again data and theory did not fit. Industrialization, urbanization, and technological advance did *not* neatly correlate with lesser church attendance, not even within the same country. In Portugal, for instance, attendance in Lisbon was higher than in the rural south. Attendance in the average American city was higher than anywhere in rural Scandinavia.

One of the contributors to *Western Religion*, David Martin (pp. 233–234), suggested that a variety of variables such as Protestant individualism, Catholic collectivism, class antagonism, religious pluralism versus state religion, minority status, and religion as the rallying point in oppressed people, would—in addition to industrialization, and in various combinations—correspond with variation in religious practices. He developed this point further in the best recent attempt to relate cross-cultural data to a theoretical frame of reference (*A General Theory of Secularization* 1978). Martin, who succeeded Bryan Wilson as president of the International Conference of the Sociology of Religion in the second half of the 1970s, has an encyclopaedic knowledge of the patterns of religious change and political power all across the globe, and he used this knowledge to differentiate among several categories of religiocultural identity (p. 77–78) as well as other kinds of identity (regional, national, ethnic and, to a lesser extent, communal) on which religion had a consolidating or destabilizing effect. He did not believe that secularization was an inevitable trend (p. 12) and went so far as to say: "If anomie, depersonalization and other characteristics of contemporary society decline then the erosion of religion may be reversed" (p. 85).

The data in *Western Religion,* together with those of *Religion in Australia* (Mol 1971), cried out for further theoretical reformulation. If variation in church attendance all over the Western world corresponds with variation in a relatively small number of variables (such as the position of a particular religious organization in a network of national, regional, class, communal, personal, church/sect alliances and conflicts), could this middle-range generalization in turn be linked to a wider theory? *Identity and the Sacred* (Mol 1976) was the result. I suggested in that book that a differentiation approach to religion was incomplete unless it was counterbalanced by an identity perspective, meaning that, through transcendental ordering, emotional anchoring, sameness enacting, and dialectic dramatization, religion restored to wholeness what change had fragmented. In other words, the sacralizing process stood in a symbiotic or dialectic relation to the secularizing process. Secularization was defined (p. 5) as "the outcome of differentiations exceeding the capacity of religious organizations to integrate them in the traditional frame of reference, with the result that, on all levels, identities and systems of meaning are becoming sacralized by agencies other than these organizations." And this meant that, like Luckmann (1967) and later Martin (1978), I felt that only a functional definition (religion defined as the "sacralization of identity") could do justice to such phenomena as rites of passage in communist countries or the ardent commitments of ecologists and feminists in the West.

In *Identity and the Sacred,* however, I relied as much on conflict as on functional theories. I postulated not only that the relation between integration and differentiation was symbiotic but also that the various units of social organization (individuals, groups, families, sects, tribes, communities, nations, etc., then still called "identities") could both be congruent and clash. How religion behaved in this field of contending and cooperating, boundary-defending and boundary-weakening forces, was elaborated on in *Identity and Religion* (Mol 1978).

This follow-up book was prepared for the 9th World Congress of Sociology at Uppsala in Sweden. In it a dozen scholars from all over the world explained how they used the identity concept in order to make sense of their religious data. Most of them wrote about religion as a consolidator of identity (whether personal, tribal, ethnic, regional, or national), particularly when it was put into jeopardy by conquest, competition, secular forces, and so on. In the introduction I tried to provide an overarching theoretical frame of reference tying together not only the variety of contributions but also the major approaches in the sociology of religion.

It was pointed out in the book that consolidation on one level might imply conflict on another and that the tendency of Feuerbach, Freud, and Fromm to link religion to its effect on personal identity had to be balanced by Durkheim's emphasis of its effect on group or social identity. It was suggested that R. D. Laing's analysis of conflict between ego and family (1971) was as true as the functionalist analysis of their congruence, leading to a dialectical approach.

Comprehension became the guiding principle of the now evolving dialectical approach to religion. The major classical and contemporary social-scientific theoreticians of religion were not wrong, it was maintained, yet neither were their approaches comprehensively true. An example can be taken from the prevailing interactionist theorizing in social psychology: Specific religious behavior is seen as the product of the interaction between upbringing and intrapsychic needs. This correctly assumes an emphasis on the building of congruence between self and group, family, or society; a common wavelength of interpretation, acting, and reacting is firmed up. Yet in this interactionist point of view, the data that separate (rather than harmonize) ego and group receive short shrift. Christianity, for example, almost always (whether in its sectarian or denominational form) stresses those values and beliefs which reinforce family or group cohesion (love, altruism, kindness, etc.) and therefore link ego and group. Yet psychoanalysts (e.g., R. D. Laing), and the Self-Realization Fellowship (a Christian/Hindu sect) emphasize the boundaries around the self rather than those around family and society. The interactionist frame of reference is therefore not large enough to accommodate the contribution religion makes in maintaining separateness as well as harmony. On a macrosociological level, some of the Jesus People (Gordon 1978:236 ff.) use theology to reinforce sect identity at the expense of family or social identity. So do Scientologists (Wallis 1976:261; Vosper 1971:16, 13, 142).

To sum up: The emerging sociological model providing the best accounting scheme for cross-cultural data treats society as a configuration of sometimes contending, sometimes conforming, units of social organizations. Whether the boundaries around these units are strengthened (allowing for more effective opposition) or weakened (allowing for greater accommodation) is determined by the push or pull of a large number of specifiable factors, some physical (e.g., famine or war may destroy a society), others social (e.g., marriage creates a new family, divorce or death destroys one), psychological, demographic, and so on.

Religion is *one* of these factors. It may reinforce personal integrity (e.g., by sacralizing self-assertion or by relativizing an existential crisis). In contrast, it may reinforce family, or community identity (e.g., by sacralizing values of humility, obedience, love, and self-denial, or by inducing respect/fear for God/authority). It may ritualize loyalties to the nation, the region, ethnic group, or race (e.g., by national anthem, flag salutation, or sacralization of a particular form of government, such as democracy). It may reinforce hierarchies and classes (e.g., by lending added prestige to the refined, rational thought of the intelligentsia, with prayers for the rulers, by preaching contentment with one's status, however lowly, but also by approving the goodness of proletarian simplicity, the virtue of poverty, equality, and brotherhood).

In so reinforcing, however, religion implicitly enters the arena of conflict; by reinforcing one unit of social organization it may diminish another. The present attention some sociologists of religion pay to power (e.g., Beckford 1982) highlights this point: If religion through its sacralizing mechanisms lends weight to existing hierarchies, it may, from the point of view of opponents to these hierarchies, abuse power, even when the latter themselves employ commitment, ideology, ritual, and myth to bolster their stance. The problem with those who exalt power as a central concept is that no attempt is made to fit the notion into a social theory that comprehensively covers all cross-cultural and cross-historical data. Yet they use the word generally as the aggressive/defensive force strengthening the place of a particular unit of social organization in a jostling, contending, but also cooperating, conglomeration of units. In this jostling, religion is almost always *either* reinforcing particular units, thereby augmenting the power of each, *or* reconciling the tension between them (providing, for instance, a perspective that transcends class, race, national, or communal divisions) *or* redressing the balance between them (defending the underprivileged, unemployed, or underpaid against the powerful corporation), thereby changing the balance of power in accordance with its transcendental frame of reference.

I am running ahead of myself, however, with this digression about power. More must be said about the fact that religion in this jostling field not only reinforces but also reconciles conflicts. In an embryonic way, for example, "The Dreaming" of the Australian Aborigines (Stanner 1972:271) unites the various units of their social organization (person, womanhood, manhood, clan, moiety, tribe, each of which is bounded off from the others by a separate totem). In a much more highly differentiated society, such as ancient Israel, a strongly objectified frame of reference (Jehovah) provides the otherworldly standards by means of which a clash between tribal authority (represented by King David) and individual rights (represented by Uriah the Hittite, 2 Sam. 11) is reconciled in the direction of the latter (David is made to repent for his abuse of power). The persistent theme of God both loving and judging persons, families, and communities in Christianity is another example of religion minimizing the strain between units of social organization by its insistence on mutual affection, understanding, and forgiveness.

Postulating a comprehensive model for religious data is one thing. Its application and verification is something else again. Even if the model works fairly well in Western societies (the cross-cultural data have generally been Western in origin), does it have to be revised when non-Western materials are studied? The F & F trilogy—*The Fixed and Fickle: Religion and Identity in New Zealand* 1982; *The Firm and the Formless: Religion and Identity in Aboriginal Australia* 1982; *Faith and Fragility: Religion and Identity in Canada* 1983—was my attempt to apply the model to native, ethnic, sectarian, and denominational religion. It seemed to work. The vigorous Maori charismatic movements in New Zealand all relativized a redoubtable, tapu-hedged, tribal and kinship identity and replaced it with a supratribal vision in which the common Pakeha enemy would be destroyed and driven into the sea. The biblical themes of exodus, promised land, and resurrection proved to be grist for the mill (Mol 1982:34).

The Aboriginal study went beyond both Frazer and Durkheim in that its consistent dialectical approach made it unnecessary to rank the individual totems above the social ones (Frazer 1910, 1:161) or the social totems above the individual ones (Durkheim 1965:219), but insisted (Mol 1982a:11–12) that the two complemented one another even when they were in conflict. Aboriginal myths (Berndt 1970:233) also proved to be prime examples of the sacralization of territorial identity as a precursor of the social/organizational one.

In the Canadian study, *Faith and Fragility*, the ecosystem was introduced as a separate form of identity (Mol 1983:24). The identity approach also fit rather well with the alternating predominance of communal identity and family identity in the 450 years of Hutterite history (Peter 1976:339). Yet the Canadian study also brought about a change in terminology. Students and other readers associated "identity" so closely with personal identity that the idea of conflicts and congruences between "identities" seemed foreign, and so the more cumbersome "unit of social organization" was used instead. "Objectification" also confused readers, as they did not associate it so readily with transcendental ordering. Therefore "transcendentalization" was used.

More importantly, a shift took place from the stress on "identity" to a stress on "dialectical." This modification took place not only because of the conservative connotation of sacralization and "sameness reinforcement" but also because it proved necessary to clarify what exactly the "dialectic" is about and what the desacralizing elements within the sacralization mechanisms consist of. The dialectic between integration and differentiation was originally perceived as the heart of evolution and the survival of the fittest; only integrated wholes (whether inorganic or organic) could maintain themselves in the environment, and yet these units could do so only by adjusting to changes in the environment through differentiation. Similarly then, the relations between units of social organization were also regarded as a dialectic of contention and cooperation. To associate sacralization too closely with just the maintenance and reconciliation of these units of social organization (as the "identity theory" tended to do) oversimplified things. The sacralization mechanisms themselves appeared to have survived as long as they did because all of them could also "de-sacralize." In other words, a dialectic with change existed even at the heart of the religious enterprise.

This final point of modification can be best illustrated by taking each of the four sacralization mechanisms in turn:

1. Transcendental ordering has two faces. Both relativize, but the conservative face manages discord, disorder, and disruption by relating them to, and placing them in, the context of transcendental order. The second face also relativizes but does so by declaring the mundane only "relatively" important, therefore less sacred and more manipulable. The first face legitimates; the second face diminishes the legitimation and can, therefore, be the catalyst for change.

2. Commitment or emotional anchoring often "de-commits" or "detaches" before actually reinforcing loyalties and allegiances. Conversion on the personal level, and charisma on the social level, almost always pass through a phase of distancing from the evil, chaotic, anxiety-ridden past before fervent witnessing to present salvation or future hopes.

3. Although there are also rites which only retrace the grooves around existing order, others, such as rites of passage, erase old lines of demarcation before drawing new lines around new or changed

identities. At marriage ceremonies a bride is dissociated from the family of origin before she is ceremoniously attached to the new family she is now forming with her new husband.

4. Myths are probably the best example of sacralization mechanisms that also absorb change and conflict. They do this by dramatizing the dialectic between chaos and order as in the first chapter of the book of Genesis, or between sin and salvation as in the letters of Saint Paul. In other religions (as in Maori myths) similar dialectic presentations between Yang (activity, dynamism) and Yin (receptivity, inclusion) or masculinity and femininity take place.

CONCLUSION

Cross-cultural data compel the search for wider horizons than those granted by most scholars in the scientific study of religion. This chapter has tried to trace the development, application, and modification of a theory of religion which originated in an attempt to embrace cross-cultural along with diachronic data into a comprehensive frame of reference. This attempt has engaged particularly those scholars associated with the two international organizations encouraging comprehensive research on religion: the sociology of religion research committee of the International Sociological Association (recent presidents: Norman Birnbaum, Hans Mol, Karel Dobbelaere, James Beckford), and the Conférence International de Sociologie Religieuse (recent presidents: Bryan Wilson and David Martin). In this chapter I have traced this search for a theoretical canopy by referring chiefly to my own cross-cultural research problems and their attempted solutions.

It might be argued, however, that no comprehensive frame of reference can arise apart from certain assumptions, such as that whatever survives has simultaneously to maintain integrity and yet also be capable of fragmentation to ensure better-fitting forms of integrity. A dialectic model of society (a field of contending and cooperating units of social organization) seems to meet best the requirements for this comprehensive frame of reference. Religion in this model is defined as the sacralization of these various units of social organization provided that the process of sacralization is also understood to contain within itself desacralizing elements. Thus transcendental ordering proves to desacralize and delegitimate the mundane on occasion. Conversion and charisma commitment also prove to go through stages of decommitment. Similarly, rites of passage go through phases of stripping before welding. And myths are analyzed as dialectic dramatizations of basic elements of human existence.

Sacralization is thus treated as the dialectical opposite of secularization, so that the latter is seen sometimes to elevate even secular movements into awe-inspiring religious phenomena.

REFERENCES

Batson, Daniel C., and Ventis, W. Larry
    1982   *The Religious Experience: A Social-Psychological Perspective.* New York: Oxford University Press.

Beckford, James A.
    1982   "The Restoration of 'Power' to the Sociology of Religion." Paul Hanley Furfey lecture delivered at the Annual Meeting of the Association for the Sociology of Religion, Providence, R.I., October.

Bellah, Robert U.
    1970   *Beyond Belief.* New York: Harper.

Berndt, Ronald M.
    1970   "Traditional Morality as Expressed Through the Medium of an Australian Aboriginal Religion." *In* Ronald M. Berndt, ed., *Australian Aboriginal Anthropology.* Nedlands, W.A.: University of Western Australia Press. Pp. 216–247.

Durkheim, Emile
    1954   *The Elementary Forms of the Religious Life.* Glencoe, Ill.: Free Press. (First published in 1912.)

Fallding, Harold
    1974   *The Sociology of Religion.* Toronto: McGraw-Hill/Ryerson.

Frazer, James George.
    1910   *Totemism and Exogamy.* 4 vols. London: Macmillan.

Gordon, David F.
    1978   "Identity and Social Commitment." *In* Hans Mol, ed., *Identity and Religion: International, Cross-Cultural Approaches.* London: Sage. Pp. 229–242.

Kelley, Dean M.
    1972   *Why Conservative Churches Are Growing.* New York: Harper.

Laing, R. D.
    1971   *The Politics of the Family and Other Essays.* New York: Random House.

Luckmann, Thomas.
    1967   *The Invisible Religion.* New York: Macmillan.

Martin, David.
  1972   "England." *In* Mol, Hetherton, and Henty, eds., 1972. Pp. 229–
            247.
  1978   *A General Theory of Secularization.* Oxford: Blackwell.
Marx, Karl.
  1974   *On Religion.* (Arranged and edited by Saul K. Padover.) New
            York: McGraw-Hill.
Merton, Robert K.
  1957   *Social Theory and Social Structure.* Glencoe, Ill.: Free Press.
Mol, Johannis (Hans) J.
  1965   *Changes in Religious Behaviour of Dutch Immigrants.* The Hague:
            Research Group for European Migration Problem.
  1966   *Race and Religion in New Zealand.* Christchurch: The National
            Council of Churches in New Zealand.
  1968   *The Breaking of Traditions.* Berkeley, Calif.: Glendessary Press.
  1969   *Christianity in Chains.* Melbourne: Nelson.
  1970   "Secularization and Cohesion," *Review of Religious Research* 11, 3
            (Spring):183–191.
  1971   *Religion in Australia.* Melbourne: Nelson.
  1974   "Marginality and Commitment as Hidden Variables in the Jel-
            linek/Weber/Merton Theses on the Calvinist Ethic." In Margaret
            Archer, ed., *Current Sociology* 22 (1974):279–297, nn. 1–3.
  1976   *Identity and the Sacred.* Oxford: Blackwell; or New York: Free Press,
            1977.
  1982   *The Fixed and the Fickle: Religion and Identity in New Zealand.* Water-
            loo, Ont.: Wilfrid Laurier University Press.
  1982a   *The Firm and the Formless: Religion and Identity in Aboriginal Au-
            stralia.* Waterloo, Ont.: Wilfrid Laurier University Press.
  1983   *Meaning and Place: An Introduction to the Social Scientific Study of
            Religion.* New York: Pilgrim Press.
  1983a   *Faith and Fragility: Religion and Identity in Canada.* Hamilton, Ont.:
            McMaster University (locally duplicated for classes).
Mol, Johannis (Hans) J., ed.
  1978   *Identity and Religion: International, Cross-Cultural Approaches.* Vol.
            16 in Sage Studies in International Sociology. London: Sage.
Mol, Johannis (Hans) J., Margaret Hetherton, and Margaret Henty, eds.
  1972   *Western Religion: A Country by Country Sociological Investigation.*
            The Hague: Mouton.
Parsons, Talcott.
  1949   *The Structure of Social Action.* Glencoe, Ill.: Free Press. (First
            published in 1937.)
  1963   "Christianity and Modern Industrial Society." *In* Edward Tirya-
            kian, Ed., *Sociological Theory, Values, and Sociocultural Change.*
            Glencoe, Ill.: Free Press.

Peter, Karl
  1976   "The Dialectic of Family and Community in the Social History of the Hutterites." *In* Lyle E. Larson, ed., *The Canadian Family in Comparative Perspective.* Scarborough, Ont.: Prentice-Hall. Pp. 337–350.

Stanner, William E. H.
  1972   "The Dreaming." In William A. Lessa and Evon Z. Vogt, eds., *Reader in Comparative Religion.* New York: Harper. Pp. 269–277.

Vosper, Cyril
  1971   *The Mind Benders.* London: Neville Spearman.

Wallis, Roy
  1976   *The Road to Total Freedom: A Sociological Analysis of Scientology.* London: Heinemann.

Weber, Max
  1952   *The Protestant Ethic and the Spirit of Capitalism.* New York: Scribner. (First published in 1904.)
  1964   The Sociology of Religion. Boston: Beacon Press. (First published in Germany in 1922.)
  1964   *The Religion of China.* New York: Macmillan. (First published in 1920–1921).

VII

Studies of Conversion: Secularization or Re-enchantment?

James T. Richardson

A partial, but significant, "paradigm shift" in research on conversion has taken place over the past two decades, and this new emergent outlook has directly contributed to moving the sociology of religion beyond the "secularization hypothesis." Secularization theory served as something of a "sacred canopy" for most research in the social sciences of religion until quite recently. It is falling into disrepute among some scholars, however, simply because it seems not to wear well when examined in the light of contemporary phenomena, such as the rise of interest in new religions in the West, particularly in America. This religious quickening among the most affluent and best-educated generation of youth in American history has delighted some, puzzled others, and caused disquiet among those to whom secularization theory has been gospel. Some, most notably Gregory Baum (1970) and Bryan Wilson (1979), have seemed to trivialize the new religions both in terms of their personal meaning for participants and in their implications for cultural change. Wilson has even suggested that the new religions are evidence *for* the secularization hypothesis (1979:96) simply because the presence of many religious alternatives demonstrates that one's religious commitment does not matter anymore. This is an appealing, but seductive, argument. This chapter will seek to establish a somewhat different interpretation of new religions which takes them more seriously and on their own terms.

PARADIGM SHIFTS

Thomas Kuhn's (1962) seminal work about the political nature of science has been widely applied to various areas of science, including the social sciences. He posits that scientific endeavor is dominated by traditional paradigms, which are a "way of seeing," or interpreting, the subjects of study. Kuhn claims that each paradigm contains within itself expectations, and rules about ways to practice science in a given area, and what he calls "normal science" is the practice whereby the reigning paradigm is expanded and extended. If difficulties are encountered in this practice of normal science—that is, if significant anomalous findings develop and persist—pressure will rise to adopt a new paradigm that can account for the anomalous findings. If such a paradigm were developed, the entire discipline (with the exception of diehards) might adopt the "new way of seeing" in what Kuhn himself ironically refers to as a "conversion experience."

THE TRADITIONAL PARADIGM

In a paper delivered in 1979, I applied the Kuhnian approach to research in conversion to explain the emergence of an apparent alternative view to the traditional way of viewing conversion as psychological and deterministic. This traditional paradigm derived from common interpretations of Paul's conversion on the road to Damascus—as sudden and dramatic, and caused by some powerful external agent. This singular event was individual in its focus, and assumed the total negation of the old self and the implantation of a new self. Emphasis was on the cognitive, assuming that, when beliefs changed, behavioral changes would follow. Most applications of this view of conversion were typically applicable to predispositions, and thus were psychological in orientation but, even when applications were more sociological, they were still deterministic, with an emphasis on situational determinants of conversion (affective ties, "networks," or intensive interaction, etc.).[1]

Although this has been the dominant view of conversion in the social and behavioral sciences for decades, some counter tendencies have been evident—more humanistic views in the social and behavioral sciences have had their followers. Carl Jung and Viktor Frankl within the psychotherapy tradition certainly professed a less deterministic view of human beings, and Jung specifically discussed religious experiences and religion in general in a more positive light than did Freud (especially see Kelsey 1968:188–199, and Jung 1933). Alfred McClung Lee and Peter Berger are two prominent sociologists who have, in somewhat different ways, contributed to the development of a more humanistic approach in sociology. This less deterministic bent has also been seen within psychology, as a number of scholars have focused on an active agency perspective more appreciative of the volitional nature of humans (see Ginsburg 1979). And even within the Christian orbit there has been some movement away from the determinism exhibited in most interpretations of what happened to Paul.

The deterministic interpretation of the Pauline experience has nonetheless been the common one. Berger's (1963) application of the market model to American religion, based in major part on the separation of church and state that forced competition among religious organizations, has fed this traditional view of conversion. Proselytizing and evangelism presupposes that people can be converted, and the focus has often been on a type of conversion deriving largely from interpretations of what happened to Paul on the road to Damascus. On the ideological level, the popularity of Freudian ideas has promoted not only the traditional view of conversion but also given it a somewhat negative slant as well. This negative perspective is clearly reflected in the contemporary efforts of a few Freudian-oriented "brainwashing" theorists such as Margaret Singer (1979), John Clark (1979) and Flo Conway and Jim Siegelman (1978), whose work has contributed importantly to the legitimation of the anticult movement (Shupe and Bromley 1980).[2] Within the sociological area this same negativism toward religion, and therefore toward religious conversion, is exemplified by those of a more Marxian or critical bent who have looked at the rise of new religion (see Nolan 1971; Marin 1972; and Foss and Larkin 1978). Deprivation and strain theories from sociology about recruitment to social movements have indirectly supported the traditional view of conversion (see Smelser 1963; Glock 1964) with their view of the individual as passive.

Secularization theory has also contributed indirectly to the maintenance of the traditional paradigm of conversion research. This is the case even though secularization theory is usually cast at the level of the society and its institutions. But this focus on the institutional and societal conceals the fact that secularization theory can also by implication refer to individual people and their religious experiences. It is worthwhile to contemplate what is being implied about these individual people.

Secularization theory generally implies that religion is something of an anachronism in our differentiated and complex modern world. Anyone who believes is basically not "with it" in the modern age, and the term *backwater believers* is used to refer to those still deeply involved in their religions. Such people may be caught up in a wave of revivalism, but such occurrences, according to secularizationists, are only temporary in the grand scheme of things. Rationality marches on, and there is something odd about those who do not get in step, even if those discussing this inexorable process lament what they are describing.

Those adhering to a secularization model have little difficulty accepting the traditional view that posits individuals as passive objects who are being pushed about by social forces over which they have little control. The mechanistic and individualistic aspects of secularization theory mesh well, in other words, with similar assumptions of the traditional model of conversion. This agreement, however, may lead some involved in a secularization view of history to miss or disregard possible counter evidence to secularization theory furnished by the rise of "conversion" to new religions in the West. It is to this new evidence that we now turn.

THE NEW PARADIGM

The seeds of a new paradigm in conversion research in the social and behavioral sciences have always been present. We have mentioned already the movement within these areas toward a more humanistic perspective that is activist in orientation. The shift in research in the related area of social movement recruitment is also significant. Research on conversion within the social scientific study of religion, however, particularly that done by sociologists, has made an important and independent contribution. This new burst of research on conversion has yielded findings that, when summarized, have the appearance of an emergent new paradigm for such research. At the same time, they offer a critique of secularization theory. The key features of this outlook have been discussed in more detail in Richardson (1982), from which the following summary is taken.

Converts to new religions are active human beings seeking meaning and appropriate life-styles (see Straus 1976, 1979; Downton 1980; Lofland 1977; Balch and Taylor 1977; Lynch 1977). Rational decisions are being made through which self-affirmation is occurring. This affirmation may involve a rejection of past beliefs and behaviors, but converts are not just "running away." They are involved in an active searching that quite often includes serious negotiations with a group concerning required beliefs and behaviors. Many are thus doing what can perhaps be described as exploiting the groups, "trying them out" but, at the same time, making no definite or long-term commitments.

Contemporary conversion is often more properly viewed as a social event. Certainly we see "intellectual conversion" (Lofland and Skonovd 1981) in which some people read a book and "convert themselves." The vast majority of conversions, however, involve people joining new communities and "coming to agree with their new friends" (Lofland and Stark 1965). The ways of joining may vary significantly (Pilarzyk 1978), but this is a quite normal process for people who have, for whatever reason, experienced a cutting of their ties with society in general and with their family and friends, as was the case with many young people in the 1960s and early 1970s.

Decisions to join may be made suddenly and dramatically, but quite often the process of affiliation is best described as a series of experiments entered into quite hestitatingly (see Straus 1976; Balch 1980; Downton 1979, 1980). People are testing the group even as the group is testing them, and a mutual decision eventually gets made. The beliefs of the potential convert do not necessarily change until later, and there may never be a complete acceptance of group beliefs by the individual. Quite often with contemporary conversion the "behaving" takes place without the benefit of a change in beliefs. As Bromley and Shupe (1979) and Balch (1980) note, most often the new members are just "playing the role" of good members while they seek information to help them decide whether or not to stay. Cognitive changes are usually much more gradual, the strongly held ideas of the "brainwashing theorists" such as Singer, Clark, and Conway and Siegelman notwithstanding.

Conversion to the new movements is seldom a once-in-a-lifetime event. It is better characterized for many as a series of affiliations and disaffiliations comprising a "conversion career" (Richardson 1979, 1980). Many young people are taking advantage of the many opportunities in our pluralistic society, trying out "serial alternatives" in life-styles and beliefs. An ideological and behavioral mobility is typical as individuals move through many different groups. High attrition rates (Bird and Reimer 1982) and data indicating that many youth have multiple, serial commitments (Richardson 1980) support this "conversion careers" view of contemporary conversion.[3]

ALTERNATIVES TO A PARADIGM SHIFT

It is possible that the notion of a paradigm shift is overstated, and that other views of contemporary conversion such as that of Lofland and Skonovd (1981) are more valid. Lofland and Skonovd argue for six major types of conversion (intellectual, affectional, revivalistic, mystical, experimental, and coercive), stating that significant shifts have occurred over the past decade or so in the actual *types* of conversion. Thus, instead of there being some major shift in how scholars view conversion, as is suggested here, Lofland and Skonovd claim that the basic reality of conversion has itself shifted over time. The debate over these perspectives is of import (see Richardson 1979 and 1982). This debate, however, is not material to the basic thesis of this chapter, which is that the new religions raise serious questions about the efficacy of the secularization model. In fact, one might claim (although they do not speak to this issue) that the position of Lofland and Skonovd is more damaging to the secularization hypothesis than my view of a more "political" paradigm change. Lofland and Skonovd are not concerned at all about secularization theories when they claim that intellectual and experimental conversions (the two types most like the new paradigm posited herein) are becoming more prevalent in the contemporary setting. But these are the two types of conversion in their scheme that most clearly involve an active subject choosing among alternatives and making potentially life-changing decisions. At least on the individual level such decisions strike at the heart of the secularization thesis. People seem to be taking their religion seriously and, even in the modern world, representatives of the most affluent and well-educated generation in American history are *choosing to be religious*. Similarly, the assertion of Lofland and Skonovd that coercive conversion is quite rare today (contrary to the view of brainwashing theorists) indirectly detracts from the secularization thesis. It is evident that people do not have to be coerced into joining a new religion because today large numbers are seeking new religions on their own. Lofland and Skonovd also note a general decline in the relative frequency of the revivalistic and mystical types of conversion, which are closely related to what I refer to herein as the "Pauline paradigm." This general decline seems indirectly supportive of the thesis that the secularization hypothesis is somewhat problematical in today's context.

Another recent theoretical statement in the area of conversion research offering an alternative to the paradigm change idea is that of Long and Hadden (1983), who discuss conflict between what they call the "brainwashing" and the "social drift" models of conversion to cults or new religions. Long and Hadden use the term *dual reality* to refer to the fact that both views have some validity, and they offer a way of integrating the two perspectives using socialization theory. Their paper is quite valuable but cannot be discussed in detail here. It is, however, noteworthy that the Long and Hadden paper supports the major thesis of this chapter just as the work of Lofland and Skonovd does. The social drift model is developing a following among researchers in the area of conversion to new religions, implying a growing recognition that conversion is a meaningful activity entered into through an exercise of volition by participants. Although Long and Hadden do not develop the idea of a possible shift in this area of research from mechanistic, deterministic psychological models through deterministic sociological models to the volitional and subject-centered model that is coming to dominate much research in the area, they do recognize the renewed appreciation in sociological circles of the more activist tradition. They cite Lofland's remark (1977:22) about the fact that his early work made use of a model that included a "thoroughly passive actor," and then briefly discuss a more activist view deriving from a focus on interaction. This focus, of course, is one implicitly recognizing that human behavior, including religious seeking, is usually meaningful to the actor who engages in such action.

IMPLICATIONS FOR SECULARIZATION THEORY

At the outset let it be said that not all conversions are the same, and not all groups are the same. Scholars in the area must be able to differentiate among various experiences and various groups. And, as Beckford (1981*b*) notes, scholars as citizens may even be called on to *evaluate* various experiences and groups in the course of debates about social policy concerning the new religions. Such possible involvement in policy recommendations by scholars carries a high responsibility that cannot be taken lightly, and every effort should be made to get beyond current fads within an area of scientific research, in order to focus on the reality of whatever is being examined.

In the case of conversion to new religions, this impartiality may be especially difficult for those who still view the world through traditional "Pauline paradigm" glasses. They may find it easy to focus on such items as the "teenyboppers for Jesus" who plainly were involved in almost blind conformity to peer expectations as they became "hangers-on" to the Jesus Movement (Adams and Fox 1972). Others dominated by the traditional paradigm may attend closely to accounts, offered by brainwashing theorists such as Singer and Clark, of ex-members, many of whom had been deprogrammed. Neither view takes very seriously the meaning of the act of affiliation with a new religious group, and instead emphasizes that the act has little real meaning or value, or means something entirely different from what the participants claim.

But views of some secularization theorists also tend to dismiss any real personal or cultural significance associated with the new religions. Gregory Baum in his provocative "Does the World Remain Disenchanted?" (1970:186–197) derides the religious significance of the new movements. He says:

Let me say at the outset that I do not attach much religious significance to these manifestations of religiosity. Most of them seem to me contrived, artificial, bizarre, and of questionable sincerity. . . . The religiosity of the youth movement, moreover, seems to have no abiding social base nor is it apt to generate one.

Baum also derides (1970:189) the "curious religious preoccupation" of young people today. However, he does not totally dismiss the meaning of the new movements among youth. He claims (1970:187) that the meaning ". . . is not principally religious at all! It is largely symbolic of the quest for a more liberated human existence." And he seems to give credence to the possibility that the youth movement in general offers needed energy for social change. But he includes in his work a warning of the "dangerous practices" of the youth movement (1970:193), among which he seems to count their strong emphasis on freedom and the experimental as part of the utopianism of the movements. He closes with the epitaph (1970:201):

The patently religious manifestations of the counter-culture, we have noted, have little religious significance. Neither the gods of the moment nor utopian expectations can survive for long in a highly rationalized society.

Baum's assessment is echoed and amplified in the writings of secularization theorist Bryan Wilson (1976), whose well-known work, *The Contemporary Transformation of Religion*, as well as his later paper, "The Return of the Sacred" (1979), are quite critical and dismissive of the new religions. In the final chapter of the 1976 volume, Wilson writes about "The Social Meaning of Religious Change," but finds little import in the development of the new religions. He summarizes Harvey Cox's interest in new religious groups and experiences (1976:93) by saying: "Salvation, it appears, is attained by learning to indulge oneself." Wilson quotes at length from Harvey Cox's 1974 description of a large experimental liturgy, and then laments the misuse and misunderstanding of the meaning of certain symbols of traditional faith described in the volume:

In such an experimental liturgy, each exotic bauble is divorced from its content, from its cultural significance, is wanted only for its brightness, to deck out a jollification. The strange symbols are not wanted for their quality as solemn communicators of values, but only as titillations for jaded palates that have experienced too much, too quickly, and too lightly. Without any sustained knowledge, without any awareness of what symbols stand for, of what choices have to be made, of what discriminations are imperative to culture and to human life, these modern men demand everything. Modern communications have produced a new liturgical emporium, from which all items may be carelessly and mindlessly brought together, not to represent an appreciation of the accumulated inheritance of past culture, but merely so that a few people may be *high* for an hour or so.

Wilson, who has done considerable research on historical and Third World religious movements, discusses earlier waves of revivalism in the West and in the Third World and concludes that these earlier movements *did* have significant social consequences. He says, however (1976:96), "The West . . . appears to have passed beyond a point at which religious teaching and practice can exercise formative influence over whole societies, or any significant segment of them." He does allow for some meaning on a personal level for individual participants, but even that is negatively assessed (1976:98):

Modern religious movements no longer have any real significance for the social system, although they may offer individual salvation—at times, explicitly salvation from the system. . . . [T]he new cults propose to take the individual out of his society, and to save him by the wisdom of some other, wholly exotic body of belief and practice.

This . . . is not so much a revival of religion in its cultural significance as its rejection, together with the rejection of the society in which it is nourished.

Wilson continues this negativism with further generalizations about new religions (1976:101):

The new cults do not serve society. They are indeed almost irrelevant to it, since their sources of inspiration are exotic, esoteric, subjective, and subterranean. . . . [The new religions] seek mystification rather than rationalization.

He makes passing reference to some of the more disciplined groups, but again finds a way to dismiss such groups as inconsequential by saying (1976:102) ". . . their discipline is for the commune and not for the world." He adds later (1976:113) a slight qualification recognizing the value of belief and commitment in the modern world, and then says, "But even those of the new movements that do mobilize commitment and do demand discipline are not organized to disseminate an effective ethic for a whole society."

Wilson closes his thoroughly pessimistic defense of secularization theory by concluding (1976:116) ". . . religions are always dying. In the modern world it is not clear that they have any prospects of rebirth."

"Other theorists supportive of the secularization hypothesis could be cited concerning their assessment of the new religions. However, the point is by now well made that the new religions concern some proponents of secularization theory, and some of those theorists have quite strong feelings about the new religions.

The views expressed by Wilson and Baum are *not* shared by all sociologists acquainted with the new religions.[4] For example, Stark and Bainbridge (1980, 1981), in two excellent papers, take strong issue with the secularization hypothesis and particularly with those who see cult development as definitive evidence for that hypothesis. They see religious history dominated by *cycles* rather than by a linear trend toward increasing secularity. They state (1981:362):

Secularization is a self-limiting process prompting religious revival and innovation. That is, we argue that secularization of the long-dominant religions is the mainspring behind current religious innovation. Particular religious bodies are withering away, and in consequence energy is pouring into new channels . . . [R]eligion is not permanently vulnerable to secularization.

Also, some of the scholars whose primary research was cited as contributing to the new activist paradigm are quite explicit about the value and meaning of the new religions for individual participants (see especially Straus's and Downton's work, as well as that of Barker 1981), and thus implicitly take issue with the secularization hypothesis. The requirements of this chapter do not allow lengthy quotes from these individual studies, but one particular assessment of the new religions offered by Joseph Fichter (1981) is worth examining in some detail.

Fichter, whose assessment appeared, ironically, in a collection edited by Bryan Wilson, examines the meaning of the new religions and focuses special attention on conversion to the new movements. He also speaks directly to the focus of this chapter: secularization theory. His assessment, based on his study of youth religions, is terse (1981:22): "It appears now that secularity, not religion, is in crisis." Fichter takes issue with sociology's traditional troika—industrialization, urbanization, and secularization—and decries the fact that "the triumph of the secular . . . has been taken as an article of faith, a practically unshakable dogma of sociological theory" (1981:23). He notes that social scientists adhering to the secularization hypothesis were sometimes quick to see defection of youth from traditional churches as evidence for secularization, but apparently the movement of significant numbers of youth into new religions has no meaning for secularization theory (or is even used as supporting data). Fichter characterizes the "secularist" view of conversion (1981:30) as follows:

It is characteristic of the secularist mentality that the religious act, the search for God, the religious conversion, must immediately be suspect. There must be "something wrong" with the individual who says that he or she has freely chosen to join a religious cult. There must have been delusion, seduction, trickery.

Fichter's own assessment is quite different (1981:31):

In spite of the hysterical charges of trickery and seduction into the religious cult, it is safe to say that the overwhelming majority of young people who become cult members do so freely and deliberately, and for reasons that make sense to them.

Fichter also alludes to the value of the new religions to the society, and takes a generally functionalist position that stresses the role played by religion in legitimation of that society's culture. And, in summary, he quotes Glick, who says (1973:228):

[T]hose of us who study people's responses to new religious ideas should not labor with the misconception that our world is one in which religion is disappearing. For, to the contrary, the evidence is that new religions are arising all the time, that people do not respond to new problems by abandoning religion but by developing a new religion on the ruins of the old.

CONCLUSIONS

The quote from Glick, in which he so easily takes for granted that new religions have meaning for both the participants and society as a whole, seems an apt description of what a number of scholars are coming to believe because of the results of research on conversion to the new religions. Although always subject to the accusation of bias, or of being taken in by gilded "conversion accounts" (Beckford 1981*b* and 1978), those researchers seem to sense signs of a possible "re-enchantment of the world." The mystification abhorred by Wilson is seen by others as a sign of hope, and an indication that the seemingly endless march of rationality may be slowed or modified significantly. The growing attention to the "communalization of religion" exhibited by some of the new groups (Kilbourne and Richardson 1983) is seen as a counter to the secularization assumptions about the privatization of religion. The experiential focus of many of the new religions, predicted years ago and now coming to flower (see Richardson and Davis 1983), is viewed positively by some scholars who, using a new paradigm of conversion, are now finding it easier to understand both how and why many people are seeking out the new religions, and managing their own conversions to them.

Long ago Feuerbach said "the secret of theology is anthropology." Perhaps the research on conversion to new religions cited here suggests that "the secret of sociology of religion is also anthropology," and the "secret" reveals secularization theory to be ill founded. Hundreds of thousands of youth in America and elsewhere, who are members of the most educated and affluent generation ever, are making conscious decisions to "convert" to new religions, even if for relatively short times for many. These events are often of individual import, but cumulatively they also have considerable cultural significance. Sociologists of religion would do well to recognize this major anomaly in the secularization theory, and seek more fruitful theoretical perspectives with which to address the continuing "species specific" interest in religion among human beings.[5]

NOTES

1. Sociological-oriented work in this more deterministic mode is sometimes quite fruitful in revealing how the conversion process works, and this discussion of a paradigm shift in conversion research is not meant to detract from

some excellent research. See Gordon (1974); Pilarzyk (1978); Hierich (1977); Lofland (1977); Stark and Bainbridge (1980); Griel and Rudy (1982); Galanter et al. (1979); and Richardson and Stewart (1977) for examples of such useful work. Quite often this research incorporates, at least implicitly, some recognition of an active subject, and thus demonstrates the evolution that has occurred from psychological determinism through sociological determinism to the more agency-oriented perspective that is being asserted in this chapter and in works of such researchers as Straus (1976, 1979), Balch (1980), and Richardson (1979, 1982).

2. See Anthony, Robbins and McCarthy (1980), Robbins and Anthony (1982), Kilbourne (1983), Richardson (1982), Richardson and Kilbourne (1983), Kilbourne and Richardson (1984), Bromley and Richardson (1983) and Melton and Moore (1982) for critiques of the brainwashing interpretation of conversion to new religions.

3. It may appear that the relative transitoriness of commitment to many of the new religions detracts from interpreting the acts of affiliation as meaningful and culturally significant. However, I would suggest that transitoriness and meaningfulness are independent in many participants, and would suggest that the actual relationship of the two variables is an empirical question, not a metatheoretical assumption.

4. This chapter must of necessity focus more on the individual level, since that is how conversion is generally considered. However, it should be appreciated that there are other signs of the import of the new religions aside from the accounts reported by converts to researchers. The tremendous attention of the media and of public officials and governmental agencies illustrates that meaning is being attached to the new religions by many in our society. And the innumerable court cases involving various aspects of the new religions drive the point home. It might be said with some seriousness that the Unificationists are the Jehovah's Witnesses of the 1970s and 1980s, since they have been responsible for the setting of a number of key court precedents, which plowed new ground in the continual societal effort to define the boundary between church and state in America. Other Western societies are focusing similar attention on new religions (see Beckford 1981*a*). Some secularization theorists may view this deluge of attention as yet another sign of growing secularization, but it seems reasonable to offer a counter interpretation.

5. Adherents of secularization theory would do well to read the remarkable discussion by Carl Jung (1933:chap. 10) of the rise of interest in new religions such as Christian Science, Rudolf Steiner's Anthroposophy, the rise of interest in spiritualism in general, and the growing following of astrology. Jung's prescient comments concern the Gnostic tendencies of the new religious phenomena and focus on the experiential demonstrated by new forms of religious thought and experience, particularly from the Hindu tradition. He apparently reaches similar conclusions to those stated herein, even though he was writing some fifty years ago. Jung says (1933:207): "The passionate

interest in these movements arises undoubtedly from psychic energy which can no longer be invested in obsolete forms of religion. For this reason such movements have a truly religious character, even if they pretend to be scientific."

REFERENCES

Adams, R. L., and R. Fox
1972 "Mainlining Jesus: The New Trip," *Society* 9:50–56.
Anthony, Dick, Tom Robbins, and Jim McCarthy
1980 "Legitimating Repression," *Society* 17(3):39–42.
Balch, R. W.
1980 "Looking Behind the Scenes in a Religious Cult: Implications for the Study of Conversion," *Sociological Analysis* 41(2):137–143.
Balch, R. W., and D. Taylor
1977 "Seekers and Saucers: The Role of the Cultic Milieu in Joining a UFO Cult." *In* J. T. Richardson, ed., *Conversion Careers* (1977).
Barker, Eileen
1981 "Who'd Be a Moonie? A Comparative Study of Those Who Join the Unification Church in Britain." *In* B. Wilson, ed., *The Social Context of the New Religious Movements.* New York: Rose of Sharon Press.
Baum, Gregory
1970 *Religion and the Rise of Scepticism.* New York: Harcourt, Brace and World.
Beckford, James A.
1978 "Accounting for Conversion," *British Journal of Sociology* 29:249–262.
1981*a* "Cults, Controversy and Control: A Comparative Analysis of the Problems Posed by New Religious Movements in the Federal Republic of Germany and France," *Sociological Analysis* 42(3):249–264.
1981*b* "Functionalism and Ethics and Sociology: The Relationship between 'Ought' and 'Function,'" *Annual Review of the Social Science of Religion* 5:101–131.
Berger, Peter
1963 *Invitation to Sociology.* New York: Doubleday.
Bird, Frederick, and Bill Reimer
1982 "Participation Rates in New Religious Movements and Para-Religious Movements," *Journal for the Scientific Study of Religion* 21(1):1–14.

Bromley, David, and J. T. Richardson, eds.
  1983   *The Brainwashing/Deprogramming Controversy.* Toronto: Edwin
          Mellen Press.
Bromley, David, and Anson Shupe, Jr.
  1979   "Just a Few Years Seem Like a Lifetime: A Role Theory Approach
          to Participation in Religious Movements." *In* L. Krisberg, ed.,
          Research in Social Movements, Conflicts, and Change. Greenwich,
          Conn.: JAI Press.
Clark, John
  1979   "Cults," *Journal of the American Medical Association* 243(3):279–281.
Conway, Flo, and Jim Siegelman
  1978   *Snapping.* New York: J. B. Lippincott.
  1982   "Information Disease: Have Cults Created a New Mental Illness?"
          Science Digest (January):87–92.
Downton, James V., Jr.
  1979   *Sacred Journeys.* New York: Columbia University Press.
  1980   "Spiritual Conversion and Commitment: The case of Divine Light
          Mission," *Journal for the Scientific Study of Religion* 19:381–396.
Fichter, Joseph
  1981   "Youth in Search of the Sacred." *In* Bryan Wilson, ed., *The Social
          Impact of the New Religions.* New York: Rose of Sharon Press.
Foss, Daniel, and Ralph Larkin
  1978   "Worshipping the Absurd: The Negation of Social Causality
          Among the Followers of the Guru Mahari'ji," *Sociological Analysis*
          39(2):157–164.
Galanter, Marc
  1980   "Psychological Induction into a Large Group: Findings from a
          Modern Religious Sect," *American Journal of Psychiatry* 137(12):
          1574–1579.
Galanter, M., R. Rabkin, J. Rabkin, and A. Deutsch
  1979   "The 'Moonies': A Psychological Study of Conversion and Mem-
          bership in a Contemporary Religious Sect," *American Journal of
          Psychiatry* 136(2):165–170.
Ginsburg, G., ed.
  1979   *Emerging Strategies in Social Psychological Research.* New York: John
          Wiley.
Glick, Leonard
  1973   "The Anthropology of Religion: Malinowski and Beyond." *In*
          Charles Glock and Phillip Hammond, eds., *Beyond the Classics?*
          New York: Harper and Row.
Glock, Charles
  1964   "The Role of Deprivation in the Evolution of Religious Groups."
          In Robert Lee and Martin Marty, eds., *Religion and Social Conflict.*
          New York: Oxford University Press.

Gordon, David
  1974   "The Jesus People: An Identity Synthesis," *Urban Life and Culture*
            3:159–178.
Greil, Arthur, and David Rudy
  1982   "What Do We Know About the Conversion Process?" Paper read
            at the annual meeting of the Society for the Scientific Study of
            Religion, Providence, R.I.
Hierich, Max
  1977   "Change of Heart: A Test of Some Widely Held Theories About
            Religious Conversion," *American Journal of Sociology* 83(3):653–680.
Jung, C. G.
  1933   *Modern Man in Search of a Soul.* New York: Harcourt Brace and
            World.
Kelsey, Morton
  1968   *Tongue Speaking.* Garden City, N.Y.: Doubleday.
Kilbourne, Brock
  1983   "An Analysis of the Conway and Siegelman Data," *Journal for the
            Scientific Study of Religion* 22(4):380–385.
Kilbourne, Brock, and James T. Richardson
  1983   "The Communualization of Religious Experience in New Reli-
            gious Movements." Paper read at the annual meeting of the
            Western Psychological Society, Sacramento, Calif.
  1984   "Psychotherapy and New Religious Groups in a Pluralistic Soci-
            ety," *American Psychologist* 39:237–251.
Kuhn, Thomas
  1962   *The Structure of Scientific Revolutions.* Chicago: University of
            Chicago Press.
Lofland, John
  1977   "Becoming a World Saver Revisited." *In* J. T. Richardson, ed.,
            Conversion Careers (1977).
Lofland, John, and Norman Skonovd
  1981   "Conversion Motifs," *Journal for the Scientific Study of Religion*
            20(4):373–385.
Lofland, John, and Rodney Stark
  1965   "Becoming a World Saver: A Theory of Conversion to a Deviant
            Perspective," *American Sociological Review* 30:863–874.
Long, Theodore, and Jeffrey Hadden
  1983   "Religious Conversion and Socialization," *Journal for the Scientific
            Study of Religion* 22(1):1–14.
Lynch, Frederick R.
  1977   "Toward a Theory of Conversion and Commitment to the Oc-
            cult." *In* James T. Richardson, ed., *Conversion Careers* (1977).
Marin, Peter
  1972   "Children of Yearning," *Saturday Review* (May 6):58–63.

Melton, Gordon, and Robert Moore
   1982   *The Cult Experience.* New York: Pilgrim Press.
Nolan, James
   1971   "Jesus Now: Hogwash and Holy Water," *Ramparts* 10(2):20–26.
Pilarzyk, Thomas
   1978   "Conversion and Alternation Processes in the Youth Culture: A Comparative Analysis of Religious Transformations," *Pacific Sociological Review* 21(4):379–406.
Richardson, James T., ed.
   1977   *Conversion Careers: In and Out of the New Religions.* London: Sage.
Richardson, James T.
   1979   "A New Paradigm for Conversion Research." Paper presented at the annual meeting of the International Society for Political Psychology, Washington, D.C.
   1980   "Conversion Careers," *Society* 17(3):47–50.
   1982   "Conversion, Brainwashing, and Deprogramming," *The Center Magazine* 15(2):18–24.
Richardson, James T., and Rex Davis
   1983   "Experiential Fundamentalism: Revisions of Orthodoxy in the Jesus Movement," *Journal of the American Academy of Religion* 51:397–425.
Richardson, James T., and B. Kilbourne
   1983   "Classical and Contemporary Brainwashing Models: A Comparison and Critique." *In* D. Bromley and J. T. Richardson, eds., *The Brainwashing/Deprogramming Controversy.* Toronto: Edwin Mellen Press.
Richardson, James T., and Mary Stewart
   1977   "Conversion Process Models and the Jesus Movements." *In* J. T. Richardson, ed., *Conversion Careers* (1977).
Robbins, Thomas, and Dick Anthony
   1982   "Deprogramming, Brainwashing and the Medicalization of Deviant Religious Groups," *Social Problems* 29:293–297.
Shupe, Anson, Jr., and David Bromley
   1980   *The New Vigilantes.* London: Sage.
Singer, Margaret
   1979   "Coming Out of the Cults," *Psychology Today* 12 (Jan.):82–82.
Smelser, Neil
   1963   *Theory of Collective Behavior.* New York: Free Press.
Snow, David A., and Cynthia L. Phillips
   1980   "The Lofland-Stark Conversion Model: A Critical Reassessment," *Social Problems* 27:430–447.
Snow, David, L. A. Zurcher, Jr., and S. Ekland-Olson
   1980   "Social Networks and Social Movements: A Microstructural Approach to Differential Recruitment," *American Sociological Review* 45:787–801.

Stark, Rodney, and William Bainbridge
   1980   "Networks of Faith: Interpersonal Bonds and Recruitment to Cults and Sects," *American Journal of Sociology* 85(6):1376–1395.
   1980   "Secularization, Revival, and Cult Formation," *The Annual Review of the Social Sciences of Religion* 20(4):360–373.
Straus, Roger
   1976   "Changing Oneself: Seekers and the Creative Transformation of Life Experience." *In* John Lofland, *Doing Social Life*. New York: John Wiley.
   1979   "Religious Conversion as a Personal and Collective Accomplishment," *Sociological Analysis* 40(2):158–165.
Wilson, Bryan
   1976   *The Contemporary Transformation of Religion*. London, New York: Oxford University Press.
   1979   "The Return of the Sacred," *Journal for the Scientific Study of Religion* 18(3):268–280.

PART THREE

The Sacred in Traditional Forms

VIII

Religious Organizations

James A. Beckford

INTRODUCTION

Unlike a number of other topics included in the sociological study of religion, religious organizations were once thought to be outcomes of, or defined in terms of, secularization. The fact that a religious sentiment, experience, or thought is expressed in regular and regulated forms of social interaction may seem to imply that it has been created by the passage of time in the human world. Religious organizations exist in time and in cultures. They cannot, according to this view, share the timelessness toward which religious expressions may strive. A tension is therefore perceived between the timeless authenticity of religious expressions and the authority invested in the social forms in which they have been organized over time. This is particularly true in the sphere of Judeo-Christian culture because of its dominant notions of linear time.

The classics of nineteenth-century sociology were concerned in part with the growing ascendancy of cultural values and norms favoring the dominance of means-end rationality within a linear, open-ended time scale. Various transitions from tradition to modernity were examined for their effects on religion, but relatively little attention was given to religious organizations because they were already assumed to be a part of the process of secularization. They were resource: not topic.

As the process of secularization has come to be taken for granted, albeit in very different ways, in the modern sociology of religion, so the specific adaptations of religious organizations to their changing environments have become a topic of interest. The very existence of religious organizations is rarely considered problematic nowadays: it is their *modus operandi* in a secularizing world which catches attention. Their significance for the broadest trends in cultural and societal change is nowadays accorded less interest than are the technical aspects of their operations.

The modern study of religious organizations departs from the tradition of the sociological classics in lacking any clear relevance to high-level theories about the development of human societies. Just as the concepts of, for example, "alienation" and "anomie" have been progressively removed from their theoretical contexts of origin in the course of successive attempts to operationalize them in universalistic terms, so the notion of religious organization has come to lose much of its rootedness in distinctive problems. It has become an apparently neutral, descriptive category lacking any particular theoretical purpose or character.

This is in itself an indirect indicator of secularization, for one is hard-pressed to think of a characteristic of religious organizations which is nowadays not also shared by nonreligious organizations. Another way of putting this is to question whether, in the present day, there are any distinguishing characteristics of religious organizations. To the extent that such characteristics are hard to isolate or few in number, one is probably justified in invoking the effects of secularization.[1] The corollary is that the sociological study of religious organizations requires no special concepts or approaches. Secularization may therefore be said to have simultaneously eroded the distinctiveness of religious organizations *and* of the sociological understanding of them. I shall demonstrate this by briefly summarizing some "classical" contributions and then by reviewing the general tendencies to be found in recent publications on religious organizations. Finally, the prospects for future research in this area will be assessed.

THE CLASSICS

Max Weber's studies of religious organization were informed by a consistent theoretical, long-term interest in the historical dynamics of Western and non-Western cultures and societies. His historico-typological accounts of the formalization of religions, practical religious ethics, religious professionals, and religious communities and collectivities were designed to illustrate their tendency in the Western world toward, first, progressive autonomization, routinization, and rationalization of their inner structures and meanings; and, second, legitimation of the material and ideational interests of various social strata. In combination, these tendencies were treated as the key to the West's distinctive path of development. Religious organizations were credited by Weber with crucial importance in the long-term processes of both rationalization and legitimation. Irony is therefore a prominent motif in his suggestion that the progressive rationalization of Western religion, especially the Protestantisms of the sixteenth and seventeenth centuries, contributed greatly to the separation of the secular and the religious and therefore toward the loss of religion's influence over the course of secular events. There is also considerable pathos in Weber's closely allied interest in the dialectic between the institutionalization of religion, charismatic breakthrough, and further routinization. This explains his fascination both with sectarian challenges to churchly adaptations to "the world" and with churchly attempts to mediate between the sacred and the human.

Emile Durkheim's studies of religious organizations were less extensive and less ironic than Weber's but no less central to his major theoretical preoccupation with the changing bases of societal integration. The sociological import of religious organizations lay therefore in their varied capacity to convey and to enact moral and ritual images of the approved relationship between the individual and society. Durkheim documented part of the historical evolution of this relationship by reference to the changing practice of religion, including speculations about the Cult of Man that he expected to be the appropriate form of religion in a future society based on an organic principle of solidarity.

It is ironic that Ernst Troeltsch is usually credited with the most systematic formulation of the basic concepts in which Western religious organizations have been constituted as sociological objects (see Séguy 1980, chaps. 17 and 18). For Troeltsch's purpose in elaborating on the main organizational types of church, sect, and mysticism was primarily to explain the variety of social forms in which Christian *ethics* had found expression and could continue to influence human affairs in the future. An all-purpose sociological typology was not intended. Troeltsch's aims were very specific and tailored by his understanding of Christianity as a complex set of ethical, social, and religious potentialities which fostered a wide variety of collective adaptations to historical contingencies.

The irony of routinized charisma and the pathos of rationalized religion were not Troeltsch's central concerns. His understanding of

Christianity's history was that it had from the very beginning represented a mixture of spiritual and worldly interests. There was no sense of progressive compromise or rationalization, only a sense of continuing interpenetration between the ideal-typical possibilities of churchlike, sectlike, and mystical forms of orientation toward the world and the spirit. His guiding concern was to ensure that Christianity would remain relevant in any of these major forms.

A not dissimilar question guided H. Richard Niebuhr's commentaries on religious organizations in the United States, with the possible difference that he was less sanguine than Troeltsch about what he considered to be the "compromise" struck between Christian ideals and the organizational reality of denominations. He characterized this reality as ". . . the accommodation of Christianity to the caste system of human society" (Niebuhr 1929:6). Christian organizations were doubly excoriated, first for being divided into separate denominations and, second, for reflecting social divisions based on class, race, region, or nation. A pathos of compromise therefore colored Niebuhr's writings on religious organization and thereby established a distinctive problematic which may paradoxically have had the effect of deterring scholarly interest in the topic (Hoge [1976] is an exception). But it certainly inspired a number of studies of the alleged transitions of sects into churches made as a result of changes in their class composition.

In sum, two general points can be made about the so-called classical studies of religious organization. On the one hand, religious organizations were regarded as important for what they revealed about the perceived dynamics of modern societies. The perceptions were varied, and the resultant interpretations of organizational structures and dynamics displayed no less variety. On the other hand, religious organizations were not considered to be especially important in themselves. That is, intensive analysis of their inner workings was not central to any of the classical works in the sociology of religion.[2] It was not until the post-World War II period that specialized sociological studies of religious organizations began to appear.

The history of sociological studies of religious organizations since 1960 represents a reversal of the classical priorities. First, religious organizations have been frequently subjected to close analysis in terms of their inner structures and dynamics, but interest has been relatively weak in their relations with their sociocultural environments.

Second, the largely implicit equation made by many sociologists between Christian religion and organized churches has been extensively challenged. In its place has dawned the recognition that religion is conveyed by a diversity of social "vehicles" which call for new conceptions of religious organization.[3]

THE MODERNS

While outstanding work was done at the beginning of the period under review within a framework of assumptions and questions derived from classical contributions dealing with bureaucratization (Harrison 1959), rationalization (Winter 1968), church-sect dynamics (Wilson 1958), and privatization (Luckmann 1967), there has subsequently been a growing tendency to adopt perspectives that owe relatively little to classical works on religious organization.

1. There is at least a degree of continuity, however, between the classical problematics and the modern interest in authority relations in religious organizations. This is part of a wider field of study concerned with the roles of religious specialists, the status of religious collectivities at various organizational levels, and the structure of communications within the organization. All these topics had a direct bearing on the classical problematics of rationalization, bureaucratization, and compromise. And they still generate numerous intellectual problems and questions about religious organizations (see Carroll 1981). Conceptual clarification has come from Bartholomew (1981), Harris (1969), and Wood (1981), while the empirical findings of research by Takayama and Cannon (1979) have illuminated the operations of various religious groups.

The general outcome of research on authority relations has underlined the importance of professionalization among religious leaders, the shifting bases of clerical authority, the encroachment of nonreligious specialists into areas that were previously the domain of religious expertise (see Dobbelaere et al. 1978), and the increasingly autonomous operation within religious organizations of agencies that are governed by mainly secular considerations. The voluminous literature on the roles of religious leaders is further testimony to this topic's central place in discussions of religious organizations.

Closely allied to questions of authority are questions about the recruitment, training, and socialization of religious professionals. This is one of the areas in which structural forces and social changes originating in the wider society are seen to press in upon religious organizations most threateningly. Studies of religious vocations

(Godin 1983; Rulla 1975) have also emphasized their declining attraction, and the recruitment of Anglican clergy is shown to fare no better (Towler and Coxon 1979). This is all consistent, of course, with classical theorizing about the effects of secularization.

Organizational responses to perceived secularization have not received the attention they deserve, but one important exception is Thompson's (1970) interpretation of the Church of England's organizational reforms in the nineteenth and twentieth centuries. Under pressure from an external world increasingly dominated by criteria of rationality, this church established numerous organizational arrangements, culminating in the present form of synodical government, which spawned bureaucratization alongside persistent elements of traditional structure.

2. There is very little continuity between classical problematics and recurrent preoccupations in the 1960s and 1970s with regard to the effects of various kinds of religious organizations on the likelihood that churches will act on radical policies in the areas of civil rights, ecumenism, and urban poverty. Pioneering studies by Hammond (1966), Hadden (1969), Wood (1970), and Quinley (1974) all recognized that the relatively liberal outlook of the clergy (especially its national leaders) in some Protestant churches was in tension with the laity's more conservative position on controversial matters. But they found that the organizational structure of the liberal denominations permitted ministers to exercise leadership functions in such a way as to overcome much grass-roots resistance without necessarily destroying denominational cohesion. Wood (1981) has more recently theorized this topic in terms of legitimation for leadership by means of "organizational transcendence."

Part of the general importance of Wood's work lies in its skepticism about Michel's so-called Iron Law of Oligarchy. But its more specific importance to the understanding of religious organizations derives from its optimistic suggestion that, as structured collectivities, they have the capacity to act on policies that would otherwise be extremely vulnerable to the conservatism of the majority of church members. This view departs sharply from classical thinking about religious organizations.

In addition to positing the power of religious organizations to facilitate change, these studies also began to acknowledge the importance of relating the organizational dynamics of churches to pressures originating in their social environments. This was later formalized in terms of open-systems theorizing (Beckford 1975a) and employed in comparative studies of American churches (Scherer 1980).

Other studies, nevertheless, have underlined the necessity of interpreting churches' organizational structures and processes in terms of their particular teachings and values (Ranson et al. 1977). The outcome has been a greater sensitivity toward the internal *and* external conditions affecting religious organizations than was displayed in the classics. A good example of this approach is Vaillancourt's (1980) analysis of the Roman Catholic Church's management of tensions between influential laity and Curial officials over the power to influence the Church's direction of development.

3. Studies of religious organization in the 1970s and early 1980s have been dominated by considerations of a wide variety of new, minority and alternative religious movements. This represents the sharpest break with classical problematics in terms of subject matter, theorizing, and methods of research. The first wave of studies challenging the equation of religion with church-type bodies brought intensive examination of the dialectical relationship between ideology and religious organization in various established sects. Wilson (1961, 1970), Beckford (1975b, 1975c), and Wallis (1974, 1976), among others, showed that the inner structures and processes of minority movements could be understood in terms of a problematic that balanced ideological purity against organizational constraints. Instead of drawing on the classical themes of irony, pathos, and compromise, however, these authors emphasized the persistent power of both ideology and organization to mobilize energies in adaptive fashion.

In fact, the old pathos of entropy in organized religion has given way in recent literature to a very different, and paradoxical, attitude. The paradox lies in the frequent finding that, even for highly enthusiastic and spiritual movements, the key to success is effective organization. Some of today's new religious movements and older established minority religions have demonstrated this point very clearly in the past two decades. It is as if their example called into question the old antinomies between spirit and letter; enthusiasm and organization; spontaneity and form. As Hirschman (1970) has demonstrated, these possibilities are more like alternates within the same organization than exclusives.

The new-found interest in minority movements is also critical toward the once dominant view concerning the role played by deprivation in the origin and continuing viability of religions. Despite various attempts to rescue the notion of deprivation in more nuanced forms, the trend has been toward approaches that emphasize the power of organization per se to sustain recruitment, socialization, and mobilization.

For example, considerable importance is attributed nowadays to the role of informal networks of social relationships in religious organizations of all kinds. Beginning with Gerlach and Hine's (1970) investigation of the reticulate character of Pentecostal groups, a large number of studies has confirmed the point that social networks are essential to the life of religious groups (see, for example, Snow et al. 1980). This has been found to be true not only for marginal movements but also for mainstream Christian churches, particularly in respect to such currents of enthusiasm as Charismatic Renewal, the Underground Church, liturgical traditionalism, and the Cursillo movement.

There is no agreed-on interpretation of the bearing of the current vitality of new religious movements on the meaning of secularization. Some see in them nothing but fads and fashions lacking relevance to crucial issues of societal integration and control; others regard them as possible sites of spiritual renewal and innovation. Of course, definitions of both "religion" and "secularization" are at stake in debates about the significance of new religious movements, and to some extent the debates are therefore bound to appear convoluted. For these reasons, it may be unwise to linger on this topic. But it is important at least to acknowledge that, irrespective of the extent to which new religious movements are considered secularizing or religious, they have stimulated several new ideas about religious organizations.

For example, one of the corollaries of the attention focused nowadays on social networks within new and old religious organizations is the diminishing value of theorizing about their churchlike or sectlike character.[4] The distinctions between churches and sects, no less than the processes of transition from one to the other, have been shown to be either overdrawn to the point of caricature or in need of such serious modification that the old terminology becomes obsolete. Not surprisingly, then, energy has been invested in schemes for subtypifying sects in ways that seek to overcome the fundamental problems of inherited, but outdated, rigidities.

At the same time, however, a new lease on life has been found for various adaptations of Troeltsch's individual mysticism type of religious orientation.[5] The term *cult* has also been pressed into service as a designation for many new religious movements; and the possibility of combining it with an updated notion of the monastic "order" has been canvassed in some places (see, e.g., Swatos 1981). It is suggested that an elective affinity links the cult type to certain sectors of the highly mobile, fragmented, rationalized, and "globalized" societies prevailing in the West in much the same way as the denomination was appropriate to the limited pluralism characterizing societies undergoing industrialization in the eighteenth and nineteenth centuries.

What has plainly *not* emerged is any comprehensive conceptual scheme that can cope with the diversity and flux of present-day religion with the sweeping economy and purposefulness of the Weberian, Troeltschian, or Niebuhrian versions of the church-sect problematic. There are many competing frameworks, but agreement is lacking on the "master" problem. Given that the social organization of religion is nowadays taken virtually for granted, it is unlikely that it *could* serve as the master principle of any would-be comprehensive framework. Since it has largely ceased to be a site of controversy and tension, it lacks theoretical interest for many sociologists.

SUMMARY

The sociological study of religious organizations has both documented and instantiated some of the effects widely attributed to the processes of secularization. It has provided empirical evidence of religious organizations' increasing differentiation from other sectors of society, bureaucratization, rationalization, professionalization, centralization, and standardization. At the same time, it has developed theoretical and methodological characteristics that reflect a declining sense of the distinctiveness of religious organizations as social phenomena. They are treated little differently from other kinds of organization; and they are expected to perform like other organizations. In other words, the boundary between the sacred and the secular has been affected in fact as well as in method.

Recent work on religious organizations has not so much challenged the classical inheritance on the sacred and the secular as it has taken it for granted and selectively adapted it for new purposes. Although reference back to the classics is still common, very few attempts are made to examine them closely or to test them systematically. In fact, studies of religious organizations have had a negligible impact on sociological conceptualizations of the sacred and the secular.

One of the reasons for this is that synchronic perspectives are predominant nowadays. Following the serious erosion of religious monopolies in many western countries, both pluralism and indifference in regard to religion have rendered the organizational aspects of religion no less optional, malleable, and interchangeable than the contents of beliefs and experiences. Long-term patterns are over-looked in preference to studies of short-term adaptations.

What is now required, therefore, is a greater sensitivity to questions about the relationship between societal change and religious change. Only in this way can we hope to understand the wider significance of the organizational adaptations which have begun to be documen-ted in recent publications.

The agenda for future research could profitably include comparative questions about religious, quasi-religious, and nonreligious organiza-tions with special reference to their relations with prevailing social forces and tendencies. Is the voluntary association, for example, be-coming the normal form for religious organizations? Is there evidence of an organizational counterpart in religion to secular processes of globalization in the late twentieth century? Have religious organiza-tions contributed any new forms of social organization to life in the modern world? ~ *multi·divisional form*?

Answers to these questions will not be generated by studies per-petuating the church-sect model of religious organization. Nor will it be helpful to approach them in terms of concepts embedded in the classical problematics of entropy and compromise. Rather, an appli-cation of theories, concepts, models, and methods deriving from general sociology offers the best prospect for progress. Interdisci-plinary approaches may also prove to be enlightening. Above all, however, it is essential that researchers should take into account current theorizing about the place of all manner of organizations in today's society. This would restore the scope of classical works on religious organizations without necessarily invoking the inherited problematics. For, if there is any agreement among the conclusions drawn from recent studies of religious organization it is that notions of the sacred can be conveyed by a wide range of organizational forms and that the fact of their being "organized" has no *necessary* implica-tions for the theory of secularization. In other words, the general pathos about the organization of religion is now giving away to a more sanguine acceptance of the importance of organization to the very existence of the sacred in the modern world. As a result, the categories of "organization" and "the sacred" are no longer conceived to be necessarily opposed to each other. This is part of a more nuanced conception of secularization in the context of societies dominated by formal organizations.

NOTES

1. In one of its strongest formulations, this view holds that "The patterns of affective neutrality, role specificity, performance expectations, self-orientation, and even universalism, which characterize the dominant organizational mode of Western society, are all, in greater or less degree, alien to religious institutions, roles, relationships, and values" (Wilson 1968:428). In an interesting qualification of this view, Richard Fenn acknowledges the progressive erosion of religion's distinctive sphere of discourse but also insists that there will be increasingly frequent eruptions of spirituality in the quintessentially secular domains of the law, education, and business (Fenn 1982).

2. If Wach's *Sociology of Religion* (1944) is considered a "classic," it constitutes an important exception to my generalization.

3. Allan Eister's far-sighted view is most appropriate here: "If it is, in fact, true . . . that 'most recent sociology of religion has been a *sociology of the churches*,' . . . then it seems reasonable to expect that, with the unmistakable surge of interest in 'religion outside of the churches'—in 'new religions', 'cults', and 'underground churches' as well as 'privatized' spiritual questing—all theories about religious organizations as such . . . might lose 'relevance' " (Eister 1973:401).

4. See Bennetta Jules-Rosette's criticisms—in her essay "The Sacred and Third World Societies" in this volume—of the influences of the church-sect model on thinking about new religious movements in Third World countries.

5. Special mention must be made of European writings that analyze organized departures from the Catholic orthodoxy in France and Italy in Troeltschian terms; for example, Séguy 1980; Pace 1983; and Léger and Hervieu 1983.

REFERENCES

Bartholomew, John Niles
1981   "A Sociological View of Authority in Religious Organizations," *Review of Religious Research* 23 (2):118–132.

Beckford, James A.
1975a   "Religious Organization. A Trend Report and Bibliography," *Current Sociology* 21 (2):1–170.

1975b   *The Trumpet of Prophecy. A Sociological Study of Jehovah's Witnesses.* Oxford: Blackwell.

1975c   "Organization, Ideology and Recruitment: The Social Structure of the Watch Tower Movement," *Sociological Review* 23 (4):893–909.

Carroll, Jackson W.
  1981   "Some Issues in Clergy Authority," *Review of Religious Research* 23
          (2):99–117.
Dobbelaere, Karel, Jaak Billiet, and Roger Creyf
  1978   "Secularization and Pillarization. A Social Problem Approach,"
          Annual Review of the Social Sciences of Religion 2:97–124.
Eister, Allan W.
 Ӿ 1973   "H. Richard Niebuhr and the Paradox of Religious Organization:
          A Radical Critique." *In* C. Y. Glock and P. E. Hammond, eds.,
          Beyond the Classics? Essays in the Scientific Study of Religion. New
          York: Harper and Row. Pp. 355–408.
Fenn, Richard K.
  1982   *Liturgies and Trials. The Secularization of Religious Language.* Oxford:
          Blackwell.
Gerlach, Luther P., and Virginia Hine
  1970   *People, Power, Change: Movements of Social Transformation.* Indian-
          apolis: Bobbs-Merrill.
Godin, André
  1983   *The Psychology of Religious Vocations.* Washington, D.C.: University
          Press of America. (First published in French in 1974.)
Hadden, Jeffrey K.
 Ӿ 1969   *The Gathering Storm in the Churches.* Garden City, N.Y.: Double-
          day.
Ӱ Hammond, Phillip E.
  1966   *The Campus Clergyman.* New York: Basic Books.
Harris, C. C.
 Ӱ 1969   "Reform in a Normative Organization," *Sociological Review* 17
          (2):167–185.
Harrison, Paul M.
  1959   *Authority and Power in the Free Church Tradition: A Social Case Study
          of the American Baptist Convention.* Princeton: Princeton University
          Press.
Hirschman, Albert C.
  1970   *Exit, Voice, and Loyalty.* Cambridge: Harvard University Press.
Hoge, Dean R.
  1976   *Division in the Protestant House. The Basic Reasons behind Intra-
          Church Conflicts.* Philadelphia: Westminster Press.
Léger, Danièle, and Bertrand Hervieu
  1983   *Des Communautés pour les Temps difficiles. Néo-Ruraux ou nouveaux
          Moines.* Paris: Editions du Centurion.
Luckmann, Thomas
  1967   *The Invisible Religion.* New York: Macmillan.
Niebuhr, H. Richard
  1929   *The Social Sources of Denominationalism.* New York: Holt, Rinehart
          & Winston.

Pace, Enzo
1983   *Asceti e Mistici in una Società Secolarizzata*. Venezia: Marsilio Editori.
Quinley, Harold E.
1974   *The Prophetic Clergy. Social Activism among Protestant Ministers*. New York: John Wiley.
Ranson, Stewart, Alan Bryman, and Christopher R. Hinings
1977   *Clergy, Ministers and Priests*. London: Routledge & Kegan Paul.
Rulla, L. M., J. Ridick, and F. Imoda
1975   *Entering and Leaving Vocation: Intrapsychic Dynamics*. Chicago: Loyola University Press.
Scherer, Ross P., ed.
1980   *American Denominational Organization. A Sociological View*. Pasadena, Calif.: William Carey Library.
Séguy, Jean
1980   *Christianisme et Société. Introduction à la Sociologie de Ernst Troeltsch*. Paris: Editions du Cerf.
Snow, David, Louis Zurcher, Jr., and Sheldon Ekland-Olson
1980   "Social Networks and Social Movements: A Microstructural Approach to Differential Recruitment," *American Sociological Review* 45:787–801.
Swatos, William H., Jr.
1981   "Church, Sect, and Cult: Bringing Mysticism Back In," *Sociological Analysis* 42 (1):17–26.
Takayama, K., Peter Cannon, and Lynn Weber Cannon
1979   "Formal Polity and Power Distribution in American Protestant Denominations," *Sociological Quarterly* 20:321–332.
Thompson, Kenneth A.
1970   *Bureaucracy and Church Reform*. Oxford: Oxford University Press.
Towler, Robert, and A. P. M. Coxon
1979   *The Fate of the Anglican Clergy*. London: Macmillan.
Vaillancourt, Jean-Guy
1980   *Papal Power: A Study of Vatican Control over Lay Elites*. Berkeley, Los Angeles, London: University of California Press.
Wach, Joachim
1964   *Sociology of Religion*. Chicago: University of Chicago Press.
Wallis, Roy
1974   "Ideology, Authority and the Development of Cultic Movements," *Social Research* 41 (2):299–327.
1976   "Observations on the Children of God," *Sociological Review* 24 (4):807–829.
Wilson, Bryan R.
1958   "Apparition et persistence des sectes dans un milieu social en évolution," *Archives de Sociologie des Religions* 5:140–150.
1961   *Sects and Society*. London: Heinemann.

1968   "Religious Organization," *In* David Sills, ed., *The International Encyclopedia of the Social Sciences* 4:428–437. New York: Macmillan.

1970   *Religious Sects*. London: Weidenfeld & Nicolson

Winter, Gibson

1968   *Religious Identity*. New York: Macmillan.

Wood, James R.

1970   "Authority and Controversial Policy: The Churches and Civil Rights," *American Sociological Review* 35:1057–1069.

1981   *Leadership in Voluntary Organizations. The Controversy over Social Action in Protestant Churches*. New Brunswick, N.J.: Rutgers University Press.

IX

Church and Sect

Rodney Stark

INTRODUCTION

For more than fifty years "church-sect theory" has been displayed as one of the major accomplishments of the sociology of religion. Yet, when I first encountered this literature more than twenty years ago, I found its merits difficult to perceive. In the hands of sociologists, church and sect had been fashioned into a host of idiosyncratic typologies that defeated the possibility of theorizing about anything.

In 1929, H. Richard Niebuhr gave theoretical life to the terms *sect* and *church* (as handed down from Weber and Troeltsch) by linking them in a process by which sects broke away from churches only to be transformed themselves into churches. Unfortunately, rather than attempting to extend and improve on Niebuhr's stimulating, but vague, process model, sociologists quickly retreated once more to the safety of mere classification (as opposed to theorizing). In the early 1960s when I first read the church-sect literature, it seemed mainly to be a game for Mandarins, each trying to name the greatest possible number of different *kinds* of sects. These writers often invoked the term *church-sect theory*, but this had only symbolic, not substantive, purpose. Ironically, scores of papers that were identified as contributions to church-sect *theory* seemed devoid of theoretical intent.

It is not uncommon for scholarly fields periodically to become like stagnant pools wherein participants, like algae, are content to add encrustation to a sunken ship. Fortunately, a pool sometimes gets drained, the wreck gets refloated, and the voyage begins again. That is precisely what has happened in the church-sect area. The first steps were conceptual and provided the tools for a resumption of theorizing. The next steps involved shifting the scope of church-sect theory from religious organizations per se to whole societies. This line of theorizing resulted in a challenge to the received wisdom from another stagnant pool: secularization theory.

In this essay, I sketch these major developments. In an initial draft I took pains to disguise and minimize my own contributions. This resulted in many oddly constructed sentences which gave the impression that ideas are but playthings of the Zeitgeist. Subsequently I have written a less modest, but more informative, version. Ultimately, of course, what is important is what we know, and what we can do with what we know, not who said what.

DOCTOR JOHNSON'S CONCEPTUAL
RUMMAGE SALE

The first, and most important step in liberating church-sect theory from its Mandarin Captivity was taken by Benton Johnson in 1963. Prior to Johnson's now famous paper, the concepts of church and sect had become encrusted with so many defining characteristics that they were all but useless for classification and hence impossible to use as terms in a theory. This was because the definitions were formed of *correlates* rather than *attributes* of the phenomena to be classified. A correlate is a characteristic of some phenomenon that is only *sometimes*, but not always, present in an instance of the phenomenon. For example, sociologists pointed out that sects tended to be small, to have a converted membership, to stress austerity, and to engage in highly emotional styles of worship (Dynes 1955, 1957; O'Dea 1966). However, *many* groups thought to be sects lacked some of these characteristics and some sects lacked them all. Inevitably the result was a maze of mixed types. Attributes, on the other hand, are present in *all* instances of a phenomenon. For example, to say that sects are religious bodies that form by breaking away from another religious body is, at least in principle, true of *all* sects. When attributes are used to form concepts, they produce no mixed types.

Why are mixed types a problem? Because they cannot be ordered. Is a religious body that lacks a converted membership, and is large, but stresses austerity and holds emotional services, more or less sectlike than one that is small and has a converted membership, but does not stress austerity or hold emotional services? There is no way to answer that question given "un-ideal types" constructed of correlates. And, without an answer to that question, it is impossible to state or to test theories about what might cause sects to be transformed into churches, for we cannot say when one group is less sectlike than some other or, worse yet, less sectlike than it used to be.

It was, therefore, of immense importance when Benton Johnson proposed to discard these immobilizing layers of correlates from the definitions of church and sect and to replace them with two attributes. First, sect and church apply to *religious* groups (thus freeing theorists from a need to account for the behavior of political movements). Second, church and sect are simply names applied to end-points of a single axis of variation formed by the *degree of tension between a religious group and its sociocultural environment*. That is, churches are religious bodies in a low state of tension with their environments; sects are bodies in a high state of tension. Given adequate indicators of the relative degree of tension it now was possible to order groups unambiguously in terms of the degree to which they were sectlike or churchlike and to detect *movement* by a given group toward lower or higher tension.

Johnson's new concepts not only made it possible to state and to test propositions about the formation and transformation of sects, it made many such propositions almost self-evident. For the many genuine insights that had been locked up in definitional schemes now could be restated as propositions about the sect to church process (for example, that when a movement becomes reliant on socialized rather than on converted members it is likely to move into lower tension). Johnson's scheme also drew attention to previously neglected issues. For example, until that time theoretical interest had been almost exclusively devoted to why sects broke away from churches—to schisms in which the dissidents moved into a higher state of tension. Given Johnson's clean axis of variation it became obvious that groups could also break off to move into a *lower* state of tension. Thus a year later Johnson's paper had led Stephen Steinberg (1965) to develop the concept of "church movement," and to illustrate it with an analysis of why and how Reform Judaism broke away from Orthodoxy. Subsequently many examples of church movements have been discovered and we have a clearer understanding of the special conditions under which they take place (Stark and Bainbridge 1984).

Johnson's paper was a breakthrough but, understandably, it left work for others. For one thing, it was necessary to demonstrate that the notion of "tension" could be stated with sufficient clarity to make it possible to operationalize it for empirical research. William Sims

Bainbridge and I (1980) undertook to fill this gap by equating tension with *subcultural deviance*, to be measured by the degree of *difference*, *antagonism*, and *separation* between a religious group and its sociocultural environment. We found a number of quantitative measures of each of these three aspects of tension and these worked very consistently and efficiently to rank religious groups. A second necessary addition to Johnson's scheme was to differentiate between several *kinds* of high-tension groups on the basis of their *origins*.

CULT MOVEMENTS

Niebuhr's theory concerns the eruption of new religious organizations from conventional churches—it is a theory of schism. However, not all new religious organizations embody old faiths, nor do they originate only via schism. Sometimes alien faiths are imported into a society. And sometimes someone discovers or invents new religious insights and thus founds a brand new faith. Johnson did not distinguish between new organizations of old faiths and organizations embodying new ones, classifying both as sects. This was in keeping with common sociological practice (see Wallis 1975). Over the decades, however, a number of scholars have pointed out the problem of mixing the new and the old and calling them all "sects" (von Wiese and Becker 1932; Yinger 1957; Glock and Stark 1965; Nelson 1969). Moreover, these same scholars have suggested that the term *cult* be used for new religions, and that *sect* be applied to schismatic movements within a conventional religious tradition.

When Bainbridge and I decided to attempt to construct a general theory of religion (Stark and Bainbridge 1980a, 1984, and forthcoming), one of our first needs was to distinguish between cults and sects (Stark and Bainbridge 1979). One could construct a full explanation of why and how schisms produce movements seeking a higher-tension version of a conventional faith, without addressing the question of why and how new religions arise. Or one could account for the formation of new religions and know nothing of how and why groups split. For this reason we proposed the term *cult movement* to identify high-tension religious movements within a *deviant* religious *tradition* (deviant in the society under examination), while applying the term *sect* to high-tension religious movements within a *conventional* religious *tradition*. We also suggested the terms *client cult* and *audience cult* to refer to deviant magical activities that had not developed into full-fledged deviant religions. We have found these distinctions vital to our theoretical progress. Of course, some scholars prefer to honor the received wisdom whatever its limitations, and condemn all newfangled schemes such as ours (Swatos 1981). As we shall see, however, the spatial and temporal distributions of sects and of cult movements are strongly negatively correlated and produce theoretically strategic diffential patterns. To lump them is to lose all.

DISCOVERING RELIGIOUS ECONOMIES

Niebuhr's original church-sect theory attempted to explain the great diversity of Christian denominations in contemporary societies. It did so by postulating a process by which religious organizations are successively captured by the middle and upper classes and accommodated to the world, thus losing their otherworldly capacity to satisfy the hopes and dreams of the deprived. His model, in effect, postulated a never-ending cycle of the birth, transformation, and rebirth of sect movements.

Following Niebuhr, sociologists gave their theoretical interest almost entirely to the process by which sects were or were not transformed into low-tension churches. Bryan Wilson's 1959 paper demonstrated how much could be learned by pursuing this matter. But Wilson's paper also displayed the inherent limits of paying too much attention to what goes on *within* religious organizations and too little attention to the external conditions they face. Indeed, it now seems likely that the environment plays the decisive role in the fate of any religious movement—particularly the other religious groups in that environment. Thus what is needed is a way to examine religious movements within a larger framework. For these purposes the concept of a *religious economy* is suitable (Stark and Bainbridge 1984).

Religious economies are like commercial economies—they comprise a market and the set of firms seeking to serve that market. And, as with commercial economies, a major consideration is the degree to which the market is regulated—that is, the extent to which it is a free market ruled by the forces of the marketplace, or a market distorted toward monopoly by use of coercion by the state. Bainbridge and I have deduced from our general theory that to the degree a religious economy is unregulated, pluralism will thrive—that the "natural" state of religious economies is one in which a variety of firms successfully cater to the special religious interests of limited market segments.

This arises because of the inherent inability of one firm to be at once both very worldly and very otherworldly, while the market will always contain segments seeking more and less worldly versions of faith. Indeed, because of this underlying differentiation within markets, religious economies can never be monopolized successfully even when a religious organization is supported by state coercion—even at the height of its temporal power, the medieval church was surrounded on all sides by heresy and dissent (Johnson 1979; Stark and Bainbridge 1984). Of course, when repression is great, black-market conditions will exist. But whenever, and wherever, repression falters, pluralism will break through.

Indeed, this line of theorizing is *implicit in church-sect theory*. Suppose we ask, what are the implications of repeated workings of the church-sect process in a society? First of all, as Niebuhr noted, there would exist a great many different religious bodies. Second, because of the tendency of religious organizations to be transformed from higher to lower tension, we would observe that the dominant religious organizations in a society will always be in transit toward lower tension, toward a more worldly, less otherworldly, version of faith. Put another way, the most influential and respectable religious bodies in any religious economy are always shedding their historic legacies of otherworldliness and adopting increasingly vague, less vivid, less active conceptions of the supernatural. Viewing it this way, we are able to see that what constitutes the transformation of a sect into a church at the level of specific organizations, constitutes at the societal level the *process of secularization*. Furthermore, once we note the correspondence between sect transformation and secularization, the traditional social-scientific view of secularization collapses.

SECULARIZATION RECONSIDERED

The famous nineteenth- and early twentieth-century founders of social science disagreed about many things, but they were nearly unanimous in predicting the rapid demise of religion (and in their desire that this occur as soon as possible). Thus social scientists have viewed secularization as a modern phenomenon, a consequence of the rise of science and rational enlightenment and the subsequent triumph of modernity over mysticism and "superstition." Yet, although generations of social scientists have diagnosed terminal ailments in religion, the patient has been uncooperative. Indeed, it is (the most "enlightened" (or secularized) churches that are in the worst organizational shape, while the "unenlightened" thrive (Kelley, 1972). For too long the strength of the more otherworldly versions of faith has been dismissed as one last hurrah.

It now seems likely that the traditional view of secularization was myopic and distorted. Examination of religious economies rather than of specific religious organizations led to the proposition that secularization is *normal*, and that it is a universal phenomenon always occurring in all religious economies. Sometimes the pace of secularization is slower and sometimes it is faster (the rise of science in the West may well have produced relatively rapid secularization). But fast or slow, if secularization is universal and normal, then it *does not* imply the demise of religion. It *does* imply the eventual failure of specific religious organizations as they become too worldly and too emptied of supernaturalism to continue to generate commitment. But, here again, application of church-sect theory to religious economies tells us to expect secularization to be *a self-limiting process* that generates countervailing responses elsewhere in religious economies. That is, secularization is to be found not only in sect transformation but also as the causative force in sect *formation*. That is, church-sect theory tells us to expect the progressive secularization of major religious organizations to touch off *revival*.

REVIVAL AND CULT FORMATION

Sect movements do not found *new* faiths. Rather they seek to restore or revive an earlier, more otherworldly version of the conventional religious culture. Indeed, sects are correct when they charge that the body from which they split had drifted away from its historic faith— that is precisely what is involved in the movement from sect to church. Conversely, in the movement from church to sect we see the process by which new firms move into openings in the religious market left by the trend toward worldliness afflicting older firms. Just as traditional church-sect theory predicts schism when a sect has developed into a church, so too the theory predicts periods of very successful sect formation to renew the balance of a religious economy when secularization has made sufficient inroads on many major firms.

It is important to see, however, that secularization and revival are not the only processes going on within religious economies. Rather, a whole religious tradition sometimes becomes weakened—perhaps by too many revolutions on the secularization-revival circuit. In any event, secularization also prompts religious innovation, or *cult formation*. That is, *new* religions arise and seek a place in the market. They succeed only as weaknesses in the established firms give them opportunity, to the extent that unserved market demand exists.

This leads to the conclusion that secularization will not usher in a postreligious era. Instead, it will repeatedly lead to a resupply of vigorous otherworldly religious organizations by prompting revival. And, once in a while, it will prompt the rise of wholly new faiths. That is, every once in a while some obscure cult movement will arise at a moment when a religious economy is in crisis and thus be able to supplant the old firms—as Christianity arose at a moment of crisis.

RECENT EMPIRICAL RESULTS

This new view of church-sect theory and its implications for the secularization thesis has led to a number of specific empirical hypotheses, which have recently received considerable empirical support.

1. If sects revive and revitalize a religious tradition, and cult movements thrive only where conventional faiths are weak, then cults should be weak where sects are strong, and vice versa. This view is incompatible with the traditional secularization thesis, which assumes that all religions will cluster where and when unenlightenment is greatest. In a series of studies, strong negative ecological correlations have been found between sect and cult strength—in the United States (Stark and Bainbridge 1980b), in Europe (Stark 1984), and in Latin America (Stark 1984a).

2. Cult movements ought to thrive wherever the conventional faiths have weakened. This has been demonstrated for the United States today (Stark and Bainbridge 1980b) and in the Roaring Twenties (Stark and Bainbridge 1981), for Canada (Bainbridge and Stark 1983), for Europe (Stark 1984), for Latin America (Stark 1984a) and for the nations of Islam (Stark 1984b).

3. Cult movements will recruit primarily from the ranks of those lacking religious affiliation—those most disaffected from conventional religious options. Although sociologists, myself included, have long supposed that people who give their religious affiliation as "None" in survey studies are mainly secular humanists, immune to mystical appeals, the results of recent research show them to be in the group

most likely to accept deviant supernatural and magical teachings (Bainbridge and Stark 1981*a*, 1981*b*). Moreover, surveys of members of a great variety of contemporary cult movements show that an extraordinary number are recruited from irreligious backgrounds (Stark and Bainbridge 1984).

CONCLUSION

During the past twenty years, church-sect theory finally began to fulfill the promise implicit in the model developed by H. Richard Niebuhr in the late 1920s. The major breakthrough came from Benton Johnson who shattered the typological chains that prevented theoretical development. Reopening of the theoretical enterprise led to further conceptual development and eventually to the application of church-sect analyses to whole religious economies. Thus did some old ideas suddenly gain new power and relevance. In so doing, they cast doubt on the secularization thesis, and perhaps just in time.

Just as religious movements can sometimes be damaged beyond repair by setting dates that too often fail to come true, so too can social scientists become a laughing stock from failed prophesy. Ever since Comte first proposed in the 1830s that sociology be developed as a substitute for religion, the leading figures in the field have been hailing the death of faith. By now these solemn prophesies are embarassingly out of joint with observable reality as religion continues to renew itself and to enjoy robust health. Given the fix we are in, the very least we must do is recognize that secularization is an "invisible" process that will not be detectable in the world of mundane appearances until another millennium has passed. If that fails to satisfy, we might want to follow where church-sect theory has long pointed and to see that, although specific religious organizations eventually are ruined by secularization, religion goes on, embodied in new organizations. In effect, the founders of social science looked only at sunsets, and never at sunrises. No wonder they couldn't tell time.

REFERENCES

Bainbridge, William Sims, and Rodney Stark
    1980   "Sectarian Tension," *Review of Religious Research* 22:105–124.
    1981*a*   "The Consciousness Reformation Reconsidered," *Journal for the Scientific Study of Religion* 20:1–16.

1981b   "Friendship, Religion, and the Occult," *Review of Religious Research* 22:313–327.

1983   "Church and Cult in Canada," *Canadian Journal of Sociology* 7:351–366.

Dynes, Russell R.

1955   "Church-Sect Typology and Socio-Economic Status," *American Sociological Review* 20:555–560.

1957   "The Consequences of Sectarianism for Political Participation," *Social Forces* 35:331–334.

Glock, Charles Y., and Rodney Stark

1965   *Religion and Society in Tension.* Chicago: Rand McNally.

Johnson, Benton

1963   "On Church and Sect," *American Sociological Review* 28:539–549.

Johnson, Paul

1979   *A History of Christianity.* New York: Atheneum.

Kelley, Dean M.

1972   *Why Conservative Churches Are Growing.* New York: Harper and Row.

Nelson, Geoffrey K.

1969   "The Spiritualist Movement and the Need for a Redefinition of Cult," *Journal for the Scientific Study of Religion* 8:152–160.

Niebuhr, H. Richard

1929   *The Social Sources of Denominationalism.* New York: Henry Holt.

O'Dea, Thomas F.

1966   *The Sociology of Religion.* Englewood Cliffs, N.J.: Prentice-Hall.

Stark, Rodney

1984   "Europe's Receptivity to New Religious Movements." *In* R. Stark, ed., *Religious Movements: Genesis, Exodus, and Numbers.* New York: Rose of Sharon Press.

"Secularization and Mormonism in Latin America," *Journal for the Scientific Study of Religion.* In press.

"Secularization and Cult Movements in Islam," *Sociological Analysis.* In press.

Stark, Rodney, and William Sims Bainbridge

1979   "Of Churches, Sects, and Cults," *Journal for the Scientific Study of Religion* 18:117–131.

1980a   "Towards a Theory of Religion," *Journal for the Scientific Study of Religion* 19:114–128.

1980b   "Secularization, Revival, and Cult Formation," *The Annual Review of the Social Sciences of Religion* 4:85–119.

1981   "Secularization and Cult Formation in the Jazz Age," *Journal for the Scientific Study of Religion* 20:360–373.

1984   *The Future of Religion.* Berkeley, Los Angeles, London: University of California Press.

A Theory of Religion. Forthcoming.

Steinberg, Stephen
   1965   "Reform Judaism: The Origin and Evolution of a Church Move-
           ment," *Journal for the Scientific Study of Religion* 5:117–129.
Swatos, William H., Jr.
   1981   "Church-Sect and Cult: Bringing Mysticism Back In," *Sociological
           Analysis* 42:17–26.
Wallis, Roy, ed.
   1975   *Sectarianism.* New York: John Wiley.
Wiese, L. von, and Howard Becker
   1932   *Systematic Sociology.* New York: John Wiley.
Wilson, Bryan
   1959   "An Analysis of Sect Development," *American Sociological Review*
           24:3–15.
Yinger, J. Milton
   1957   *Religion, Society and the Individual.* New York: Macmillan.

X

Conservative Protestantism

James Davison Hunter

It has been noted that of all the world religions Protestantism has confronted modernity more intensely and for a longer period of time. If one concedes this point, then one must allow that Protestantism bears a special relationship to the processes of secularization as well. In theology, as Peter Berger has argued, the Protestant case is paradigmatic; throughout the nineteenth century and indeed to the present, Protestant theology has attempted to come to grips with secular intellectual thought, the diffusion of secular consciousness among the wider population, and the churches' increasingly limited role in the social world. Protestantism's protracted struggle with modernity and secularization may thus be paradigmatic for understanding the theological enterprise generally in the modern world, but it may also be paradigmatic for an understanding of the nature and limits of secularization itself. At least it will prove to be an important test case for the secularization hypothesis at the end of the twentieth century.

Yet it is not Protestantism as a whole that provides the crucible for the secularization postulate. In its liberal expression, Protestantism has maintained the posture of compromise—from unwitting accommodation to aggressive capitulation to the secularizing constraints of modernity—so that the liberal Protestant world view functions as a deeply secularized cosmology. In contrast, within the numerous traditions of conservative Protestantism one may find secularism's greatest challenge, for what these traditions share precisely is an attempt to retain the integrity of orthodox Christian (Protestant) symbols in a context presumed hostile to that integrity.

PRELIMINARY ASSESSMENTS

The results of early studies of conservative Protestantism all seemed
to support the contention that religion was retreating in the face of
modernization. Weber's (1958) classic thesis, of course, was that, as
industrial capitalism matured, the religious asceticism of the Puritan
would no longer be needed to sustain it. Writing in 1904, Weber
maintained that Protestant culture, like all religious traditions, would
give way to "rationalization, intellectualization, and the 'disenchantment of the world.'" Robert and Helen Lynd's study of Middletown
two decades later confirmed this thesis. In 1925, the evangelical
Protestant church continued to dominate the religious life of
Middletown as it had in 1890 (Lynd and Lynd 1929:402), yet church
attendance, they noted, had been steadily declining since that time
(1929:359). Ten years later, in *Middletown in Transition* (1937), the
pattern had not changed. Quoting a "local editor" in 1935, they
reported that ". . . all churches in town, save a few denominations
like the Seventh Day Adventists, are more liberal today than in 1925.
Any of them will take you in no matter what you believe doctrinally"
(1965:308).

Though the Lynds' study provided the most important evidence,
other community studies of the period corroborated this theme.
Liston Pope's study of Gastonia, North Carolina, in 1929 during the
turbulent "Loray Millworker's Strike" showed that the churches there
(liberal or conservative) had become ancillary to economic realities,
except insofar as they were instrumental in creating a manipulable
labor force. Church leaders of all classes legitimated plainly exploitive
management practices and resisted, with management, the union's
efforts to bring about fair wages and working conditions. They were
also silent about the violent recriminations exerted by the community
against union organizers. Underwood's study of Holyoke, Massachusetts, in 1946 showed that religious affiliation (whether in Catholic
parishes or in Protestant churches and sects) was politically token;
religious knowledge and its relevance to everyday life for the working
class and for the business leaders was nebulous. Its greatest import
was for ethnic identification, which did have consequences for political action and occupational mobility. So too did Morland's 1958 study
of the mill village sections of Kent in the South. Morland found, like
Pope, that Protestant conservatism existed predominantly among the
lower class mill workers, as opposed to the people in the upper class
section of town, where religion's role was principally to provide a

measure of private-sphere respectability. Its chief contribution to the economic and political life of Kent was the encouragement of a high level of passivity among the mill workers and farm people.

The net conclusion of these studies and others was that conservative Protestantism was well on its way out. When it existed at all, it was at the sectarian margins of society. As Niebuhr put it as early as 1929, it existed as a "religion of the disinherited"—lower class, rural, politically impotent—precisely in those areas of society farthest removed from the secularizing influences of modernity. This assessment on the part of the social scientific community held fast through the end of the 1960s, when Berger noted that a milieu of Protestant conservativism still existed, yet "these are typically located on the fringes of urban, middle-class society. They are like besieged fortresses, and their mood tends toward a militancy that only superficially covers an underlying sense of panic" (1969:11). Berger was not alone. As social scientific convention would have it, the acids of secularization were ubiquitous and unyielding, and conservative Protestantism would prove no exception to the rule.

RECENT TRENDS

Prevailing opinion about the decline of conservative Protestantism, however, changed abruptly with the publication of Dean Kelley's *Why Conservative Churches Are Growing* (1972). Kelley documented that, while mainstream Protestant church bodies in the United States were declining numerically, conservative Protestant churches were showing sharp increases in membership. Membership and church school enrollment declines in the mainstream bodies began in the mid-1960s with denominations such as the United Methodist Church, the Episcopal Church, the United Presbyterian Church, and the United Church of Christ all showing losses of 1 percent to 3 percent a year. Similarly, church construction, religious publishing, and overseas missionary personnel in the mainstream churches also declined at significant rates. In contrast, such conservative denominations as the Southern Baptist Convention, Church of the Nazarene, the Salvation Army, Christian and Missionary Alliance, and smaller independent pentecostal sects, continued to show strong numerical increases—from 2.5 percent (Southern Baptist) to 9.2 percent (Assemblies of God) each year from 1958 to 1975. Catholic and Protestant charismatic fellowships also experienced considerable revitalization and growth (McGuire 1982; Paloma 1983). Kelley's explanation for this trend was that, in contrast with the liberal churches, conservative churches were providing people with answers to ultimate questions and were thus sufficiently serious in character to evoke high levels of personal commitment from their constituencies.

Needless to say, Kelley's thesis spawned considerable debate in both religious and social scientific circles, but during the 1970s consensus emerged that Evangelical Christianity was experiencing some revival. Kelley reiterated his argument in 1978, and Carroll et al. (1979) and Roof (1982) updated this analysis and assessment. Coverage in the popular media throughout the decade further encouraged this perception (*Time* 1976; *The Wall Street Journal* 1980). Others, however, were skeptical. In one of the first empirical analyses of the issue, Bibby and Brinkerhoff (1973) argued that growth was not caused by new converts to conservative churches but by a recycling process in which members were added by reaffiliation (switching from other churches) and by the matriculation of the offspring of church members. The proselytization factor, they argued, was negligible in all of this. Bouma (1979) followed this up with an analysis of the church membership rates of the Christian Reformed Church and concluded that the growth of the church was largely due to immigration and birth, and not to the evangelization of nonbelievers. This skepticism was reiterated by Bibby and Brinkerhoff (1982) in a ten-year followup of their earlier study, as well as by Wills (1978) and Hunter (1983a) who suggested that what had been called religious revival may have been at heart a revival of awareness of evangelicalism in America—a revival encouraged if not manufactured by the mass media.

It is quite possible that proponents of the revival thesis and their critics are both correct, the real issue being the degree to which each is correct. Thus far, however, this question remains open and unanswered. What may be more important is simply the fact that conservative Protestantism is surviving against all odds that it would. Its survival is confirmed not only in the United States—where estimates of its demographic base range from between one-fifth (Hunter 1983a:49) and one-third (Gallup 1976) of the American population—but in Canada (Bibby and Brinkerhoff 1973; Tipp and Winter 1970) and the United Kingdom (Bruce 1983a, 1983c) as well.

On the American scene, the survival of conservative Protestantism must be partially attributed to the postwar development and consolidation of a complex institutional infrastructure—a network of parallel institutions encompassing and supporting the totality of the Evangelical subculture (Sandeen 1970). Thus, while program development within traditionally conservative denominations is one important area of growth, the most significant and visible area has been in the para-church field. In the United States, one could note the many evangelical agencies in existence, such as the Evangelical Family Service, the Evangelical Child and Family Agency, Family Ministers, the Evangelical Purchasing Service, Evangelical Social Action, World Relief, World Vision, Medical Assistance Program, the Christian Service Corps, and the Christian Service Brigade (Hunter 1983a:56–58). Apart from these agencies, institutional entrenchment has been greatest in four areas: education, publishing, the mass media and the "electronic church," and politics.

EDUCATION

Evangelical higher education is a concern shared by all traditions in conservative Protestantism—from the pentecostal sects to the European reformational denominations. The United States is unparalleled on this count with over 450 Evangelical liberal arts colleges, Bible colleges, and seminaries (Hunter 1983a:58). More astonishing than the growth and stability of these institutions is the growth of independent private evangelical primary and secondary schools, which form the Christian School movement. Protestant schools of this sort increased in number by 47 percent between 1971 and 1978, with a 95 percent increase in student enrollment (Wuthnow 1984). Current estimates are that 18,000 such schools representing roughly 2.5 million students are now operating (Kienel 1983). A study by Ballweg (1980) of parents sending their children to Christian schools found resentment toward the public school environment and the public school professional establishment to be the principal reason parents sent their children to Christian schools. Social class, political orientation, religious conviction, and other cultural factors were related to some degree but were not nearly as important as the attitude of resentment.

Organizations serving the secular university and secondary school populations have also been central to the institutional entrenchment of evangelicalism. Denominational support systems are more numerous than the para-church support organizations, but the latter are more visible and more active on most campuses. Oldest among these interdenominational campus ministries is the Inter-Varsity Christian Fellowship (IVCF). With a staff of several thousand, it is represented at universities in local chapters around the world, though mainly in the United States. Organizationally more diverse, Campus Crusade for Christ surpasses IVCF with a staff of over 16,000 and involvement in 150 countries around the world. Smaller organizations such as the Navigators and Youth for Christ have made an impact as well.

PUBLISHING

Evangelical publishing has been tremendously active in the post-World War II era. The Evangelical Press Association represents the journalistic side of Evangelical publishing. Founded in 1949, it now represents 275 periodicals, showing a net increase in membership of 15 to 20 new periodicals a year. Its greatest increase reportedly came in the mid- to late 1970s, doubling its previous membership. Overall, these periodicals claim to reach in excess of twenty-two million people. In the United Kingdom, Bruce (1983c) points out that, while liberal Protestant religious publishing has sharply declined since the 1970s, conservative Protestant periodical publishing has increased in the same time period. (This is small by comparison to the conservative efforts in the United States, but vital by comparison to liberal efforts in the U.K.)

The book-publishing dimension is best represented by the Christian Booksellers Association. The CBA was founded in 1950 and currently encompasses 3,300 member stores out of a reported (and estimated) total of 5,500 to 6,000 Christian bookstores in America. On its own, CBA stores account for roughly $600 million in gross sales per year (Alm 1983). Most of the books represented in these figures are published by specifically Evangelical publishing houses. In the early 1980s, these numbered approximately 70, ranging, of course, in size and quality.

MASS MEDIA AND THE "ELECTRONIC CHURCH"

The third areas of institutional growth for conservative Protestantism are the religious electronic media. They are, of course, mainly an American phenomenon, since in Canada and the United Kingdom, radio and television are largely controlled by centralized and provincial governments. The development of the religious electronic media

has roughly paralleled the development of the mass media generally—slow but steady growth from the early part of the century,
expanding after the Second World War and proliferating rapidly from
the 1960s to the present. At present, 16 percent of all radio stations
operating in the United States are classified as predominantly religious (see Stacey and Shupe 1982). The majority of these are Evangelical in orientation. Further, there are at least sixty-five television
stations broadcasting nearly exclusively programs of Evangelical content (Mariani 1979:23; Ostling 1983). Dominating this scene is the
Christian Broadcasting Network, currently fed to 3,200 local cable
systems which claim access to twenty million homes, offering pro-
gramming twenty-four hours a day (Commuta 1983). In global terms,
the 1007 units (including 922 radio stations, 65 television stations, 535
radio producers, and 280 television/film producers) handled, as of
1983, 85 percent of all Protestant religious broadcasts in the United
States and 75 percent of all Protestant religious broadcasts in the
world (Barrett 1982; see also Hadden and Swann 1981:61–83).

   In spite of this display of religious machismo, analyses of television
viewer data collected by Arbitron show that the claims of certain
"televangelists" to be reaching tens and even hundred of millions of
people is grossly exaggerated. As of 1980, Arbitron estimated the total
number of persons viewing sixty-six syndicated religious programs
to be, at best, twenty million people (Hadden and Swann 1981:50).
Other estimates suggest the figure is even smaller, somewhere between seven and twelve million people. Notably, most of these view-
ers are from the working class, the greatest percentage are women,
and they are slightly older than nonviewers. Moreover, they tend to
be predisposed to Evangelical Christianity, being actively involved in
traditional forms of religiosity in their own local churches (Stacey and
Shupe 1982).

   This interplay of conservative religious ideology and sophisticated
communications technology is interesting in light of the secularization
hypothesis, and yet it is an issue virtually unexamined in empirical
research. Some evidence suggests that conservatives see technology
as either neutral and thus not challenging to their faith, or positive—
as a gift from God to further his work on this earth—and, thus, an
enhancement to faith. Bruce (1983a) has argued that conservative
Protestants continue to operate out of a "Baconian inductionism"
positing no sharp dichotomy between natural and supernatural reality. Developments in science and technology can then be seen as
congruent with God's intentions in human affairs.

POLITICS

The interplay of conservative Protestantism and the technology of the communications media is interesting for yet another reason: the potential for political mobilization. Though some television evangelists have deliberately avoided politicizing their religious message (e.g., Oral Roberts, Rex Humbard, Jimmy Swaggart) others (such as Jerry Falwell, James Robison, and Pat Robertson) use their access to the powerful communications media for promulgating a conservative political agenda. This development, along with the rise of new political organizations such as the Moral Majority, Christian Voice, Religious Roundtable, Coalition for Better Television, and others, signaled the reawakening in the late 1970s and early 1980s of the "Christian Right" in America (Kater 1982; Crawford 1980; Lienesch 1982; Hill and Owen 1982).

The last time the Christian Right emerged as a visible political force was in the late 1950s and early 1960s when its principal feature was its alliance with the nationalistic, anti-Communist initiatives of Senator Joseph McCarthy, the Committee on Un-American Activities, the John Birch Society, and other organizations making up the "radical right" (Bell 1964; Epstein and Forster 1967). Its main organizations were Christian Crusade (Billy James Hargis), Church League of America (Edgar Bundy), The Christian Anti-Communist Crusade (Fred Schwartz), and the American Council of Christian Churches (Carl McIntyre). Survey data of this period documented the relationship between "ascetic Protestantism" and Republican conservatism, even when controlling for region and social class (Johnson 1962, 1964; Grupp and Newman 1973). It also documented a positive correlation between adherence to fundamentalist beliefs and racial prejudice (Feagin 1964), anti-Semitism (Glock and Stark 1966; Stark et al. 1971) and intolerance for civil liberties generally (Selznick and Steinberg 1969; Stellway 1973).

The shape and agenda of the current Christian Right is altogether different. Although intolerance for civil liberties remains in conservative Protestantism, it does so only among a fairly small minority in this subculture. Largely because of increasing levels of education among evangelicals generally, support for religious liberty has been on a sharp incline (Hunter 1984; Quinley and Glock 1979). In fact, Evangelicals have cooperated with conservative Catholics and conservative Jews to mobilize against a new enemy—what is perceived as a pervasive relaxation of moral standards in American culture. "Life-style" concerns such as abortion, homosexuality, feminism, sexual permissiveness, and the progression of "secular humanism" in the communications media, the schools, and in government and law have now replaced anti-Communism and "Wasp" supremacy as the focal points of the Christian Right (Page and Clelland 1978; Lorentzen 1980). Surveys show that in a stark departure from the past, evangelicals, more than any other major religious grouping, now endorse a political role for religion (Hunter 1984; Wuthnow, 1983). This notwithstanding, in analyzing 1980 election data, Lipset and Raab (1981) conclude that the conservative Protestant factor was negligible in determining the outcome of presidential and senatorial races. Other analyses of national survey data substantiate this general thesis: (a) Evangelical attitudes are not uniform on a range of public policy issues (Gallup 1980b, 1980c; Simpson 1983), in fact they basically parallel the attitudes and opinions of the general population (Lipset and Raab 1981; Mueller 1983); (b) the religious communications media have been, to the present, ineffective in mobilizing Evangelicals for coherent political action (Stacey and Shupe 1982); (c) the New Christian Right has only a small active constituency in the American population, so that the majority even of evangelicals themselves are either neutral toward or opposed to the goals of the Moral Majority (Hunter 1980, 1983c, 1984); and (d) the greatest support for the Christian Right comes from religious professionals in Conservative Protestantism, not least from Southern Baptist clergy (Guth 1983; Hunter 1984).

In light of these facts, one might well wonder why so much attention has been given to the new Christian Right by the communications media, and why the reaction in the liberal community has been so strong (Hunter 1983b). Lipset and Raab (1981) suggest that the response to the Christian Right is appropriate because, though Evangelicals do not exercise measurable power, politicians believe that they do and, as long as they continue to believe it, the vanguard of the New Christian Right can have political consequences. Along a different vein, Hunter (1984) points out that a large percentage of those working in the communications media share a left-liberal political orientation and represent perhaps the most vocal part of the left-liberal coalition in the United States. Moreover, they reflect this bias in their collective activity. These opposing coalitions, by exaggerating and sensationalizing each other's influence, then, use each other as ideological scapegoats. The net effect has been the galvanizing of their own constituencies.

Equally speculative is the question of why the new Christian Right reemerged in the first place. Lipset and Raab (1981), Simpson (1983) and Page and Clelland (1978) reinvoked the status-politics argument fashioned in the late 1950s and early 1960s to account for the radical right: disenfranchised groups engage in political action as an attempt to regain lost power and social prestige. Along a different line, Wuthnow (1983) argued that the national prominence Evangelicals experienced in the 1970s reawakened a collective sense of entitlement and responsibility on the part of evangelicals to take part in the political process. Still a third perspective interpreted the rise of conservative Protestant political action as a defensive reaction to the de-institutionalization or erosion of traditional definitions of reality (in this case, moral codes)—a process which, like secularization, appears to be intrinsic to the modernization process. Intensifying this reaction, though, is a conflict with elements of the "new class" of cultural elites whose structural interests are the further erosion of those traditional moral meanings (Hunter 1983a:102–119). In this sense it is, as Heinz (1983) puts it, a struggle among various sectors of the population to define/redefine America's past history and future direction.

Questions of religious revival apart, all of these areas of institutional growth and activity in themselves represent an important challenge to the secularization hypothesis, a challenge of a particular sort. Each of these areas concerns either the consolidation, dissemination, or mobilization of conservative Protestant symbols. This is important because secularization is as much a symbolic phenomenon as it is a structural phenomenon. What this means is that the symbolic universe of orthodox Protestantism is not only holding its own but is making gains within a symbolic environment hostile to it. The evangelical gains may or may not be numerical, but they are cultural, and the latter may be as important as the former.

SECULARIZATION RECONSIDERED

The survival and success of conservative Protestantism, especially in America, would appear, then, to dispose handily of the secularization hypothesis. Yet this judgment would be premature. Conservative Protestantism's survival in the modern world can also be brought into question. Modernization, in other words, exacts costs from orthodoxy—costs expressed in terms of accommodation.

Accommodation, though, results from specific pressures. To the pressures of modern functional rationality, Evangelical orthodoxy has become rigorously codified. The spiritual aspects of Evangelical life are increasingly approached and interpreted in terms of principles, rules, steps, guidelines, and the like (Hunter 1983a; Bruce 1983b). Packaging spirituality in this way has the effect of harnessing the charismatic and supra-empirical aspects of conservative Protestant faith. Similarly, to the pressures of cultural pluralism, Evangelical orthodoxy has adopted the demeanor of civility. The offensive aspects of the Evangelical world view (e.g., sin, hell, judgment, and so on) are de-emphasized while its positive side is accentuated (e.g., joy, spiritual wholeness, peace, love). "Fanaticism" and "zeal" are moder-ated by "good sense" and the quest for respectability (Hunter 1983a:84–91). Finally, to the pressures of structural pluralism (the pressures of privatization), Evangelical orthodoxy has become en-tangled in modern subjectivism. It is increasingly fixated on the new psychological and emotional problems and "needs" of contempo-rary living, even to the point of fetishism (Hunter 1982b). In this, orthodoxy has abandoned the asceticism characteristic of Protestant-ism in earlier periods in favor of a softness that arises in a milieu of personal and social ambiguity.

Overall, the concessions evangelicalism has made thus far have been cultural and not doctrinal (the latter being the heart of the faith). Even so, the world view of contemporary evangelicalism is hardly comparable to its Reformational predecessor. What is more, a posture of adaptation may yet have consequences for its theology. The more evangelicalism engages in the mainstream of modern society, the more likely this is to occur. An important example of this is higher education. Even in Evangelical colleges, education has been shown to lessen the degree to which the Evangelical world view coalesces—it weakens the plausibility of the Evangelical world view for the Evangelical student (Hammond and Hunter 1984). Secularization, then, appears to have subtle effects—effects not easily assessed by church membership trends, trends on per capita church donations, or by other quantifiable measures.

CONCLUSIONS

Research on a topic may be as much a commentary on the researchers as it is on the topic of inquiry. So it is with conservative Protestantism. It is not tangential to the concern of this chapter to make the sociology of knowledge observation that most of the scholarship on conservative Protestantism in America in the past two decades emerged when this movement entered the political realm with a public agenda. As expected, most of the research analyzes Evangelical political ideology and assesses the potential for political mobilization. It was true in the late 1950s/early 1960s; it is true in the 1980s. Interest in the subject all but disappears in calmer days. Such an approach betrays an academic opportunism and/or an attitude of resentment against the subject (Warner 1979; Ribuffo 1980; Hunter 1983*b*). Both are probably true, but the latter is more intriguing for it suggests that the researchers' liberal bias against the subject predisposes them to accept uncritically assumptions about secularization generally and the secularization of conservative Protestantism particularly. (It is ironic, after all, that commentators would make claims about the decline of conservative Protestantism as late as the 1970s when in fact it had, during the two or three preceding decades, experienced unprecedented numerical and institutional growth.) A less tendentious approach to the subject is clearly warranted, for such an approach taken previously might have signaled problems with the secularization model much earlier.

In light of the conservative Protestant case, the secularization hypothesis would seem to require revision. Secularization may yet prove to be the ultimate design for contemporary society, but that is unlikely. Minimally, one can say that it is not a straight-line occurrence, as is often assumed; cycles of secularity and religious upsurge are evident. Moreover, secularization can also be a subtle process, eroding all but the core of an orthodoxy, thus having mixed effects. If the conservative Protestant case *is*, therefore, paradigmatic for religious orthodoxy in contemporary society, the coming decades will prove to be important not just for conservative Protestantism but also for what it tells us about the secularization hypothesis.

REFERENCES

Alm, Robert, Christian Booksellers Association
   1983   Telephone interview with author, 8 September.
Ballweg, George Edward
   1980   "The Growth in the Number and Population of Christian Schools since 1966: A Profile of Parental Views Concerning Factors Which Led Them to Enroll Their Children in a Christian School." Unpublished Ph.D. dissertation, School of Education, Boston University.

Barrett, Donald
  1982   *World Christian Encyclopedia*. Nairobi: Oxford University Press.
Bell, Daniel
  1964   *The Radical Right*. New York: Doubleday.
Berger, Peter L.
  1969   *The Sacred Canopy*. New York: Doubleday.
Bibby, R.
  1979   "Religion and Modernity: The Canadian Case," *Journal for the Scientific Study of Religion* 19:1–17.
Bibby, R., and M. Brinkerhoff
  1973   "The Circulation of the Saints," *Journal for the Scientific Study of Religion* 12:273–285.
  1982   "The Circulation of the Saints Revisited." Presented at the annual meetings of the Society for the Scientific Study of Religion, Providence, R.I.
Bloesch, Donald
  1973   *The Evangelical Renaissance*. Grand Rapids: Erdmans.
Bouma, Gary
  1979   "The 'Real' Reason One Conservative Church Grew," *Review of Religious Research* 20:127–137.
Bruce, Steve
  1982   "Born Again: Conversions, Crusades and Brainwashing," *The Scottish Journal of Religious Studies* 3,2;107–123.
  1983a   "The Persistence of Religion: Conservative Protestantism in the United Kingdom," *Sociological Review* 31:3.
  1983b   "Religion, Science and Epistemology: The Conservative Protestant Case." Unpublished manuscript. The Queen's University, Belfast.
  1983c   "A Sociological Account of Liberal Protestantism." Unpublished manuscript. The Queen's University, Belfast.
Carroll, Jackson W., Douglas W. Johnson, and Martin E. Marty
  1979   *Religion in America: 1950 to the Present*. New York: Harper and Row.
Commuta, John, National Religious Broadcasters
  1983   Telephone interview with the author, 8 September.
Crawford, Allen
  1980   *Thunder on the Right*. New York: Pantheon.
Elinson, Howard
  1965   "The Implications of Pentecostal Religion for Intellectualism, Politics, and Race Relations," *American Journal of Sociology* 70:403–415.
Epstein, Benjamin, and Arnold Forster
  1967   *The Radical Right*. New York: Vintage.
Ethridge, F. M., and J. R. Feagin
  1979   "Varieties of 'Fundamentalism': A Conceptual and Empirical Analysis of Two Protestant Denominations," *Sociological Quarterly* 20:37–48.

Fackre, Gabriel
1982 *The Religious Right and Christian Faith.* Grand Rapids: Eerdmans.
Feagin, J. R.
1964 "Prejudice and Religious Types: A Focused Study of Southern Fundamentalists," *Journal for the Scientific Study of Religion* 4:3–13.
Gallup, George
1976 *Religion in America, 1976.* Report no. 130. Princeton: The Gallup Organization, Inc.
1978 *The Unchurched Americans Study.* Princeton: Princeton Religion Research Center.
1980a "The Political Impact of Evangelicals." Pt. 1. News release from the Gallup Poll.
1980b "The Political Impact of Evangelicals." Pt. 2. News release from the Gallup Poll.
The Gallup Organization, Inc.
1982 *The Robert Schuller Survey of Self-Esteem.* Princeton: The Gallup Organization, Inc.
Glock, C. Y., and R. Stark
1966 *Christian Beliefs and Anti-Semitism.* New York: Harper and Row.
Grupp, F. W., and W. Newman
1973 "Political Ideology and Religious Preference: The John Birch Society and the Americans for Democratic Action," *Journal for the Scientific Study of Religion* 12:401–413.
Guth, James L.
1983 "Southern Baptist Clergy: Vanguard of the Christian Right?" *In* Robert Liebman and Robert Wuthnow, eds., *The New Christian Right: Mobilization and Legitimation.* New York: Aldine.
Hadden, J. K., and Charles E. Swann
1981 *Prime Time Preachers.* Boston: Addison-Wesley.
Hammond, Phillip E.
1981 "An Approach to the Political Meaning of Evangelicalism in Present-Day America," *Annual Review of the Social Sciences of Religion* 5:187–201.
Hammond, Phillip E., and James Davison Hunter
1984 "On Maintaining Plausibility: The World View of Evangelical College Students," *Journal for the Scientific Study of Religion,* vol. 23.
Harpers, Inc.
1971 "The Rush for Instant Salvation," *Harper's* (July).
Heinz, Donald
1983 "The Struggle to Define America." *In* Robert Liebman and Robert Wuthnow, eds., *The New Christian Right: Mobilization and Legitimation.* New York: Aldine.
Hill, Samuel S., and Dennis E. Owen
1982 *The New Religious Political Right in America.* Nashville: Abingdon.
Hunter, James Davison
1980 "The Young Evangelicals and the New Class," *Review of Religious*

Research 22(2):155–169.

1982a   "Operationalizing Evangelicalism: A Review, Critique, and Proposal," *Sociological Analysis* 42:363–372.

1982b   "Subjectivization and the New Evangelical Theodicy," *JSSR* 20,1:39–47.

1983a   *American Evangelicalism: Conservative Religion and The Quandary of Modernity.* New Brunswick: Rutgers University Press.

1983b   "The Liberal Reaction to the New Christian Right." *In* Robert Liebman and Robert Wuthnow, eds. *The New Christian Right* Chicago: Aldine.

1983c   "The Perils of Idealism: A Reply," *Review of Religious Research* 24:3.

1984   "Evangelicals and Political Civility: The Coming Generation." Unpublished manuscript.

Johnson, Benton

1962   "Ascetic Protestantism and Political Preference," *Public Opinion Quarterly* 2:35–46.

1964   "Ascetic Protestantism and Political Preference in the Deep South," *American Journal of Sociology* 69:356–366.

Kater, John L., Jr.

1982   *Christians on the Right: The Moral Majority in Perspective.* New York: Seabury.

Kelley, Dean

1972   *Why Conservative Churches Are Growing.* New York: Harper and Row.

Kienel, Paul, Director, Association of Christian Schools International

1983   Telephone interview with author, 15 July.

Liebman, Robert

1983   "Mobilizing the Moral Majority." *In* Robert Liebman and Robert Wuthnow, eds., *The New Christian Right: Mobilization and Legitimation.* New York: Aldine.

Lienesch, Michael

1982   "Right-Wing Religion: Christian Conservatism As a Political Movement," *Political Science Quarterly* 97:403–425.

Lipset, S. M., and Earl Raab

1981   "The Election and the Evangelicals," *Commentary* 71 (March):24–32.

Lorentzen, Louise

1980   "Evangelical Lifestyle Concerns Expressed in Political Action," *Sociological Analysis* 41,2:144–154.

Lynd, R. S., and H. M. Lynd

1929   *Middletown.* New York: Harcourt, Brace and Jovanovich.

1937   *Middletown in Transition.* New York: Harcourt, Brace and World.

Mariani, John

1979   "Milking the Flock," *Saturday Review* (February).

Martin, William
1982   "Waiting for the End," *The Atlantic Monthly* (June):31–37.
McGuire, Meredith
1982   *Pentecostal Catholics*. Philadelphia: Temple University Press.
Morland, John Kenneth
1958   *The Millways of Kent*. Chapel Hill: University of North Carolina Press.
Mueller, Carol
1983   "In Search of a Constituency for the 'New Religious Right,'" *Public Opinion Quarterly* 47:213–229.
Newsweek, Inc.
1976   "Born Again!" *Newsweek* 88 (October 25):68–70.
Ostling, Richard
1983   "Evangelical Publishing and Television." Paper presented at the conference on Evangelical Christianity and Modern America, 1930–1980. Illinois: Wheaton College.
Page, Ann L., and Donald A. Clelland
1978   "The Kanawha County Textbook Controversy: A Study of the Politics of Life Style Concern," *Social Forces* 57:265–281.
Paloma, Margaret M.
1983   *A Sociological Analysis of the Charismatic Movement: Is There a New Pentecost?* Boston: Twayne.
Patel, K., D. Pilant, and G. Rose
1982   "Born-Again Christians in the Bible Belt: A Study in Religion, Politics and Ideology," *American Politics Quarterly* 10:255–272.
Pope, Liston
1965   *Millhands and Preachers*. New Haven: Yale University Press.
Quebedeaux, Richard
1974   *The Young Evangelicals*. New York: Harper and Row.
1976   *The New Charismatics*. New York: Doubleday.
1978   *The Worldly Evangelicals*. New York: Harper and Row.
Quinley, Harold, and Charles Glock
1979   *Anti-Semitism in America*. New York: Free Press.
Ribuffo, Leo
1980   "Liberals and That Old-Time Religion," *The Nation* (November): 570–573.
Roof, Wade Clark
1982   "America's Voluntary Establishment: Mainline Religion in Transition," *Daedalus* (Winter).
Sandeen, Ernest
1970   "Fundamentalism and American Identity," *Annals of the American Academy of Politics and Social Science* 38:56–65.
Selznick, Gertrude, and Stephen Steinberg
1969   *The Tenacity of Prejudice*. Westport, Conn.: Greenwood.

Simpson, John
    1983   "Support for the Moral Majority and Status Politics in Contempo-
              rary America." In Robert Liebman and Robert Wuthnow, eds.,
              The New Christian Right. Chicago: Aldine.
Stacey, William, and Anson Shupe
    1982   "The Electronic Church," Journal for the Scientific Study of Religion
              21,4:291–303.
Stark, Rodney, Bruce Foster, Charles Glock, and Harold Quinney
    1971   Wayward Shepherds: Prejudice and the Protestant Clergy. New York:
              Harper and Row.
Stellway, R. J.
    1973   "The Correspondence Between Religious Orientation and Socio-
              Political Liberalism and Conservatism," Sociological Quarterly
              14:430–439.
Time, Inc.
    1971   "The New Rebel Cry: Jesus Is Coming!" Time (June 21).
    1976   "Born-Again Faith." Time 108 (September 27):86–87.
Tipp, Charles, and Terry Winter
    1970   "The Christian Church in Canada: A Summary of Protestant
              Churches and Organizations." Unpublished manuscript. Ottawa.
Underwood, Kenneth W.
    1957   Protestant and Catholic. Boston: Beacon Press.
U.S. News and World Report
    1972   "The Jesus Movement: Impact on Youth and the Church." U.S.
              News and World Report 72 (March 20):59–65.
Warner, R. S.
    1979   "Theoretical Barriers to the Understanding of Evangelical Chris-
              tianity," Sociological Analysis 40:1–9.
Warner, W. Lloyd
    1961   The Family of God. New Haven: Yale University Press.
Weber, Max
    1958   The Protestant Ethic and the Spirit of Capitalism. New York:
              Scribner's.
Wills, Gary
    1978   "What Religious Revival?" Psychology Today (April):74–81.
Wuthnow, Robert
    1983   "The Political Rebirth of American Evangelicalism." In Robert
              Liebman and Robert Wuthnow, eds., The New Christian Right.
              Chicago: Aldine.
Wuthnow, Robert
    1984   "Religious Movements and Counter-Movements in North
              America." In James A. Beckford, ed., New Religious Movements and
              Rapid Social Change. Paris: UNESCO.

XI

The Sacred in Ministry Studies

Edgar W. Mills

The ambiguous role of the sacred has generated dilemmas and crises for religious leaders. This ambiguity, abetted by major trends in Western society, has shaped much of the research on religious leadership since World War II. In this chapter I will describe some converging results of that influence and some important lacunae in the research.

"The sacred" refers here not to God or the gods in some objective, "out-there" sense, but to human *apprehension* of reality that transcends empirical experience and to which power and purpose are attributed. In a secondary sense, the sacred also refers to the symbolic and social forms by which this apprehension is organized and made meaningful.

In the Weberian tradition, the relationship of the sacred to the secular is complex and ambiguous. On the one hand, the sacred sanctifies, stabilizes, legitimates, and gives meaning to taken-for-granted structures and processes in daily life; it strengthens people's loyalties to existing frameworks of power. It brings out the best in ordinary pursuits and relationships, enhancing rather than upsetting the existing order of things. On the other hand, the sacred criticizes and finds fault, pointing out finitude and error in human efforts, directing goals and hopes beyond the present and the mundane, pressing for reform and renewal. In the name of transcendent standards and holy values, it disturbs daily life and makes problematic much that is taken for granted. In its troubling of the existing order, the sacred moves either against or away from existing forms, either to reform them or to abandon them for new symbolic and communal structures.

The secularization thesis begins by stating that both sides of the sacred's ambiguous role have been steadily excluded from larger and larger portions of the society. It seeks to provide a framework for this observation in a number of ways, notably by Weber's emphasis upon rationalization and its consequences. That secularization has been a long-term trend in industrializing societies is hardly in doubt. That the secularization process is a necessary and irreversible consequence of modernization is somewhat in doubt. But that slow death by secularization is the fate of religion in the modern age is very much in doubt. During recent decades, religious vitalities have been revealed that are more consistent with concepts of religious transformation than with the death of religion in secularized society (McGuire 1981).

The ambiguity of the sacred/secular interface creates stress and crisis among religious leaders as they are drawn both to priestly and to prophetic roles and thus into conflicting pressures.[1] In addition, secularization and related trends undermine the social framework on which the plausibility of ministry traditionally has rested. In the process, the place of religion (and thus of its leaders) in the larger society is fundamentally changed.

In order to connect recent research on religious leadership with the changing fortunes of the sacred, two points must be understood. First, the secularization debate has largely ignored the role of clergy in the process[2] and in turn has rarely been considered explicitly in studies of clergy. Thus one's first impression is that ministry studies have little to do with secularization. Second, however, in spite of general silence on the theory, the most promising research on clergy is in the direct line of the secularization argument.[3] What follows will show that ministry studies have (usually implicitly) articulated secularization theory, from which causal variables are often drawn, with clergy behavior and morale as dependent variables, using a variety of intervening contextual factors.

SOCIOCULTURAL TRENDS THAT HAVE CHANGED MINISTRY

The principal focus of ministry studies has been upon strain and crisis among clergy, and the twin touchstones of that work have been conflicts over purpose and authority. Although much of the empirical research has been atheoretical and limited to specific operational concerns, a few theorists have advanced significant explanations for these conflicts, emphasizing more the effects of social change than those of the intrinsically ambiguous role of the sacred. In these theories, social change is represented by four somewhat overlapping historical trends: increasing secularization, the professionalization of occupations, the rise of individualism/personalism, and the conditions of a voluntaristic society.

The clearest statements about the effects of *secularization* upon clergy have been made by Wilson (1966, 1982) and Martin (1978). Religion's declining influence in social and personal life creates problems of legitimacy for religious leadership, problems that in turn cause clergy to seek greater role specialization (Gustafson 1963) and to assert more forcefully the religious bases of their ministries (Martin 1978). Martin applies his three-phase theory of secularization to clergy roles, with successive phases requiring different legitimating grounds.[4] Goldner et al. (1973) identify the intervening mechanism in this process as twofold: reduction in the range of role functions over which clergy have exclusive domain, and reduced prestige for the remaining clergy functions. Wilson (1982) traces one major component of secularization to "societalization" by which the communal bonds underlying religion are progressively weakened, and thoroughgoing rationalization of social forms leaves little place for the mysteries of religion (and thus for their priests). As a result, clergy, whose callings are rooted in communal religion, suffer major dislocation. For each of these writers, and for those whose treatment of secularization is only implicit (e.g., Hadden 1969), the principal impact is felt in problems of authority, whether in relation to the hierarchical tradition, as in Catholicism, or in relation to lay-clergy conflict among Protestants and Jews.

A second social trend with major impact upon ministry is the *professionalization* of occupations, arising in part out of the same rationalizing impetus that underlies the secularization process (Hagstrom 1957). The concepts of profession and of professionalization have been the subject of much debate among sociologists over several decades. There is little doubt, however, that the earlier constellation of a few learned professions making up a cultured elite has given way in the twentieth century to a spectrum of occupational strata that exhibit only some of the traditional characteristics of professions. Among the most important of these characteristics, however, are the development of professional identity and loyalty across work organization lines, and the emphasis upon professional autonomy and self-regulation (Gannon 1971; Hughes 1960). The formation of professional associations and formal institutions for socialization and certification provide structural support for these marks of a profession, as does the social legitimation of professional mandate by law and custom in the larger society.

The impact of professionalizing tendencies upon the clergy has been noted by many authors (Hagstrom 1957; Fichter 1961; Ference et al. 1971; Gannon 1971; Ebaugh 1977; and others). The issue is not whether the ministry can be properly labeled a profession in some formal sense, but rather the degree to which crises and problems in the ministry have arisen from changes induced by professionalizing tendencies in occupations generally (Vollmer and Mills 1966). In this sense, the issues of professional autonomy and of peer association loyalties seem to be of greatest significance in the study of clergy and thus are clearly linked to secularization processes.

Particularly among Roman Catholics, the conflict between the growing professional attitudes of clergy and the hierarchical-bureaucratic character of the authority structure of the church has been frequently remarked (Fichter 1961; Bell and Koval 1972; Seidler 1979). In a series of papers Ference, Goldner, and Ritti consider several aspects of the professionalization and secularization of the Catholic priesthood, pointing out the links between rationalized work roles and the transformation, among lay and clergy alike, of traditional beliefs about the sanctity and functions of the priesthood. Devaluation of traditional sacerdotal roles and loss of exclusive domination over education, welfare, and other social functions have restricted the priest's legitimate domain and pushed him toward nontraditional activities (see Wilson 1966). These changes shift the focus of the clergy's work from simply fulfilling a traditional calling to the gaining of results (Gustafson 1963).

Among non-Catholic clergy, professionalization also involves conflicts over authority and self-regulation. In the more democratic structures of most Protestant and Jewish bodies, professionalization often creates lay-clergy conflict over purpose and authority in the ministry (Hadden 1969). In at least one study (Hammond 1966), professionalization was seen as a facilitator by which a specialty (the campus ministry) is institutionalized, the implication being that occupational specialization is both a consequence of the development of professional characteristics and a partial solution to the conflicts thereby created. Others have emphasized the link between secularization, professionalization, and specialization in the ministry (Gustafson 1963; Goldner et al. 1973).

The third major social trend to which theorists have attributed a continuing impact on ministry is an increasing emphasis upon values of self-determination, personal gratification, individual rights, and interpersonal communication in the society at large. Also related to the secularization process, this modern form of classical *liberal individualism* has led to the questioning of traditional church authority structures in the name of personal preferences as well as of professional autonomy. Democratic ideals and movements for social justice likewise challenge older institutional and evangelical priorities for ministry. "Modern values" have been measured in several studies: as personalism (Ebaugh 1977; Schallert and Kelley 1970) or interpersonalism (Goldner et al. 1973), as a desire for personal fulfillment or a marriage partner (Schoenherr and Greeley 1974), and as social change values (Hadden 1969; Quinley 1974). The shifting of values takes many forms that reflect the ascendancy of individualism in American culture, but their net effect is further to undermine the ancient traditions of authority and practice in the churches, and thus to increase conflict and distress between age and status groups. (Neal [1965] shows the affinity of value and social change orientations among priests.)

The fourth social trend affecting ministry is the *voluntarism* that has long been a hallmark of American religious life. Clergy are increasingly "responsive to the desires and needs of the laity. . . . Traditional functions must be adapted to be accepted by the laity, and new functions must be created to win their continuing support" (Gustafson 1963:729). Although voluntarism has historically been more characteristic of Protestant and Jewish polities than of Catholicism (prior to Vatican II), the long-standing voluntarism of religion in America has been intensified for all. Increasing rationalization of the clergy's work has resulted in emphasis on legitimation by visible results rather than by traditional expectations (Ference et al. 1971), with consequently increased vulnerability to failure or at least to role confusion (Blizzard 1958). The keystone of voluntarism is consent by members of the community (Gustafson 1963:729), which has led both to instrumentalism and to increased role socialization in the interests of greater expertise among clergy. Ebaugh (1977) documents changes in religious orders of women from utopian communities with traditional hierarchical control to voluntary associations with democratic control and individualized life-styles. The effect which extreme voluntarism can have upon the work of clergy has been shown by Campbell and Pettigrew (1959), Wood (1970), and others, in the power with which congregational resistance can inhibit clergy leadership in churches without centralized denominational authority. Finally, Lehman (1980, 1981) has shown that the placement of ordained women depends to a significant degree on lay estimates of the effect of a woman minister on the viability of the congregation, as well as on the degree to which denominational placement mechanisms are used. In all these ways, voluntarism, as reflected in the degree to which the clergy's mandate depends upon work results and approval by lay members, has had a profound effect upon ministry.

DEPENDENT AND INDEPENDENT VARIABLES IN RESEARCH ON MINISTRY

Secularization, professionalization, liberal individualism, and voluntarism have thus been seen to generate crisis in the ministry, and the resulting distress has been the most frequent source of dependent variables in American ministry studies. Much of the best work has concerned three possible expressions of underlying crises: exit, voice, and stress. Hirschman (1970) introduced the terms *exit* and *voice* as the primary options of members in troubled organizations, voice referring to attempts to change the organization and exit to actual departure from it. As *behavioral* outcomes, clergy exit and voice have frequently been dependent variables. Research focusing upon *subjective* responses such as satisfaction, role commitment, morale problems, or hope/frustration balance can be grouped as stress-related studies, reflecting motivational states that may lead either to exit from ministry or to active voice.

Exit increased during the 1960s, particularly among Catholic clergy, along with reduced rates of entry. In the same period, clergy were increasingly visible both in social change movements and in church reforms, promoting change along lines generally perceived as "liberal." These latter activities, belonging to Hirschman's voice option, were accompanied by growing conflict between parish clergy and those in authority within the churches: hierarchical leaders in Catholicism and lay leaders within Protestant and Jewish groups. Authority conflicts and other pressures arising out of major social change created severe stress.

For Catholic clergy, the reformist Vatican II Council of the early 1960s stimulated and legitimized both voluntarism and modern values to an unprecedented degree. Clergy also assumed increasingly professional attitudes within the traditionally bureaucratic hierarchy (Fichter 1961). For women religious professionals, additional impetus came from the papal injunction of 1952 to obtain "knowledge and skills necessary for becoming better qualified professionally" (Ebaugh

1977:6). For all groups of American clergy the civil rights, antiwar, and feminist movements of the later 1960s and early 1970s also precipitated the long-gathering effects of secularization and other social change trends. Studies of ministry over the past two decades have been especially stimulated by policy concerns arising out of the increased problems of clergy exit, voice, and stress.

Many independent variables that account empirically for exit, voice, and stress among clergy are indicators of the four major social trends discussed earlier. For example, the demand for *professional autonomy* is a predictor of exit (Ebaugh 1977; Fichter 1961), voice (Seidler, 1979), and stress (Hall and Schneider 1973; Ritti et al. 1974). The related variable *inner-directedness* contributes to exit plans (Schoenherr and Greeley 1974). Conflict over the *exercise of authority*, arising both from secularization and voluntarism, is associated with exit (Ebaugh 1977; Jud et al. 1970), voice (Greeley and Schoenherr 1972; Seidler 1979), and stress (Hadden 1969; Mills and Koval 1971). The adoption of *modern beliefs and values*, including personalism, predicts exit (Ebaugh 1977; Schoenherr and Greeley 1974), voice (Seidler 1979), and stress (Ritti et al. 1974; Ference et al. 1971). Increased *professionalization* and *specialization* brings stress (Goldner et al. 1973; Wilson 1959) as well as facilitating voice (Hammond 1966). The availability of *authoritative support* influences exit (Jud et al. 1970; Schallert and Kelley 1970), as well as voice (Ammerman 1980; Campbell and Pettigrew 1959; Wood 1981) and stress among clergy (Mills and Koval 1971). These and other indicators in research on ministry reveal profound (and often unstated) dependence upon the secularization thesis and its corollaries.

CONTEXT EFFECTS AS INTERVENING FACTORS

To identify the mechanisms by which clergy adapt to social change, research has tended to focus upon contextual effects that mediate the impact of that change. These context factors are of two general types: *interaction effects* involving individual and structural predictors, and *social support networks* from which coping resources are drawn.

One of the best examples of an explanation by interaction is Ebaugh's account of exits among women religious (1977). Change-oriented women's exits from a rapidly liberalizing order were more difficult to explain than were exits from a conservative order. But interviews showed that leaving the order held different meaning according to the organizational context: exit from the conservative order was most often a protest against the lack of change in the order, whereas women most often left the liberal order because the new values had raised doubts about the advantages of life under vows as compared with lay life. Interaction between personal and social change variables meant that the meaning of each variable for exit depended upon the value of the other.

This type of interaction factor is often a *prevalence* effect, in that the prevalence of a phenomenon in a group determines its meaning for individual behavior. A similar effect can be seen in Schoenherr and Greeley's (1974) search for structural sources of exit decisions, using aggregated variables for dioceses. They found, after controlling for individual-level measures, that the principal structural characteristic affecting a priest's decision to resign is the prevalence of such decisions in his diocesan environment. Hammond and Mitchell (1965) found that segmentation of social activist clergy to high-prevalence fields, such as campus ministry where social change voice is prevalent, allowed them to be accepted within the churches, whereas, when located in parishes, social critics because seen as deviant, become dangerous. Hadden (1969) also noted the flow of liberal clergy into nonparish positions where prevalence buffered voice from conservative opposition.

A related form of interaction factor is the *facilitator* variable, as seen in Lehman's analyses of the placement of women clergy (1980, 1981). The effect of the candidate's gender upon placement depended to a significant degree upon estimates of the congregation's viability, suggesting interaction between gender and organizational maintenance needs in the determination of placement. In other research, measures of church resources or affluence have been found to affect lay people's acceptance of clergy leadership in ways that imply interaction effects (Campbell and Pettigrew 1959; Wood 1981).

In general, interaction between individual- and collective-level variables provides one approach to contextual explanation of clergy responses to social-change pressures. Univariate data analyses have gradually been replaced in recent years by more sophisticated multivariate and multistage models of explanation, but these continue to be designed with additive rather than interactive assumptions. The consequence is that the causal meanings of variables are interpreted as though independent of one another, whereas both common sense and the persistent findings of qualitative field studies suggest that behavior arises out of interacting forces and differential judgments. The links between broad historical trends and religious leader behavior will be understood far better as research designs take account of the contextual meaning of hypothesized relationships.

A second general type of contextual factor that has appeared frequently in ministry studies is that of *social support network*. In exit, voice, and stress situations, clergy draw heavily upon emotional support, financial aid, organizational assistance, and other resources made available by role partners. The presence of a social support framework made up of role partners with deliverable resources mediates the impact of social change on religious leadership.

The importance of the support system is evident in Seidler's (1979) finding that cross-status friendships within the diocese decrease the likelihood of priestly protest against misuse of church authority, whereas solidarity among dissident priests increases that likelihood. He also observes that "a general deprivation theme runs throughout the research on priest resignations" (779). In addition to his own data, he cites Schallert and Kelley (1970) on deprivation of both personal and professional support, and Schoenherr and Greeley (1974), whose predictors of exit include indicators both of professional isolation and of loneliness and the desire to marry. Research on Protestants also emphasizes social support resources as mediating variables. Jud et al. (1970) found that the reasons reported by Protestant parish clergy for both stress and exit decisions were weakness in denominational career support services, low levels of perceived support from denominational officers and fellow ministers, and reduced support from spouses. (See also Mills 1969; Mills and Koval 1971.)

The importance of official support in facilitating clergy voice has been shown by Seidler's (1979) finding that episcopal policy, along with clergy climate, provided the principal explanation of priestly protest; this was also shown to be the case by Campbell and Pettigrew (1959), Wood (1970), and Ammerman (1980) in their research on civil rights activists. In these latter studies, clergy in denominations with strong official positions legitimizing pro-civil rights activity were more likely to engage successfully in such activity. Hall and Schneider (1973) also showed a related way in which the support system mediates social change trends, in this case professionalization, by finding that "psychological success" is most likely for priests who received both supportive autonomy and confirming feedback from their ecclesiastical superiors.

In summary, recent research in religious leadership assumes that secularization and other social change processes are major causes of widespread exit, voice, and morale crises among clergy. Research

shows that the most promising mediators of these effects are contextual: interactions between individual and social structural variables, and support networks. These contextual factors determine in
significant part the response of clergy to social change pressures.

UNGRASPED OPPORTUNITIES IN
RESEARCH ON LEADERSHIP

In spite of what I have summarized above, explanatory arguments in
ministry studies mainly deal with a needlessly limited range of dependent variables associated with the institutional crises of the 1960s and
1970s. Perhaps this is due to the interests of religiously based funding
agencies. Another source of limitation is that most of the theoretically
informed, methodologically sound studies that built upon previous
research and address issues of broad significance have come from
sociologists (and not many of those). Survey methodology dominates
much of the good research. While this work has produced some
converging results, as outlined above, there remain several important
lacunae. In addition to strengthening our knowledge of leadership in
religion, the grasping of these research opportunities will reveal more
clearly where the sacred is to be found today.

1. *Qualitative field studies* are sorely needed to provide current and
accurate descriptions of the world and work of the clergy. Although
qualitative research may sometimes appear to be an easy alternative
to careful design and rigorous measurement, it is in reality, when
well done, the best way to discover the meaning of ministry from
within. The movement toward contextual explanations documented
above leads directly to the definition of meaning contexts through
ethnographic and phenomenological research. The religious leader's
world is not the same now as it was three decades ago. Both the
selection and quantitative measurement of survey research variables
risk error in ways that we cannot detect without knowledge of how
that world has changed. There is some justification for the view that
explanatory research always strains toward quantification, since both
causal and system feedback models require it for specification and
testing. However, because the validity issue logically precedes reliability, *what* we are measuring is a bigger problem at this stage than
how precisely we do it. With measurement error playing so large a

part in the low levels of explanatory power of causal models, reconceptualization based on careful field studies would seem to offer great dividends.

2. Listening to clergy and observing them in vivo will, in addition to yielding greater confidence in measurement, tell us much about how (or whether) the *sacred* appears in religious leadership. Wilson (1982:80) points out that historically the demystification of the priesthood has "reduced [it] to the role of ministry." Virtually no empirical research on clergy deals substantively with sacerdotal functions, that is, with the sacred/secular interface as actually performed by religious leaders. Only in field studies of premodern societies are the most religious functions of religious leaders seriously studied. Secularization has transformed the plausibility structure of priestly practice—so how *do* clergy perceive, communicate, and act out their modern apprehensions of God? So far, the research does not tell us.

3. Studies of leadership in *new religious movements* are relatively few. Even though excellent case studies of such movements have been published, the comprehensive review by Robbins, Anthony, and Richardson (1978) found so little attention to leadership that it was not useful in typology construction or in the categorization of groups. Bainbridge and Stark (1979), in proposing an entrepreneurial theory of cult formation, lament the lack of leader-oriented models in the study of cults. We lack both descriptive accounts of leadership and analyses of the sources and consequences of leader behavior in such groups. For example, the missionary role of Baptist and Pentecostal workers was quite different from the indigenous leadership of converts in organizing and spreading the Jesus Movement of the late 1960s and early 1970s, but existing studies largely ignore leadership factors. A couple of good exceptions to this (and to my first-mentioned lacuna) are Johnson's analysis of charismatic leadership in the People's Temple (1979) and Alfred's attention to sources of charisma in the Church of Satan (1976).

4. The term *religious leadership* has generally denoted a working *elite* of leaders rather than the *processes* by which religious groups are led. This is partly owing to the structural and role models that have been drawn from elsewhere in the social sciences, and partly to the general neglect of leadership processes in social movement research (McCarthy and Zald 1977). Wood (1981), however, has applied organizational analysis to church leadership and shown how groups can be led collectively in actions that members would not go along with individually. Some excellent analyses of leadership processes

can be found in studies of religious movements, all of them in the qualitative tradition (Beckford 1975; Lofland 1977; McGuire 1982.) What is needed is that researchers give serious attention within the same study, both to leaders *and* to their leading.

5. *Comparative* research on ministry is largely lacking, with existing studies segmented along denominational or faith-group lines. Perhaps the policy-oriented funding of much research accounts for the absence of samples that include Roman Catholics, a broad range of Protestants, the Jewish groups, black Christian and Muslim leaders, and Eastern Orthodox within a single design, although the distaste of government agencies for religiously defined research questions is probably more responsible. The awesome difficulty of assembling data from such a sample is inhibiting as well. As a result, the parallels and divergences between respective ministry groups are simply not well known, and thus comparisons of the impact of social change on them and of the forms in which the sacred prospers among them are impossible to make.

6. Although frequent references to age, gender, and socio-economic status are to be found, little systematic attention has been paid to *ascriptively based cleavages* in ministry, particularly as these have been affected by major social changes such as secularization. Increasing proportions of women clergy, increasing age among clergy, and deepening conflict between rich and poor peoples (and churches) of the world demand inclusion in research. As a rare example of such work, Schoenherr and Sorenson (1982) present evidence that current demographic changes among Catholic clergy will profoundly affect church policy and clergy leadership. There is also reason to believe that one major mechanism of social change in religion, as elsewhere, is cohort flow (Wuthnow 1976).

7. In general, though not primarily in the studies reported herein, research on religious leadership has suffered from simplistic methodology and theoretical weakness. Dittes (1971) especially laments the undue influence of available data, handy measurement techniques, and practical interests, rather than theory, in guiding research. He regards the atheoretical approaches of most researchers as "the root obstacle to progress." His criticism is warranted and his example should be followed. Among recent ministry studies evidence is growing of theoretical and methodological sophistication, but there is still much "implicit theory" that could powerfully shape research on leadership if it were to be linked explicitly to broad theoretical streams in the social sciences.

THE SACRED IN RESEARCH ON
RELIGIOUS LEADERSHIP

In the modern transformation of religion, leaders find themselves both fighting a delaying action and leading their people in new directions. The sacred is both back there and up ahead, always ambiguous in implication and conflicting in demand. Research on ministry has largely concentrated upon the crises of clergy within the conflicted condition. I have suggested directions that would throw more light upon current leadership in new and old religions.

In reflecting upon the argument, I believe ministry studies have a great deal more to tell us about religion than our recent work has revealed. If the sacred—our apprehension of some ultimate reality— has the quality of unpredictability and uncontrollability, then the life and practice of the religious leader ought to yield a unique view of contemporary forms of the sacred. Because of the massive social-change trends outlined above, clergy, whose livelihoods, reputations, and very identities require that the sacred be real, are constantly structuring the sacred—in rules and principles, in organizational effectiveness, in professional disciplines, in the rights and needs of individuals, and in countless daily, rational means-ends calculations. As the structuring goes on, religion repeatedly "breaks out" into new expressions, both collective and individual, both spiritual and physical. Sometimes the clergy are themselves the "breakers-out" (the new breed of the 1960s, from the charismatic healers to the missionaries to the hippies) and sometimes they are embattled defenders of the structures. The relationship of the sacred to religion, as well as to the secular, is ambiguous, and the leaders reflect that ambiguity.

The ungrasped opportunities offer researchers on leadership a fresh look at the sacred, provided the research transcends the ways in which clergy have segmented and managed their sacred apprehensions. By transcending I do not mean ignoring the structural lines but rather looking always both for the structure and for its antithesis in leadership. Each set of role preferences will have its residual of dissatisfaction with role preference categories; each organizational variable will have its error component—not only measurement error but a more fundamental error as the result of inner contradiction in the concept itself. The ambiguous sacred creates ambivalence, both sociological and psychological, in leadership. It should be studied.

If such a proposal sounds slightly mystical, it is because we are accustomed to think linearly rather than dialectically, and because, when we see inherently conflicting forces, we have learned to look for homeostasis or equilibrium as the "normal" result. But suppose the dissonance is itself the normal state of things, and measurement error is only a tiny part of the unexplained variance in linear models? The study of religious leaders and of their ambivalent work would in fact yield knowledge of the building and the breaking of structures. That, I think, could be interpreted as a view of the sacred in action in religious leadership.[5]

NOTES

1. To provide some limits to the discussion, I will use "clergy" and "ministers" interchangeably, to include both designated career leaders of religious groups and religious persons under vows. "Ministry studies" and "clergy studies" will be convenient labels for social science research on religious leaders. I am excluding from attention the religious functionaries of premodern societies.

2. Wilson (1966, 1982) and Martin (1978) are exceptions that will be considered later in this chapter.

3. From more than 150 published studies reviewed, I am reporting on about three dozen that constitute the majority of theoretically informed, methodologically sound work explicitly linked to previous research and addressed to relevant issues of ministry. I offer apologies to authors of the few excellent works that are not discussed herein.

4. See, for example, Martin's theory of the origin of "new breed" clergy protests from third-phase processes (1978:291–297).

5. I am grateful to Robert E. Davidson, Helen Rose Ebaugh, Phillip E. Hammond, and Meredith B. McGuire who commented on an earlier draft of this chapter and gave much good advice, some of which I took.

REFERENCES

Alfred, Randall H.
    1976   *The Church of Satan. In* Charles Y. Glock and Robert Bellah, *The New Religious Consciousness.* Berkeley, Los Angeles, London: University of California Press. Pp. 180–202.
Ammerman, Nancy
    1980   "The Civil Rights Movement and the Clergy in a Southern Community," *Sociological Analysis* 41,4 (Winter):339–350.

Bainbridge, William S., and Rodney Stark
1979   "Cult Formation: Three Compatible Models," *Sociological Analysis*
40,4 (Winter):283–295.
Beckford, James A.
1975   *The Trumpet of Prophecy: A Sociological Study of Jehovah's Witnesses.*
Oxford: Basil Blackwell.
Bell, Richard W., and John P. Koval
1972   "Collegiality and Occupational Change in the Priesthood," *Kansas
Journal of Sociology* 7,2 (Summer):47–61.
Blizzard, Samuel W.
1958   "The Minister's Dilemma," *The Christian Century* 73,17 (April
25):508–510.
Campbell, Ernest Q., and Thomas F. Pettigrew
1959   Christians in Racial Crisis. Washington, D.C.: Public Affairs
Press.
Dittes, James E.
1971   "Psychological Characteristics of Religious Professionals." *In* Mer-
ton P. Strommen, ed., *Research on Religious Development: A Com-
prehensive Handbook.* New York: Hawthorn Books. Pp. 422–460.
Ebaugh, Helen R. F.
1977   *Out of the Cloister: A Study of Organizational Dilemmas.* Austin:
University of Texas Press.
Ference, Thomas P., Fred H. Goldner, and R. Richard Ritti
1971   Priests and Church: The Professionalization of an Organization,"
American Behavioral Scientist 14:507–524.
Fichter, Joseph H.
1961   *Religion As an Occupation: A Study in the Sociology of Professions.*
Indiana: University of Notre Dame Press.
Gannon, Thomas M., S. J.
1971   "Priest/Minister: Profession or Nonprofession?" *Review of Reli-
gious Research* 12,2 (Winter):66–67.
Goldner, Fred H., Thomas P. Ference, and R. Richard Ritti
1973   "Priests and Laity: A Profession in Transition," University of
Keele: *The Sociological Review* monograph no. 20 (December):119–
137.
Greeley, Andrew M., and Richard A. Schoenherr
1972   "The Catholic Priest in the United States: Sociological Investiga-
tions." Paper delivered at the United States Catholic Conference,
Washington, D.C.
Gustafson, James M.
1963   "The Clergy in the United States," *Daedalus* 92,4 (Fall):724–744.
Hadden, Jeffrey K.
1969   *The Gathering Storm in the Churches.* New York: Doubleday.
Hagstrom, Warren
1957   "The Protestant Clergy As a Profession: Status and Prospects,"
Berkeley Journal of Sociology 3(1):54–69.

Hall, Douglas T., and Benjamin Schneider
   1973   *Organizational Climates and Careers: The Work Lives of Priests.* New
            York: Seminar Press.
Hammond, Phillip E.
   1966   *The Campus Clergyman.* New York: Basic Books.
Hammond, Phillip E., and Robert E. Mitchell
   1965   "Segmentation of Radicalism: The Case of the Protestant Campus
            Minister," *American Journal of Sociology* 71,2 (September)133–143.
Hirschman, Albert O.
   1970   *Exit, Voice and Loyalty.* Cambridge: Harvard University Press.
Hughes, Everett C.
   1960   "The Professions in Society," *Canadian Journal of Economics and
            Political Science* 26:54–61.
Johnson, Doyle Paul
   1979   "Dilemmas of Charismatic Leadership: The Case of the People's
            Temple," *Sociological Analysis* 40,4 (Winter):315–324.
Jud, Gerald J., Edgar W. Mills, and Genevieve Burch
   1970   *Expastors: Why Men Leave the Parish Ministry.* Philadelphia: United
            Church Press.
Lehman, Edward C., Jr.
   1980   "Patterns of Lay Resistance to Women in Ministry," *Sociological
            Analysis* 41,4 (Winter):317–338.
   1981   "Organizational Resistance to Women in Ministry," *Sociological
            Analysis* 42,2 (Summer):101–118.
Lofland, John
   1977   *Doomsday Cult* (enlarged edition). New York: Irvington.
Martin, David
   1978   *A General Theory of Secularization.* New York: Harper and Row.
McCarthy, John D., and Mayer Zald
   1977   "Resource Mobilization and Social Movements: A Partial Theory,"
            American Journal of Sociology 82,6 (May):1212–1241.
McGuire, Meredith B.
   1981   *Religion: The Social Context.* Belmont, Calif.: Wadsworth.
   1982   *Pentecostal Catholics: Power, Charisma and Order in a Religious Move-
            ment.* Philadelphia: Temple University Press.
Mills, Edgar W.
   1969   "Career Change in the Protestant Ministry," *Ministry Studies* 3,1
            (May):5–21.
   1983   "The Sociology of Religion As an ASA Subdiscipline," *Sociological
            Analysis* 44,4 (Winter):339–353.
Mills, Edgar W., and John P. Koval
   1971   *Stress in the Ministry.* Washington, D.C.: Ministry Studies Board.
Neal, Marie Augusta, S.N.D.
   1965   *Values and Interests in Social Change.* Englewood Cliffs, N.J.:
            Prentice-Hall.

Quinley, Harold E.
  1974   *The Prophetic Clergy: Social Activism Among Protestant Ministers.* New York: John Wiley.

Ritti, R. Richard, Thomas P. Ference, and Fred H. Goldner
  1974   "Professions and Their Plausibility: Priests, Work and Belief Systems," *Sociology of Work and Occupations* 1,1 (February):24–51.

Robbins, Thomas, Dick Anthony, and James Richardson
  1978   "Theory and Research on Today's 'New Religions,'" *Sociological Analysis* 39,2 (Summer):95–122.

Schallert, Eugene J., and Jacqueline Kelley
  1970   "Some Factors Associated with Voluntary Withdrawal from the Catholic Priesthood," *Lumen Vitae* 25,3:425–460.

Schoenherr, Richard A., and Andrew M. Greeley
  1974   "Role Commitment Processes and the American Catholic Priesthood," *American Sociological Review* 39,3 (June):407–426.

Schoenherr, Richard A., and Annemette Sorenson
  1982   "Social Change in Religious Organizations: Consequences of Clergy Decline in the U.S. Catholic Church," *Sociological Analysis* 43,1 (Spring):23–52.

Seidler, John
  1979   "Priest Resignations in a Lazy Monopoly," *American Sociological Review* 44,5 (October):763–783.

Vollmer, Howard M., and Donald Mills, eds.
  1966   *Professionalization.* Englewood Cliffs, N.J.: Prentice-Hall.

Wilson, Bryan
  1959   "The Pentecostalist Minister: Role Conflicts and Status Contradictions," *American Journal of Sociology* 643 (March):494–504.
  1966   *Religion in Secular Society.* Baltimore: Penguin Books.
  1982   *Religion in Sociological Perspective.* New York: Oxford University Press.

Wood, James R.
  1970   "Authority and Controversial Policy: The Churches and Civil Rights," *American Sociological Review* 35,6 (December):1057–1068.
  1981   *Leadership in Voluntary Organizations: The Controversy over Social Action in Protestant Churches.* New Brunswick: Rutgers University Press.

Wuthnow, Robert
  1976   "Recent Patterns of Secularization: A Problem of Generations?" *American Sociological Review* 41,5 (October):850–867.

PART FOUR

Culture and the Sacred

XII

Science and the Sacred

Robert Wuthnow

Most of the empirical research devoted to examining the relations between religion and science has been heavily influenced by secularization theory, positing in particular that the rapid expansion of modern science and the dissemination of a scientific attitude among the general public should result in an erosion of conventional religious commitments. Further posited is that this erosion is due to such self-evident conflicts between science and religion as the proverbial "warfare" between reason and faith, between the results of modern astronomy and the medieval religious conception of a three-tiered universe, between evolutionary theory and biblical creationist views, between the causal determinism of science and the espousal of individual free will (and, hence, responsibility) by religion or, more broadly, between the cognitive, positivistic approach to knowledge of the sciences and the subjective, hermeneutic orientation to knowledge found in most contemporary religions. In this view, secularization comes about as a result of direct conflict between religion, which appears to consist largely of beliefs about the nature of reality, and science, which offers different interpretations of the same phenomena (Moberg 1962:334; Glock 1972).

STUDIES OF THE RELATION

In efforts to subject these arguments to empirical test, a wide variety of data has been examined over the past half century, which has generally been claimed to show unqualified support for the religion/

187

science conflict hypothesis. The clearest support has come from studies of scientists and academicians themselves, because they (unlike the general public) can be assumed to have actually thought seriously enough about science and to have grasped its implications well enough to have had it influence their religious views. One of the first quantitative studies of religious views ever conducted was psychologist James Leuba's (1916, 1934) examination of the religious beliefs of scientists listed in the 1913–1914 edition of *American Men of Science*. This study showed that scientists tended less than other professionals to believe in God or in immortality, and that faculty members were less likely to hold these beliefs than were nonacademicians. More recent studies have generally confirmed these results. A study of data from a national survey of graduate students found them to be nonreligious in far greater proportion than the general public and demonstrated negative relationships between religious involvement and a variety of scholarly orientations, including attendance at high-quality graduate and undergraduate schools, cosmopolitanism, identifying oneself as an intellectual, and valuing self-expression (Stark 1963). Another analysis of these data confirmed the relation between low religiosity and intellectualism and also showed the less religious to feel alienated in general from nonacademic settings (Hajda 1961). Another graduate-student survey found a positive correlation between religious apostasy and a preference for academic careers (Zelan 1968; see also Salter and Routledge 1974; Campbell and Magill 1968). An analysis of national data on faculty members collected by the Carnegie commission in the late 1960s revealed a negative relation between religiosity and university quality, and found that the less religious were more likely to identify themselves as intellectuals, preferred research over other academic activities, and published more (Steinberg 1974). Another analysis of these data showed the latter findings to hold true when differences in specialties were taken into account (Faia 1974, 1976). Finally, a survey of faculty members in a midwestern city, designed especially to examine their religiosity, found negative relations between the ideological, ritual, and experiential dimensions of religious commitment and various measures of scholarly orientation, including identification with one's field and valuing research, in both nonsectarian and sectarian schools (Lehman 1972).

Some additional evidence which appears to support these earlier studies was provided by the *Connecticut Mutual Life Report on American Values in the '80s*, a national study conducted in 1980, which included interviews with randomly selected "leaders" in a variety of institutional areas, among which was "science." In comparison with the general public, scientists were far less likely to indicate religious involvement: only 31 percent said they frequently feel that God loves them, compared with 73 percent of the general public; only 8 percent had frequently had a religious experience, compared with 25 percent of the public; 64 percent had never had a religious experience, compared with 34 percent of the public; only 28 percent had ever encouraged others to turn to religion, compared with 57 percent of the public; 62 percent ever read the Bible compared with 75 percent of the public; only 28 percent said they attended church frequently, compared with 44 percent of the public; 27 percent prayed frequently, compared with 57 percent of the public; 18 percent said they had made a personal commitment to Christ, compared with 47 percent of the public; and 50 percent thought they were religious persons, compared with 74 percent of the public. Some of these differences may have been due to the fact that educational levels of leaders are generally higher than those of the public. Nevertheless, even among the leaders sampled, scientists scored at the very bottom of the list on virtually every question about religion.

While these kinds of studies represent the most straightforward tests of the religion/science conflict thesis (in that they focus on scientists and academicians themselves), a variety of other evidence also appears to lend indirect support to the thesis. For instance, virtually all surveys and polls, whether of the general public, college students, church members, or clergy, show inverse relations between exposure to higher education and adherence to core religious tenets, such as the existence of God, the divinity of Christ, the divine inspiration of the Bible, life after death, religious conversion, and the necessity of faith in Christ for salvation. Few of these studies have actually proven that exposure to science is the reason why the better educated turn out to have lower measures of religious commitment, but this has generally been assumed to be a factor. Other research has indicated the differences in life-styles and attitudes associated with scientific or social scientific meaning systems as opposed to theistic meaning systems; in particular, the former appear to be considerably more willing, at least in the present cultural context, to experiment with social reform and with alternative life-styles or leisure activities in their personal lives than the latter (Wuthnow 1976; Aidala 1984). Cross-national studies have shown, perhaps obviously, that growth in scientific knowledge has led religion to represent a declining share of scholarly output in many modern or modernizing countries (Wuthnow 1977). As another indication of the potential for perceived trade-offs between science and religion, 89 percent of a national sample surveyed in 1979 identified "scientific research" as making a major contribution to America's greatness; by comparison, only 57 percent listed "deep religious beliefs" in this role (National Science Foundation 1981:337). Another survey in 1979 showed that 46 percent of the public thought "technological know-how" contributes most to the influence of the United States in the world, whereas only 15 percent thought this about "our religious heritage" (Miller et al. 1980:251–253). Similar studies over the past decade have shown rising levels of faith in science at the same time that confidence in religion's ability to solve major problems has declined (National Science Foundation 1981:335; Gallup 1982). And numerous historical studies have focused on the declining significance of religion in areas ranging from schoolbooks and popular fiction to medicine and law as scientific theories and evidence have become accepted as standard criteria of truth or professional practice in place of religious world views (e.g., Elson 1964; Schneider and Dornbusch 1958; Babbie 1970).

SOME ANOMALIES

Despite the seemingly overwhelming nature of the evidence supporting the idea of conflict between religion and science, some peculiar aspects of the research results do not seem to fit very well into the conventional view of this relationship. First, it appears that *historically* there was a positive relation between religion, particularly Puritanism, in the seventeenth and eighteenth centuries and the rise of modern science, or so Robert Merton argued in his famous thesis (1970). Second, contemporarily, there is the fact that the *more scientific disciplines,* such as physics and chemistry, usually turn out to have *higher* rates of religiosity among their practitioners than do the less scientific specialties, such as the social sciences or the humanities. For instance, the Carnegie data on faculty members showed that 49 percent in the social sciences were indifferent or opposed to religion, compared with 46 percent in the humanities, 41 percent in the biological sciences, and only 37 percent in the physical sciences (Steinberg 1974). Another study of faculty members showed similar patterns: 41 percent of the social scientists did not believe in God, compared with 36 percent of those in the humanities and 20 percent in the natural sciences; similarly, 48 percent, 45 percent, and 34 percent, respectively, said they never attended church (Thalheimer 1973). Several studies of graduate students and a host of undergraduate surveys also reveal these patterns (see, for example, Feldman and Newcomb 1970).

Third, many of the studies done among students and aspiring scientists or academicians indicate that it is the irreligious who are selected into academic careers in the first place, not that the process of being socialized into the academic life causes them to become less and less religious as time goes on. For example, further analysis (as yet unpublished) of panel data among University of California, Berkeley, students (discussed in Wuthnow 1978) suggests that religious nonconventionality—indeed, nonconventionality in general— leads subsequently to higher academic performance and identification with the intellectual role, controlling for earlier measures of academic standing, but the data show no tendency for high academic performance or intellectualism to result in subsequent shifts toward religious nonconventionality. In short, the conflict between religion and academic careers does not seem to occur as part of the socialization process into those careers, but *prior to it.* Again, there are some striking differences by discipline. In the Berkeley data, those majoring in the social sciences were most likely to have been raised in nonreligious families, humanities students were most likely to have defected from the religion in which they were brought up, and natural science students were more likely to have retained their religious faith. Perhaps more to the point, a study that sought to determine why some students choose to embark on careers as college professors found that religiosity was not a factor affecting the choices of students in the natural sciences, but that it was an important factor in the choices of social sciences and humanities students (Currie et al. 1966). The point is that people in the natural sciences not only have higher levels of religiosity later in life than do their counterparts in the social sciences and the humanities but are also less deterred by religiosity from embarking on these careers in the first place.

Fourth, longitudinal evidence in the United States over the past several decades reveals very little tendency for the rapid growth in science to have been accompanied by an equally dramatic decline in religious commitment. The growth in science and, more generally, in higher education and in other professions, since World War II has been nothing short of spectacular: quantitative indices show that expenditures for R & D increased from $6 billion in 1955 to $61 billion in 1980—adjusting for inflation, this was still a rise of more than 300 percent (National Science Foundation 1981). Over the same period, the number of college or advanced degrees conferred annually rose

from about 350,000 to about 1,300,000; expenditures on higher education grew from about $2 billion to more than $50 billion annually; the
proportion of young people enrolled in higher education tripled; and
the average level of educational attainment rose by almost three full
years. As early as the middle 1960s, the United States had more than
half a million research scientists in the labor force, the highest proportion of any country in the world; it produced almost 40 percent
of all scientific and technical articles in the world; and almost two-
thirds of its exports were produced by industries that relied heavily
on science and technology (*Statistical Abstract* 1981; National Science
Foundation 1978). But over the same period, quantitative indices of
institutional religion held remarkably steady: church membership
hovered at about 60 percent; clergy and religious workers made up
about the same proportion of the labor force that they had for the
past fifty years; the number of nonprofit religious organizations held
its own as a proportion of all such organizations; and, although
church attendance dropped slightly, most of this decline seemed to
be a function of changes in morality and life-styles rather than exposure to science (Wuthnow 1983*b*).

Finally, cross-sectional studies of the public and of religious groups
have shown that individuals have a remarkable propensity actually
to *mix* religious and scientific world views. For instance, Gallup polls
asking about creation and evolution show that the largest segment of
the public adheres to some combination of these views (only a small
fraction believes exclusively in evolution), and other studies in both
the United States and Canada show that people frequently mix
theistic and scientific or positivistic understandings (Gallup 1982;
Wuthnow 1976; Bibby 1979). Case studies have also shown that religious groups and movements of all theological varieties have a pronounced tendency to rely heavily on scientific evidence and testimony
to *support* their religious claims (Barker 1979; Wuthnow 1983*a*).

AD HOC REVISIONS

These anomalies have not gone unnoticed in the literature on religion
and science, for their cumulative impact is, at least on the surface,
disarmingly devastating to the standard religion/science conflict
hypothesis. In defense of this hypothesis a variety of counterargu-
ments and *ad hoc* revisions of the overall thesis have been put forth.
The Merton thesis relating Puritanism and science has been roundly

attacked on the basis of more elaborate data and cross-national comparisons, and even defenders of the thesis point out that an initially reinforcing relation between Puritanism and science does not rule out the possibility of subsequent conflict once science had become institutionalized (Greaves 1969; Hall 1963; Mulligan 1973; Wuthnow 1980). On the issue of the social sciences and humanities showing more religious apostasy than the natural sciences, an intriguing argument has been advanced which suggests that the conflict is more pronounced in the former than in the latter precisely because the latter enjoys more "scholarly distance" from religion; in other words, social scientists and humanists study religion itself and therefore run into a conflict of paradigms, whereas the natural sciences usually do not study religion (Lehman and Shriver 1968; Faia 1976). The same argument, it appears, could be applied to the evidence on early selection patterns among aspiring academicians. The evidence on long trends in religion and science is easiest to refute by pointing to *attitudinal* data on religion which suggest that religiosity has in fact declined sharply over the past thirty years. For instance, Gallup polls conducted since the early 1950s show significant declines in the percentages of people who believe religion can answer their problems, who say religion is important in their personal lives, who pray, and who think religion's influence in society is increasing (Gallup 1982). Finally, the evidence of people mixing religion and science has been interpreted, from a different perspective, as evidence of secularization itself; namely, that science has begun to penetrate previously sacred realms and, in the future, will likely dominate these realms to an even greater extent.

At present, therefore, the secularization thesis as it pertains to religion and science is by no means without defenders. And a large share of these defenders work primarily in the sociology of religion. To be sure, there are those in sociology and in religious studies who have sought to circumvent the secularization perspective by reconceptualizing religion and its functions in such a way that it avoids any appearance of inevitable conflict with science. If religion consists of a special kind of symbolism whose purpose is to evoke the wholeness of life, as Bellah (1970) has argued, or if it mediates between world views and ethos, in Geertz's (1973) terms, or is, more importantly, faith rather than belief (Smith 1979), then clearly its conflict with science should be minimal. The key phrase, however, is "should be." What these arguments have done is to posit ways of reconciling religion and science at a highly intellectual level or in the far distant future, rather than address the conflicts that may in fact presently exist. It has been, perhaps ironically, from the sociology of science, rather than from the sociology of religion, that the most telling challenges to the traditional secularization view have taken place.

In essence, many of the workers in sociology of science have recently begun to take seriously the idea that science is a socially constructed reality, just as other forms of knowledge and belief are. Accordingly, heavy emphasis has been placed on the ways in which scientific work and the products of that work reflect the social environment in which they occur. Approaches vary from the so-called "strong programme," represented best in Scottish sociology of science, which argues that even simple and seemingly irrefutable scientific facts, such as $2 + 2 = 4$, are really reflections of social experience in ways exactly parallel to Durkheim's arguments about religion (Bloor 1976; Barnes 1974); to the new "anthropology of science," which examines the social processes involved in the laboratory to elicit consensus (Latour and Woolgar 1979) and the structure of scientific discourse (Mulkay 1979, 1980); to theories of scientific method which debunk textbook descriptions of scientific procedure as being *post hoc* reconstructions and which argue for an anarchistic approach to science (Feyerabend 1978). While none of these approaches has yet addressed the relation between religion and science frontally, they have laid the groundwork for such a reexamination by relativizing the reality (the sacredness) of science. Whereas the conventional view of this relation, adopted from secularization theory, has tended to view science as an unquestionable description of fact, against which religious belief has inevitably been put to rout, the more recent view of science suggests it to be a precarious reality in need of constant social construction and reaffirmation. From this perspective, the relation between science and religion may be reconceptualized as a kind of reality-maintaining process as far as science itself is concerned.

SCIENCE AS CONSTRUCTED REALITY

The precariousness of science can be demonstrated from a source more familiar to most students of religion than the recent work of Bloor, Mulkay, Feyerabend, and others; namely, Alfred Schutz's (1962) famous essay on multiple realities. In this essay, which Berger (1967), Luckmann (1967), and others have drawn on as a basis for their interpretations of religion, Schutz draws a sharp contrast between "scientific theorizing"—a "finite province of meaning"—and the paramount reality of everyday life. Specifically, scientific theorizing is nonpragmatic, universalistic, governed by norms of personal detachment, oriented toward the past and future of the problem at hand, revocable in the sense that hypotheses are subject to constant revision, and dominated by an attitude of critical skepticism. By comparison, everyday reality is pragmatic, particularisticly oriented to the here and now of the individual, governed by norms of self-interested involvement ("wide-awakeness"), oriented toward standard linear time, irrevocable, and dominated by a "willing suspension of doubt." In short, there is a fundamental opposition between the norms of science and the norms governing conduct in everyday life. Moreover, the practitioner of science is constrained to live in both worlds, causing the sense of reality that accompanies one to fade from view when living in the other, and vice versa. If the scientist is to maintain the reality of science against the alternative and more prevailing reality of everyday life, therefore, he or she must *engage in certain reality-maintaining activities,* and the very quality of the scientist's work is likely to depend on this reality-maintaining process.

One method by which science, as any reality, is maintained is communication—the face-to-face interaction which Berger (1967) has labeled a "plausibility structure." Not only do scientists engage in frequent communication activity with other scientists but this activity is generally a powerful predictor of research productivity and scientific innovativeness (Garvey and Griffith 1967; Crane 1972; Breiger 1976; Blau 1978; Wuthnow et al. 1982). A second mechanism of reality maintenance is the codification of a concise theoretical paradigm which specifies important research problems, promotes communication, and clarifies standards of evaluation and reward (Kuhn 1970). As Merton and Zuckerman (1973) have observed, scientific disciplines vary widely in the degree to which "codification" has been achieved. In disciplines such as the social sciences and the humanities, codification is low relative to the physical and biological sciences, resulting in wide variations among these disciplines, variations ranging from lower rates of communication in the social sciences and humanities to greater variability in citations to the literature to higher rejection rates in leading journals as a result of greater ambiguity concerning relevant problems and procedures. Thus, in the less codified disciplines some other mechanism of reality maintenance must be brought into play.

The argument to be suggested here is that scientists, especially those in the less codified disciplines, frequently rely on values, attitudes, and life-styles to maintain the reality of science by setting up *external boundaries* between themselves and the general public or those who represent the realm of everyday reality. In other words, scientists who lack clearly codified paradigms and strong communication networks turn to symbolic modes of differentiating themselves from everyday reality in order to maintain the plausibility of their scientific orientations—orientations that are inevitably precarious in relation to the paramount reality of everyday life. These "boundary-posturing mechanisms," to give them a name, create a diffuse social space in which the scientist can function and with which the scientist identifies as a person. To the extent that the scientist can maintain these boundaries he or she is likely to be more productive, just like the scientist who relies on professional communication as a reality-maintaining device. Moreover, this boundary-posturing activity is likely to be especially important during the early process of socialization and selection into the scientific role.

IRRELIGIOSITY AS SCIENTIFIC BOUNDARY POSTURING

With this argument in hand, some of the anomalies observed earlier in the religion/science literature—anomalies that make little sense in terms of the standard secularization thesis—can be interpreted more readily. Studies of the values and life-styles of scientists have shown them consistently to differ from nonscientists (and to vary in predictable ways from discipline to discipline) on a variety of characteristics, including political orientations, feelings of alienation, nonconventionality, and irreligiosity (e.g., Becker and Carper 1956; Eiduson 1962; Ladd and Lipset 1975). In the context of a more complete examination of these findings it could probably be shown that all of these characteristics function as boundary-posturing mechanisms. In the present context, only the evidence on irreligiosity is of relevance.

   It was observed earlier that academic scientists and graduate students in general are more likely to identify themselves as intellectuals, and more likely to value research and produce more scholarly work when they are irreligious than when they are religious. These findings can be interpreted to suggest that irreligiosity helps to maintain the plausibility of the scientific province by differentiating scientists (in their own minds) from the larger public who represent everyday reality and generally maintain stronger religious identifications. By helping to maintain the plausibility of the scientific role for the scientist, irreligiosity contributes to his or her role performance as a scientist, as indicated by higher productivity and greater attachment to the values of science. The studies showing early irreligiosity leading to subsequent high levels of academic performance and to a likelihood of selecting academic careers point to the importance of this boundary-posturing mechanism during the selection and socialization process in leading to scientific roles. Indeed, selection and early socialization appear to mark the critical stages as far as the relation between irreligiosity and science is concerned, because cohort comparisons of older scientists fail to show any tendency for extended work in science to result in declining levels of religious commitment (as the religion/science hypothesis would predict). In short, the more successfully scientists can extricate themselves from the realm of everyday reality, of which conventional religion is an important aspect (at least in the United States), the more likely they are to make the transition successfully into the scientific role.

A more interesting anomaly that can also be given an interpretation is the variation in irreligiosity by discipline; that is, why the most irreligious persons should be found in the *least scientific* disciplines, rather than in the most scientific disciplines. The high levels of irreligiosity observed in the social sciences and the humanities can be understood in terms of the *low levels of paradigmatic codification* in these disciplines and, therefore, the greater tendency of these disciplines to rely on boundary-posturing mechanisms such as irreligiosity (the same patterns prevail, incidentally, on traits such as political radicalism, nonconventionality, and alienation from the public). These disciplinary differences have been interpreted as being the result of differences in "scholarly distance" from religion, but this interpretation proves insufficient in itself, because it implies that people in the social sciences and humanities actually study religion (giving them low scholarly distance in comparison with practitioners of the natural sciences). In actuality, this is not the case for the vast majority of persons in the social sciences or the humanities (in sociology, for example, fewer than 10 percent of its practitioners list sociology of religion as one of their specialties). Furthermore, the logical extension of the scholarly distance argument leads to some strikingly implausible predictions: for example, that theologians and professors of religious studies will be the *least religious*, that political scientists will be the most likely to reject the family! The present interpretation is broader in that it suggests that people in the social sciences and humanities reject religion not so much because of what they dislike about religion specifically (otherwise, why should they also differ on political and life-style issues?) but because of the ill-codified reality they need to protect within their own discipline.

Further support for this interpretation comes from the fact that there is, indeed, greater boundary-maintaining activity among *religious people* in the social sciences and humanities than in the natural sciences. In Thalheimer's (1973) study of faculty members, those in the social sciences or the humanities who *believed in God* were far more likely to say they had to keep their religious convictions and their research separate than those in the natural sciences, who felt they did not have to keep the two separate. In other words, work in the social sciences and humanities needed to be protected from religious convictions; work in the physical sciences did not.

Studies like Thalheimer's, Lehman's, and others', it should be noted, typically show that people in the applied sciences and the professions resemble the natural scientists in religious convictions and, indeed, often display higher levels of religiosity. This pattern again is consistent with the idea of irreligiosity as a boundary-posturing mechanism. The applied sciences generally operate from better-codified paradigms than the social sciences and the humanities (Merton and Zuckerman 1973) and, unlike the more purely academic disciplines, have less need to separate their reality from the reality of everyday life. Schutz (1962) specifically draws his distinction between pure scientific work (which he calls "scientific theorizing") and everyday reality, rather than between the application of scientific knowledge and everyday life.

Two other features of the religion/science relation also appear consistent with the boundary-posturing interpretation. One is that the general public, not being actively involved in maintaining the scientific role, can be (as it has in fact been shown to be) more eclectic by combining religious and scientific views. As numerous studies in other areas have demonstrated, the average person displays a high capacity for mixing beliefs which social scientists have been prone to regard as inconsistent (see Wuthnow 1981). This is not to deny the inverse relation shown in most studies between people with high levels of education and irreligiosity, but these relations probably reflect broader socialization experiences than they do direct exposure to science. The other phenomenon that can be interpreted is the fact that scientists seem more likely to *think of themselves* as religious persons than they are actually to engage in any of the conventional practices or beliefs associated with religion (*Connecticut Mutual Life Report* 1980). This fact, coupled with (largely anecdotal) evidence of scientists and academicians pursuing idiosyncratic, syncretistic, and mystical religions or quasi religions, suggests that scientists may be able to maintain private, nonconventional religious orientations at the same time that their public boundary-posturing activity calls on them to disidentify with the conventional religious performance that are tainted by everyday reality.

CONCLUSION

In conclusion, the evidence on religion and science, one of the areas in which the processes of advancing secularization should be most evident, points largely to the survival of religion in the postsecular era. While the evidence clearly documents the irreligiosity of scientists themselves, it shows that this irreligiosity is far more pronounced among the least scientific disciplines—the social sciences and humanities—than it is among the natural sciences. And closer inspection of the scientific role itself suggests that scientists in these fields may adopt an irreligious stance chiefly as one of the boundary-posturing mechanisms they use to "distance" themselves from the general public and, thereby, to maintain the precarious reality of the work they do. If this interpretation is correct, the proverbial conflict between religion and science may be more a function of the precariousness of science than of the precariousness of religion. Rather than religion being constantly on the run, so to speak, in the face of ever advancing scientific knowledge, scientists have had to carve out a space in which to work by dissociating themselves from the powerful claims which religion has had traditionally, and which it still appears to command over the everyday life of contemporary society.

BIBLIOGRAPHY

Aidala, Angela A.
  1984   "Worldviews, Ideologies and Social Experimentation: Clarification and Replication of 'The Consciousness Reformation,'" *Journal for the Scientific Study of Religion*. In press.
Babbie, Earl R.
  1970   *Science and Morality in Medicine: A Survey of Medical Educators.* Berkeley, Los Angeles, London: University of California Press.

Barker, Eileen
  1979   "Thus Spake the Scientist: A Comparative Account of the New
            Priesthood and Its Organisational Bases," *Annual Review of the
            Social Sciences of Religion* 3:79–103.
Barnes, Barry
  1974   *Scientific Knowledge and Sociological Theory*. London: Routledge &
            Kegan Paul.
Becker, Howard S., and James Carper
  1956   "The Elements of Identification with an Occupation," *American
            Sociological Review* 21 (June):341–348.
Berger, Peter L.
  1967   *The Sacred Canopy*. Garden City, New York: Doubleday.
Bellah, Robert N.
  1970   *Beyond Belief*. New York: Harper & Row.
Bibby, Reginald W.
  1979   "Religion and Modernity: The Canadian Case," *Journal for the
            Scientific Study of Religion* 18 (March):1–17.
Blau, Judith R.
  1978   "Sociometric Structure of a Scientific Discipline." *In* Robert Alun
            Jones, ed., *Research in Sociology, Sciences, and Art*. Greenwich,
            Connecticut: JAI Press. Pp. 191–206.
Bloor, David
  1971   "Two Paradigms for Scientific Knowledge?" *Science Studies* 1:101–
            115.
  1976   *Knowledge and Social Imagery*. London: Routledge and Kegan Paul.
Breiger, Ronald L.
  1976   "Career Attributes and Network Structure: A Blockmodel Study
            of a Biomedical Research Specialty," *American Sociological Review*
            41:117–135.
Campbell, Douglas F., and Dennis W. Magill
  1968   "Religious Involvement and Intellectuality Among University
            Students," *Sociological Analysis* 29 (Summer):79–93
"Connecticut Mutual Life Report on American Values in the '80s: The Impact
  1981   of Belief." New York: Research & Forecasts, Inc.
Crane, Diana
  1972   *Invisible Colleges: Diffusion of Knowledge in Scientific Communities*.
            Chicago: University of Chicago Press.
Currie, Ian D., Henry C. Finney, Travis Hirschi, and Hannan C. Selvin
  1966   "Images of the Professor and Interest in the Academic Profes-
            sion," *Sociology of Education* 39 (Fall):301–323.
Eiduson, Bernice T.
  1962   *Scientists: Their Psychological World*. New York: Basic Books.
Elson, Ruth Miller
  1964   *Guardians of Tradition: American Schoolbooks of the Nineteenth Cen-*

tury. Lincoln: University of Nebraska Press.
Faia, Michael A.
1974   "The Myth of the Liberal Professor," *Sociology of Education* 47 (Spring):171–202.
1976   "Secularization and Scholarship Among American Professors," *Sociological Analysis* 37 (Spring):63–74.
Feldman, Kenneth A., and Theodore M. Newcomb
1970   *The Impact of College on Students*. San Francisco: Jossey-Bass.
Feyerabend, Paul
1978   *Against Method*. London: Verso Books.
Gallup, George, Jr.
1982   *Religion in America, 1982*. Princeton: Princeton Religion Research Center.
Garvey, W. O., and B. C. Griffith
1967   "Scientific Communication as a Social System," *Science* 157:1011–1016.
Geertz, Clifford
1973   *The Interpretation of Cultures*. New York: Harper & Row.
Glock, Charles Y.
1972   "Images of 'God,' Images of Man, and the Organization of Social Life," *Journal for the Scientific Study of Religion* 11 (March):1–15.
Greaves, Richard L.
1969   "Puritanism and Science: The Anatomy of a Controversy," *Journal of the History of Ideas* 33 (July):345–368.
Hajda, Jan
1961   "Alienation and Integration of Student Intellectuals," *American Sociological Review* 26 (October):758–777.
Hall, A. Rupert
1963   "Merton Revisited: Science and Society in the 17th Century," *History of Science* 11:1–16.
Kuhn, Thomas
1970   *The Structure of Scientific Revolutions*. 2d. ed. Chicago: University of Chicago Press.
Ladd, Everett Carll, Jr., and Seymour Martin Lipset
1975   *The Divided Academy: Professors and Politics*. New York: W. W. Norton.
Latour, Bruno and Steve Woolgar
1979   *Laboratory Life: The Social Construction of Scientific Facts*. Beverly Hills, Calif.: Sage.
Lehman, Edward C., Jr., and Donald W. Shriver, Jr.
1968   "Academic Discipline as Predictive of Faculty Religiosity," *Social Forces* 47 (December):171–182.
Lehman, Edward C., Jr.
1972   "The Scholarly Perspective and Religious Commitment," *Sociolog-*

ical Analysis 33 (Winter):199–213.
Leuba, James
   1916   *The Belief in God and Immorality.* Boston: Sherman French &
            Company.
   1934   "Religious Beliefs of American Scientists," *Harper's Magazine* 169
            (August):291–300.
Luckmann, Thomas
   1967   *The Invisible Religion.* New York: Macmillan.
Merton, Robert K.
   1970   *Science, Technology and Society in Seventeenth-Century England.* New
            York: Harper & Row.
Merton, Robert K., and Harriet Zuckerman
   1973   "Age, Aging, and Age Structure in Science." *In* Robert K. Merton
            ed., *The Sociology of Science.* Chicago: University of Chicago Press.
            Pp. 497–560.
Miller, Jon D., Kenneth Prewitt, and Robert Pearson
   1980   *The Attitudes of the U.S. Public Toward Science and Technology.*
            Chicago: National Opinion Research Center, University of
            Chicago.
Moberg, David O.
   1962   *The Church as a Social Institution.* Englewood Cliffs, N.J.: Prentice-
            Hall.
Mulkay, Michael
   1979   *Science and the Sociology of Knowledge.* London: Allen & Unwin.
   1980   "Accounting for Error," Department of Sociology, University of
            York, England.
Mulligan, Lotte
   1973   "Civil War Politics, Religion and the Royal Society," *Past and
            Present* 59:92–116.
National Science Foundation
   1978   *Science Indicators, 1978.* Washington, D.C.: U.S. Government
            Printing Office.
   1981   *Science Indicators, 1980.* Washington, D.C.: U.S. Government
            Printing Office.
Salter, Charles A., and Lewis M. Routledge
   1974   "Intelligence and Belief in the Supernatural," *Psychological Reports*
            34 (February):299–302.
Schneider, Louis, and Sanford M. Dornbusch
   1958   *Popular Religion.* Chicago: University of Chicago Press.
Schutz, Alfred
   1962   "On Multiple Realities." *In* Alfred Schutz, *Collected Papers.* vol. 1.
            The Hague: Nijhoff. Pp. 209–259.
Smith, Wilfred Cantwell
   1979   *Faith and Belief.* Princeton: Princeton University Press.

Stark, Rodney
1963   "On the Incompatibility of Religion and Science," *Journal for the Scientific Study of Religion* 3 (Fall):3–20.
Statistical Abstract
1981   *U.S. Statistical Abstract, 1981.* Washington, D.C.: U.S. Bureau of the Census.
Steinberg, Stephen
1974   *The Academic Melting Pot: Catholics and Jews in American Higher Education.* New York: McGraw-Hill.
Thalheimer, Fred
1973   "Religiosity and Secularization in the Academic Professions," *Sociology of Education* 46:183–202.
Wuthnow, Robert
1976   *The Consciousness Reformation.* Berkeley, Los Angeles, London: University of California Press.
1977   "A Longitudinal, Cross-National Indicator of Cultural Religious Commitment," *Journal for the Scientific Study of Religion* 16 (March):87–99.
1978   *Experimentation in American Religion.* Berkeley, Los Angeles, London: University of California Press.
1980   "The World-Economy and the Institutionalization of Science in Seventeenth-Century Europe." *In* Albert Bergesen, ed., *Studies of the Modern World-System.* New York: Academic Press. Pp. 25–55.
1981   "Two Traditions in the Study of Religion," *Journal for the Scientific Study of Religion* 20 (March):16–32.
1983*a*   "The Political Rebirth of American Evangelicals." *In* Robert Liebman and Robert Wuthnow, eds., *The New Christian Right: Mobilization and Legitimation.* New York: Aldine. Chap. 13.
1983*b*   "Indices of Religious Resurgence in the United States." Paper presented at the Conference on Religious Resurgence in Comparative Perspective, State University of New York at Binghamton, January 1983.
Wuthnow, Robert, James Beniger, and Wesley Shrum
1982   "Networks of Scientific and Technological Information in the Technical Innovation Process: Final Report." National Science Foundation, Washington, D.C. (Grant PRA-7920573).
Zelan, Joseph
1968   "Religious Apostasy, Higher Education, and Occupational Choice," *Sociology of Education* 41:370–379.

XIII

Gender, the Family, and the Sacred

Barbara Hargrove

Twenty years ago, the primary social scientific model on which the study of the relationships of religion to the institutions of the family and gender role could be based was that of secularization. The number of those who were interested in the field was relatively small, since religion in the secular model was seen as a vanishing institution. To study religion was somewhat like studying rural life, an attempt to catch before it was too late a dimension of human life passing out of existence under the relentless march of industrial modernization, which has no need of a transcendent dimension, mystery, or ancient ritual. The family was only slightly less threatened by the secularization model, since it was understood to have lost many functions to such public institutions as the school and the marketplace. The family had become strictly a voluntary affair for mutual enjoyment, just as the church was a voluntary institution for personal enrichment. Their power in the society at large was understood to be minimal.

As far as gender roles were concerned, this subject in the early 1960s was not part of the purview of most scientific students of religion. The interest in the field seems to have grown in direct proportion to the number of women now active in scholarly societies in the field, though not all of the work is done by women. Their very presence, apparently, has made the issue seem real to their colleagues.

In research on religion and gender roles, primary focus had to do with assumptions that women are more religious than men, or at least different in the ways in which they practice or are affected by religion. Studies of college students or more general populations thus show women more likely to attend religious services, and more accepting of church strictures on sexual activity. This has been a continuing focus during the years and still gets its share of research attention, as can be seen, for example, in Dickinson (1976), Hunsberger (1978), and Suzredelis and Potvin (1981). Beyond that, discussions of sex roles have largely been subsumed, until recently, under the general rubric of studies of the family.

The secularization model, assuming the more mysterious or transcendent elements of religion to be essentially incredible to the modern mind, has explained the survival of religion primarily by recognizing the functions it has continued to serve in modern society. In relation to the family, therefore, religion was recognized as a source of social control: regulating sexual activity and enforcing commonly held models of appropriate behavior for men, women, and children, particularly in the home environment. Gerhard Lenski, in *The Religious Factor* (1961), enriched that view by demonstrating in his Detroit study the place of religion in supporting identity through the family, and those extensions of families he called socioreligious groups. These were particularly evident in his research among ethnic groups, whose religion was a symbol of that ethnicity.

Even by then, however, the situation was in flux. Herberg's *Protestant-Catholic-Jew* (1955) spelled out probable sources of disintegration of that pattern: second-generation ethnics left their family enclaves (and churches) to become secular Americans, and the third generation then returned to major denominations purged of their ethnic and, perhaps, family ties. By the middle of the 1960s this return to religion was therefore less evident, and studies of religion came to focus on questions of religious social control.

Social control by religious groups in a pluralistic society is necessarily predicated on effective boundary maintenance by such groups. A primary measure of that boundary maintenance has been the rate of marriage within the group as compared with religious exogamy. One piece of evidence of the changing focus of studies of religious social control in this area is the diminution in the number of studies of this phenomenon over the past two decades. Boundary maintenance was a common topic into the 1960s but by the end of that decade it became more problematic. Questions arose concerning appropriate definitions of interreligious marriage, questions therefore indicating some confusion in the definition of religious boundaries. (See, for example,

Cavan 1970; Yinger 1971*a*, 1971*b*.) By the end of the 1970s the subject was seldom addressed, though some attention was still being given to such interfaith differences as could be found in divorce rates, for example (see McCarthy 1979). It may support the secularization thesis that religion seems to have become increasingly irrelevant to the choice of mates in modern society.

The sexual revolution of the sixties led to a considerable number of studies concerning both sexual behavior and efforts to limit its potential products. Many studies of sexual behavior have compared self-reported behavior or attitudes of members of various religious groups, in an attempt to trace the interaction between acceptance of sexual intimacy outside marriage and religious values and proscriptions. In some cases, such as the greater toleration by Catholics (particularly the men) for a double standard of sexual behavior, traditional attitudes tend to confound any understanding of change in sexual mores (see, for example, Alston 1974*a*). Over time, Mormons have tended to replace Catholics as the exemplars of effective boundary maintenance vis-à-vis sexual activity and family roles, but by the mid-1970s even they were showing trends related to those in the society around them (see Bahr 1982; Thomas 1983).

Perhaps a more significant topic has been religious control over pregnancy, whether that concerns premarital and extramarital intercourse (where no progeny are desired) or the limitation of family size within marriage. One clear trend over the past two decades has been the change of focus in this issue from contraception to abortion. In the mid-1960s, Carl Reiterman (1965) provided a masterful survey of changes in the Catholic position on family size limitation. When those Catholics who hoped they would be allowed to consider "the pill" a licit form of family planning found their hopes dashed, studies showed a reversal of the usual paradigm. Among Catholics already committed to contraception, defection from the church took place rather than acceptance of its control. (See, among others, Greeley 1976, 1979.) Mainstream Protestant churches had long ago essentially given up efforts to control the contraceptive behavior of members, instead approving the idea of limited family size in pursuit of a higher quality of life (see, for example, Hargrove 1983*b*). Now they are dealing with both sides of the controversy over abortion as a legitimate means of terminating unwanted pregnancies. Although abortion is still anathema to many Catholics (though on this subject, see Westhoff 1979) and others as well, in most areas usually assumed to relate to the family, religion seems to have become a weak source of social control. The secularization model seems to hold.

Many of those who have been studying the interrelation of church and family, however, have come to question the secular model as the only paradigm for their study. At least two sources of their dissatisfaction with the model can be found. One source questions the value of concentrating almost exclusively on the function of social control as the variable relating to family. The other, more important source is the rise of new religious movements and the related demand for reestablishing a sacral view of the universe. The rise of these movements greatly expanded the number of persons interested in the social-scientific study of religion, as it attracted to that study persons whose fields had been those of social movements or social problems. Suddenly religion had come to have relevance for a wider area of study. That in itself led to a questioning of the secularization model. It became a problem of study to learn why this turn to religion—albeit not "standard brand" institutional religion—was occurring.

The relation of these movements to the family has, in itself, had several dimensions. For many members, the new religions have served as substitute families, and many of them emphasize this function through the use of family terminology, calling one another "brother" or "sister" and holding leaders to be their spiritual parents. This only increases the agony of the biological families of members, who may assume that conversion to such groups is a symptom of the failure of the family unit. Social scientists tend to blame, however, not any individual family but the larger social trends of urbanization, modernization, and industrialization for weaknesses in all modern families. (See, for example, Clayton 1979; Kilbourne and Richardson 1982; and Hargrove 1983*a*.) Secularization is a primary factor in this approach, of course, sometimes blinding researchers to new forms that may be arising in the groups, even as those researchers concentrate on the pain and frustration felt in the "normal" family as it loses members. For example, in the book *Cults and the Family* (Kaslow and Sussman 1983), first published as two consecutive issues of *Marriage and Family Review*, among twelve articles on "cults" and families, only two deal with definitions or practices within the "cults" regarding families. The rest are focused on the families that have been deserted by those joining the new movements.

Whether because of the dominance of the secularization model or the natural conservatism of those who take established social institutions as their major focus, little has been written about the possible use of religious enthusiasm to provide an alternative world view to undergird changes in major family or sex roles. What can be gleaned from studies of various movements is that new forms being developed by them include definitions of sexual practice, relations between men and women, child-rearing practices, and the like. In some new movements, as in historic religious movements, commitment to the cause outweighs considerations of gender, so that the equality between the sexes is far greater than that experienced even in societies priding themselves on equal treatment of all their people. Not only are gender roles seen anew but parental roles as well. Members may be sent on missions, leaving children with other members for long periods of time or, indeed, children may be raised by the community as a whole, with little identification with their biological parents. Chastity is often enforced as a way of showing religious devotion, with the side effect of reducing sexual competition and jealousy in tightly knit groups. In a few groups (many fewer than expected by their detractors) overt sex is used as a form of recruitment or of ministry. Case studies of particular groups have provided the outlines of these factors, leading as least some researchers to see in them a model of social transformation that would relate to religion more in terms of revitalization movements than as steady new trends. (For bibliographical resources on these movements, see Robbins 1978, 1983).

A number of studies, however, have shown that many new religious groups have arisen as a reaction to modern society, not to bring about a new order, but rather as nativistic movements that would restore the old order. Nowhere is this more evident than in the case of sexual activity and gender roles, in which members seem to be reacting to the sexual revolution and the ambivalence about sexual and gender behavior accompanying it. In these groups, the power of religion to exercise control over sexual activity is recognized and practiced. Many demand of members very traditional gender behavior. (See, for example, Richardson, Stewart, and Simmonds 1978; Bromley, Shupe, and Oliver 1982.) In this they join those movements seldom classified as new, such as the evangelical sectors of established denominations, which make a shibboleth of family as defined in middle-class America, and of gender roles that assume the "headship" of the man in the home and in public. (See Robison 1980; Ammerman 1983; Hunter 1983:103–105.)

The effect of the variety of religious prescriptions and proscriptions on the psychological health of many women has led to other sorts of studies. While those engaged in "pure" areas of scholarly theory and research tend to denigrate those involved in more practical fields, in the field of gender roles the practitioners seem to have been ahead of the theoretical types. In the mid-seventies, when little was being published in other scholarly journals, those devoted to pastoral care and counseling began a series of studies concerning the place of women, the effects on women of sexism in the society, and so forth (See, e.g., Ford 1967; Edson 1973; Ulanov 1975; Stewart 1978.) This concern has gradually spread into the more traditionally scholarly areas (see, for example, Meadow 1980, Stoudenmire 1976) to consider the effects of sexist ideology on men as well as on women in clerical positions (Morgan 1980).

Although they date from the early 1970s, internal changes regarding gender roles in the mainstream churches have only begun to receive the attention of those interested in the social scientific study of religion. One reason may be the antireligious rhetoric of many feminists, which lead some researchers to ignore churchly feminists as an unlikely group. (McClain 1979, is a good example of this approach.) So far, most of those involved in the studies conducted within the churches assessing their growing feminist movement assume the secularization model. They tend to take their methodology from the sociology of occupations, studying the rise in number of women clergy as an example of professionalization and of social justice issues involving equal employment opportunity. (See Wallace, 1975; Lehman 1980; Carroll et al. 1983.) Although the attitude of some women to their careers as clergy seems dissimilar to that of men (see Carroll et al. 1983:132–124, 169–175), there are as yet few studies taking those differences seriously enough to suggest that the change in gender of church leadership might affect the style of church activity or programs.

Yet it is here we may find the cutting edge of research in this area, for it is here that gender role research meets research on the family in relation to religion.

A NEW PARADIGM?

In his presidential address to the Society for the Scientific Study of Religion in 1979, William D'Antonio challenged his colleagues to move beyond the conservative notion that religion functions only as social control in their studies of family and gender relations. He suggested that, in a society undergoing rapid change, one demand of religion is to support persons as they move into new forms of relationships. Moreover, he suggested, religious values, traditionally supportive of such family values as love, could provide that sort of grounding. In studies of students, he said, "A significant percentage see the issue 'how to love' as the fundamental problem of human societies" (D'Antonio, 1980:102; see also D'Antonio et al. 1983*a*). While much of the study of changing gender roles has centered around competitive models of the job market for clergy or social justice issues of equal rights, some of the material coming from the study of women entering new religious roles indicates a closer relationship to the sort of perspective D'Antonio has posited. In *Families and Religions,* edited by D'Antonio and Aldous (1983*b*), a number of colleagues follow his lead in their discussions. In the meantime, studies of women in religious institutions have been broadened and researchers are beginning to consider the effects of marginality upon women as they come into more prominent places in the churches. Haywood (1983) showed the effect of this marginality in churches not part of the mainstream. Similarly, Gilfeather (1977) has shown that the increase of leadership roles among Catholic women in Chile, though brought about by the shortage of priests rather than by any ideological commitment on the part of the bishops, has put into positions of influence women whose views are in sharp contrast to those of the bishops—women who are demanding greater religious commitment and a more seriously critical view of the society at large. Much of this approach is coming from the increasing number of women in the field of the social scientific study of religion, who can relate such phenomena to their own experience (Wallace 1975; Neal 1975).

More studies of this sort need to be undertaken. Do religious values reflect what seems to be taken for granted in modern secular society? And are those values being conveyed by churches and by women who are gaining more formal power, not only in those churches but in the society at large? Or is the gaining power related to the abandonment of those values, an abandonment of the family, of love and personal support, as conservative critics have claimed?

At the beginning of the Industrial Revolution, Protestantism provided an economic ethic that assisted new social classes to achieve public responsibility and build a new society. As we now move into a postindustrial age, is Naisbitt (1982) right (in spite of the shallowness of his data) that we are moving into a "high tech/high touch" era where new forms of personal relationships will be essential to the survival of the society? If he is, are families as we have known them—or as they are becoming—the social purveyors of those relationships? Will new movements for gender equality also be the sources of a new ethic of love? How is religion related to all this? Can a truly new social paradigm arise unless it is perceived as grounded in the sacred? It is to such problems that we might well address our future research.

REFERENCES

Alston, Jon P.
1974*a* "Review of the Polls: Attitudes of White Protestants and Catholics toward Nonmarital Sex," *Journal for the Scientific Study of Religion* 13:73–74.
1974*b* "Review of the Polls: Attitudes toward Extramarital and Homosexual Relations," *Journal for the Scientific Study of Religion* 13:479–481.
Ammerman, Nancy T.
1983 "The Fundamentalist World View: Ideology and Social Structure in an Independent Fundamental Church." Ph.D. dissertation, Yale University.
Bahr, Howard
1982 "Religious Contrasts in Family Role Definitions and Performance: Utah Mormons, Catholics, Protestants, and Others," *Journal for the Scientific Study of Religion* 21:200–217.
Bromley, David G., Anson D. Shupe, Jr., and Donna Oliver
1982 "Perfect Families: Visions of the Future in a New Religious Movement." *In* Florence Kaslow and Marvin B. Sussman, eds., *Cults and the Family*. New York: Haworth.
Carroll, Jackson W., Barbara Hargrove, and Adair Lummis.
1983 *Women of the Cloth*. San Francisco: Harper & Row.
Cavan, Ruth Shonle
1970 "Concepts and Terminology in Interreligious Marriage," *Journal for the Scientific Study of Religion* 9:311–320.
Clayton, R. R.
1979 *The Family, Marriage, and Social Change*. 2d. ed. Lexington, Mass.: D. C. Heath.
Cox, Harvey
1965 *The Secular City*. New York: Macmillan.
1969 *Feast of Fools*. Cambridge: Harvard University Press.
1977 *Turning East*. New York: Simon and Schuster.
D'Antonio, William V.
1980 "The Family and Religion: Exploring a Changing Relationship," *Journal for the Scientific Study of Religion* 19:89–104.
1983*a* With William M. Newman and Stuart A. Wright. "Religion and Family Life: How Social Scientists View the Relationship," *Journal for the Scientific Study of Religion* 21:218–225.

1983*b*   With Joan Aldous, eds. *Families and Religions*. Beverly Hills, Calif.:
           Sage.
Dickinson, George E.
1976   "Religious Practices of Adolescents in a Southern Community,"
           Journal for the Scientific Study of Religion 15:361–364.
Edson, Cynthia J.
1973   "Male and Female, Created He Them: An Encounter of Sex-Role
           Stereotypes in CPE," *Journal of Pastoral Care* 45:159–171.
Ford, J. Massingberd
1967   "The Apostolates of the Sick and Women in Pastoral Care," *Jour-
           nal of Pastoral Care* 21:147–162.
Gilfeather, Katherine
1977   "The Changing Role of Women in the Catholic Church in Chile,"
           Journal for the Scientific Study of Religion 16:39–54.
Greeley, Andrew M.
1976   With William McCready and Kathleen McCourt. *Catholic Schools
           in a Declining Church*. Kansas City: Sheed & Ward.
1979   *Crisis in the Church*. Chicago: Thomas More.
Hargrove, Barbara
1983*a*   "The Church, the Family, and the Modernization Process." *In*
           D'Antonio and Aldous.
1983*b*   "Family in the White Protestant American Experience." *In* D'An-
           tonio and Aldous, eds., 1983*b*.
Haywood, Carol Lois
1983   "The Authority and Empowerment of Women in Spiritualist
           Groups," *Journal for the Scientific Study of Religion* 22:157–166.
Herberg, Will
1955   *Protestant-Catholic-Jew*. Garden City, N.Y.: Doubleday.
Hunsberger, Bruce
1978   "The Religiosity of College Students: Stability and Change over
           Years at the University," *Journal for the Scientific Study of Religion*
           17:159–164.
Hunter, James Davidson
1983   *American Evangelicals*. New Brunswick, N.J.; Rutgers University
           Press.
Kaslow, Florence B., and Marvin B. Sussman, eds.
1983   *Cults and the Family*. New York: Haworth Press.
Kilbourne, Brock K., and James T. Richardson
1982   "Cults Versus Families: A Case of Misattribution of Cause?" *In*
           Kaslow and Sussman, 1983.
Lehman, Edward C., Jr.
1980   "Placement of Men and Women in Ministry," *Review of Religious
           Research* 22:18–40.
Lenski, Gerhard
1961   *The Religious Factor*. Garden City, N.Y.: Doubleday.

McCarthy, James
  1979   "Religious Commitment, Affiliation, and Marriage Dissolution."
          In Robert Wuthnow, ed., *The Religious Dimension: New Directions
          in Quantitative Research.* New York: Academic Press. 1979.
McClain, Edward W.
  1979   "Religious Orientation the Key to Psychodynamic Differences
          between Feminists and Nonfeminists," *Journal for the Scientific
          Study of Religion* 18:40–45.
Meadow, Mary Jo
  1980   "Wifely Submission: Psychological/Spiritual Growth Perspec-
          tives," *Journal of Religion and Health* 19:103–120.
Morgan, Edward
  1980   "Implications of the Masculine and the Feminine in Pastoral
          Ministry," *Journal of Pastoral Care* 34:268–277.
Naisbitt, John
  1982   *Megatrends.* New York: Warner.
Neal, Marie Augusta
  1975   "Women in Religion: A Sociological Perspective," *Sociological
          Inquiry* 45:33–39.
Reiterman, Carl
  1965   "Birth Control and Catholics," *Journal for the Scientific Study of
          Religion* 4:213–233.
Richardson, James T., Mary Stewart, and R. B. Simmonds
  1978   *Organized Miracles.* New Brunswick, N.J.: Transaction.
Robbins, Thomas
  1978   With Dick Anthony and James T. Richardson. "Theory and
          Research on Today's 'New Religions'," *Sociological Analysis* 39:95–
          122.
  1983   "Sociological Studies of Selected New Religious Movements: A
          Selective Review," *Religious Studies Review* 9:233–239.
Robison, James
  1980   *Attack on the Family.* Wheaton, Ill.: Tyndale Press.
Stewart, Dorothy Cox
  1978   "Sex Role Values in Pastoral Care," *Journal of Pastoral Care* 32:111–
          117.
Stoudenmire, John
  1976   "The Role of Religion in the Depressed Housewife," *Journal of
          Religion and Health* 15:62–67.
Suzredelis, Antanas, and Raymond H. Potvin
  1981   "Sex Differences in Factors Affecting Religiousness Among Cath-
          olic Adolescents," *Journal for the Scientific Study of Religion* 20:38–
          50.
Thomas, Darwin L.
  1983   "Family in the Mormon Experience." *In* D'Antonio and Aldous,
          eds., 1983*b*.

Ulanov, Ann Belford
1975   "The Feminine and the World of CPE," *Journal of Pastoral Care*
          29:11–22.
Wallace, Ruth A.
1975   "Bringing Women In: Marginality in the Churches," *Sociological
          Analysis* 36:291–303.
Westoff, Charles F.
1979   "The Blending of Catholic Reproductive Behavior." *In* Wuthnow,
          1979.
Wuthnow, Robert, ed.
1979   *The Religious Dimension: New Directions in Quantitative Research.*
          New York: Academic Press.
Yinger, J. Milton
1971a   "A Research Note on Interfaith Marriage Statistics." *Journal for the
          Scientific Study of Religion* 7:97–103.
1971b   "On the Definition of Interfaith Marriage." *Journal for the Scientific
          Study of Religion* 7:104–107.

XIV

The Sacred and
Third World Societies

Bennetta Jules-Rosette

Dramatic social upheavals in the Third World over the past twenty years have been accompanied by the rise of new religious movements, including indigenous churches, separatist groups, and politico-religious movements of various sorts. These movements have been characterized by symbolic protest and a search for cultural continuity that involves a redefinition of what is perceived to be sacred on the cognitive and institutional levels. Concurrent with this trend, interdisciplinary research on the role of religion in the Third World has increased enormously.[1] In this chapter, I shall explore concepts of the sacred that have emerged from cross-cultural studies of Third World religions during the past two decades and examine the implications of these findings for the present and future state of research in the field.

RE-ENVISIONING THE SACRED AND THE SECULAR

Emile Durkheim (1915:52) posited that "all known religious beliefs, whether simple or complex" presuppose the classification of the world into sacred and profane domains. For Durkheim, no particular entity, object, or event is intrinsically sacred. Instead, the sacred consists of collective moral and symbolic expressions projected and reinforced by the social group (see Douglas 1966:21), meaning that

social processes generate and sustain the sacred.[2] Durkheim's definition of the sacred refers to a way of seeing and thinking about the
world as much as it does to a set of social institutions.

This approach contrasts with Max Weber's view that the sacred is
embodied in religious institutions and must be studied in terms of
their relationship to the rest of society (Weber 1963:207–208). It is from
the latter perspective that the opposition between the sacred and the
secular as a source of social change has developed as a tool for
analyzing historic and contemporary religions. The much-debated
problem of secularization, which became a major scholarly and popular concern for Western researchers and theologians in the 1960s and
is still a source of controversy, was partially set in motion by Weber's
approach.[3]

Researchers have both debated and refined Weber's initial assumptions. For example, in his introduction to the English translation of
Weber's *The Sociology of Religion,* Talcott Parsons (1963:lxii) argues that
the rise of interdenominationalism and liberal Protestantism in the
United States seriously challenges Weber's view of how the secularization process would unfold in contemporary Western societies. But
neither did Weber ever envision the processes of rapid social change
and cultural contact resulting from decolonization and development;
the notion that the people of the Third World would have a voice in
redirecting the course of religion and institutional change in the West
did not appear as an empirical possibility at the beginning of the
twentieth century. As movements of protest, many new religious
groups in the Third World have become vehicles for the creation,
exercise, and legitimation of power by their adherents. Those who
were formerly powerless have found in religion a means of altering
their situation, even reversing their status in both symbolic and social
terms. The adherents of these new movements have created and
manipulated sacred symbols to attain secular goals. Therefore, the
existence of these movements will necessarily modify future conceptualizations of the relationship between the sacred and the secular.

Another fundamental question lingers when assessing U.S. research on Third World religious movements. This concerns the comparative lens through which such studies are conceived and developed. The church-denomination-sect typology, which has been
widely debated since Troeltsch and Weber, and probably reached its
peak as an analytical tool by 1970 (see Eister 1967:85–90; Demerath
and Hammond 1969; Johnson 1971:124–137), has done much to obscure research on new religious movements in the Third World and
elsewhere, growing as it did out of historical studies of European

Christianity. Its effects on research into the Third World have been particularly misleading because it promoted a tendency to view new religious developments as "sectarian" responses rather than as developments with alternative or parallel cultural and historical roots to those of more established churches and denominations. The rise of new religions and cults in the United States since the 1960s has already called this typology into serious question. The wide range of cultural combinations and socio-political goals in Third World groups renders the church-sect typology almost ineffective, even as a descriptive device.

RELIGIOUS RESEARCH ON THE THIRD WORLD:
AN OVERVIEW OF RECENT DEVELOPMENTS

The term *Third World* presents nearly as many definitional problems as the church-sect typology, although it has received far less attention in scientific studies of religion. Some scholars (see Berreman 1972:285–414; Goldthorpe 1975:2–4) have described the Third World as consisting of societies that have not yet reached the advanced stages of industrial development. Bryan Wilson (1973:1) begins his comprehensive study of Third World religious groups by defining them as "movements arising among less-developed peoples following cultural contact with westerners." This assertion is both descriptive and causal. Third World religious movements have been equated with what Vittorio Lanternari (1963:19) termed "religions of the oppressed," which he considered to be "the spontaneous result of the impact of the white man's presence on the native society." Each of these definitions views Third World religious movements as responses to external pressures rather than as independent initiatives. The concept of "Third World religion" also assumes a cultural and social equivalency among diverse movement types on an international scale, both in non-Western countries and among marginal people and minorities in Western nations.[4] To the extent that the goal of comparative study is to illuminate potentially universal concepts and processes, these definitions of Third World religions may be acceptable. However, they may also lead to distortion about the degree of similarity among these groups.

In spite of these difficulties, there are several themes shared by new movements arising in areas moving from traditional to post-traditional cultures. For example, it has been argued that the Western model of "church and state," with clearly separated sacred and secular domains, often does not apply neatly to these movements in either a historical or a cultural sense. Larry Shiner (1966:218) comments on this problem: "When we apply this spiritual-temporal polarity to non-Western situations where such differentiations did not originally exist, we falsify the data."

Versions of the secularization thesis, in which the separation of the sacred and the secular is inherent, have nevertheless been applied successfully to studies of religious movements in the Third World, following a neo-Weberian model. A landmark study in this regard is Norman Long's (1968) monograph on the religious and social responses to modernity among the Jehovah's Witnesses of Kapepa village in Zambia. The Weberian view posits that modernity is accompanied by the increasing "rationalization" of activities in the religious and social spheres (e.g., a structuring of religious activities according to secular ideals). Religious motivations for action are redirected into the secular domain. Long found a classic version of the Protestant Ethic operative among the Witnesses of Kapepa. Most of them were relatively young villagers with little urban experience. They equated hard work and economic success with the process of preparing themselves for the millennium and entry into the "New Kingdom" (Long 1968:241). Relative to their fellow villagers, the Witnesses made a rapid transition from hoe to plow agriculture with notable commercial success. Long (1968:239–240) remarks:

I . . . concluded that like the correlations that Weber suggested between the Protestant ethic and "the spirit of capitalism," there existed in Kapepa a close correspondence between Jehovah's Witnesses and their social and economic behavior. . . . But social, economic and cultural factors also play their part.

Religion, in this case, helped the Witnesses of Kapepa adapt to change. They did so by redefining their social world in millenarian religious terms and acting upon these beliefs in their economic lives. Long's study thus exemplifies the secularization thesis in the Third World, but it also demonstrates the involvement of African Witnesses in an overwhelming religious redefinition of every aspect of their daily lives. Moreover, the Kapepa Witnesses are atypical of many Central African groups that developed as offshoots of the Watch Tower movement during the colonial period (see Biebuyck 1957:117–140).[5] These movements, tending to exhibit extreme millenarian religious and political responses to European domination, were without specific social programs for their members.

Another important theme found in Third World religious movements is their status as alternative avenues to power. Much has been made of the overtly apolitical character of many of these groups (see Murphree 1969:109), the adherents being either not interested or not successful in creating significant political changes within their societies. However, the formal political sphere is not the only arena in which power can be exercised, and new religious movements in the Third World have redefined power and its contexts in several ways.

Of course, one line of research has indeed explored the extent of direct political involvement of millenarian and messianic movements, particularly in Africa and Latin America, but the net can be cast wider. Robert Janosik (1974:161–175) contrasted African religious movements of the millenarian and spirit types in terms of the extent of political activism among their respective followers and the influence of these movements on the development of nationalist ideologies and social policies. He establishes a continuum ranging from politico-religious movements, such as "Mau Mau" in colonial Kenya (see Rosberg and Nottingham 1966:320–347), to apolitical groups with an emphasis on salvation and spiritual redemption, such as Zulu Zionism.[6] Although Janosik clearly does not compare the larger political pictures in Kenya and South Africa and the sources of domination and repression that generate structural differences, he touches upon two contrasting relationships between religion and society: (1) the tendency of new religious movements to insulate themselves from the secular society, as opposed to (2) the process by which these movements, through their symbolic content, challenge and alter aspects of the societies in which they appear.

This contrast is also reflected in Wilson's (1973) study of new religions in the Third World. His typology compresses a number of empirical movement types into two doctrinal and cultural orientations: the thaumaturgist and the revolutionist, or the magical and the millennial. Although this distinction refers to both world views and specific movements, a concern with supernatural powers—magic, healing, and purification—is, for Wilson, the major thrust of *all* Third World religions emerging in so-called tribal societies. What the sociologist considers "magical" in this context, of course, may be viewed by movement followers as a set of rational alternatives logically derived from tradition or from innovative doctrinal combinations. Wilson's "magic" is a catch-all description for both a wide variety of indigenous customs and beliefs and for new conceptions of symbolic action. For Wilson, millenarian movements of protest contain much that is "magical" and, therefore, have little broad, lasting political or social impact. He cites the case of new West African religions (see Peel 1968:209) and of some American Indian movements in support of this tendency of millenarian movements to be temporary and localized. When such movements of protest do arise, they are often, in Wilson's opinion, so replete with supernatural and otherworldly elements that they are only marginally effective as movements of protest. I would argue, however, that a challenge to the existing social order is implicit in many Third World religious movements, regardless of the specific traditional or "magical" elements present. In this regard, the meanings and functions of new religious movements for their own group members must become central issues for study. Several researchers have emphasized the redefinition of social status among members of spirit-type religious movements in Africa (see Daneel 1971; Sundkler 1976). The Zionist movements of southern Africa stress faith-healing and the unique status of their members, the unique status being derived from their charismatic gifts and spiritual ordination. These movements establish leadership patterns fueled by the charismatic authority, as opposed to the secular roles, of their members.

Emilio Willems (1966:253–258) analyzes related problems of power distribution with respect to Pentecostal groups in Brazil and Chile. He claims that these movements attract socially marginal individuals with low social status. Using their charismatic authority and with their sense of becoming the spiritual elect, members of these movements establish a status hierarchy reversing the assumptions and values of the external society. Formal education for leaders is devalued at the expense of spiritual inspiration. The leaders of these movements thus establish new roles for themselves in an alternative social order. Mary O'Connor (1979:260–268) notes a similar process of group validation taking place among the Mayo Indians of Mexico who have become involved with evangelical Protestant movements. The members of such movements challenge both the existing social order and established Catholicism with an alternative ecclesiastical order.

In the Caribbean, movements such as Ras Tafarianism and Santeria seek to redefine values by withdrawing and establishing an alternative social order. Orlando Patterson (1964:17) has referred to the Ras Tafari movement as an "extroverted, aggressive type of withdrawal." Sheila Kitzinger (1969:259), in a detailed description of the Ras Tafari movement, has noted its "dysfunctional" tendencies in seeking "the destruction of the very social system in which the cult operates." In this case, millenarian revolt has become institutionalized through the establishment of alternative communities with practices considered to be hostile, deviant, and even illegal in the wider society. The veneration of the late Emperor Haile Selassie and the wish to return to Africa constitute a reactionary definition of the sacred which, at the same time, reinforces the symbolic and political protest of the Ras Tafari group. Such movements also represent a collective search for identity in their turn toward core religious ideals and psychological reversal of the values of the external society.

Both the Latin American Pentecostal cases and the Ras Tafari movement illustrate important tendencies in Third World religions. These include offering spiritual mobility as a substitute for social mobility, dispensing with a specialized clergy, and defining salvation and other religious goals in terms that can be easily grasped and applied by their members. These processes have been identified by some researchers with a simplification of doctrine and ritual (see Wilson 1982:124), but such simplification does not always occur and may often be a product of the sociologist's analytic reductionism. In fact, ritual processes and ceremonies in Third World religions may be more complex than those in established churches because of the necessity of redefining the meaning and source of the sacred in these religions.

This point reinforces the methodological concern in some recent studies with defining the cosmology and belief systems in traditional and new religions. On the ethnographic level, this defining is essential in order to assess the greater influence of new movements on the societies in which they appear. Steven Piker (1972:210–229) does this when he analyzes the relationship among Buddhist, Hindu, and animistic beliefs in the religious practices of a Thai village using the concept of *Kamma* (receiving good for good or evil for evil). Building upon the research of Ames (1964:21–52) on Sinhalese religion, and Spiro (1967) on Burmese Buddhism, Piker argues that numerous inconsistent doctrines are maintained simultaneously in Thai religion and are balanced by applying a principle of coherency. Piker attempts to analyze these belief systems from the point of view of the villagers who adhere to them.[7] He outlines a set of cognitive and cultural categories and demonstrates how they are used in daily religious practice. Building upon a semantic anthropological approach to religion, this line of research suggests that the comparative study of Third World religions must be preceded by a schematic treatment of the content of religious doctrines and practice. This suggestion raises issues of both theological and sociological import. Specifically, how do the members of new religious movements conceive of the sacred, of categories of religious belief and practice, and of the distribution of ecclesiastical authority within their groups? Beyond simply noting that these categories challenge or differ from those of Western religious belief and practice, we must examine the new terms in their own right.

THE PROBLEM OF SECULARIZATION IN
THIRD WORLD RELIGIONS

Just as the interpretation of the sacred takes a unique form in Third World religions, so too does the process of secularization.[8] Peter Berger (1967:171) argues on the one hand that the worldwide spread of the structures of the modern industrial state triggers religious change in non-Western societies and is an important catalyst for the secularization process. On the other hand, Wilson (1973:499) points to the decline of traditional authority structures and religious beliefs as a fact of colonial domination and "Westernization." The implication of both assertions is that tendencies toward secularization are introduced to Third World societies from the outside as a by-product of the eventual movements of all societies toward industrial and post industrial socioeconomic structures (see Parsons 1966:109–114). These changes are accompanied by cultural pluralization, frequent contact between diverse social groups, and an increase in bureaucratic forms of organization and in impersonal social relationships. Similarly, Shiner (1967:209–217) has noted three important characteristics of secularization that can be associated with this transition to modernity: (1) desacralization or decline in the role of religion in defining the social world, (2) the process of structural differentiation by which religious and secular social institutions become distinct and autonomous, and (3) the transference of religious knowledge and activities to the secular domain.[9] As a result of these processes, individuals reorder their religious beliefs so they will meet the demands of modern society—a society that Western theologians and social scientists have argued has become increasingly secular, but which nonetheless contains unmistakable elements of the sacred.

This combination of the sacred and secular domains in the religions of many "tribal" groups, particularly in Africa and Asia, creates thorny problems when analyzing the process of secularization (see Nash 1971:105–122; Turner 1974:697–705).[10] In these groups, the political domain has traditionally been defined and reinforced by religious beliefs and sacred symbols, so change-oriented movements that draw upon customary religious and political symbolism have often been regarded with a mixture of alarm and suspicion by both colonial governments and new regimes. When these cultural combinations are aggravated by millenarian tendencies in religious groups, the issue becomes even more complex. It is thus difficult to disentangle a nostalgic return to traditional notions of the sacred from new political and social demands. Desacralization and resacralization, in this context, may actually constitute two complementary poles of a single phenomenon. Hence, the concept of secularization offers an incomplete framework for analyzing what actually takes place when old and new symbolic categories are combined.

In defining secularization in the Third World context, one must also consider the problem of symbolic realism (see Bellah 1970:89–96). How do members of these groups see their own religious claims vis-à-vis the emerging secular society? Berger (1966:8) suggests that recent research on religion often takes for granted the predominance of a universal "secularized consciousness," or total acceptance of a scientific reality, without considering the possibility that for some people the standard of cognitive validity may be the sacred—a "nonscientific reality that has been lost to modern man." The quest to regain a sense of the sacred through religious, cultural, and national identity is a common response to social change in the Third World.

Secularization is often assumed to be a linear and uniform process, with predictable economic and social changes accompanying industrialization viewed as equally applicable to the cultural domain. In fact, however, many new religious movements in the Third World react to industrial change and the new social orders accompanying it by seeking to create a sense of unity and group identity characteristic of preindustrial communities. Elsewhere, I have referred to this process as the impossible arcadian wish to return to old values and a simpler form of life (Jules-Rosette 1979:219–229). In this case, the growth of modern institutions results not just in "secularizing" but also in an effort to "resacralize" Third World societies through new religious groups and nationalistic political movements.

Liberation theology, particularly in Latin America, is one such product of this process of secularization in the Third World (see Brown 1974:269–282). Using this approach, theologians operating within established Catholic and Protestant traditions view the Bible as a revolutionary book which documents the process of religious liberation and the goal of freedom. Their objective is to redefine the sacred as a set of moral principles which should be invoked in the wider society to reduce social inequities and injustice. Although liberation theology shares some features with millenarian movements, it differs in its direct equation of secular goals such as social justice with religious ideals. Liberation theology is both a product of and a reaction to the worldwide process of secularization and the spread of modern industrial structures to all corners of the globe.[11]

The example of liberation theology suggests that secular goals directly influence the formation and growth of Third World religious movements. Accordingly, it is important to analyze how tendencies toward secularization have actually shaped new religious movements in the Third World. One method used to explore this problem is to examine tensions in the relationship between church and state in Third World nations. In many African nations, such as Zaire, Zambia, and Malawi, the growth of new religions takes place under close government scrutiny, and many movements (e.g., the Watch Tower spin-offs) are outlawed as threats to nation building. A similar reaction may be noted in the response of the Vietnamese state to the Buddhist and Taoist secret societies that arose under authoritarian rule (see Sacks 1971:44–66). In all of these cases, new religions are seen as potential sources of trouble—capable of weakening civic political commitments by virtue of their ability to mobilize masses of people in activities that are not directly supervised or controlled by the state. Political forces attempt to control and thereby restrict the sphere of influence of the new religious movements in a secularizing society.

There are currently more new religions in non-Western nations than ever before, and their fragmentation may be viewed as a characteristic of secularization. Many Third World religious movements (whether separatist break-offs, liberation theologies within established religious organizations, or independent developments) are influenced by contact with diverse "unorthodox" Western movements. Government persecution creates further external pressures toward schism, but so is fragmentation an internal characteristic of many of these movements, particularly in Africa (see Barrett 1968:223–224; Wilson 1982:142). Internally, conditions of plural culture contact and the failure to stabilize leadership roles promote schism, a by-product of the decline of customary religious authority and the transference of many of the functions of religion to the secular domain. This suggests that subjective secularization, or the manifestation of secularization as a psychological orientation, may be less prevalent in the Third World than structural changes resulting in new tensions in the relationship between religion and society.

A counterbalancing tendency in the secularization process is one toward ecumenical cooperation among the new religious groups. Martin West (1975:142–170) analyzes the rise of ecumenism among South Africa's indigenous churches based upon two large-scale surveys of these movements. Unlike Janosik, he notes efforts toward cooperation among these groups, particularly in education and financial programs, if not on the level of doctrine and ritual. Similar tendencies have appeared among indigenous churches in Zambia and East Africa. Some scholars have argued that this process of cooperation ultimately results in the secularization of doctrine and leadership structures within new religious movements. In describing an African spirit-type movement, for example, Angela Cheater (1981:45) has argued that pragmatic concerns of economic success and secular social ties have actually diminished the scope of the sacred within the group. She sees cooperation with other groups in the larger society as a major force in modifying the doctrinal and organizational structure of the religious groups. This argument suggests that social differentiation and change may eventually cause subjective secularization as well.

Individual Third World religious movements have thus adopted a variety of psychological and cultural responses to the process of secularization. These responses may be summarized in terms of four basic tendencies, according to which several movement types can be classified:

1. *Traditionalism* retains the myth of an ideal past and is often accompanied by an attempt to reconstruct an authoritative religious tradition. The persistence of traditional religious forms in Africa and Asia within the contemporary context are cases in point.

2. *Revitalization* introduces new concepts to regenerate the old. On the psychological level, this response is perceived as *comprehensive* and seeks an explanation of the sacred in both old and new terms. African indigenous churches and Buddhist revitalization movements are examples.

3. *Syncretism* is the process through which former definitions of the sacred are combined with innovative patterns to produce a satisfying definition of the whole and an expression of core values which is both in line with the past and adaptive to new institutions.[12] Santeria, Latin American Pentecostalism, and many African movements exhibit this process.

4. *Millenarianism* creates a myth of the ideal future which attempts to construct a new definition of the sacred and a new social order in ways that yield pragmatically effective results for members of new

movements. New African movements and, to a lesser extent, liberation theologies use this approach.

Although these four options do not exhaust empirical movement types, they point to ways in which new religious movements in the Third World have attempted to redefine the sacred in a secularizing society. In some instances, a direct redefinition of political and social values is involved, as in the case of millenarianism and liberation theology. In other instances, the sacred is revalidated through efforts to preserve customary notions of community and conventional expressive symbols, as evidenced in revitalistic, evangelical, and spirit-type movements. In the latter case, a resacralization of dominant traditional symbols occurs, often in reaction to the decline of religious values and institutions in the rest of society.

In spite of the sacralization process, some scholars like Robin Horton (1971:107) have argued that religion in Third World societies will ultimately move in an increasingly secular direction in terms of doctrine and organization and will survive primarily "as a way of communion but not as a system of explanation, prediction, and control." At present, however, a more prevalent trend in Third World religious movements is the attempt to create cohesive forms of community in which religious values are more coherent and exercise a larger influence on social life. This tendency also appears to characterize new religious movements that emphasize community and a personal idiom of expression in the West.

PROSPECT FOR FUTURE RESEARCH

One of the major research problems confronting those who study religion in the Third World is the appearance of articles in disparate anthropological, sociological, and area studies journals, thereby scattering documentation of new studies and making comparisons difficult.[13] Much of the best recent research on the topic has not been published in U.S. journals devoted to the scientific study of religion, such as *JSSR* and *Sociological Analysis*, which have been heavily oriented toward research on Western religion. Furthermore, many studies of Third World religious movements do not contain a systematic comparative treatment of secularization but instead focus on the details of individual cases. Such case studies, however, are not counterproductive since much ground-breaking research remains to be done on new Third World groups and on non-Western religious movements generally. There is also a critical need to define the major conceptual issues related to the emergence and spread of new religious movements outside of the West. Apart from Wilson's (1973 and 1982) studies, and a handful of continent-focused collections on new African or Asian religions (Thomsen 1973; Barrett 1968; Spencer 1971; Bond et al. 1979), relatively few attempts have been made to bring these new developments together from either a regional or an international comparative perspective.

It has been proposed that more refined comparative analysis will enable "the historian and ethnographer to make better bricks" in building their accounts of Third World religions (Wilson 1973:502). Conversely, there is an urgent need for more systematic and careful use of basic ethnographic data in structuring comparative studies. Specifically, many of the studies of Third World religions lack a model for including a phenomenology of the sacred from the perspective of members of these societies.[14] I have attempted to demonstrate that the processes of fragmentation and redefinition of leadership roles and goals in the new religions of the Third World take place under unique cultural conditions. These processes are often counterbalanced by attempts to redefine the sacred as part of a new search for collective identity and a reinterpretation of tradition. Paradoxically, these processes may involve a challenge to definitions of the sacred in Western religious traditions—a challenge, however, that is not always synonymous with secularization.

The cultural transmission of new Eastern religions to the West in both direct and diluted forms renders these research questions even more complex and pressing. Parallel developments, such as the transplanting of U.S. movements like the People's Temple to the Third World (see Richardson 1980:239–253), suggest that centralizing and consolidating research efforts on Western and Third World religions is a both pragmatic and theoretical necessity. Speculating on the future of new religions in Africa, Asia, and Latin America may provide social scientists with not only a mirror but also a new model for interpreting what has happened in the West. The rise of new non-Western theocracies, such as that in Iran, and the resacralization of the state appear to present challenging alternatives to the case for secularization that has been described for the postindustrial West. Paralleling Berger's (1967:128) notion of subjective secularization is a new subjective sense of the sacred contained in the innovative cultural combinations of many Third World religious movements. By suggesting new ways in which a sense of the sacred may be reintegrated into contemporary life, these movements offer an empirical challenge to theories that propose that secularization is an essential feature of the incorporation of Third World communities into the industrial and postindustrial social order.

NOTES

1. Over the past two decades, in excess of thirty articles have been published on cross-cultural research in the *Journal for the Scientific Study* of *Religion*. Of these articles, less than half have been devoted to Third World and non-Western religions. An additional six articles have been published on the topic of black religion in the United States according to the *Journal's* twenty-year index. (See Palmer, Michael D., with George Kier, *Journal for the Scientific Study of Religion: 20-Year Index, 1961–1981*, especially pp. 30–32.)

2. Durkheim considered the concept of the sacred to refer to the symbolic, categorical, and moral aspects of social life. His view has been refined and reemphasized in contemporary studies of the social institutions that support religious world views and concepts of the sacred (see Berger 1967:33–34).

3. Peter Berger's presidential address to the Society for the Scientific Study of Religion (1966:3–16) summarizes the influence of the secularization thesis on contemporary theology before the impact of new religious movements and the rise of the new evangelical Christianity in the United States had been fully assessed by researchers. His concerns have been reflected and debated in a large number of articles published in the *Journal for the Scientific Study of Religion*. Larry Shiner (1967:207–220) presents an excellent overview of the problems of using the concept of secularization in empirical research. Although many new empirical developments have taken place since Shiner's article was published, the methodological issues he proposes are still fundamental to the discussion of secularization.

4. The societies of Latin America, Asia, and Africa which are just entering the stages of industrial and advanced industrial development are generally considered to make up the "Third World." Recently, economists and sociologists have divided developing nations into Third and Fourth worlds based on average capital income (see Goldthorpe 1975:4; Graburn 1976:1–2). Another distinction has been made between Third World nations as industrializing states and Fourth World peoples who are underprivileged or exploited minorities within both advanced industrial and Third World nations (Berreman 1972:385–414). Clearly, this issue poses complex definitional problems which cannot be resolved here.

5. For example, the Watch Tower movement that began in 1908 under Elliot Kamwana can be viewed as an ephemeral millenarian response to the colonial regime of Nyasaland (see Barrett 1968:29). Although this movement resurfaced later in other forms, it never assumed the characteristics of the Zambian group described by Long.

6. The term *Zionist* as used here was derived from the activities of John Alexander Dowie's evangelical church, which originated in Zion City, Illinois. This church began missionary activities in South Africa at the turn of the century and baptized its first group in Johannesburg in 1904 (Sundkler 1961:48).

7. Piker's (1972:211–299) analysis of Thai religion is one of the few studies of non-Western religion in the *Journal for the Scientific Study of Religion* which focus on an anthropological definition of the categories of religious experience and their internal coherence. Such studies are essential in order to lay the groundwork for further comparative studies of Third World religious groups. In his methodological discussion of the new ethnography and the study of religion, John Saliba (1974:145–159) makes a similar point.

8. Along these lines, Ted Solomon (1977:1–14) suggests that the transference of concepts of the sacred to the secular domain and the bureaucratization of religious movements may be productively analyzed through the new religions of Japan including Sokka Gakkai, Rissho Kosei-kai, and PL Kyodan. These groups have been politically active and have used Nichiren Soshu Buddhism to reshape the expression of Japanese nationalism.

9. This process is distinct from the decline of the social influence of religion (see Wilson 1982:149). Instead, the concept of transferal takes Parsons's notion of social differentiation a step further. When applied to Third World religious movements, it suggests that these groups retain aspects of customary religion and newly introduced cultural elements without being associated exclusively with either alternative.

10. Revitalistic and millenarian movements in Africa, as well as Hindu and Buddhist reform movements in India and Burma respectively, have exhibited this close unity between the sacred and secular domains because of the influence of customary religions on the new organizations. In these cases, political ramifications may not always be the result of secularization but may instead constitute carry-overs from the past. See also Spencer (1971:3–13).

11. Theologians such as James Cone (1970) have also applied the concepts of religion of the oppressed and liberation theology to black American religion. See also Banks (1969:263–268).

12. Robin Horton (1971:106–107) argues that members of the Aladura Church in Nigeria are able to reconcile custom with Christianity by focusing on those aspects of Western religion which are most consistent with their own beliefs, for example, faith-healing, spiritualism, and occultism. They thereby minimize the discrepancy between Western religions and their own traditions through innovative strategies of interpretation.

13. Much firsthand research on the new religions of Africa and Asia has been published in journals of area studies. Detailed analyses of the content and structure of non-Western religions often appear in anthropological publications. The *Journal for the Scientific Study of Religion* provides an outlet in which some of these studies could appear together. This might foster further, more comprehensive comparative research.

14. Egon Bittner (1963:928–940) suggests a model for the study of social movements which incorporates both their structural features and the motivations of participants. It might be productive to use such an approach as a point of departure for redefining the sacred and the process of secularization in a manner that accounts more fully for the subjective categories and assumptions of group members.

REFERENCES

Ames, Michael M.
  1964   "Magical-Animism and Buddhism: A Structural Analysis of the Sinhalese Religious System," *Journal of Asian Studies* 23 (June):21–52.
Banks, Walter R.
  1969   "Two Impossible Revolutions? Black Power and Church Power," *Journal for the Scientific Study of Religion* 8 (Fall):263–268.
Barrett, David B.
  1968   *Schism and Renewal in Africa: An Analysis of Six Thousand Contemporary Religious Movements.* Nairobi: Oxford University Press.
Bellah, Robert
  1970   "Christianity and Symbolic Realism," *Journal for the Scientific Study of Religion* 9 (Summer):89–96.
Berger, Peter
  1966   "A Sociological View of the Secularization of Theology," *Journal for the Scientific Study of Religion* 6 (Spring):3–16.
  1967   *The Sacred Canopy: Elements of a Sociological Theory of Religion.* Garden City, N.Y.: Anchor Books.
Berreman, D. G.
  1972   "Race, Caste, and Other Invidious Distinctions," *Race* 13:385–414.
Biebuyck, M. O.
  1957   "La Société Kuma Face au Kitawala," *Zaire* 11:7–40.
Bittner, Egon
  1963   "Radicalism and the Organization of Radical Movements," *American Sociological Review* 28:928–940.
Bond, George, Walton Johnson, and Sheila S. Walter
  1979   *African Christianity: Patterns of Religious Continuity.* New York: Academic Press.
Brown, Robert McAfee
  1974   "Reflections on 'Liberation Theology,' " *Religion in Life* 43 (Fall):269–282.
Cheater, Angela
  1981   "The Social Organisation of Religious Difference Among the Vapostori weMaranke," *Social Analysis* 7:24–49.

Cone, James H.
  1970   *A Black Theology of Liberation.* New York: Lippincott.
Daneel, Marthinus L.
  1971   *Old and New in Southern Shona Independent Churches.* Vol. 1: *Back-
           ground and Rise of the Major Movements.* The Hague: Mouton.
Demerath, N. J., III, and Phillip E. Hammond
  1969   *Religion in Social Context.* New York: Random House.
Douglas, Mary
  1966   *Purity and Danger: An Analysis of Concepts of Pollution and Taboo.*
           New York: Praeger Publishers.
Durkheim, Emile
  1915   *The Elementary Forms of Religious Life.* Joseph Ward Swain, trans.
           London: Allen and Unwin.
Eister, Allan W.
  1967   "Toward a Radical Critique of Church-Sect Typologizing: Com-
           ment on 'Some critical observations on the church-sect dimen-
           sion,' " *Journal for the Scientific Study of Religion* 6 (Spring):85–90.
Goldthorpe, J. E.
  1975   *The Sociology of the Third World: Disparity and Involvement.* Cam-
           bridge: Cambridge University Press.
Graburn, Nelson H. H.
  1976   *Ethnic and Tourist Arts: Cultural Expressions from the Fourth World.*
           Berkeley, Los Angeles, London: University of California Press.
Horton, Robin
  1971   "African Conversion," *Africa* 41 (April):85–108.
Janosik, Robert J.
  1974   "Religion and Political Involvement: A Study of Black African
           Sects," *Journal for the Scientific Study of Religion* 13 (Summer):161–
           175.
Johnson, Benton
  1971   "Church and Sect Revisited," *Journal for the Scientific Study of
           Religion* 10 (Summer):124–137.
Jules-Rosette, Bennetta, ed.
  1979   *The New Religions of Africa.* Norwood, N.J.: Ablex Publishing.
Kitzinger, Sheila
  1969   "Protest and Mysticism: The Rastafari Cult of Jamaica, *Journal for
           the Scientific Study of Religion* 8 (Fall):240–262.
Lanternari, Vittorio
  1963   *Religions of the Oppressed. A Study of Modern Messianic Cults.* Lisa
           Sergio, trans. New York: Alfred A. Knopf.
Long, Norman
  1968   *Social Change and the Individual: A Study of the Social and Religious
           Responses to Innovation in a Zambian Rural Community.* Manchester:
           Manchester University Press.
Murphree, Marshall W.
  1969   *Christianity and the Shona.* London: The Athlone Press.

Nash, Manning
    1971   "Buddhist Revitalization in the Nation State: The Burmese Experi-
            ence." *In* Robert F. Spencer, ed., *Religion and Change in Contempo-
            rary Asia.* Minneapolis: University of Minnesota Press. Pp. 105–
            122.
O'Connor, Mary
    1979   "Two Kinds of Religious Movements Among the Mayo Indians
            of Sonora, Mexico," *Journal for the Scientific Study of Religion* 18
            (Fall):260–268.
Palmer, Michael D., with George Kier, comps.
    1981   *Journal for the Scientific Study of Religion: 20-year Index, 1961–1981.*
Parsons, Talcott
    1963   Introduction. *In* Max Weber, *The Sociology of Religion.* Ephraim
            Fischoff, trans. Boston: Beacon Press. Pp. xix–lxvii.
    1966   *Societies: Evolutionary and Comparative Perspectives.* Englewood
            Cliffs, N.J.: Prentice-Hall.
Patterson, Orlando
    1964   "Ras Tafari: The Cult of Outcasts," *New Society* 12 (November):92–
            118.
Peel, J. D. Y.
    1968   *Aladura: A Religious Movement Among the Yoruba.* London: Interna-
            tional African Institute.
Piker, Steven
    1972   "The Problem of Consistency in Thai Religion," *Journal for the
            Scientific Study of Religion* 11 (Fall):211–229.
Richardson, James T.
    1980   "People's Temple and Jonestown: A Corrective Comparison and
            Critique," *Journal for the Scientific Study of Religion* 19 (Fall):239–253.
Rosberg, Carl G., and John Nottingham
    1966   *The Myth of "Mau Mau" Nationalism in Kenya.* New York: Praeger
            Publishers.
Sacks, Milton
    1971   "Some Religious Components in Vietnamese Politics." *In* Robert
            F. Spencer, ed., *Religion and Change in Contemporary Asia.* Min-
            neapolis: University of Minnesota Press. Pp. 44–66.
Saliba, John A.
    1974   "The New Ethnography and the Study of Religion," *Journal for
            the Scientific Study of Religion* 13 (Summer):145–159.
Shiner, Larry E.
    1967   "The Concept of Secularization in Empirical Research," *Journal for
            the Scientific Study of Religion* 6:207–220.
Solomon, Ted J.
    1977   "The Response of Three New Religions to the Crisis in the
            Japanese Value System," *Journal for the Scientific Study of Religion*
            16 (Spring):1–14.

Spencer, Robert F., ed.
    1971   *Religion and Change in Contemporary Asia*. Minneapolis: University of Minnesota Press.
Spiro, Melford E.
    1967   *Burmese Supernaturalism*. Englewood Cliffs, N.J.: Prentice-Hall.
Sundkler, Bengt G. M.
    1961   *Bantu Prophets in South Africa*. London: International African Institute.
    1976   *Zulu Zion and Some Swazi Zionists*. London: Oxford University Press.
Thomsen, Harry
    1973   *The New Religions of Japan*. Rutland, Vt.: Charles E. Tuttle.
Turner, Harold
    1974   "Tribal religious movements, new," *The New Encyclopaedia Britannica* 18:697–705.
Weber, Max
    1963   *The Sociology of Religion*. Ephraim Fischoff, trans. Boston: Beacon Press.
West, Martin
    1975   *Bishops and Prophets in a Black City: African Independent Churches in Soweto, Johannesburg*. Cape Town: David Philip.
Willems, Emilio
    1966   "Validation of Authority in Pentecostal Sects of Chile and Brazil," *Journal for the Scientific Study of Religion* 6 (Fall):253–258.
Wilson, Bryan R.
    1973   *Magic and Millennium: A Sociological Study of Religious Movements Among Tribal and Third-World Peoples*. New York: Harper and Row.
    1979   "The Return of the Sacred," *Journal for the Scientific Study of Religion* 18 (Fall):268–280.
    1982   *Religion in Sociological Perspective*. Oxford: Oxford University Press.

PART FIVE

Private Life and the Sacred

XV

Religion and Psychological Well-Being

Donald Capps

The idea that religion has something to do with psychological well-being is hardly new. It saturates William James's discussion of sick and healthy mindedness in *The Varieties of Religious Experience* (1958: 76–139); it influences Gordon Allport's discussion of the role of religion in contributing to personal growth and maturity (1950, 1955); and it underlies Erik Erikson's view that religion reinforces the individual's sense of basic trust (1959:64–65). What is relatively new is the effort to clarify the relationship between religion and psychological well-being through empirical investigation (Hadaway 1978; Hadaway and Roof 1978; McNamara and St. George 1979; Steinitz 1980; Bahr and Martin, 1983).

These efforts, however, have been seriously impeded by the imprecision of the term *psychological well-being*. In a recent unpublished paper, Arthur St. George and Patrick McNamara (1983) cite as examples of studies of the effect of religion on psychological well-being studies of anomie, self-esteem, individual integration, psychiatric impairment, positive adjustment to old age, proneness to committing suicide, alcohol abuse, and marital adjustment. Undoubtedly, these are all relevant to psychological well-being, but they do not reflect a clearly articulated theory or concept of psychological well-being. St. George and McNamara recognize this, and therefore suggest using recent "quality-of-life" studies to bring the relationship of religion to psychological well-being into coherent theoretical focus.

QUALITY-OF-LIFE STUDIES

As St. George and McNamara point out, the major quality-of-life study (Campbell, Converse, and Rodgers 1976; Campbell 1981) gave only cursory attention to the relationship of religion to quality-of-life factors. Another important study (Andrews and Withey 1976) did not even utilize their two religiosity indicators in assessing "specific life concerns" such as education, friends and associates, home, leisure time, family, self, and interpersonal relations. Furthermore, Campbell and his associates compounded the problem by misinterpreting their data, erroneously suggesting a *negative* association of religiosity and quality of life, when in fact their data supported a positive, albeit quite small, relationship (Hadaway 1978; Hadaway and Roof 1978). Subsequent studies (Chalfant, Beckley, and Palmer 1981; McNamara and St. George 1979; Hadaway and Roof 1978) have found a small but positive relationship between religion and various quality-of-life indicators, such as global happiness, excitement in life, satisfaction with family life, satisfaction with community, friendships, perceived state of physical and mental health, and marital satisfaction. Hadaway and Roof found that religion explains more of the variance between people of high and low well-being than do number of friends, marital status, age, education, health, income, and race, whereas St. George and McNamara found that religious effects do a better job of explaining the variance for blacks than for whites, and for black men than for black women.

Use of quality-of-life research to assess the relationship of religion and psychological well-being holds promise because it includes many more personal and psychosocial factors than were included in previous studies. But, as St. George and McNamara point out, the original quality-of-life studies lacked adequate measures of religiosity or failed to employ them in analyzing people's sense of well-being in specific areas where some impact might be expected.

Other researchers have begun to solve these problems by using more complex measures of religiosity. Lucy Steinitz (1980), for example, used four religious measures (frequency of church attendance, strength of denominational affiliation, confidence in organized religion, and belief in life after death) in her study of the relation between religion and well-being in old age. She found that belief in life after death was the strongest and most discriminating predictor of well-being. Frequency of church attendance was associated with well-being, but more because it was an indicator of physical health than for its religiosity per se. Since relationships between well-being and denominational affiliation and confidence in organized religion were negligible, Steinitz's study suggests that the "meaning" dimension of religion may be more important than the "belonging" dimension for psychological well-being.

Hadaway and Roof's study supports this conclusion. Using "importance of religious faith" as their meaning indicator, church membership and attendance as belonging indicators, and sense of the "worthwhileness of life" or "life satisfaction" as their quality of life measure, they found that religious belonging is not nearly as good a predictor of quality of life as religious meaning. They believe this is because church attendance, church membership, number of friends, and marital status all imply some degree of social integration, whereas importance of faith represents a more subjective, personal resource: "Since life satisfaction itself is a psychological trait, and one which is interrelated with other aspects of personal meaning, the smaller relationship between church attendance and worthwhileness of life is not surprising" (303).

SPIRITUAL WELL-BEING STUDIES

Another research area of considerable relevance to the religion and psychological well-being issue is spiritual well-being (Moberg 1979). Blaikie and Kelsen (see Moberg 1979:133–151) suggest that spiritual well-being is a subtype within the larger category of *existential* well-being. Existential well-being involves a sense of meaning and purpose, a secure and stable identity, and a feeling of belonging. For existential well-being, "individuals need to know what to do and why, who they are, and where they belong" (p. 137). For Blaikie and Kelsen, spiritual well-being is a "type of existential well-being which incorporates some reference to the supernatural, the sacred, or the transcendental" (p. 137). Since psychological well-being is virtually synonymous with existential well-being, spiritual well-being may be viewed as a type of psychological well-being, one of critical importance for the study of the relationship of religion and psychological well-being.

Among the various studies of spiritual well-being in the volume Moberg edited, his own study of the development of social indicators of spiritual life for quality-of-life research is particularly valuable (1979:1–13). This study indicates that 80 percent or more of the persons who are sure they personally have spiritual well-being believe the following characteristics are either essential or present: peace with God, inner peace, faith in Christ, good morals, faith in people, and helpfulness toward others. Only a minority of persons with spiritual well-being felt that good physical health and being successful in life are associated with spiritual well-being. The majority of persons attesting to spiritual well-being attends church regularly, and believes that organized religion helps more than it hinders the acquisition of spiritual well-being. But it should also be noted that more persons credited friends and personal prayer with influencing their spiritual well-being than credited church attendance.

One virtue of the "spiritual well-being" literature is that it recognizes the need for theoretical discussion of what well-being involves. But the sheer diversity of theoretical approaches represented in Moberg's volume indicates that there is little agreement as to how to initiate such theoretical discussion. Some authors turn to traditional religious and theological concepts of spirituality (for example, Christian and Hindu mysticism, and biblical concepts of spiritual well-being). Others explore conceptions of spiritual well-being in specific religious groups, such as Catholic devotionalism, Mormonism, the Mennonites, and new religious movements. Still others turn to contemporary sociological theory, including reference and role theory (Garrett) and secularization theory (Barker). Still others use psychological concepts, including concepts of identity, the self, life stages, and personal maturity. None of these latter studies, however, makes any significant use of the psychological theories behind these concepts. This is understandable, of course, because the authors in these cases are sociologists, not psychologists.

THE SELF AND PSYCHOLOGICAL WELL-BEING

In the following pages, I will take up one of these psychological concepts—the self—to provide a more adequate theoretical foundation for the relationship of religion to psychological well-being. The concept of the self is an important issue in this regard because there is broad consensus among psychologists that a requisite for psychological well-being is a coherent sense of self. Erik Erikson's theory of the self is especially useful here because for him a coherent self-image has an ultimately religious grounding.

For Erikson, any consideration of the self needs to begin with the fact that we are composed of "various selves which make up our composite Self" (1968:217). Psychological well-being depends on our having a "reasonably coherent Self," where our various selves are held together in a coherent "sense of I."

> There are constant and often shocklike transitions between these selves: consider the nude body self in the dark or suddenly exposed in the light; consider the clothed self among friends or in the company of higher-ups or lower-downs; consider the just awakened drowsy self or the one stepping refreshed out of the surf or the one overcome by retching and fainting; the body self in sexual excitement or in a rage; the competent self and the impotent one; the one on horseback, the one in the dentist's chair, and the one chained and tortured—by men who also say "I." It takes, indeed, a healthy personality for the "I" to be able to speak out all of these conditions in such a way that at any given moment it can testify to a reasonably coherent Self. (1968:217)

Thus psychological well-being requires a coherent sense of self. This means sensing that "I am the center of awareness in a universe of experience in which I have a coherent identity" (1968:220).

But Erikson also goes beyond a concern for psychological well-being, and shows how a coherent self-image is necessary for spiritual well-being. In his view, our sense of being a coherent self is ultimately confirmed by our perception of God as an eternal center of awareness: "The counterplayer of the 'I' therefore can be, strictly speaking, only the deity who . . . is Himself endowed with an eternal numinousness certified by all 'I's' who acknowledge this gift [of self-awareness]. That is why God, when Moses asked Him who should he say had called him, answered: 'I AM THAT I AM' " (1968:220). Thus, a coherent sense of self is essential to psychological well-being, and its confirmation by God—the Eternal Self—is essential to spiritual well-being. One author in Moberg's volume who articulates this view is William Garrett, who develops H. Richard Niebuhr's emphasis on the "disclosiveness" of the "Divine Other" wherein "the self knows himself to be known from beginning to end and discovers himself to be valued by the activity of the universal valuer" (1979:80). For Garrett, as for Erikson, awareness of oneself as known and valued by the Divine Other is essential for spiritual well-being.

Another self theory that is relevant to psychological well-being and also has direct bearing on the major theme of this book (the sacred in a secular world) is Heinz Kohut's views concerning the narcissistic self. Many psychoanalysts agree that the narcissistic personality is the predominant character type seen in therapy today, replacing the obsessive-compulsive type of an earlier era. The narcissistic personality structure has its origins in infancy and very early childhood; unlike the obsessive-compulsive type, it is preoedipal. In infancy, one becomes the object of considerable attention and admiration. When expectations of continued admiration go unmet in early childhood, the frustration this causes results in internalized rage against those from whom one anticipated admiration, especially the mother, and the formation of a "grandiose self" that continues in fantasy to merit and receive adulation and acclaim. This grandiose self forms the core of the narcissistic personality, whose major characteristics are (1) resistance to being subject to the claims of others on oneself, (2) a shallow emotional life to protect oneself from further emotional hurt (narcissistic injury), (3) manipulation of the impressions one makes on others, and (4) inability to acknowledge one's finitude (see Lasch, 1979).

These are characteristics of "primitive narcissism." But Kohut also proposes that narcissism can be transformed into a more mature form of narcissism. By exploring his views on transformed narcissism (1978:427–460) we will be able to make the following important points concerning religion and psychological well-being:

1. If religion exerts less influence on the social order but retains its influence on personal life, as various secularization theories suggest (Wilson 1982; Luckman 1967), this "privatization" of religion provides a favorable context for an increasingly close association of religion and narcissism. We would predict that religious institutions capitalizing on this trend will be those responding to the interests of the narcissistic self. This prediction is not made with cynical intent because, as our discussion will show, the narcissistic self has features clearly compatible with the Judeo-Christian meaning system, though not so compatible with traditional styles of "belonging," especially as articulated in liturgical language.

2. The survival of the sacred in a highly secular world will depend to a significant degree on whether the narcissistic self is not deposed but transformed. Religious institutions and movements would be better advised to devote themselves to its transformation than to attack it as morally or spiritually bankrupt. A transformed narcissism may provide the foundation not only for psychological well-being but also for such spiritual well-being as can realistically be expected in a secular world.

3. The previously cited findings concerning the relationship between religion and spiritual well-being can be understood in terms of Kohut's notion of transformed narcissism. This concept provides

a theoretical foundation, therefore, for the study of religion and well-being.

4. In popular discussions of narcissism in the 1970s, there was much emphasis on the narcissism of younger members of our society—the so-called "me generation." But the narcissistic self is not limited to the younger generation or to any specific cohort. Indeed, if it is especially problematic for any single generation, it is the old. The need for a transformed narcissism is especially acute for the post-retirement adults.

To support these four important points, we need to take a closer look at Kohut's views on the narcissistic self.

TRANSFORMED NARCISSISM AND
PSYCHOLOGICAL WELL-BEING

Narcissism, which psychoanalysis defines as the "libidinal cathexis of the self" or "self-love," is usually thought of as a more primitive or immature form of love than "objective love" or "love for others." Kohut notes that, in psychoanalytic theory, narcissism is neither pathological nor obnoxious. Yet "there exists an understandable tendency [among psychoanalysts] to look at it with a negatively toned evaluation as soon as the field of theory is left" (1978:427). Kohut attributes this negative evaluation to an improper intrusion of the altruistic value system of Western civilization into clinical practice. It does not derive from an "objective assessment of either the developmental position or adaptive value of narcissism" (p. 427). He argues that the clinical objective ought not be the replacing of self-love with object love, but a working toward a transformed narcissism, "a redistribution of the patient's narcissistic libido" and "the integration of the primitive psychological structures of narcissism into the mature personality" (p. 428). The opportunity to initiate this transformation typically arises when an individual has suffered "narcissistic injury" (for example, a threat to self-esteem, or rejection, humiliation, or shame). Such experiences can become the occasion for "harnessing" the narcissistic energies and transforming them into new and more differentiated psychological configurations. The narcissistic self's desire to be admired, affirmed, and appreciated is not challenged, but the primitive narcissism of exhibitionism and grandiose fantasies is replaced with a more mature narcissism. Kohut cites the following capacities as expressions of transformed narcissism: (1) personal creativity, (2) capacity for empathy, (3) capacity to contemplate one's own impermanence, (4) a sense of humor, and (5) wisdom. I will comment on each of these capacities because, together, they reflect psychological well-being.

PERSONAL CREATIVITY

Kohut acknowledges that a major impetus behind creativity is the narcissistic desire for fame or acclaim. But he contends that creative activity itself needs to be considered among the *transformations* of narcissism. Narcissism is involved in creative activity because the "object" being created is viewed as an extension of oneself, and ambitions one holds for oneself (for example, self acclaim) are transferred to the object. Creative persons "are attempting to re-create a perfection that formerly was directly an attribute of their own" (p. 450). This is not object-love because the product of one's creativity is related to as part of a narcissistically experienced world: "The well established fact . . . that creative people tend to alternate during periods of productivity between phases when they think extremely highly of their work and phases when they are convinced that it has no value is a sure indication that the work is cathected with a form of narcissistic libido. . . . They do not relate to their work in the give-and-take mutuality that characterizes object love" (p. 450).

EMPATHY

Kohut points out that the "groundwork for our ability to obtain access to another person's mind is laid by the fact that, in our earliest mental organization, the feelings, actions and behavior of the mother prepares us for the recognition that to a large extent the basic inner experiences of other people remain similar to our own. Our first perception of the manifestations of another person's feelings, wishes, and thoughts occurred within the framework of a narcissistic conception of the world" (p. 451). But unfortunately in the adult, nonempathic forms of cognition and perception have become dominant. Effective empathy among adults entails the recovery of one's "original empathic mode of reality perception" while, at the same time, emancipating it from conflicts that were part of this original experience. Such empathy draws on the narcissistic experience of knowing the "other" through being recognized oneself. But this is a transformed narcissism because the focal point is the empathy learned in this experience, not one's original experience of recognition by one's mother.

ACKNOWLEDGE FINITENESS OF ONE'S EXISTENCE

Kohut says that our capacity to acknowledge the finiteness of our existence and to act in accordance with this painful discovery may well be our "greatest psychological achievement, despite the fact that it can often be demonstrated that a manifest acceptance of transience may go hand in hand with covert denials" (p. 454). The acknowledgment of our finiteness is associated with narcissism because it entails an emotional acceptance of the fact that "the self which is cathected with narcissistic libido is finite in time" (p. 454). Yet it is not simply a victory of reason and objectivity over the claims of narcissism, but the creation of a higher form of narcissism. Those who have achieved this outlook on life do not display resignation and hopelessness but a quiet pride and assurance. Kohut calls this a new "cosmic narcissism" which has transcended the bounds of the individual.

CAPACITY FOR HUMOR

Kohut suggests that when a person responds with humor to the recognition of the unattainable realities opposing the assertions of the narcissistic self, we may assume that a transformation of narcissism has occurred. Any circumstance that frustrates one's desire for admiration or approval may occasion humor, which reflects greater self-possession and personal maturity than the rage or resentment of primary narcissism. When addressing the narcissistic desire to overcome death, for example, humor does not present "a picture of grandiosity and elation but that of a quiet inner triumph with an admixture of undenied melancholy" (p. 458). This "quiet inner triumph" is an expression of transformed narcissism. It is not a shift from self-love to object-love, but the capacity of the narcissistic self to accept the frustration of its self-interest. Kohut acknowledges that there may be disregard for one's own self-interest in object-love. But when disregard for self is expressed through humor, we may assume that what is involved here is narcissistic love in the process of transformation.

WISDOM

Kohut says that "wisdom is achieved largely through man's ability to overcome his unmodified narcissism, and it rests on his acceptance of the limitations of his physical, intellectual and emotional powers" (p. 458). If humor concerns the limitations posed by the real world, wisdom addresses our own limitations. For Kohut, wisdom may be defined as a "stable attitude of the personality toward life and the world" (p. 458). It is attained relatively late in life because it depends on the prior acceptance of the inevitability of death and the attainment of humor, both of which are not normally realized until one becomes a mature adult. Wisdom is based in cosmic narcissism because it involves "a sense of supraindividual participation in the world," and in humor, because it involves the transformation of the humor of one's maturity "into a sense of proportion, a touch of irony toward the achievements of individual existence." This transformation is not merely a resigned attitude toward one's physical, emotional, and cognitive limitations, but instead reflects the "ultimate insight" that human achievements pale in comparison to the supreme powers of nature. (Of course, humanity's power to destroy with nuclear weaponry rivals the destructive powers of nature. Still, the wise response to this new state of affairs is not to claim human supremacy over nature [as unmodified narcissism would do] but to recognize that with the acquisition of such destructive capabilities the physical, emotional, and cognitive limitations of the human species are even more self-evident.)

Kohut concludes that "such wholesome transformations of narcissism" are a "more genuine and valid result of therapy than the patient's precarious compliance with demands for a change of his narcissism into object love" (p. 460). Similarly, if religion is to contribute to psychological well-being, its goal is like that of therapy: not demanding a change of narcissism into object-love, but supporting a transformed narcissism. To make this case, we need to consider that religion today functions in a secular context. Any consideration of the role of religion in fostering psychological well-being must include this fact.

TRANSFORMED NARCISSISM AND THE
RECOVERY OF THE SACRED

Larry E. Shiner (1967) has identified five types of secularization concepts in sociological literature. 1. *Decline of religion:* previously accepted symbols, doctrines, and institutions lose their prestige and influence. 2. *Conformity with this world:* a religious group or the religiously informed society turns its attention from the supernatural and becomes more and more interested in "this world." 3. *Disengagement of society from religion:* a society separates itself from the religious understanding that has previously informed it in order to constitute itself an autonomous reality and consequently to limit religion to the sphere of private life. 4. *Transformation of religious beliefs and institutions:* knowledge, patterns of behavior, and institutional arrangements which were once understood to be grounded in divine power are transformed into phenomena of purely human creation and responsibility (Shiner also uses the more common term, *differentiation*, to describe this process). 5. *Desacralization of the world:* the world is gradually deprived of its sacral character as man and nature become the object of rational-causal explanation and manipulation. Shiner argues that the disengagement (or privatization), transposition (or differentiation), and desacralization concepts are the most valuable for sociological analysis because they are concerned with secularization as a social and cultural process, providing explanations of a sociological nature. The decline theory is mainly useful for describing historical trends (e.g., the declining influence of religion from the time of the "great medieval synthesis" of religion and society in the Middle Ages). The conformity concept is mainly useful for describing the assimilation of religious groups into the larger society. Neither has much explanatory power.

For our purposes here, the critical concept is *desacralization of the world*. Most sociologists of religion agree that there has been privatization (Wilson 1982; Berger 1969) and differentiation (Bellah 1970; Greeley 1969; Berger 1969) in the modern era. The question is whether this necessarily entails desacralization of the world (Berger 1970). Does it necessarily lead to the "loss" of the sacred? Or does the sacred become less closely associated with specific social institutions (churches), and more widely diffused throughout the culture?

Peter Berger discusses this issue of the desacralization of the world in *A Rumor of Angels* (1970). His well-known discussion there of "signals of transcendence" (pp. 49–75) can be read as an appeal for the survival of the sacred in modern society in spite of seemingly inexorable trends toward increasing privatization and differentiation. These signals of transcendence assume the privatization of religion (Luckmann 1967) because none of them is dependent on religious institutions as such. Indeed, because of widespread differentiation, they are diffused throughout the culture. Religious institutions may mediate these signals of transcendence, but individuals' access to these signals is not limited to such institutional channels.

These signals of transcendence are also remarkably similar to Kohut's characteristics of transformed narcissism. What this means is that religion is deeply implicated in psychological well-being (here understood as transformed narcissism). Similarly, transformed narcissism has a central role in spiritual well-being (here understood as the perception that one's well-being is ultimately grounded in the sacred). Thus transformed narcissism provides the psychological condition for psychological well-being, but, more importantly, it also provides the psychological condition for such spiritual well-being as can realistically be expected in a world in which the privatization of religion has become a fact of life.

I will not attempt here a detailed discussion of the close fit between Berger's five signals of transcendence and Kohut's five characteristics of the transformed narcissistic self. A few brief comments will have to suffice.

PERSONAL CREATIVITY (KOHUT) AND ARGUMENT FROM PLAY (BERGER)

For Berger, play is a form of creativity in which individuals experience transcendent joy. In play, one steps out of normal time and becomes a participant in eternal time. Joyful play suspends or brackets the reality of our "living towards death." Berger acknowledges that this experience of transcendent joy could be interpreted as "regression to childish magic (along the lines, say, of the Freudian theory of wishful fantasy)" (p. 60). But he prefers to view it as the adult counterpart of the experience of "the deathlessness of childhood," and thus unwittingly but perceptively grounds the experience of transcendent joy (in play or other forms of creativity) in a transformed narcissism.

EMPATHY (KOHUT) AND ARGUMENT FROM DAMNATION (BERGER)

Berger points out that there are certain human acts of atrocity that so outrage us that "the only adequate response to the offense as well as to the offender seems to be a curse of supernatural dimensions" (p. 65). Such deeds are curiously immune to relativizing analysis. We refuse to accept the argument that the act might be defensible "in light of the circumstances." For Berger, the transcendent element of this condemnation of atrocities has two aspects. First, our condemnation is absolute and certain: "It does not permit modification or doubt, and it is made in the conviction that it applies to all times and to all men." Second, the condemnation does not seem to exhaust its intrinsic intention in terms of this world alone. "Deeds that cry out to heaven also cry out for hell. . . . These are deeds that demand not only condemnation, but *damnation* in the full religious meaning of the word—that is, the doer not only puts himself outside the community of men; he also separates himself in a final way from a moral order that transcends the human community, and thus invokes a retribution that is more than human" (pp. 67–68).

In my judgment, our visceral response of outrage in such cases of atrocity derives not from "object-love" for the victim but from a narcissistically grounded empathy. Our condemnation is so absolute and certain because *we* are victimized by the deed and experience the atrocity as a personal assault. Thus the atrocity violates our narcissistic sense of self-love. In effect, we "empathize" with the victim through role-taking (i.e., putting ourselves in the victim's place). What gives this reaction to such atrocities a transcendent dimension is that we also "take the role" of God (see Garrett 1979; Capps 1982*a*), and view the atrocity as an "offense against God." Put this way, transformed narcissism is not without a moral dimension. However, this moral dimension is not based on the precarious foundation of the transfer of self-love to object-love but on the empathy of transformed narcissism.

ACCEPTANCE OF FINITENESS OF ONE'S EXISTENCE (KOHUT) AND ARGUMENT FROM HOPE (BERGER)

We have seen how, for Kohut, acceptance of our finitude is not an act of resignation and hopelessness, but of quiet pride and assurance based on a "cosmic narcissism" transcending personal identity. Berger's argument from hope addresses essentially the same issue of human finitude. He notes that "human hope has always asserted itself most intensively in the face of experiences that seemed to spell utter defeat, most intensely of all in the face of the final defeat of death" (p. 61). Berger calls such hope "death refusing" to distinguish it from "death denial." Such hope depends on full awareness of human finitude and acceptance of the fact that on empirical grounds assertions of individuals' victory over death are futile and vain. But Berger says that such hope has its roots in "the intentions within our 'natural' experience of hope that point toward a 'supernatural' fulfillment" (p. 64). This hope does not contradict the explanations of empirical reason, but encompasses them. Psychologically, therefore, this hope is based not on primary narcissism (unawareness or denial of personal finitude) but on transformed narcissism (saying "no" to death in full awareness of human finitude).

CAPACITY FOR HUMOR (KOHUT) AND ARGUMENT FROM HUMOR (BERGER)

Berger views humor as a response to "the imprisonment of the human spirit in the world" (p. 70), one that relativizes this imprisonment by implying "that this imprisonment is not final but will be overcome." Thus for Berger and Kohut, humor has a similar function. For both, it is addressed to certain unalterable realities. But it deprives these realities of their victory over the self by refusing to concede that they have ultimate power. As Berger puts it: "At least for the duration of the comic perception, the tragedy of man is bracketed. By laughing at the imprisonment of the human spirit, humor implies that this imprisonment is not final but will be overcome, and by this implication provides yet another signal of transcendence—in this instance in the form of an intimation of redemption. I would thus argue that humor, like childhood and play, can be seen as an ultimately religious vindication of joy" (p. 70).

WISDOM (KOHUT) AND THE ARGUMENT FROM ORDER (BERGER)

For Kohut, wisdom is a "stable attitude" of the personality toward life and the world. This stability may be viewed in terms of what Berger calls "a human propensity for order," which is ultimately based on a "faith in order as such, a faith closely related to man's fundamental trust in reality" (p. 54). Berger suggests that the most fundamental human gesture of order is the assurance a mother offers her anxious child. This locates the propensity for order in the narcissistic self. But Berger links this fundamental experience of order to *transformed* narcissism when he points out how the mother's reassurances that "everything is in order" transcend the immediate present of two individuals and their situation, and imply a statement about reality itself. The statement "everything is in order" can be "translated into a statement of cosmic scope—'have trust in being.' This is precisely what the formula intrinsically implies. And if we are to believe the child psychologists . . . this is an experience that is absolutely essential to the process of becoming a human person" (pp. 55–56). Thus the "sense of order" is critical to psychological well-being, and thus the basis for spiritual well-being. But so is it the foundation for adult wisdom, which also is reflected in a fundamental trust in being.

TRANSFORMED NARCISSISM AND RELIGIOUS INSTITUTIONS

These parallels between Kohut's capacities of transformed narcissism and Berger's signals of transcendence support the claims made earlier regarding the importance of the narcissistic self for the continuing role of the sacred in secular society. Psychologically speaking, both analyses suggest that attempts by religion to replace narcissism with object-love are doomed to failure. In a secular world in which religion is increasingly privatized, transformed narcissism is the psychological condition for the survival of the sacred. Moreover, because awareness of the sacred is vital for maintaining a religious orientation to life, transformed narcissism is critical to spiritual well-being. In fact, the very idea that religion contributes to a sense of spiritual well-being reflects the degree to which our society already implicitly looks to religion to assist individuals in the *transformation* of their narcissistic selves.

In *The Heretical Imperative* (1979), Berger links the theological method underlying his "signals of transcendence" discussion (i.e., the method of "inductive faith") to theological liberalism. Thus his discussion is compatible with at least one major theological approach to maintaining the Judeo-Christian *meaning system* in modern society. (The link between these signals and the *belonging system* of the Judeo-Christian tradition is much more attenuated.) But the fact that none of these signals is directly dependent on religious institutions is also instructive. Privatization and disengagement concepts of secularization provide sociological explanations for this. A more psychological explanation is that religious institutions have as their objective the replacing of narcissism with object-love. This is perhaps most evident in their liturgical language, especially prayers of confession ("We confess that we have not loved our neighbors as ourselves") and petition (where prayers of self-interest are discouraged or severely qualified—"not my will but thine be done").

In spite of widespread changes in liturgical language, often toward more secular forms of language (Fenn 1982), confessional prayer has been highly immune to basic changes. The language of guilt (for failure to replace narcissistic propensities with object-love) continues to prevail over the language of shame, and this is clear evidence that religious institutions have not been able to come to terms with the narcissistic self's most profound experience of personal fault or unworthiness. As Kohut points out, it is "the ambitious, success-driven person with a poorly integrated grandiose-self concept and intense exhibitionistic-narcissistic tensions who is most prone to experience shame. If the pressures from the narcissistic self are intense and the ego is unable to control them, the personality will respond with shame to failures of any kind, whether its ambitions concern moral perfection or external success" (1978:441). For the narcissistic self, shame and not guilt is the deepest threat to both psychological and spiritual well-being.

Similarly, liturgical forms of petitionary prayer continue to reflect a negative attitude toward praying for one's own self-interests. Desires that have their roots in self-love are invariably judged to be incompatible with a mature religious orientation to life. Prayers expressing such desires are considered the least likely to meet with God's approval. The more acceptable petitionary prayers are those that reflect a transfer of self-love to object-love. Yet such prayers are often desultory and insincere because they are not rooted in real desire (Capps 1982; see also Gay 1978). A better approach would be to take a less critical view of prayers of self-interest (see Heiler 1932) and to rewrite liturgical prayers of petition according to the norms of transformed narcissism.

In general, religious institutions do not support the goal of transformed narcissism, probably on the assumption that any form of narcissism is incompatible with a religious orientation to life. Our analysis here would suggest that, whereas primary narcissism may be incompatible with a mature religious orientation, transformed narcissism is not only compatible with it, but may well be essential to its very survival.

TRANSFORMED NARCISSISM AND THE ACCESSIBLE GOD

If transformed narcissism is critically important to the continuing role of the sacred in secular society, what kind of sacredness does this entail? Does it imply any particular image or conception of God? A recent essay by Guy Swanson (1980) suggests that what we are see-ing today is a new evolutionary stage in the continuing elaboration and modification of the Protestant formulation of the divine-human relation. His argument is based on an analysis of the organizational styles of post-industrial corporations, firms, and agencies. But it is directly relevant to our concern with the narcissistic self because he argues that corporate styles of management and human relations have direct bearing on "the formation of a personal identity" (p. 210).

Significantly, Swanson's delineation of the major principles under-lying the formation of the personal identity fostered by post-industrial corporate life has major parallels to Kohut's transformed narcissistic self. These principles emphasize the freedom of each individual to develop his own talents and interests, the acceptance of each indi-vidual as a whole person, and the expectation that each individual will be open and flexible to changing conditions, prepared to change even himself if this does not violate his freedom as a person. These principles, with their emphasis on personal interests, suggest that the narcissistic self has gained wide acceptance in corporate life. But not in its primary form. Individuals are expected to manifest a higher form of narcissism, one reflecting greater attention to how one's personal creativity may contribute to the well-being of others, and a capacity to modify one's self-interests in light of changing institutional goals, as long as this does not entail self-denial.

Swanson claims that this new understanding of personal identity is reflected in the conception of divine-human relations in today's "popular" Christian theology. This theology emphasizes God's accep-tance of the individual as inherently worthy of his love ("The Second Commandment means that one must love God, one's neighbor, *and oneself*"); de-emphasizes guilt ("But guilt should not be the center of your actions. You are needed and wanted for what you freely are"); and stresses mutual supportiveness ("Each is obligated to be at least tolerant and supportive of all who open themselves to him"). These theological understandings are clearly consistent with Kohut's view of transformed narcissism. But what does this all add up to? What does it mean for the role of the sacred in contemporary secular society?

In my judgment, the emergence of the narcissistic self is effecting a new emphasis on God as the "accessible Self." As accessibility to self and others has become a human priority, it has also become an expectation of God. If the Catholic era drew our attention to God as responsible self, and the Protestant Reformation focused on God as a believable self, the present era is concerned with the accessibility of God. The accessibility of the "other" is a central motif in Berger's signals of transcendence, Swanson's description of human relations in modern corporate life, and Kohut's description of the narcissistic self. It is also central to Erikson's view that one's religious orientation is formed in the first stage of life through the accessibility of the mother. The primary threat to spiritual well-being in our era is the inaccessibility of the sacred. We are less likely than our predecessors to expect God to respond to our specific needs, or to prove his credibility, but more likely to expect God simply to be "present" and "available" to us. We are also less likely to accept the idea that God's presence is a mediated one, whether through a sacred text, a holy personage, a religious institution, or a major historical event. Narcissistic selves expect face-to-face recognition, as reflected in the dramatic revival of interest in spirituality and prayer. The transformation of the narcissistic self does not change this fundamental expectation. The Protestant Reformation supported respect for the privacy of God and his accessibility only through careful mediation, whereas we expect the sacred to be immediately accessible. Religion has become more privatized, but this has only increased the expectation that the sacred will be open and available to all—that is, if this expectation is consistent with God's own freedom to be what he chooses to be.

REFERENCES

Allport, Gordon W.
 1950   *The Individual and His Religion.* New York: Macmillan.
 1955   *Becoming: Basic Considerations for a Psychology of Personality.* New Haven: Yale University Press.
Andrews, F. M., and S. B. Withey
 1976   *Social Indicators of Well-Being.* New York: Plenum Press.
Bahr, Howard M., and Thomas K. Martin
 1983   "'And thy neighbor as thyself': Self-Esteem and Faith in People as Correlates of Religiosity and Family Solidarity Among Middletown High School Students," *Journal for the Scientific Study of Religion* 22:132–44.
Barker, Eileen
 1979   "Whose Service Is Perfect Freedom: The Concept of Spiritual Well-Being in Relation to the Reverend Moon's Unification Church." *In* David O. Moberg, ed., *Spiritual Well-Being: Sociological Perspectives.* Washington, D.C.: University Press of America.
Bellah, Robert N.
 1970   *Beyond Belief.* New York: Harper and Row.

Berger, Peter L.
  1969   *The Sacred Canopy.* Garden City: Anchor Books.
  1970   *A Rumor of Angels.* Garden City: Anchor Books.
  1979   *The Heretical Imperative.* Garden City, N.Y.: Anchor Books.
Blaikie, Norman W. H., and G. Paul Kelsen
  1979   "Locating Self and Giving Meaning to Existence: A Typology of
          Paths to Spiritual Well-Being on New Religious Movements in
          Australia." *In* David O. Moberg, ed., *Spiritual Well-Being: Sociolog-
          ical Perspectives.* Washington, D.C.: University Press of America.
Campbell, A., P. E. Converse, and W. L. Rodgers
  1976   *The Quality of American Life.* New York: Russell Sage Foundation.
Campbell, A.
  1981   *The Sense of Well-Being in America.* New York: McGraw-Hill.
Capps, Donald
  1982a   "Sunden's Role-Taking Theory: The Case of John Henry Newman
          and His Mentors," *Journal for the Scientific Study of Religion* 21:58–
          70.
  1982b   "The Psychology of Petitionary Prayer," *Theology Today* 39:130–
          141.
Chalfant, H. Paul, Robert E. Beckley, and C. Eddie Palmer
  1981   *Religion in Contemporary Society.* Sherman Oaks, Calif.: Alfred
          Publishing Company.
Erikson, Erik H.
  1959   *Identity and the Life Cycle.* New York: International Universities
          Press.
  1968   *Identity: Youth and Crisis.* New York: W. W. Norton.
  1977   *Toys and Reasons: Stages in the Ritualization of Experience.* New York:
          W. W. Norton.
Fenn, Richard K.
  1982   *Liturgies and Trials: The Secularization of Religious Language.* New
          York: The Pilgrim Press.
Garrett, William R.
  1979   "Reference Groups and Role Strains Related to Spiritual Well-
          Being." *In* David O. Moberg, ed., *Spiritual Well-Being: Sociological
          Perspectives.* Washington, D.C.: University Press of America.
Gay, Volney
  1978   "Public Rituals versus Private Treatment: Psychodynamics of
          Prayer," *Journal of Religion and Health* 17:244–60.
Greeley, Andrew M.
  1969   *Religion in the Year 2000.* New York: Sheed and Ward.
Hadaway, C. K.
  1978   "Life Satisfaction and Religion: A Reanalysis," *Social Forces* 52:636–
          43.
Hadaway, C. K., and W. C. Roof
  1978   "Religious Commitment and the Quality of Life in American
          Society," *Review of Religious Research* 19:295–307.

Heiler, Friedrich
  1932   *Prayer: A Study in the History and Psychology of Religion.* Trans.
            Samuel McComb. New York: Oxford University Press.
James, William
  1958   *The Varieties of Religious Experience.* New York: Mentor Books.
Kohut, Heinz
  1978   "Forms and Transformations of Narcissism." *In* Paul H. Ornstein,
            ed., *The Search for the Self: Selected Writings of Heinz Kohut 1950–
            1978,* vol. 1. New York: International Universities Press.
Lasch, Christopher
  1979   *The Culture of Narcissism.* New York: Warner Books.
Luckmann, Thomas
  1967   *The Invisible Religion: The Problem of Religion in Modern Society.* New
            York: Macmillan.
McNamara, P. H., and A. St. George
  1979   "Measures of Religiosity and the Quality of Life: A Critical
            Analysis." *In* David O. Moberg, ed., *Spiritual Well-Being: Sociolog-
            ical Perspectives.* Washington, D.C.: University Press of America.
Moberg, David O., ed.
  1979   *Spiritual Well-Being: Sociological Perspectives.* Washington, D.C.:
            University Press of America.
Moberg, David O.
  1979   "The Development of Social Indicators of Spiritual Well-Being for
            Quality of Life Research." *In* David O. Moberg, ed., *Spiritual
            Well-Being: Sociological Perspectives.* Washington, D.C.: University
            Press of America.
Shiner, Larry E.
  1967   "The Concept of Secularization in Empirical Research," *Journal for
            the Scientific Study of Religion* 6:207–220.
Steinitz, Lucy Y.
  1980   "Religiosity, Well-Being, and *Weltanschauung* among the Elderly,"
            Journal for the Scientific Study of Religion 19:60–67.
St. George, A., and P. H. McNamara
  1983   "Effects of Religion on Psychological Well-Being." Unpublished
            paper.
Swanson, Guy E.
  1980   "A Basis of Authority and Identity in Post-Industrial Society." *In*
            Roland Robertson and Burkhart Holzner, eds., *Identity and Au-
            thority: Explorations in the Theory of Society.* Oxford: Blackwell.
            Pp. 190–217.
Wilson, Bryan
  1982   *Religion in Sociological Perspective.* New York: Oxford University
            Press.

XVI
Psychoanalysis and the Sacred
Paul W. Pruyser

The formative years of psychoanalysis, roughly 1895 to 1930, coincide with the declining years of another noteworthy intellectual undertaking known as the Science of Religions. Through the works of such scholars as Burnouf, Müller, Smith, Strauss, Taylor, Vacherot, and Westermarck and the more widely disseminated works of Spencer and Frazer, the idea of the sacred had, since the last quarter of the nineteenth century, become a respectable research domain that could be approached from many technical vantage points outside theology. Thus religion and the sacred were also studied in a spirit that reflected in various proportions the major ideational passions of the times: empiricism, positivism, and evolutionism. In addition, throughout the nineteenth century there had been an increasingly pronounced psychological analysis of religion, whether for criticism or advocacy, that runs from Schleiermacher the theologian, via Feuerbach the philosopher, to Wundt and Ribot the psychologists, and James the physician-psychologist-philosopher. Notwithstanding their widely different agendas, all these investigators took religion and the sacred seriously—if only because of the manifest power that the sacred appears to have, or to have had, over the minds of people.

It is just this power of religious belief over the mind, which "overwhelms reason and science" (1939:123), which Freud singled out at the end of his life as the reason for his fascination with religion. As I indicated in an earlier review article (Pruyser, 1973),[1] there is no question that Freud was fascinated by religion (he addressed the topic repeatedly from 1893 until 1939)—and that he saw his own psychology of religion as a new branch of that Science of Religion that had furnished him some of the data and constructs on which he was to lean for his own contribution.

What aspects of the sacred are addressed in Freud's works? In *Totem and Taboo* (1913) the sacred[2] is a complex of powers and power relations that center around the need to constrain by sacred ordinances (customs, taboos) the incestuous Oedipal wish, and to produce by rituals and ceremonies a compromise act that symbolically satisfies a part of both sides of the deep-seated ambivalence (loving and hating, making love and killing) that has beset parent-child relations from the dawn of civilization. The taboos, the prohibitions, the avoidance maneuvers themselves are sacred; whoever personifies or whatever symbolizes them is also sacred. Similarly sacred are the sacrifices made ceremonially, or as expiation for transgressions. Following Wundt, Freud held that this context for the sacred dates from before the development of religions; the taboo is older than any god and belongs to the animistic stage of civilization. In stressing as essential the *ambivalence* inherent in any taboo-morality, Freud's intuition about the sacred runs parallel with Rudolf Otto's idea of the Holy as an ambiguous *mysterium tremendum et fascinosum*, in which awe and bliss are jointly experienced.

A different intimation of the sacred occurs in *The Future of an Illusion* (1927) and *Civilization and its Discontents* (1930), in both of which Freud's focus is no longer on primitive mentality and archaic culture but on the contemporary world in which religion is a mass phenomenon. The focus is now on the idea of god, and on the agenda of religions to inculcate and buttress this idea by doctrinaire instruction involving a degree of thought control. Religion is here seen as a halfway station between magic and science. It serves to secure for humans some kind of mastery (albeit an illusory one) over the whimsical powers of nature, as well as to subordinate individuals to the culture's mandates. Culture had been created for protecting humanity from the ruthlessness of nature, at the price of demanding from each individual some renunciation of instinctual impulses.

It is implied in these two essays that what the ordinary person holds as sacred are not only the gods and the ceremonial transactions between believers and their gods but the very thought structures and operational frameworks of institutional religion as well. Nay, what is more, the believer also holds as sacred the social order, inasmuch as it is sanctioned by a religious tradition, and the human conscience, which is the internalization of both religion and the social codes. Although Freud's only explicit mention of Durkheim's works is in the 1913 book, the knowledgeable reader can detect in the 1927 and 1930 essays an awareness of the Durkheimian thesis that religion is functionally the weft or woof of the social fabric. In this sense Freud extends the idea of the sacred from the religious circle to the larger orbit of the social order.

While the Ur-father of *Totem and Taboo* is a brutal power whose memory image is almost totally repressed, the deity of the two later essays is a much more benign and accessible, providential figure, many of whose attributes the believer can freely admit to consciousness. The believer can worship, pray to, and even bargain with his god in verbalizable transactions. Ask a member of a totemic taboo culture about the why's of the prescriptions and proscriptions he follows, and he can only answer with a dumb "Because!" But the theistic believer can give all kinds of reasons for obeying the divine commandments and for the human ways of worshiping.

Freud visits the sacred once more, in his very last work, *Moses and Monotheism.* It contains his definition of the "remarkable concept of holiness" (1939:120). What really is holy or sacred? Freud's answer is that "everything religious is sacred" (1939:120). But he notes that the term is also used tendentiously for nonreligious situations involving prohibitions that are staged as self-evident: for example, the taboo on incest that proscribes touching a blood relative. Why is such a prohibition considered sacred? Freud's explanation is that ". . . what is sacred was originally nothing other than the prolongation of the will of the primal father" (1939:121). He feels satisfied that this definition also throws light on the ambiguity inherent in the Latin term *sacer,* which means both *sacred* or *consecrated* and *infamous* or *detestable;* this semantic ambiguity reflects the affective ambivalence that has always dominated the relation of child to father.

A running theme throughout this work is the determination of Moses (conjectured to be an Egyptian Akhnaton devotee) to make his people (i.e., those who fled with him into Canaan) *holy* by the mark of circumcision. As this fledgling Aton-Mosaic religion develops into Judaism it comes to include sacred books, sacred prohibitions and, eventually, sacred feelings of awe and respect and a reverence for ethical principles. Looking forward beyond Moses' time to developed Judaism and Christianity, as well as backward to prehistorical antecedents, Freud finds the truth content of religion to be "historical" (rather than material) in the sense that it resides in mankind's archaic experiences of sexuality and power, perennially repeated in myth, ritual, dreams, folklore, and religious ideas.

One of Freud's contemporaries and personal friends, the Swiss pastor-psychoanalyst Pfister, was greatly concerned with the "hygiene of religion." Seeing considerable religion-induced, religion-reinforced, or religiously toned psychopathology in his pastoral practice, he began to stress the difference between two models of the sacred. The older and still persisting model (epitomized in Freud the critical scholar) sees the sacred as instilling taboos and inducing fear and guilt feelings; the newer model (in part epitomized by Freud the healer) defines the sacred as love, proclaimed as the highest mandate by the great Hebrew prophets and by Jesus. Pfister was a pioneering psychoanalyst who stressed prevention of neurotic distortions in all spheres of life by arguing for mental hygiene endeavors in schools, churches, and medicine; whatever is done out of love, and for the sake of enhancing love, operationally defines the sacred for this arch-meliorist. "Love through faith and faith through love" (1948:210) was Pfister's slogan, the highest hygienic aim and the essence of what deserves to be called sacred.

Freud's preoccupation with an archaic image of the sacred tied up with taboos, compulsivity, guilt feelings and the Oedipus and castration complexes was seconded by many other psychoanalysts, such as Jones, Rank, and Reik, all of whom contributed to a further understanding of the archaic roots of religion by analyzing both religious practices (rituals) and religious ideation (concepts, myths, arts, literature). Pfister's orientation, however, never blossomed into a definite position concerning religion within psychoanalysis, although several other individuals sought to gain within the movement some appreciation for the healthy, nonneurotic, nondefensive, freeing, or "genital" positions of belief, feelings, and practices that religion offers. I would count in this category Flugel, Brierley, and Guntrip in England, and Zilboorg and Stern in North America, albeit some of these psychoanalysts had reservations about major parts of Freudian theory and entertained revisionist ideas that affect more than Freud's views of religion.

Within the psychoanalytic mainstream, a truly new appreciation of the sacred comes with Erikson's description of the spontaneous and genuine joy experienced by mother and infant in their mutual greeting rituals. Erikson does not hesitate to call these tender situations *numinous* (1966:603) and to see them as manifestations of a disposition that is psychodynamically of crucial importance for the rest of life. While other psychoanalysts accentuated in various ways some kind of basic fear as an organizer of life, Erikson laid stress on basic trust. And his description of the greeting ritual promotes in one fell swoop recognition of a whole class of symbolic behaviors that the classical psychoanalytic tradition up to that time had disregarded: numinous acts and their accompanying attitudes and feelings that are not primarily in the service of defense, but arise from free energy, bubbliness, or spontaneity—in a word, which occur in a psychic economy of abundance rather than scarcity.

Moreover, Erikson (1958) took for his demonstration piece of "psychoanalysis and history" (soon to be called "psychohistory") an acknowledged religious genius, Martin Luther, portraying him in the protracted act of resolving a profound emotional crisis of early adulthood. Here, in Luther's struggle of faith, psychodynamic forces are traced in which personal identity and religious integrity are interlinked to produce a developmental movement from a sick to a healthy, from a neurotic to a relatively conflict-free, from an obsessionally doubting to a heartfelt affirmative credo, with the accompanying emotional liberation of the person and his considerable talents. Where Freud (1923) had confined his works on religion to phylogenetic and collective events, his only individual religious case study being a short piece on an obscure seventeenth-century figure who had sold his soul to the devil, Erikson did a fulsome case study on a well-documented, publicly known, and vivid religious leader who had made a great impact on human history.

If the idea of the sacred includes the demonic, as it does for most students of religion or animistic beliefs and practices, attention should be paid to Melanie Klein (1965) and her followers who have placed great stress on the gruesome, hellish, almost satanic fantasies that they allege to occur in infants and young children, and in adults with profound mental disturbances. Klein herself hardly mentioned religion in her works, but did influence some psychoanalysts who had religious interests (e.g. Guntrip, originally a Congregational minister in England who later became a psychotherapist). Both he (Guntrip 1961) and his mentor Fairbairn (1954), who had laid the theoretical groundwork for the British Object Relations school, were impressed by so-called schizoid phenomena. These comprise patients of shy, withdrawn, and socially awkward conduct, distrustful and often complaining of emptiness, who in analysis proved to have an extremely intense fantasy life that was shaped in dreams and reveries as an interior theatrical stage on which persons, including various projections of their own selves, would engage in all kinds of scenes, often of the greatest cruelty. Fairbairn's theoretical centerpiece is the "inner world" complementing the outer world and sometimes outweighing the latter in dynamic importance for behavior; it is an inner world of human object *imagos* created by the infantile imagination in response to its own needs and the human caretakers on which the infant depends. These *imagos* are frequently the product of emotionally induced cognitive distortions and are beset by intensely polarized affective charges that make their being felt (and seen) as either good or bad, seductive or attacking, praising or blaming, solacing or threatening, exciting or depressing, accepting or rejecting.

Aside from Fairbairn's almost pious emphasis on human relatedness and his subsequent radical rejection of psychoanalytic drive theory and drastic revision of the structural point of view, neither he nor Guntrip (the latter despite writing a book on psychotherapy and religion [1957]) seem to have had the interest in the sacred that is so noteworthy in Freud. There is no hint in their works that they even had the feeling for, the sensitivity to, or the sense of the sacred that we see in Freud's *Totem and Taboo*, Reik's *Ritual*, or Erikson's *Luther*. Instead, we find in their clinical and theoretical works a preoccupation with the fiendishness and savageness of the human imagination which dwells on such cannibalistic themes as devouring and being devoured, assaulting and being persecuted. The lurid and the gory hold the center stage in this school's account of the dynamic content of the unconscious, in contrast to the libidinal wishes and pleasurable make-belief that prevail in Freud's account.

But perhaps more important than this difference is the status given to these demonic "bad internal objects"—bad, because they devour, accuse, assault, or reject, or else because they excite too much. They are part of an inner world that is *imaginary*, and typically quite at variance with the person's actual outer world. They do not depend on Freud's "historical truth" of the Ur-Oedipus and the Ur-Menelaus, nor on the taboos, rituals, and beliefs presented and transmitted to each new generation by organized religion and morality. Moreover, for these Object Relations devotees, the generalized "youngster" from which their theory takes its cues is the highly dependent, autistic, preverbal infant already haunted by a cruel primitive superego; whereas for Freud it is the half-civilized, verbal, Oedipal child who has already gained some degree of autonomy, knows quite a bit about the real world, and has just begun to acquire superego control. Curiously, despite the status of the internal objects as figments of the imagination, there is a tendency among the Object Relations clinicians to concretize them as if they were living *things*, quasi *persons*, or dynamic *substances*. Their parlance often takes a digestive or alimentary turn (e.g., "undigested" or "unmetabolized" object), or else is crudely demonological (e.g., when therapy is described as if it were an act of exorcising a devil). It is for this reason, I think, that Glover, a classical analyst, accused Klein of the "creation of a kind of slang" (1945:85), and Rapaport (1958:750) called her theory an "id mythology."

At any rate, the Kleinians have managed: (1) to shift attention from the sacred to the demonic, (2) to relocate the demonic from the exterior world of cosmos or nature into the inner world of the personal imagination, (3) to privatize the demonic by discounting the culture-historical pressures and traditions that shape the content of the conscious and unconscious human mind, (4) to shift from the sacred image of the deity as exalted father to the (often demonic) image of the terrifying mother. Those are important shifts in emphasis in their own right, but their impact is enhanced further by the typically Kleinian minimizing of a person's traffic with the outer world and maximizing the relations with internal objects.

In two books of my own (Pruyser 1968, 1974) I have sought to deal with the sacred by combining Otto's phenomenology of the Holy with classical psychoanalytic conceptions, emphasizing the ego's psychological and adaptational processes set forth in the Hartmann tradition (1958). Otto's insistence on the ambiguity of the Holy's self-presentation and the combined awe and bliss experienced by believers is a wonderful demonstration of Freud's correctness in considering ambivalence an essential quality of the sacred object and of the human response to it. In fact, Goodenough (1965) was sufficiently impressed by both writers to spot that Otto's *tremendum* is not only exterior to mankind but has also an interior locus in each individual's unconscious as conceived by Freud in the structural and dynamic Id. Concurring with that proposition, I gave detailed accounts of the various psychological processes (such as perception, cognition, language, emotion, motor behavior, motivational states, and relationship paradigms) whereby the sacred (including the demonic) is individually approached, recognized, represented, symbolized, or dealt with, placing considerable emphasis on the cultural transmission of religious objects and ideas. Few people have to invent the sacred all by themselves, from scratch; the culture teems with highly stylized and institutionalized symbolizations of it which are hard to ignore even if one would like to escape exposure to them. Most people are trained to seek a personal alliance with the *tremendum* both for its benefits and as a way of protecting themselves from its power to harm them—according to psychoanalysis, the latter concern is partly achieved at all times in all cultures by the mental mechanism of repression. This repression is a psychological necessity that has become an integral function of the human species, and is to be differentiated from neurotic or other symptomatic hyper-repression.

In the course of this work, I became aware of the need to distinguish the private, solipsistic, *autistic*, and essentially unspeakable fantasy that operates in dreaming and the forming of primitive object representations, from the *tutored* imagination that is nurtured on the culture's abiding symbol systems. The latter fantasy products can be talked about, for they are shared; children are actively instructed in their appropriation by the use of books, pictures, songs, rituals, and parental demonstrations of devout and reverential attitudes. Most children acquire some skill in dealing with the entities and modes of thought and feeling appropriate to religion, with the result that an aura of sacredness, or holiness, can become attached as a special value to ideas, things, persons, institutions, paraphernalia, and activities over and beyond its being a singular attribute of the deity and divine ordinances.

The private fantasy can distort or significantly alter the culturally transmitted ideas about the sacred. But distortions of the sacred, including displacement of the holy from proper to improper objects, can also be induced by religious institutions beset by power struggles or engaged in unholy liaisons with other institutions such as the state, political parties, an economic system, or the military. The holy can turn into the demonic, as it has done on a massive scale in historical bloodbaths, and on a smaller scale in individual delusional derangements. In the form of religion, of whatever kind, the idea of the sacred exerts power over the minds of men and women. It has done so in all ages and is bound to continue to wield this power.

It seems to me that precisely on this point of religion's power—and the associated questions about that power's origins or causes and eventual destiny—psychoanalytic studies of the sacred are liable to a flaw (Pruyser 1983). That flaw becomes manifest when reductionism combined with positivism forces the scholar to suppose that religion must come from something else that is clearly not religion; for example, an economic arrangement, a hygienic consideration, a needed food selection, a mating pattern, a protection against natural disaster. It seems to me safer, because more realistic and more historical, to say: Religion comes from religion—and will give rise to religion. It is an abiding preoccupation of humanity, perhaps a Kantian category of the mind. It cannot be reduced to something else. Precisely when religion as such is seen as an irreducible pursuit, just as original and abiding as the visual arts, the sciences, literature, and music, psychoanalysis has much to offer (as it has already done up to a point) in refining our understanding of the phylogenetic and ontogenetic development of religion, the human uses and abuses of the sacred, the distinction between the divine and the demonic, and the forces that cause progressive or regressive movements in religion. All kinds of interesting questions about religion can be pursued from a psychoanalytic angle.

For instance, Rizzuto using object relations theory has sought to trace rather minutely by clinical interviews and drawings what kind of mental images or representations of God are in people's minds, and how such images compare with these same persons' parental images, self-images, and other significant objects. While Rizzuto oddly insists that her book is not about religion but about object relations, she nevertheless demonstrated in her small published sample an interesting diversity. For instance, in one case God is devoid of any *tremendum* but is "a domestic divinity of simple human characteristics" (1979:106) replicating the woman's much beloved father. In another case there is a rageful striving toward self-sufficiency that rejects a disappointing but very pious mother as well as the god seen as the mother's extension; this person wants to be left alone by both objects, but cannot quite shake off their presence. While it may not be clear what such data contribute to an understanding of the *essence* of the sacred, they do illustrate the varied kinds of traffic that people have or seek with it. These data also illustrate the negotiations people make with the sacred objects to which they have been introduced by instruction, the sacred ordinances or rules to which they are subjected, and the sacred institutions in which they are embedded. And the weight of the cognitive and emotional relations one may have with any and all of these items presses eventually toward an existential decision: Shall I recognize (i.e., honor) them or shall I withhold recognition from them?

Apart from the attention the sacred has received in the psychoanalytic psychology of religion or the "science of religion," how does it fare in the clinical practice of psychoanalysis? The answer is bound to be ambiguous—bespeaking an ambiguity that is proper both to the holy and to psychoanalysis. Psychoanalytic practice can be described as an exercise in demythologizing, and to this extent it may contribute to secularization. It destroys those myths that individuals and families produce to shield themselves from unpleasant events, feelings, and realities. It exposes the personal "demons," which mask as symptoms, to the general effect of making them manageable and subjecting them to conscious mastery by the ego. Psychoanalytic treatment fosters rationality and seeks to provide insight in situations where the dominance of affect has led to poor coping behavior. But it does all these things by means of a special and rare contract that not only allows transference reactions by the patient to the analyst to occur but actively elicits such transferences, thereby charging the clinical situation with a great deal of primitive affect and primitive attitudes. Inasmuch as the latter put the analyst into the role of the powerful parent as seen by the very young child, God-like parental qualities are attributed to the analyst, and there are moments such as those described by Ostow: "When an illusion of merging develops, the transference acquires a mystical quality. It creates the impression of reunion with a parental object, the precursor of the image of God" (1982:7). Because of its maximizing and concretizing of both reason and emotion, the clinical psychoanalytic situation is not without its own sacred aspects; how could it be otherwise for a therapy that seeks depth in dealing with personal integrity and autonomy, with selfhood and alienation, and with the relations between fantasy and reality? All of these existential motifs are quite mysterious.

NOTES

1. The reader is referred to this 1973 article also for its extensive bibliography.

2. Freud's original word choice in German comprises: *heilig, das Heilige, Heiligkeit* for holy, the holy, and holiness; *unheimlich* for uncanny; *geweiht* for consecrated. These are all standard words in common use, as are their English translations by Strachey.

REFERENCES

Erikson, Erik
    1958   *Young Man Luther.* New York: W. W. Norton.
    1966   "Ontogeny of Ritualization." *In* Rudolph M. Lowenstein, Lottie M. Newman, Max Schur, and Albert J. Solnit, eds., *Psychoanalysis—A General Psychology.* New York: International Universities Press. Pp. 601–621.
Fairbairn, W. Ronald D.
    1954   *An Object Relations Theory of the Personality.* New York: Basic Books.
Freud, Sigmund
    1913   "Totem and Taboo," *Standard Edition*, vol. 13. London: Hogarth Press, 1955.

1923   "A Seventeenth-Century Demonological Neurosis," *Standard Edition;* vol. 19. London: Hogarth Press, 1961.
1927   "The Future of an Illusion," *Standard Edition,* vol. 21. London: Hogarth Press, 1961.
1930   "Civilization and Its Discontents," *Standard Edition,* vol. 21. London: Hogarth Press, 1961.
1939   "Moses and Monotheism," *Standard Edition,* vol. 23. London: Hogarth Press, 1964.

Glover, Edward
1945   "Examination of the Klein System of Child Psychology," *The Psychoanalytic Study of the Child* 1:75–118.

Goodenough, Erwin R.
1965   *The Psychology of Religious Experiences.* New York: Basic Books.

Guntrip, Henry, J. S.
1957   *Psychotherapy and Religion.* New York: Harper.
1961   *Personality Structure and Human Interaction.* New York: International Universities Press.

Hartmann, Heinz.
1958   *Ego Psychology and the Problem of Adaption.* Trans. D. Rapaport. New York: International Universities Press.

Klein, Melanie
1965   *Contributions to Psychoanalysis, 1921–1945.* London: Hogarth Press.

Ostow, Mortimer
1982   Introduction. *In* Mortimer Ostow, ed., *Judaism and Psychoanalysis.* New York: KTAV Publishing House. Pp. 1–44.

Pfister, Oskar
1948   *Christianity and Fear.* Trans. W. H. Johnston. London: George Allen and Unwin.

Pruyser, Paul W.
1968   *A Dynamic Psychology of Religion.* New York: Harper & Row.
1973   "Sigmund Freud and His Legacy." *In* Charles Y. Glock and Phillip E. Hammond, eds., *Beyond the Classics: Essays in the Scientific Study of Religion.* New York: Harper & Row. Pp. 243–290.
1974   *Between Belief and Unbelief.* New York: Harper & Row.
1983   *The Play of the Imagination: Towards a Psychoanalysis of Culture.* New York: International Universities Press.

Rapaport, David
1958   "A Historical Survey of Psychoanalytic Ego Psychology." *In* Merton M. Gill, ed., *The Collected Papers of David Rapaport.* New York: Basic Books, 1967.

Reik, Theodor
1931   *Ritual: Psychoanalytic Studies.* Trans. D. Bryan. New York: W. W. Norton, 1946.

Rizzuto, Ana-Maria
1979   *The Birth of the Living God—a Psychoanalytic Study.* Chicago: University of Chicago Press.

XVII

Religion and Healing

Meredith B. McGuire

Until relatively recently, social scientists were uninterested in exploring any connection between religion and healing. These linked concepts evoke images of tent evangelists claiming faith healings or of earnest Christian Scientists doing their mental "work"—little enclaves of believers who seem outside the mainstream of the modern world and contemporary religiosity. The healing focus of such groups is viewed as a remnant of an earlier folk religiosity or as a commitment mechanism, a ritual support of group beliefs of a cognitive minority (Allen and Wallis 1976; Nudelman 1976; Pattison 1973, 1974; Wardwell 1965).

If religion's impact on healing is, indeed, even considered, it is typically in terms of inadvertent psychotherapeutic benefits (Frank 1973; Kiev 1973; Torrey 1972). Some authors argue that psychoanalytic methods, as opposed to faith healing, are more appropriate to modern goals of developing insight and individual independence (Prince 1972). Other observers note the extent to which psychoanalysis itself represents a world view in competition with traditional religious world views for hegemony in social control mechanisms in the public sphere and identity-maintenance functions in the private sphere (Berger 1965). There has also been a recognition that religious specialists in mainstream churches were doing effective counseling; however, pastoral counseling was generally modeled after the dominant secular therapeutic methods, although it was less bound by the orthodoxy of these therapeutic models (Spencer 1982).

On the whole, then, social scientists merely reflect a more general societal notion: Religion and healing are two *separate* spheres, with little mutual influence. Separate specialists are appropriate to each arena. Any serious overlapping of religion and healing is viewed as a quaint relic of folk or ethnic religiosity, an anachronism in the modern world.

THE SECULARIZATION OF HEALTH AND HEALING

This view of religion and healing as separate spheres reflects the secularization of health and the process of healing in Western societies.[1] For the purposes of this essay, "secularization" means the removing of belonging- and meaning-providing elements from an institutional area (i.e., healing). A number of historical developments has led to this separation of religion and healing.

Western medicine has, over the years, gradually *differentiated* itself from other institutions, such as religion or the family. This differentiation is characterized by the development of a distinctive body of knowledge, a corps of specialists with control over this body of knowledge and its application, and public acknowledgment (or legitimacy) of the specialized authority of medical specialists (Freidson 1970; Turner 1980). Before the development of medical specialists, healing was the function of mothers and other nurses, religious persons, midwives, diviners, herbalists, barbers, and an array of folk healers (e.g., persons with a special gift for setting bones).

Routine reliance on medical professionals is a relatively new phenomenon; the medical profession has achieved its dominance over the area of healing only in this century. The roots of institutional differentiation of healing, however, go back to Greek and Persian medicine, with the beginning of a rationalized approach to medicine: observation, description, generalization, and prediction (Freidson 1970). The foundations of "secularized" medical practice thus antedate the advent of capitalism and industrialization, and this secular medical approach was subject to religious critique in several subsequent centuries (such as the medical theories of Paracelsus [1493–1541]; see Turner 1980).

The specialized occupation of "doctor" began to develop in the Middle Ages. Since healing was highly supernaturalized in this period, the church attempted to control healing. Nonclerical healing was severely limited and suspect of being aided by the devil. Two groups of healers were in conflict with church-approved healing: Jewish doctors and "white" witches (typically women)—members of the community who used herbs, potions, magic, charms, and elements of pre-Christian religions to cure disease and ward off evil influences (see Ehrenreich and English 1973). These healers were a special target of the Inquisition and witch-hunts in several countries. When the church declared that "if a woman dare to cure without having studied, she is a witch and must die," it was legitimating only its own controlled version of medicine and the medical occupation (Szasz 1970:91). The specialized occupation of doctor developed largely through the establishment of university medical schools and the creation of medical guilds, which increased the authority of physicians against the claims of other healers. Indeed, church-approved physicians were often called upon to identify and certify witches. Nevertheless, formally recognized physicians were unable to command a monopoly over healing services, largely because the state of their craft did not inspire public confidence.

The modern medical profession owes its preeminence largely to the *rationalization* and further specialization of medicine which began during the Renaissance and proceeded rapidly after about 1850. Two spheres of rationalization are relevant: the application of rational science to medical discoveries, and the rational organization of the profession. Medical knowledge was increasingly based upon scientific methods of discovery and utilization of technology and technique. Breaking free of religious normative constraints, medical science began to treat the human body as an object—open to observation, dissection and autopsy, and pharmacological experimentation. Technological developments (such as the invention of the microscope and other diagnostic tools) were also a part of this rationalization process. Especially important was the development, in the latter part of the nineteenth century, of the idea that specific agents (e.g., bacteria) caused specific diseases (Freidson 1970:16). Access to specialized knowledge and specialized technologies uniquely "qualified" the physician.

Medical knowledge increasingly focused on *disease*, a biophysical condition, rather than on *illness*, the complex social, psychological, and spiritual condition of the sick person (Kleinman 1978). Rational medicine has an inherent tendency to treat the human body as an object rather than as a person. This biological determinism is linked to professional dominance. It promotes the image of the physician as active and powerful, the client as passive and objectlike. The sick person must give up control of his or her own body and rely upon the knowledge and power of the professional (Young 1976:18, 19).

Similarly, the organization of the medical profession itself became increasingly rationalized; as knowledge and technical skill became more specialized, physicians' areas of expertise became more compartmentalized. As physicians divided specialties among themselves, they also consolidated their control and prestige by annexing and subordinating a number of competing medical workers such as nurses, pharmacists, and medical technicians. Other competitors, such as midwives and bone-setters, were effectively driven out of practice and their functions taken over by the medical profession (Friedson 1970:52). This process of increasing medical control was not without its detractors; for example, there were popular movements in the eighteenth and nineteenth centuries which opposed medical dominance and promoted self-care, but these proved ephemeral (Risse et al. 1977).

In America, one specific medical approach (called "allopathy") gained a monopoly over medical practice, education, and licensing. This monopoly excluded from legitimacy most competing medical approaches, such as homeopathy, osteopathy, chiropractic, and naturopathy (Wardwell 1972). The dominant medical system also reduced the legitimacy of other institutional areas, such as religion. In a number of court cases in this century, religious groups have had their involvement in healing censured or circumscribed (Burkholder 1974; Szasz 1970).

The medical profession today has thus achieved an officially approved monopoly over the definition of health and illness and the treatment of persons defined as "sick" (Freidson 1970:5). Indeed, through the increasing *medicalization of deviance*, the medical profession has claimed jurisdiction over a wide range of disapproved behavior: alcoholism, homosexuality, promiscuity, drug addiction, arson, suicide, child abuse, and civil disobedience (Conrad and Schneider 1980). There is a widespread shift from defining such deviance as "sin" to considering it to be "sickness." The concept of sickness, however, far from being a neutral scientific concept, is ultimately a moral one, establishing an evaluation of normality or desirability (Freidson 1970:208). The seeming rationality of medical diagnosis thus masks the evaluative process. Medical jurisdiction over deviant behaviors does not depend upon medical knowledge of their causes or cures, for medicine is no better able to cure alcoholism or homosexuality than can religion or law. The dominance of medical definitions is due to popular and juridical acceptance of medical authority (Bittner 1968; Freidson 1970:251–253). Control over the definition of deviance leads to power in other areas of social control: certifying deviance and applying therapy. Social control may seem pleasanter or more humane when the deviance is considered to be sickness rather than crime or sin, but the potency of the control agencies is just as great.

Another important characteristic of the institution of medicine in modern Western societies is the separation of the functions of curing disease from the functions of providing meaning and belonging to the sick person. Medicine limits itself to the cure of disease (a biophysical entity) and the physical tending of the diseased person. The meaning and belonging functions of healing are treated as relatively unimportant and are relegated to the private-sphere institutions of family and religion. If one views the Western medical system from a cross-cultural perspective, this segregation can be more clearly seen (Kleinman 1978).

All medical systems, no matter how "scientific" or "primitive," address similar functions: construction of the illness experience; cognitive organization and management of the illness experience; healing practices per se; and management of death (Young 1976). Construction of the illness experience involves giving symbolic form (i.e., meaning) to the illness (Kleinman 1973:160–161). Each culture attaches different meanings to different biophysical situations; members learn how to feel, experience, and interpret the illness itself. For example, the meaning attached to pain determines how it will be experienced. Illness is not a simple biophysical fact but—through symbolic interpretation—is shaped into a human experience.

Western medicine, in contrast with traditional (folk) healing systems, has seriously truncated these meaning-providing aspects. Likewise, management of death is limited in Western medicine. Although the medical profession has gained authority to define death and to control its usual social setting, it has generally avoided the problem of what dying means or how the dying person and family feel about the process of dying. Instead, the meaning-providing functions are segregated and relegated to separate agencies, usually the family and religious representatives, such as hospital chaplain. Because Western medicine is focused on the curing of "disease," rather than on the healing of illness, the provision of meaning is privatized and undermined. Secularized medicine is generally unable to deal with *illness*—the complex of perceptions and experiences of the sick person.

The secularization of health and healing is the process by which the Western medical system has come to adopt (and defend) the notion that health, illness, and dying have no real meaning beyond their biophysical reality determinable by empirical, rational means.

Institutions of the private sphere are allowed to provide meaning, as voluntary and purely subjective interpretations, only so long as that interpretive scheme does not interfere with the medical dominance and its biophysical treatment of the disease.

NEW SOURCES OF THINKING ABOUT RELIGION AND HEALING

The secularization model, as defined here, clearly applies to the Western medical system. Recent developments in theory and research, however, are leading Western medicine to a renewed respect for the role of religion in health and healing. Simultaneously, new social phenomena are challenging the medical establishment on issues arising from its secularization.

NEW THEORETICAL APPROACHES

Interesting new approaches are developing in sociology, anthropology, and medicine itself. Medical researchers have begun to document the powerful impact of the individual's social and emotional situation on the causation of disease and on the healing process. These findings suggest a number of ways in which religious beliefs, symbols, rituals, and communities can be important influences in health and healing.

Increasing evidence in Western medical terms suggests that illnesses previously thought to be purely biogenic are related to social and psychological states such as stress, conflict, sense of "threat," role dissatisfaction, rapid social change, and sense of powerlessness (House 1974; Kiely 1972; Rahe et al. 1964; Selye 1975; Wolff 1962). One medical interpretation suggests that stress and emotional distress may influence the immunologic system through the central nervous system and possibly through the stress-responsive endocrine system (Solomon 1969). If this is the case, then social-emotional supports, such as might be provided by religious and other nonmedical healing groups, may indeed be therapeutic—physically as well as emotionally.

Furthermore, studies of the impact of stress now emphasize that the individual's response is not based solely upon the stimulus/ stressor (e.g., life crisis) but rather upon the meaning or appraisal of that stimulus (Lazarus 1975). Thus nonmedical healing may work through the impact of individuals' meaning systems (i.e., religion) on their experience and self-regulation of emotions (see Schwartz 1982; Hochschild 1979; Lazarus 1975). Another approach emphasizes the psychotherapeutic effects of ritual and symbolism. For example, properly "distanced" ritual may produce the catharsis necessary for emotional healing (Scheff 1979). Religious meditation, ritual life, and social support networks may provide significant coping responses for anxiety, stress, and other emotionally and physically debilitating situations (Caplan and Killelea 1976; Cobb 1976; Levin and Idler 1981; Ness 1980; Turner 1982).

Another line of investigation shows the significance of helplessness and hopelessness in bringing on illness (Rogers 1979; Schmale and Iker 1971; Schmale 1972). Conversely, raising the sick person's hope and sense of personal empowerment is found to be physically, as well as emotionally, therapeutic (Rogers 1979; McGuire 1982, 1983). For example, oncologist Carl Simonton and his associates teach cancer patients to mobilize their personal resources to fight their illness by using vivid imagery and visualization (Simonton 1975).

Many researchers are taking the "placebo effect" more seriously, suggesting that the healing that takes place this way is linked to the symbolic empowerment of the sick person (Brody 1977:121, 122). A chemically inert pill is not real medicine, but the sense of power the individual gains by that symbol is real. The "placebo effect" may be merely one way of describing an individual's response to his or her society's peculiar symbolization of empowerment—be it an amulet, ritual word, pill, or something else. Medication (especially "pills") is a major contemporary symbolization of the power to heal and the power of medical technology (Pellegrino 1976). Religious rituals and symbols may impart a similar sense of empowerment to those who believe in them. This symbolic empowerment may, indeed, have concrete physical and psychological effects (Frank 1973; Shapiro 1964).

There is a growing medical and social-psychological literature suggesting that biophysical conditions are intimately intertwined with a sense of well-being, mastery, and harmony in one's social environment (Fabrega 1974; Freund 1982; Hayes-Bautista and Haveston 1977). If this is the case, the idea that religion may be able to address those problems as well as, if not better than, the dominant scientific medical system is plausible.

These theories from psychosomatic medicine dovetail remarkably with a number of sociological and anthropological interpretations that emphasize the role of power, domination, and control in illness and healing (Freund 1982; Glick 1967). Likewise, a sociology of the body illustrates the wealth of meanings attached to the human body (Douglas 1966, 1970; Dreitzel 1981; Durkheim 1965; Turner 1974). These theories suggest that religious ritual may address the healing of the metaphorical body as well as the individual's physical body.

NEW EMPIRICAL DEVELOPMENTS

Two recent social developments challenge the secularization of healing. One is the increasing prominence of healing in new religious movements, both outside and within the churches. Many of the new religious movements emphasize physical, emotional, and spiritual healing. At the same time, quite a few established churches have renewed interest in their healing ministry. Faith healing previously carried the connotation of being invariably limited to uneducated, lower-class sectarians; now, however, it is prominent in numerous middle-class churches and movements, such as the Catholic Charismatic Renewal, Order of St. Luke (Episcopalian), and Women Aglow (an interdenominational pentecostal association). Faith healing is typically used in addition to medical treatment. Few middle-class healing movements recommend foregoing secular medicine; rather, they generally emphasize the limitations of modern medicine—especially its inability to heal the whole person.

The second development is the parallel rise of a number of alternative therapies.[2] Some of these alternative therapies draw heavily upon the Christian tradition; others are adaptations of Eastern practices. Many more are eclectic combinations: Christian and Western occult traditions, Eastern thought and practice, native American healing, elements of psychotherapeutic approaches, science and pseudoscience. Although some of these alternative therapies are organized or otherwise embodied in movements, others operate simply as proprietary courses.

A strong case could be made that these alternative therapies are, in effect, new religions on the American scene. They do appear to function as religions for many adherents—providing cosmologies, rituals, a language for the interpretation of believers' worlds, a social context for belief and practice, and a group of fellow believers. One observer suggests that they be considered "self-religions" because, although they do have notions of transcendence, their focus is more on the believing *individual,* and the motivation to participate is frequently one's *self*-enhancement or realization (Heelas 1982).

Alternative therapeutic approaches are widespread among middle-class, relatively well-educated persons—sometimes as adherents' sole belief system and sometimes in combination with more traditional religious belief systems. For example, a 1976 Gallup poll found that 4 percent of those polled had engaged in transcendental meditation and another 3 percent had practiced yoga; a further 1 percent were involved in an Eastern religion. Projecting from this sample, these figures suggest that over ten million Americans are involved in just a few of these "alternatives" (Gallup 1976). A 1973 study in California found a predictably higher percentage of participants in the San Francisco Bay Area: approximately 8 percent had participated in yoga, 5 percent in transcendental meditation, 3 percent in Zen, 1.5 percent in est, and 1.1 percent in Scientology. Furthermore, this study documented the fact that there were more respondents who considered getting to know the inner self and becoming aware of their own bodies to be important than there were respondents who attached importance to having a high-paying job, having a beautiful home, or belonging to church or synagogue (Wuthnow 1976, 1978). A recent study in a relatively staid East Coast suburban community likewise found alternative therapies widespread; hundreds of suburbanites in this catchment area were found to have employed nonmedical healing, and over eighty-five different healing methods were found in use (McGuire 1983). These figures are merely suggestive of the scope of this phenomenon, which deserves much more empirical investigation.

It appears that, while members of "modern" Western societies are utilizing secularized medicine, they are also seeking something more. A number of similarities between the new Christian healing movements and the other alternative healing systems emphasizes the challenge of these movements to the secularization of health and healing. Both the Christian and alternative healing groups assert the need for *wholeness*. They emphasize that true healing depends on the recognition that social, emotional, and spiritual aspects are intimately intertwined with the physical. In contrast, secularized medicine has difficulty dealing with the whole person. The specialization of medical tasks, segregation of the sick person from other aspects of social life, together with physicians' "disease model" concept (i.e., the notion that what they are treating is a discrete physical entity) make it unlikely that medicine can address the whole person.

Another parallel between Christian healing movements and other alternative therapies is that both proffer alternative *norms for healthiness*. Their definitions of health are far broader than those used by the medical profession. These broad definitions imply that healing is an appropriate response to a wide range of physical, emotional, spiritual, social, economic, and political "problems." The symbolic and metaphorical signficance of health and healing are highlighted. Spiritual values, such as oneness with God, balance, and harmony with the universe, are critical.

The main point of divergence between Christian healing movements and many of the other new alternative healing systems is on the relative importance of the self. While both types of healing promote the empowerment of the sick person, their conceptions of the source of healing power are very different. Christian groups typically view the power as transcendent, external to the individual. Most (but not all) alternative healing groups considered individual power to be an expression of some greater power, but individuals need not look outside themselves for the source of the empowerment they need. Accordingly, if they are weak, it is because they are not in touch with their own power. Healing, in the Christian tradition, emphasizes the self in "proper" (i.e., subordinate) relationship to a transcendent deity. The renewed emphasis on healing in Christian groups may, indeed, be a ritual response to contemporary urges to "free" the self from constraints of roles, norms, and other "hang-ups." Therapy/healing thus realigns the individual with the group-prescribed ways of thinking, feeling, and believing. In contrast, many of the other alternative modes of healing emphasize a flexible self with a different conception of individual role, responsibility, and moral accountability (see Bird 1979; Tipton 1982). Accordingly, therapy/healing frees the self and the body from many learned constraints, opening new possibilities and potentials for choice and continued "growth."

More data are needed before comprehensive theoretical interpretations of these phenomena are possible. A productive line of questioning would include: What are the socio-economic contexts of these developments regarding attitudes toward the self and the body? Do these alternative health/healing movements possibly reflect internal contradictions in the structure of production in modern society? For example, the nature of much work (especially that of the middle classes) requires considerable investment of self, as well as management of body and emotions, but involves the problem of different appropriate selves for different tasks and roles. Furthermore, the public-private split highlights the discrepancies between a seemingly autonomous self in the private sphere and the controlled self in the bureaucratic structure. Do emphases on the self actually challenge the production sphere, for example by minimizing workers' motivation to sacrifice their health to success on the job?

Are contemporary healing movements adaptations to or assertions against such features of modern socioeconomic life? Likewise, we could ask: Do such movements represent features of consumption in contemporary society? On one hand, they resemble items of consumption like other life-style factors; yet, at the same time, they emphasize that enhancing one's self and one's health is not a commodity. They also affirm the power of the individual, as consumer of medical services, to choose a course of healing for him or herself. Thus they represent a political statement against medical professional dominance. One hypothesis worth exploring is that much of the "new" therapy offered in such alternative healing groups may represent an attempt at the symbolic creation and socialization of a new kind of identity—a new mode of self-in-relation-to-the-world. The resulting mode of individualism may be one in which the self would have the flexibility to move between constantly changing roles and attachments, able to choose the quality of its emotional and physical experiences (Dreitzel 1981; see also Bird 1978; Lifton 1968; Luckman 1967; Robertson 1977, 1978).

An investigation of alternative healing in the context of the secularization of health and healing thus brings us squarely to some central classical issues about the relationship between various modes of individualism and their socioeconomic context. Both the revival of traditional Christian healing and the development of various alternative healing belief systems illustrate the elective affinity of these ideas to their adherents' social locations and social structural needs. The study of religion and healing appears to be an ideal focal point for understanding these broader sociological issues.

CONCLUSION

Although the history of the development of medicine in modern Western societies exemplifies the process of secularization, many new developments challenge both the continuation and the desirability of that trend. New movements have arisen which run counter to the secularized approach to health and healing; they proclaim the importance of treating the whole person—body, mind, and spirit, and they affirm the value of spiritual meaning, ritual, symbol, and community in the healing process. At the same time, new developments in psychosomatic medicine are evidence of a recognition that the prevention and healing of illness involves factors that are strongly influenced by religious belief, ritual, imagery, and social group support.

In the face of these developments, is the secularization model still useful in understanding religion and healing? Probably, yes. These developments demonstrate the complexity of the secularization process. It is clearly not unilinear or nonreversible. Also, some aspects of an institutional area may be undergoing secularizing tendencies, while other parts may be moving away from a secularized approach. At the same time, structural arrangements built into the fabric of modern society orient medical responses to human needs toward a secularized model. For example, the centrality of criteria such as cost-efficiency, insurance coverage, or scientific accountability make it unlikely that religious approaches to healing will receive much societal legitimacy. Professional dominance and the structure of the medical profession also mitigate against inroads by nonmedical healing; if anything, the medical profession may attempt to co-opt some aspects of nonmedical healing. The basic structural arrangements of Western medical practice thus work against desecularization. Although religion and healing may not, in reality, be such separate spheres as they previously appeared to be, whether desecularized healing achieves legitimacy may be essentially a political issue.

NOTES

1. Portions of this analysis are adapted from chapter 8 of my book, *Religion: The Social Context* (Belmont, Calif.: Wadsworth Publishing, 1981). Work on this essay was made possible by a grant of released time from Montclair State College. My thanks to Peter Freund and Edgar Mills for their thoughtful comments on this essay.

2. "Alternative therapies" here refers to a wide variety of nonmedical approaches to health and healing; they are typically based on a larger medical paradigm but few exclude the use of medical diagnosis and/or treatment. Some examples include Silva Mind Control, Shiatsu, Rebirthing, Jain Yoga and Meditation, TM, psychic healing, est, Psychosynthesis, Astara, Cornucopia.

REFERENCES

Allen, Gillian, and Roy Wallis
  1976   "Pentecostalists as a Medical Minority." *In* R. Wallis and P. Mor-
            ley, eds., *Marginal Medicine.* New York: Free Press. Pp. 110–137.
Berger, Peter
  1965   "Toward a Sociological Understanding of Psychoanalysis," *Social
            Research* 32(1):26–41.
Bird, Frederick
  1978   "Charisma and Ritual in New Religious Movements." *In* J.
            Needleman and G. Baker, eds., *Understanding the New Religions.*
            New York: Seabury. Pp. 173–189.
  1979   "The Pursuit of Innocence: New Religious Movements and Moral
            Accountability," *Sociological Analysis* 40, 4:335–346.
Bittner, Egon
  1968   "The Structure of Psychiatric Influence," *Mental Hygiene* 52:423–
            430.
Brody, Howard
  1977   *Placebos and the Philosophy of Medicine.* Chicago: University of
            Chicago Press.
Burkholder, John Richard
  1974   "The Law Knows No Heresy: Marginal Religious Movements and
            the Courts." *In* I. Zaretsky and M. Leone, eds., *Religious Move-
            ments in Contemporary America.* Princeton: Princeton University
            Press.
Caplan, Gerald, and Marie Killelea
  1976   *Support Systems and Mutual Help: Multidisciplinary Explorations.*
            New York: Grune and Stratton.
Cobb, Sidney
  1976   "Social Support as a Moderator of Life Stresses," *Psychosomatic
            Medicine* 38(5):300–314.
Conrad, Peter, and Joseph W. Schneider
  1980   *Deviance and Medicalization: From Badness to Sickness.* St. Louis:
            Mosby.
Douglas, Mary
  1966   *Purity and Danger.* London: Routledge and Kegan Paul.
  1970   *Natural Symbols.* New York: Pantheon.
Dreitzel, Hans P.
  1981   "The Socialization of Nature: Western Attitudes towards Body
            and Emotions." *In* P. Heelas and A. Lock, eds., *Indigenous
            Psychologies: The Anthropology of the Self.* New York: Academic
            Press. Pp. 205–223.
Durkheim, Emile
  1965   *The Elementary Forms of the Religious Life.* New York: Collier/Free
            Press. (Originally published in 1915.)

Ehrenreich, Barbara, and Deidre English
1973 "Witches, Midwives, and Nurses: Historical Review of Women as Healers," *Monthly Review* 25(5):25–40.

Fabrega, Horacio
1974 *Disease and Social Behavior: An Interdisciplinary Perspective.* Cambridge: MIT Press.

Frank, Jerome D.
1973 *Persuasion and Healing.* New York: Schocken.

Freidson, Eliot
1970 *Profession of Medicine: A Study of the Sociology of Applied Knowledge.* New York: Dodd, Mead.

Freund, Peter
1982 *The Civilized Body: Social Domination, Control, and Health.* Philadelphia: Temple University Press.

Gallup Poll
1976 "Americans taking up religious, spiritual experimentation." Princeton, N.J.: Gallup International. 18 November.

Glick, Leonard B.
1967 "Medicine as an Ethnographic Category: The Gimi of the New Guinea Highlands," *Ethnology* 6 (1):31–56.

Hayes-Bautista, D., and D. Haveston
1977 "Holistic Health Care," *Social Policy* 7(5):7–13.

Heelas, Paul
1982 "Californian Self-Religions and Socializing the Subjective." *In* E. Barker, ed., *New Religious Movements: A Perspective for Understanding Society.* New York and Toronto: Edwin Mellen Press. Pp. 69–85.

Hochschild, Arlie R.
1979 "Emotion Work, Feeling Rules, and Social Structure," *American Journal of Sociology* 85(3):551–575.

House, James
1974 "Occupational Stress and Coronary Heart Disease: A Review and Theoretical Integration," *Journal of Health and Social Behavior* 15:17–21.

Kiely, W. F.
1972 "Coping with Severe Illness." *In* Z. Lipowski, ed., *Advances in Psychosomatic Medicine: Psychosocial Aspects of Physical Illness.* Basel: Karger. Pp. 105–118.

Kiev, Ari
1973 "Magic, Faith and Healing in Modern Psychiatry." *In* R. Cox, ed., *Religious Systems and Psychotherapy.* Springfield, Ill.: Chas. C. Thomas. Pp. 225–235.

Kleinman, Arthur M.
1973 "Some Issues for a Comparative Study of Medical Healing," *International Journal of Social Psychiatry* 19 (3/4):159–165.
1978 "The Failure of Western Medicine," *Human Nature* 1:63–68.

Lazarus, Richard S.
  1975   "The Self-Regulation of Emotion." *In* L. Levi, ed., *Emotions—Their Parameters and Measurements*. New York: Raven Press. Pp. 47–67.
Levin, Lowell, and Ellen Idler
  1981   *The Hidden Health Care System: Mediating Structures and Medicine*. Cambridge, Mass.: Ballinger.
Lifton, R. J.
  1968   "Protean Man," *Partisan Review* 35:13–27.
Luckmann, Thomas
  1967   *The Invisible Religion: The Problem of Religion in Modern Society*. New York: Macmillan.
McGuire, Meredith B.
  1982   *Pentecostal Catholics: Power, Charisma and Order in a Religious Movement*. Philadelphia: Temple University Press.
  1983   "Words of Power: Personal Empowerment and Healing," *Culture, Medicine, and Psychiatry* 7:1–20.
Ness, Robert
  1980   "The Impact of Indigenous Healing Activity: An Empirical Study of Two Fundamentalist Churches," *Social Science and Medicine* 14B (3):167–180.
Nudelman, Arthur E.
  1976   "The Maintenance of Christian Science in Scientific Society." *In* R. Wallis and P. Morley, eds., *Marginal Medicine*. New York: Free Press. Pp. 42–60.
Pattison, E. Mansell
  1973   "Faith Healing: A Study of Personality and Function." *Journal of Nervous and Mental Disease* 157 (6):397–409.
  1974   "Ideological Support for the Marginal Middle Class: Faith Healing and Glossolalia." *In* I. Zaretsky and M. Leone, eds., *Religious Movements in Contemporary America*. Princeton: Princeton University Press. Pp. 418–458.
Pellegrino, E. D.
  1976   "Prescribing and Drug Ingestion: Symbols and Substances," *Drug Intelligence and Clinical Pharmacy* 10:624–630.
Prince, Raymond
  1972   "Fundamental Differences of Psychoanalysis and Faith Healing," *International Journal of Psychiatry* 10:125–128.
Rahe, Richard, M. Meyer, M. Smith, G. Kjaer, and T. Holmes
  1964   "Social Stress and Illness Onset," *Journal of Psychosomatic Research* 8:35–44.
Risse, Guenter et al., eds.
  1977   *Medicine Without Doctors: Home Health Care in American History*. New York: Neale Watson Academic Publishers.
Robertson, Roland
  1977   "Individualism, Societalism, Worldliness, Universalism: Thematizing Theoretical Sociology of Religion," *Sociological Analysis* 38

(4):281–308.

1978   "Theoretical Comments on Religion and Society in Modern America: Weber Revisited." Paper presented to the World Congress of Sociology.

Rogers, William R.
1979   "Helplessness and Agency in the Healing Process." *In* W. R. Rogers and D. Barnard, eds., *Nourishing the Humanistic in Medicine.* Pittsburgh: University of Pittsburgh Press. Pp. 25–51.

Scheff, Thomas J.
1979   *Catharsis in Healing, Ritual, and Drama.* Berkeley, Los Angeles, London: University of California Press.

Schmale, A. H.
1972   "Giving Up as a Final Common Pathway to Changes in Health." *In* Z. Lipowski, ed., *Advances in Psychosomatic Medicine: Psychosocial Aspects of Physical Illness.* Basel: Karger. Pp. 20–40.

Schmale, A. H. and I. V. Iker
1971   "Hopelessness as a Predictor of Cervical Cancer," *Social Science and Medicine* 5:95–100.

Schwartz, Gary
1982   "Physiological Patterning and Emotion: Implications for the Self-Regulation of Emotion." *In* K. R. Blankstein and J. Polivy, eds., *Self-Control and Self-Modification of Emotional Behavior.* New York: Plenum. Pp. 13–27.

Selye, Hans
1975   *Stress Without Distress.* New York: Signet.

Shapiro, A. K.
1964   "Factors Contributing to the Placebo Effect," *American Journal of Psychotherapy,* suppl. 1 (18):73–88.

Simonton, Carl
1975   "The Role of the Mind in Cancer Therapy." *In* S. Dean, ed., *Psychiatry and Mysticism.* Chicago: Nelson-Hall. Pp. 293–308.

Solomon, George F.
1969   "Emotions, Stress, the Central Nervous System, and Immunity," *Annals of the New York Academy of Science* 164(2):335–343.

Spencer, Metta
1982   "Therapy and Eastern Religion: A Study in Cultural Evolution." Paper presented to the Society for the Scientific Study of Religion.

Szasz, Thomas
1970   *The Manufacture of Madness.* New York: Dell.

Tipton, Steven M.
1982   *Getting Saved from the Sixties: The Transformation of Moral Meaning in American Culture by Alternative Religious Movements.* Berkeley, Los Angeles, London: University of California Press.

Torrey, E. Fuller
1972   *The Mind Game: Witchdoctors and Psychiatrists.* New York: Emerson Hall.

Turner, Bryan S.
   1980   "The Body and Religion: Towards an Alliance of Medical Sociol-
             ogy and Sociology of Religion," *The Annual Review of the Social
             Sciences of Religion* 4:247–286.
Turner, R. Jay
   1982   "Direct, Indirect and Moderating Effects of Social Support upon
             Psychological Distress and Associated Conditions." *In* H. B. Kap-
             lan, ed., *Psychosocial Stress: Trends in Theory and Research.* New
             York: Academic Press.
Turner, Victor
   1974   *Dramas, Fields, and Metaphors: Symbolic Action in Human Society.*
             Ithaca: Cornell University Press.
Wardwell, Walter I.
   1965   "Christian Science Healing," *Journal for the Scientific Study of Reli-
             gion* 4(2):175–181.
Wolff, Harold G.
   1962   "A Concept of Disease in Man," *Psychosomatic Medicine* 24(1):25–
             30.
Wuthnow, Robert
   1976   *The Consciousness Reformation.* Berkeley, Los Angeles, London:
             University of California Press.
   1978   *Experimentation in American Religion.* Berkeley, Los Angeles, Lon-
             don: University of California Press.
Young, Allan
   1976   "Some Implications of Medical Beliefs and Practices for Social
             Anthropology," *American Anthropologist* 78(1):5–24.

XVIII
Mysticism
Ralph W. Hood, Jr.

Social scientists continue to develop theory and research strategies without specific reference to the validity of references to the sacred. Although such strategies can have limited methodological usefulness, ultimate questions concerning the sacred cannot be forever avoided. This is particularly evident in the study of mysticism, in which questions concerning the persistence of the sacred and its diverse manifestations become crucial. Whether in new settings, undeniably religious, or in new modes of experience, undeniably holy, mysticism forces the scientist and the theologian to be at least familiar with each other's concepts. Here questions concerning the meeting of the sacred and the solitary person raise crucial issues at the interface of the social sciences and theology, which cannot be ignored either by a methodological stance that dogmatically forces the sacred out the front door or by one that surreptitiously sneaks the sacred in through the back door. The study of mysticism requires the reconceptualization of areas of concern that have become sterile insofar as their relationship to the sacred have been ignored.

The centrality of mysticism to the study of religious experience remains unquestioned. Yet mystical claims to an unmediated union with an ultimate transcendent reality appear perpetually problematic—both for theologies and for social scientific theories. While the profundity of mysticism as a human experience is usually accepted by both theologians and scientists, mystical interpretations of such experiences are seldom given much credence. In Scharfstein's (1973:45) quaint phrasing, the mystics' claims to knowledge based upon their experiences are but "ontological fairy-tales." Thus, as a general rule, mystical experience has been a constant target for reductionistic explanations. Certainly among classic theorists, whether sociologists or psychologists, mystical experiences have been analyzed as experiences of union *misinterpreted* by those who would think they have been united with an ultimate transcendent reality (whether interpreted as God or not). Although sociologists and psychologists differ in easily predictable ways in terms of the broad nature of the conceptual categories they use to define the "real" object to which the mystic feels united, seldom have social scientists seriously entertained the notion that mystics might be correct in their claims to have directly experienced ultimate reality.

Sociologically, mystical claims to "know" ultimate reality in a direct experiential sense are often seen as threatening to religious institutions and dogmas whose very authority is thereby undermined. As the Bishop is reported to have said to Joan of Arc at her trial, "Between you and God there stands the church" (Stobart 1971:157).

Historically, religious institutions have a varied record of reacting to mystical experiences. They have attempted to discredit some mystics while accepting others within the folds of a particular institutional dogma. Whatever the ultimate nature of mystical experience, its proper reporting and interpretation have always been of prime concern to religious institutions. This is the root of the paradox of mysticism noted by classical theorists—its Janus-faced nature. On one hand it supports and revitalizes established religious institutions when it is normatively interpreted and channeled; on the other hand it challenges and rebels against religious institutions when interpreted independently of established dogmas and sacraments.

In this context, Ozment's (1973) historical work provided a theretofore neglected theoretical basis for sociological studies of mysticism. Focusing on the sixteenth century, Ozment argues persuasively for the conceptual basis on which mysticism, typically assumed to be linked with asceticism and conservatism, is also linked to activism and radical protest. Ozment notes that medieval theology distinguished between *potentia Dei ordinata,* or the mere facticity of God's acts in history, and *potentia Dei absoluta,* or the facticity of God's absolute freedom. While the former identifies "what is," the latter emphasizes that "what is" need not be. God's freedom is absolute and never limited by its revealed actuality in human history. In a similar vein, Ozment suggests a *potentia hominis absoluta* as the subjective basis for human transcendence postulated upon a parallel for unmediated contact with ultimate reality that transcends apparent limitations of physiological states and structures. Ozment's suggestion is relevant to proposals we shall make later regarding the inclusion of theological assumptions within a social science of mysticism. For now it is sufficient to note that a mysticism rooted in a *potentia hominis absoluta* can be socially threatening to those who fear a loss of authority in any contact with ultimate reality, unmediated by the authority of dogma or sacrament. This fact is emphasized in the classic work of Troeltsch (1931) in which two senses of mysticism are noted.

In one sense, mysticism is simply a profound, primary religious awareness of transcendent reality that serves as a human experiential basis for religious institutions and dogmas. Such a mysticism is compatible with almost any dogma or structure and is simply the existential foundation that religion molds into its various social forms. As such it has no unique sociological importance. In another sense, mysticism as a separate form emerges historically as a deliberate cultivated act of transcendence, often rising in opposition to established religious institutions, if not independently of them altogether. As such, it is an independent religious form, distinct from both church and sect. Garrett's (1975) recent reemphasis of Troeltsch's analysis of mysticism aptly refers to the "maligned mysticism" within contemporary sociology. His point is well taken and, as we shall note shortly, of immense value in clarifying the limited empirical studies of mysticism within sociology. Yet in this context it is worth noting that classical theorists saw the emergence of mysticism as problematic, a point Robertson (1975) reminds us of concerning Weberian mysticism, and a point also characteristic of Troeltsch's analysis. Such negative views of mysticism are to be contrasted with modern empirical studies of mysticism which are often apologetic in tone. The difference is largely due to the fact that current empirical research in the sociology of mysticism takes place within a theoretical vacuum, a point leading to some unnecessary confusion. Nowhere is this more evident than in the survey studies typical of contemporary sociology of mysticism.

Contemporary survey studies of mysticism are largely linked to rather simple empirical findings regarding relationships between reports of mystical experiences and demographic variables. In some ambitious efforts, such as the Religious Experience Unit at Oxford University (Hardy 1979), data are severely limited by sampling procedures (e.g., mail responses to newspaper solicitations). Yet other studies have used rather sophisticated sampling procedures in both America (Greeley 1974; Wuthnow 1978) and Britain (Hay and Morisy 1978). Overall, this research is remarkably consistent in its findings in at least three senses. First, at least one-third of all respondents indicate a positive response to questions variously worded to reflect a report of mystical experience; second, reports increase in frequency among females, the educated, the privileged, and the older. Third, while reports of mystical experience relate positively to church membership, significant percentages of nonchurch members also report mystical experiences. For instance, despite the three to one difference in rate of church attendance between America and Britain, national surveys in both countries indicate similar percentages of reported mystical experience.

Obvious methodological issues in such survey research have been noted elsewhere (Spilka et al., forthcoming), yet here I want to emphasize the need to link classical social theory on mysticism with this empirical research. Two examples should suffice.

First, the consistent finding of increased reports of mystical experience among the educated and advantaged has often been discussed in terms of a crude Marxism in which such findings are "unanticipated." Yet clearly Troeltsch's discussion of mysticism anticipates its emergence as the religion of the educated insofar as it is a reflective and rational pondering upon a directly cultivated awareness of transcendent reality. In this sense of mysticism, discussed previously, one should anticipate not only the demographic relationships typically reported but also the association of this type of mysticism with social experimentation, as in Wuthnow's data. Likewise, if the fundamental capacity of humans to relate to transcendent reality is shaped by religious institutions, then one might expect more reports of mysticism among church members. Hence, classical theory can serve to provide theoretical clarification of reports of mysticism among different groups (church members and nonmembers) insofar as a different sense of mysticism is likely to be operative in each group. In this sense Gaede's recent (1981) addition of an inductive-orthodoxy category to Berger's inductive-heterodoxy category is pure Troeltsch. There are mysticisms within and outside institutions. While Berger's conceptualizations lead him to classify mysticism only as encouraging "heterodoxy," Gaede's addition (accepted by Berger [1981]) once again emphasizes mysticism's Janus nature. The relevance of these natures remains unquestioned, and their roots in Troeltsch need to be emphasized if for no other reason than that some theoretical continuity in the study of mysticism is necessary. Such an awareness belies the confusion in contemporary empirical research in which the tendency is to "test" two opposing views of the relationship between mysticism and institutional support as if it were an "either/or" issue.

Yet as Troeltsch's own work suggests, a mysticism reported in nondogmatic and nonsacramental language is likely to be a mysticism of protest and change, as opposed to one reported in dogmatic and sacramental language which serves to support a particular church. Hence, the paradox some find in empirical studies of mysticism is but a reflection of the paradox of mysticism itself in its various senses suggested by classical theory, of which Troeltsch is but one example.

The second point to note is that, among contemporary researchers, the inclusion of a methodological theism often treats the report of mystical experience in a nonproblematic sense. The research is simply descriptive and merely assumes the validity of the report—that is, persons in fact experienced transcendent reality. As such, there is no need to develop reductionistic theories. Yet even assuming a methodological theism, why it is that God or transcendent reality is differentially revealed and socially situated is curiously unconfronted by critical theory. What is needed is a critical sociological theory informed by theological concepts which permits the reality of mysticism to be confronted within its differing social situations. Until then, neither classic theory, unfettered by empirical constraints, nor crude empirical generalizations, unharnessed by critical theory, will do much to illuminate the social aspects of mysticism.

We will return to the controversial issue of a methodological theism later. For now it is sufficient to note that, as Jaki (1978:97–98) has emphasized in a broader context, classical theorists sought a scientific orientation within the confines of theological assumptions: "Meinecke, Mannheim, Troeltsch and others would have also said with Dilthey that their whole life was devoted to overcoming the ensuing 'anarchy of opinions.' " Only with a methodological theism can a crude relativism associated with the uncritical evaluation of reported mystical experiences be overcome.

If the contemporary sociology of mysticism is uninformed by classical theory, its appeal to phenomenology to clarify mystical experience is curious—especially since it is precisely phenomenological works on mysticism that have led to the extensive resurgence of empirical research on mysticism in contemporary psychology. As R. J. Morris and I have shown (1981), virtually all contemporary empirical studies of mysticism can be traced either directly or indirectly to Stace's (1961) now classic phenomenological "common core criteria" of mysticism. While Stace's work has recently generated an entire volume of critical philosophical response (Katz 1978), his illumination of the phenomenology of an experience of unity at the center of mysticism remains unchallenged. Stace's criteria, operationalized in a paper/pencil scale

(Hood 1975) or in other forms, provide an important link to classical sociological theory that has yet to be explicitly noted.

While Stace distinguishes introvertive (imageless) and extrovertive (imagery) mysticism, factor analyses of scales based on Stace's criteria are consistent in discovering two factors that cut across the imagery distinction. In particular, as both Holm (1982) and I (Hood 1975) have argued, a distinction can be made between minimal phenomenological properties of mysticism—such as ego loss, experience of unity— and interpretive evaluations, especially religious evaluations, of such properties. As such, a crucial theoretical link can be made to our discussion of Troeltsch's two "senses" of mysticism. On one hand, religiously interpreted mysticism is rooted within traditions and institutions and serves to support and sustain them in a rather sociologically "neutral sense." On the other hand, the more phenomenologically basic mystical criteria are linked to mysticism in Troeltsch's sense of a religious orientation that can be an alternative to established institutional religious forms. Holm's cross-cultural replication of much of my work points to this same distinction. While the parallels to Troeltsch may not be precise, research on mysticism in psychology can be clarified by these two dominant "senses" of mysticism. Nowhere is this more clear than in one of the major areas of psychological research on mysticism—its relationship to religious orientation.

A wide variety of studies has continually demonstrated a positive relationship between intrinsic religiosity and mysticism (Spilka et al., forthcoming). Yet in light of our discussion above, it is perhaps more important to note that such studies using the Mysticism scale I developed find that intrinsic persons differ from extrinsic persons primarily in the interpretative factor. Likewise, research relating reported mystical experience and church membership has rather consistently shown that while both church and non–church members have high reports of mystical experience, non–church members score higher on the phenomenological factor, church members higher on the religious interpretative factor. Hence, a fair summary of this empirical research is that it meshes nicely with classic sociological theory. It is less the case that mysticism per se is differentially situated in society than that the two senses of mysticism are differentially situated, as Troeltsch predicted. On one hand, intrinsic religiosity with its firm church commitment is linked to mysticism, especially, as one might expect, to a religiously interpreted mysticism. Mysticism is here the experiential foundation on which social institutions base experiential orientations to transcendence. On the other hand, mysticism cultivated and sought outside institutions, as indicated by the minimal phenomenological factor of Hood's Scale, reflects an orientation toward transcendence cultivated independently of traditional dogma and sacraments and leads to innovative religious alternatives much as Troeltsch predicted.

If religious orientation differentially relates to the two basic senses of mysticism suggested by Troeltsch, studies of mysticism and psychopathology can also be linked to this distinction. Classic psychological theorists attempted to link mysticism with psychopathology on purely conceptual grounds, a position I have criticized elsewhere (Hood 1976). Yet it is true that some investigators continue to link mysticism and pathology using inappropriate indices of pathology whose items often reflect mystical claims. To wit: insofar as the empirical indices of mysticism are often also used as indicators of psychopathology, independent assessments of mysticism and psychopathology become impossible (Hood 1974). Likewise, *functioning* religious groups are by definition adjusted, despite "pathological" indices of their members. Hence, empirical studies of mysticism and psychopathology remain rather trite conceptually: indices are chosen that demonstrate "pathology" or "psychological well-being" dependent on whatever criteria the investigator has selected. Typically Jamesean claims to assess mysticism "by its fruits" are fraught with conceptual and evaluative confusions. This issue has been raised particularly with studies indicating that pathological tendencies are more likely to be related to the phenomenological properties of mystical experience than to the religious interpretative factors except in cases in which religion and pathology are defined as one and the same thing. Yet here the issue is precisely put by Troeltsch—given that mysticism in the minimal phenomenological sense arises in opposition to established norms, normative criteria of judgment by definition will find such mysticism lacking. This is precisely what the empirical research has shown, and its conceptual impoverishment is obvious. What is critically needed are reevaluations of the entire realm of pathology and religion, something Hillman (1975) has recently attempted. To extend the point one step further, theological criteria must be linked with psychological criteria to make any conceptual sense of the empirical options which, to date have been only trivially investigated where mysticism and psychopathology are concerned.

The final area of research on mysticism that needs noting is what Laski (1961) has termed triggers of mysticism. The term is deliberate and appropriate, pointing to situations and circumstances in which mysticism is likely to be reported, while avoiding claims as to the determinants of such experiences, a rather sophisticated scientific move to allow for the theological concept of "grace." Again, the two senses of mysticism noted by Troeltsch can serve us well in organizing this literature. Repeatedly, across numerous studies, it has been shown that mystical experiences occur among diverse social groups but with one consistent pattern: Institutionally oriented persons report religiously interpreted mystical experiences, triggered in normatively expected circumstances (for instance, church members report mysticism during prayer). Noninstitutionally oriented persons, however, report mysticism in its minimal phenomenological sense, not normatively religiously interpreted but triggered in deviant normative contexts (for instance, through the use of drugs or sex). In this latter case it is worth noting the long history of linking mysticism in its alternative and protesting sense of deviant activities designed to trigger it. Also, an overlooked fact emphasized by myself and J. R. Hall (Hood and Hall 1980) and others (Robertson 1975; Troeltsch 1931:731–732) is the intimate relationship between eroticism and mysticism in which both senses of mysticism are paralleled—one linking eroticism to the normative context of marriage, the other to the protesting notion of romanticism paralleling Ozment's term, *an erotic hominis absoluta*, in which a "cosmic" love is divorced from its "impure" containment and linked with mysticism (Harper 1969).

Efforts have been made to develop higher level conceptualizations of mystical triggers. Mere listing of triggers has proven of minimal value, however, given the immense variety of triggers. Thus, outside of normative contexts determining the legitimacy of triggers for each of the "senses" of mysticism noted by Troeltsch, little advancement seems possible. Two exceptions can be noted. One is physiological efforts to link explanations of mysticism to altered states of the body. While such theories are tentative, the overall direction is one in which the classic medieval identification of the *apex mentis* as the structure by which persons contact transcendent reality is replaced by the more scientifically appropriate search for physiological structures that presumably allow for transcendence. Such theories have minimal psychological or sociological import, however, in that at best they serve to identify structures by which experiences are possible, something hardly likely to advance truly critical theory in the social sciences, especially if the object of transcendence remains unspecified.

The other exception is the effort to find higher order conceptualizations in which transcendence is described in nonreductive physiological terms. Here our effort to link set and setting incongruities to the elicitation of mystical experience is worthy of note. As Ellwood (1980) has noted, the suddenness of many mystical experiences may be elicited by incongruities in which one is suddenly confronted with a transcendent reality made obvious by any situation in which set and setting clash. Such midrange theorizing incorporates physiological data on drugs and other triggers insofar as their effects are precisely to produce set/setting incongruities which then bring about mystical experiences. In addition, Ellwood's theory explains the lack of reported mystical experiences in normative contexts in which routinization produces what Laski termed *anti-triggers*.

The areas of religious orientation, pathology, and triggers fairly identify the major directions of current empirical research in the psychology of mysticism. As with sociological studies, however, psychological studies of mysticism have yet to be critically guided by theory or theology. In the former case, I have tried to show the relevance of Troeltsch's "senses" of mysticism in support of Garrett's claim that their "maligned" status is undeserved. As Robertson continually reminds us, classic theory is relevant, and in mysticism research we have yet to go beyond it. A start has been made, however, especially in the psychology of mysticism, in which reductive theories have simply been abandoned in favor of more systematic empirical efforts, some of which at least promise to bear fruit. Yet more controversial is the claim that theology is relevant to mysticism, and I shall close with a brief argument on its behalf.

Mystic claims to union with transcendent reality must at some point be evaluated in terms of critical theory concerning that reality. Theological assumptions must be incorporated into empirical research much as psychological theories of acting must take account of physiological realities concerning capabilities of human movement. Either social-scientific theories assume a methodological atheism, in which theories of union with transcendent reality are capable only of reductionistic "illumination," or else social-scientific theories assume a methodological theism, in which the nature of transcendent reality as theologically illuminated is taken into account in describing and evaluating mystical experiences (Hutch 1982). In this sense, as Mannheim (1936) long ago noted, the focus on subjective process, while enlightening, must eventually approach the object of concern in order to rise to the level of critical theory about reality. After all, the *noetic* claims of mystics at some point are right or wrong, and critical theory must evolve to evaluate such claims. Without theological sensitivities such theory risks incurring the same charge of ideological naivete that would cause wonder at the small number of Christian Science students in medical schools.

In this light, we (Spilka et al.) have proposed that a typology for mysticism that suggests both the "senses" of mysticism noted by Troeltsch, the distinction between mysticism "types" proposed by Stace, and a link to those theological views we consider essential to theoretical advancements. Basically, four mysticisms along two dimensions are proffered. One dimension is the personal vs. impersonal dimension; the other dimension is imagery vs. nonimagery. This creates a fourfold typology in which personal/imagery; personal/nonimagery; impersonal/imagery; and impersonal/nonimagery result. Each of these mysticisms can be conceived in Troeltsch's two senses, noted above, and each has a long tradition of historical and philosophical support. (For instance, "nature" mysticism as imagery/impersonal; Christian mysticism as personal/imageless; Jewish mysticism as personal/imagery; and Buddhist mysticism as impersonal/imageless). What is crucial is that this typology allows for critically confronting mysticism in various forms whose consequences are capable of empirical investigation. For instance, mysticism in which reality is confronted in personal terms differs in crucial ways from a mysticism in which reality is confronted as impersonal. Likewise, contrary to Stace's claim, an imageless mysticism (introvertive) is not a higher form of imagery mysticism; one could cite within the Jewish mystical tradition but one obvious example.

This typology also links with theological claims about the nature of ultimate reality and what consequences, sociological and psychological, might reasonably follow. For instance, each one of the proposed types is illuminated by elaborate theologies, thus making it of little value for the social scientist to assume the theological equivalency of all types. Clearly debates as to the ultimate nature of reality—for instance, whether personal or not—will be crucial in developing a psychology of mysticism. Or, the claim that differences in mysticism are "merely" interpretations can be taken too far insofar as at some point interpretations are part of the experience. Hence, mystics confronting their personal God within the boundaries of noetic claims are making more than a *mere* interpretation of their experience. And even if such a claim is an "ontological fairy-tale," by what ontology is that known?

If the sacred persists in what may be secular times, some form of a theologically informed science of mysticism is needed. The fact of a diversity of religious forms need no longer bother us if only we remember that the sacred has always expressed itself in diverse forms. Moreover, specific theological traditions often provide clear maps for the experience of the sacred which, if ignored, may result only in confusion and misunderstanding. For scientists not to utilize concepts from these traditions is to lose a rich source of concepts that can provide theoretical clarity and empirical ordering. Likewise, the emergence of new sacred forms provides the basis for ordering and structuring new modes of experiencing the sacred which the scientists must acknowledge if these experiences are to be appropriately understood theoretically. Clearly Troeltsch's two senses of mysticism intermingle and infuse each other. As Mannheim noted (1936:92):

May it not be possible that the ecstatic element in human experience which in the nature of the case is never directly revealed or expressed, and the meaning of which can never be fully communicated, can be discovered through the traces which it leaves on the path of history, and thus be disclosed to us?

Only theologically informed research promises to rise to the level of critical theory by doing more than relativizing perceptions of the absolute, and hence confronting the noetic claims of the mystics seriously as well as critically.

REFERENCES

Berger, P.
  1981   "Review Symposium: The Heretical Imperative," *Journal for the Scientific Study of Religion* 20:193–196.
Ellwood, R. S., Jr.
  1980   *Mysticism and Religion.* Englewood Cliffs, N.J.: Prentice-Hall.
Gaede, S. D.
  1981   "Review Symposium: The Heretical Imperative," *Journal for the Scientific Study of Religion* 20:181–186.
Garrett, W. R.
  1975   "Maligned Mysticism: The Maledicted Career of Troeltsch's Third Type," *Sociological Analysis* 36:205–223.
Greeley, A.
  1974   *Ecstasy: A Way of Knowing.* Englewood Cliffs, N.J.: Prentice-Hall.
Hardy, A.
  1979   *The Spiritual Nature of Man.* Oxford: Clarendon Press.

Harper, R.
   1969   *Human Love Existential and Mystical.* Baltimore: The John Hopkins
             Press.
Hay, D., and Morisy, A.
   1978   "Reports of Ecstatic, Paranormal, or Religious Experience in Great
             Britain and the United States: A Comparison of Trends," *Journal
             for the Scientific Study of Religion* 17:255–268.
Hillman, J.
   1975   *Re-visioning Psychology.* New York: Harper and Row.
Holm, N. G.
   1982   "Mysticism and Intense Experiences," *Journal for the Scientific
             Study of Religion* 21:268–276.
Hood, R. W., Jr.
   1974   "Psychological Strength and the Report of Intense Religious Ex-
             perience," *Journal for the Scientific Study of Religion* 13:65–71.
   1975   "The Construction and Preliminary Validation of a Measure of
             Reported Mystical Experience," *Journal for the Scientific Study of
             Religion* 14:29–41.
   1976   "Conceptual Criticisms of Regressive Explanations of Mysticism,"
             Review of Religious Research 16:179–188.
Hood, R. W., Jr., and Hall, J. R.
   1980   "Gender Differences in the Description of Erotic and Mystical
             Experiences," *Review of Religious Research* 21:195–207.
Hood, R.W., Jr., and Morris, R. J.
   1981   "Knowledge and Experience Criteria in the Report of Mystical
             Experience," *Review of Religious Research* 23:76–84.
Hutch, R. A.
   1982   "Are Psychological Studies of Religion on the Right Track?" *Reli-
             gion* 12:277–299.
Jaki, S. L.
   1978   *The Origin of Science and the Science of its Origin.* South Bend:
             Regnery/Gateway, Inc.
Katz, S. T., ed.
   1978   *Mysticism and Philosophical Analysis.* New York: Oxford University
             Press.
Laski, M.
   1961   *Ecstasy.* New York: Greenwood Press.
Mannheim, K.
   1936   *Ideology and Utopia.* New York: Harcourt, Brace and World, Inc.
Ozment, S. E.
   1973   *Mysticism and Dissent: Religious Ideology and Social Protest in the
             Sixteenth Century.* New Haven: Yale University Press.
Robertson, R.
   1975   "On the Analysis of Mysticism: Pre-Weberian and Post-Weberian
             Perspectives," *Sociological Analysis* 36:241–266.

Scharfstein, Ben-Ami
  1973   *Mystical Experience*. New York: Bobbs-Merrill.
Spilka, B., R. W. Hood, Jr., and R. Gorsuch
          An Empirical Psychology of Religion. Englewood Cliffs, N.J.: Prentice-Hall. Forthcoming.
Stace, W. T.
  1961   *Mysticism and Philosophy*. Philadelphia: Macmillan.
Stobart, St. Clair
  1971   *Torchbearers of Spiritualism*. Port Washington, N.Y.: Kennikat Press. (First published in 1925.)
Troeltsch, E.
  1931   *The Social Teaching of the Christian Churches*. 2 vols. New York: Macmillan.
Wuthnow, R.
  1978   *Experimentation in American Religion*. Berkeley, Los Angeles, London: University of California Press.

PART SIX

The Sacred and the Exercise of Power

XIX

Religion and Politics in America: The Last Twenty Years

Benton Johnson

In the early 1960s it was widely believed among social scientists that religion had become irrelevant to the major social processes of modern societies. The prevailing opinion was that religion no longer exerted an independent influence on public affairs. Will Herberg argued (1955) that in the United States the historic religions had lost their distinctive character and now simply apotheosized the American Way of Life. A few years later Peter Berger (1961) elaborated this theme by claiming that the sacred symbols of American religions really reinforced the influences of class, ethnic, racial, and regional traditions. This point of view was associated with a theory of secularization, most prominently articulated by Bryan Wilson (1966), which held that religion was losing its impact on political, economic, and intellectual life throughout the industrial world. If religion continued to have any independent impact at all, some argued, it was exerted only in the private sectors of life—in family affairs and in personal life-styles, for example.

Twenty years later it is clear that this broad picture of the retreating influence of religion in American life is seriously distorted. There have been too many surprising developments and too much empirical research providing contradictory data for any responsible social scientist to claim that religion has no influence on public affairs in the United States or that it has retired quietly to the sidelines of social life. In retrospect, it is clear that a serious problem with such a claim was that it was not based on a careful investigation of American religion. Insightful and provocative as Herberg's, Wilson's, and Berger's treatments were, they were largely speculative. William Petersen was correct when he complained in 1962 that "even the most elementary data" concerning American religion were either "faulty or absent."

The two classic voting studies of Paul Lazarsfeld and his associates (Lazarsfeld et al. 1948; Berelson et al. 1954) provided the first solid evidence of religious differences in American political party preference and voting behavior. These studies, both conducted in religiously heterogeneous northern communities, revealed that Protestants tend to be Republicans and Catholics tend to be Democrats and that these tendencies cannot be fully explained on the basis of socioeconomic status. To be sure, class status has an effect on political preference, as do region and race, but religious affiliation has an independent effect as well, especially among those with strong religious identifications. Moreover, the two studies were conducted during election campaigns that did not involve religious issues. Although these studies were widely read by sociologists and political scientists, their findings concerning religion were difficult to interpret and they had no immediate influence on sociologists of religion. In fact, they came as a complete surprise to Lazarsfeld himself, as they did to George Gallup, who greeted them with skepticism. As late as 1959 Elmo Roper remained unconvinced (Lipset 1964). Subsequent studies, however, have consistently reproduced Lazarsfeld's basic findings. As might be expected, Protestant-Catholic differences peaked in the 1960 presidential election but since then there has been no clear tendency for them to fade away. Although they are sharpest among nonsouthern whites, in recent years regional differences have tended to diminish. Studies have also repeatedly shown that Jews and those with no religious affiliation are strongly inclined toward the Democratic party. Despite election-to-election variations, these patterns have proved both enduring and pronounced. In the decade of the seventies, for example, about 41 percent of white Protestants considered themselves Republicans, as opposed to 21 percent of Catholics and only 11 percent of Jews (Opinion Roundup 1978).

Interpreting these patterns has not been a simple task. They cannot be derived from an examination of formal creeds or professions of faith. Clearly other factors are also at work. In a long and important essay published in 1964, Seymour Martin Lipset reviewed existing historical materials concerning American religion and politics and concluded that several factors, including class, social status, and moral and theological tenets, had combined by the time of the Civil

War to produce the basic political tendencies observed today among Catholics and northern white Protestants. The political traditions of religious communities, once established, form an important part of their members' sense of identity and tend, like religion itself, to be passed on from parents to children. Realignments have occurred, as when black Protestants left the Republican party for good in 1936, and many white southern Protestants began boycotting Democratic presidential candidates in 1948, but permanent realignments have been rare and occur only when radically changed circumstances challenge the political tradition of communities with a common culture. Despite the privations of the Great Depression, many Protestant workers in the North found it hard to vote for Roosevelt, just as it was hard for Irish Catholics to vote for Goldwater or Nixon even after acquiring a prestigious education, climbing the corporate ladder, and moving to an expensive suburb.

Although Lipset's 1964 essay was not read by all sociologists of religion, Robert Bellah's famous civil religion essay of 1967 almost certainly was, for it achieved a very wide circulation among students of American religion and provoked a spate of commentaries and rejoinders that has kept its memory alive to this day. More than any other single piece of writing, this essay has given sociologists of religion a sense of the long-term importance of religion in the political life of the American nation, especially its role in shaping and guiding the national political community and hence the national sense of identity and purpose that transcends denominational identities.

Voting studies utilizing a simple three-faith breakdown demonstrated the persistence of traditional political legacies, but they threw little light on whether religion has anything to do with the ideological struggles of contemporary politics. In most nations these struggles involve a contest between the forces of the left and the right. In the United States in the twentieth century the Republican party has represented the interests of established privileged groups, whereas since New Deal times the Democratic party has tended to support labor and, more recently, an array of other traditionally underprivileged segments of society.

Have religious commitments anything to do with the sides people take on these political issues of the twentieth century? In 1960 almost everyone would probably have doubted that they do. But a close look at modern church history might have dispelled their doubts. Among American Protestants, serious controversies broke out early in the century, which have persisted to the present. Although the controversies have featured theological issues, they have also contained an important political dimension. The theological issues concern the extent to which traditional doctrines remain tenable in the light of modern science and philosophy. The parallel political controversies concern the extent to which Christians and their churches should become actively involved in causes of the political left. By 1914 a vocal and influential interdenominational party had emerged within Protestantism arguing that the true mission of the church is not to save souls and promote traditional godliness but to fight politically for freedom and justice for oppressed people. In reaction, an opposing interdenominational party, soon known as fundamentalists, attacked this argument. The result was a new alignment of forces within and between denominations. Because basic issues of belief and practice were involved, they had implications for a very wide range of actions and attitudes. Sociologists of religion were slow, however, to investigate these implications systematically. It was not until 1965, when Glock and Stark published their research on the "new denominationalism," that sociologists got a clear picture of how wide the range was.

I was one of the first to investigate whether theological differences among Protestants were related to political party preference and voting behavior. In two studies of the Protestant laity, one in the Pacific Northwest and the other in the Deep South, small but consistent differences appeared between the political preferences of those who attended theologically liberal and theologically conservative churches. Regardless of socioeconomic status, churchgoers who attended liberal churches were more likely than those who attended conservative churches to prefer the Democratic party and to vote for Democratic candidates. Later studies of the laity suggest that these patterns are neither uniform nor pronounced except among those for whom religion or the church is highly salient. Stronger and more consistent relationships emerged, however, from studies of the clergy. My study of the Baptist and Methodist clergy of Oregon showed theological commitment to be strongly related to political preference, self-designation as politically liberal or conservative, voting behavior, and position on a variety of public issues (Johnson, 1966, 1967). The numerous follow-up studies (e.g., Hadden 1969; Quinley, 1974), some conducted on national samples, have consistently shown the same basic patterns among the Protestant clergy. Now well established, there is a marked tendency for theological liberals to prefer the political left and for theological conservatives to prefer the political right.

After 1965, the new political alignments of liberal Protestants ceased to be matters for academic investigation alone and became visible to the public at large. In the early 1960s, following more than a decade of relative inattention to social issues, the leadership of the theologically liberal denominations began emphasizing them once again, and a "new breed" of younger clergy, freshly exposed to the liberal influences of seminary teachers, became actively involved in political causes. Liberal theologians launched a fresh wave of highly publicized attacks on traditional doctrines. In his provocative and widely read *The Secular City* (1965), Harvey Cox proclaimed that the basic task of Christianity is the political one of liberating the captive peoples of history. The first of the new liberation struggles to command the energies of church people in the 1960s was the civil rights movement. Church lobbying efforts had much to do with securing passage of the Civil Rights Act of 1964, and the clergy was conspicuously involved in the struggles that followed (e.g., in the famous march at Selma, Alabama). Beginning in 1966, an enormous amount of clerical energy was also spent on opposing the Vietnam War. Although students made up the bulk of the antiwar movement, the clergy was arguably the most active of all the professional groups involved. Moreover, a high percentage of those who did oppose the war had previously worked in the civil rights movement. Jews were also prominently involved in both movements. Studies have consistently shown that American Jews tend to be more liberal than either Catholics or Protestants. A nationwide survey of Jews conducted in 1970–1971 also revealed an inverse relationship between religious traditionalism and political liberalism. The most liberal Jews are those who identify with no denomination. Those identifying with Reform are a bit less liberal, while the least liberal identify themselves as either Conservative or Orthodox (Harrison and Lazerwitz 1982).

The militant phase of the civil rights movement began in 1955 with the celebrated Montgomery bus boycott. Its leader, Martin Luther King, Jr., was a black Baptist pastor, and much of the support that eventually assured its success was mobilized by the black churches of the city. This development surprised many sociologists, for they accepted the prevalent view that black religion encourages political passivity and a preoccupation with otherworldly concern. Despite the importance of black churches and ministers in the civil rights movement, many social scientists continued to regard the black church as more a refuge from the world than as a resource for changing it. In fact, in 1964, near the height of the movement, E. Franklin Frazier reiterated this view. Gary T. Marx (1967) was the first sociologist to analyze national survey data designed to throw light on the relation between religiosity and civil rights militancy among blacks. His findings lent support to the conventional view of black religion; the more religious tended to be less militant on the issue of civil rights. The majority of militants, however, did consider themselves religious, and Marx reported evidence that among those who did, militancy was enhanced by a "temporal" as opposed to an otherworldly outlook. Subsequent studies, some of them reanalyses of Marx's data, suggest that thematic variations in black religion are indeed related, though not strongly, to degree of militancy. In this connection it is worth noting that although King's indebtedness to Gandhi's example has received wide attention, King was also thoroughly trained in the theological and political perspectives of liberal Protestantism. Although the evidence is far from conclusive, it also appears likely that, among black Christians, militancy is associated with middle-class status, rejection of extreme otherworldly or "sectarian" forms of religion, and being Baptist or Methodist (Hunt and Hunt 1977).

Among those who marched at Selma were Catholic priests and nuns. This was mildly surprising to some, for although the American church had never endorsed racist ideology, it had no record of supporting black struggles for freedom. Moreover, some of the nuns who marched defied the wishes of their superiors despite the fact that nuns had a reputation for strict obedience. Still more surprising were the dramatic and well-publicized antiwar efforts of certain priests, notably the Berrigan brothers. For years the hierarchy had voiced strong anticommunist views, and leading prelates were voicing them again in their support of the Vietnam War. By 1970 it was clear that the theological and political division long evident in white Protestantism, and present to some extent among Jews and black Protestants, had also emerged within Catholic ranks. These divisions had been in the making for some time, at least among intellectuals, but they did not become pronounced or visible until the vast changes and expectations set in motion by Vatican II. Freed from traditional restraints and open to new possibilities, many Catholics began rethinking their theological and political positions as well as their commitment to the Church itself. A few moved far to the left, embraced the Marxist-influenced liberation theology, and supported revolutionary movements in the Third World.

Studies of the Catholic laity show, as do studies of the Protestant laity, a relation between theology and political outlook somewhat different from that of its leaders and opinion makers. A nationwide survey of Catholics conducted in the early 1960s revealed what may well have been a long-standing pattern among the laity, namely, a tendency toward traditionalism on religious issues, liberalism on domestic economic issues, and authoritarianism on issues involving civil liberties, including civil rights for blacks. These patterns were especially marked among those identifying with the Democratic party, the traditional party of American Catholics (Henriot 1966). Exposure to the new liberalizing influences of Catholic intellectuals may be changing this traditional pattern, as suggested by Andrew M. Greeley's findings that graduates of Catholic colleges score higher on all measures of both political and social liberalism than other Catholics and even than graduates of non-Catholic colleges. Moreover, the Irish, who are the most educated, affluent, and historically the most politically and ecclesiastically influential of all American Catholic ethnic groups, are also the most liberal on a wide variety of issues. On the whole they are more liberal, as well as more inclined to vote Democratic, than white Protestants (1969, 1977).

In their rejection of "establishment" America, including "establishment" religion, some counterculture youth experimented with mystical and spiritual regimens foreign to their own backgrounds. One result was a highly visible upsurge of new religious movements which immediately became the object of numerous sociological studies. In view of the revolutionary hope generated by the counterculture it is not surprising that many of these new movements promised an early transformation of the social order or that their adherents tended to be more radical than their peers who still belonged to conventional churches (Wuthnow 1981). But virtually none of the new religions emphasized radical social action in the usual sense, and a few, like the Unification Church, were strongly anticommunist. Many of them taught that social change could be accomplished by meditation, chanting, or other spiritual exercises. To date, the new religions have had no discernible political impact beyond the legal problems raised by efforts to restrict their operations. Moreover, most of them have stopped growing rapidly and some have probably declined. In the meantime, large numbers of counterculture veterans are in sympathy with the loosely knit New Age Movement, a congeries of tendencies with common spiritual themes, including a persistence of "Aquarian" hopes. They have received little sociological attention.

In the early 1970s the religious left lost the momentum it had generated in the sixties. Faced with membership losses and declining revenues, the liberal Protestant denominations began curtailing social action programs. Although for the most part the clergy did not change its theological or political views, many former activists felt demoralized and "burned out." They supported the women's movement and gay rights, but much of the energy they spent on these causes went into struggles for reforms in their own parishes and denominations (e.g., the removal of sexist language from the liturgy). The political left lost its steam as well. George McGovern's attempt to unite minorities, women, intellectuals, and radical youth in 1972— an attempt that neglected and alienated the Democrats' traditional Catholic and white working-class constituencies— met with crushing defeat. Jimmy Carter, elected in 1976, was the most conservative Democratic president since Woodrow Wilson. And in 1980 Ronald Reagan became the most conservative Republican to win the presidency in more than half a century. The fate of the Equal Rights Amendment to the Constitution is symptomatic of the trend. Passed by Congress in the early seventies, it was soon ratified by over half the states. But by 1976 the ratification process had come to a halt. A few years later ERA was dead, the victim of a newly militant religious right.

In the middle 1960s the liberal Protestant ministry had a large following at campuses across the United States. Campus ministers, who tend to be more radical than parish ministers, were successfully involving students in the civil rights and antiwar movements. The United Christian Movement, an interdenominational association of liberal Protestant students, was strong and vigorous and committed to the same causes. But only a few years later many campus ministers found themselves with no one to talk to. Their student following had vanished and the UCM had dissolved itself. This rapid and unforeseen change, which has not been reversed to this day, is only the most dramatic sign of a larger trend that thinned the ranks of liberal Protestant denominations. Although sociologists were slow to investigate this trend, enough research has now been done to conclude that the single most important source of the unprecedented decline in the membership of liberal Protestant denominations that began in the late 1960s was the failure of their young people to become affiliated. The tensions between the liberal clergy and the relatively conservative laity, well documented by Hadden (1969), may have played a small part in this decline, but it was mainly due to the defection of youth (Carroll et al. 1979). Their defection was only one manifestation of an alienation from all the major institutions and from much of the life-style of "establishment" America—an alienation that found its most vivid and radical expression in the counterculture made by white middle-class youth in the late 1960s.

By the mid-1970s the evangelical, or theologically conservative, wing of Protestantism was much in the news and was acquiring a reputation for influence and growth. Jimmy Carter announced that he had been "born again." National polls revealed that fully 46 percent of American Protestants made this claim, as did a third of the population at large. Twenty-one percent of the population could be classified as evangelicals by a very exacting test, and an astonishing 48 percent of Protestants reported that they interpreted the Bible literally (Carroll et al. 1979). In 1976 the Gallup Organization claimed to detect early signs of a national religious revival. If liberal denominations were losing members, conservative denominations were growing rapidly. The Jesus Movement was attracting young people. Bob Dylan, Eldridge Cleaver, and other unlikely notables were finding the Lord. In the late 1970s a host of TV evangelists invaded prime time and a new Christian television network was launched. By the end of the decade Christian Voice and the Rev. Jerry Falwell's Moral Majority were busy enlisting conservative Christians for right-wing political action. In 1980 all three presidential candidates could lay some claim to be evangelicals.

Most sociologists of religion were unprepared for these developments. Studying the evangelical community had not been one of their major concerns. Some had their own roots in it but few nourished them and many seemed to know as little about it as the average college sophomore (a trivial but telling example is the fact that although authors and editors can spell Presbyterian and Episcopalian, they sometimes have trouble spelling Pentecostal). Moreover, as Stephen Warner has argued (1979), sociologists of religion have tended to identify with the liberal tendency in American religion and politics, with its disdain for positions deemed historically outmoded and hence irrational. They were inclined to see evangelicalism, or fundamentalism, as it was often called, as a waning influence in American life, an otherworldly faith catering to the economically and culturally impoverished.

But events of the seventies made it impossible to ignore another side of the picture. For one thing, a lively intellectual subculture had emerged within the evangelical community. For another, a great many evangelicals were both prosperous and well educated. Among the throngs attending Billy Graham's 1970 Knoxville rally were numerous managers but virtually no laborers (Clelland et al. 1974). Finally, as a result of concerted interdenominational efforts dating from the 1940s, evangelicals had been making vigorous efforts to expand their numbers and influence in American life. While liberal denominations were diverting funds from church-growth programs to social action in the sixties, evangelicals were planting new congregations and actively recruiting young people through such agencies as Young Life and Campus Crusade for Christ. Perhaps this is one reason why they have been more successful than either the liberal churches or the Catholics in retaining their own youth and converting young outsiders. In 1975 no less a church watcher than Martin Marty suggested that evangelicals may be the new mainstream of American religion.

Another common view of evangelical religion was that it discouraged political activism. Sociologists knew about Fred Schwartz's and Billy James Hargis's Christian campaigns against communism, but they had good reason to believe that most evangelicals were reluctant to become politically involved in the name of religion. For example, although the evangelical clergy tended to support the Vietnam War, it was much less likely than the liberal clergy to preach or make public statements about it (Quinley 1974). Evangelicals had a rich history of political activism, but the premillennial theology that became so popular in evangelical circles after 1900 had discouraged human efforts to change society. The political militancy of evangelicals after 1975 was therefore something of a surprise (Wuthrow 1983). The stands they took—for traditional family values, school prayer, a strong national defense—were not surprising, but the political mobilization of the evangelical community did require a great deal of effort, including that of well-known persons such as Anita Bryant, Bill Bright, and James Robison, and such "media events" as the 1980 National Affairs Briefing in Dallas, at which Ronald Reagan was the featured speaker.

Reagan's 1980 electoral college victory was impressive, as was the defeat of several liberal Democratic senators opposed by the Moral Majority. Jerry Falwell immediately gave evangelical voters much of the credit for the Republican successes and announced they had become an important new political force. Follow-up studies suggest that evangelical votes were not a decisive factor in the elections. For example, a study of "Middletown" residents found that economic issues far outweighed moral issues in influencing voting (Johnson and Tamney 1982). An NBC news poll found that a clear majority of those who had heard of Falwell disapproved of his activities (Yinger and Cutler 1982). An exit poll conducted by the *Des Moines Register* on election day found that although two-thirds of self-identified born-again Christians had voted Republican, they had done so in previous elections, which is not surprising in view of the tradition of Republican voting among white northern Protestants (Zwier 1982). Although the matter has not been thoroughly investigated, it is possible that Moral Majority efforts may have made some difference in the South, where evangelicals are proportionately more numerous and tradition-ally less inclined to vote Republican. And the defeat of ERA and the various local victories of anti-gay forces do show that conservative Christians, both Protestant and Catholic, can achieve success in cer-tain single-issue campaigns.

There are good reasons for doubting that evangelicals will prove to be a strong or coherent conservative political force in the future. In the first place, although evangelical denominations are growing, their growth is not exceeding that of the population as a whole. They are not attracting large numbers of converts from outside their own ranks. Their growth is mainly the result of a favorable birthrate and an ability to retain members, including their own children (Bibby and Brinkerhoff 1983). In the second place, although evangelicals are more conservative than other Americans on certain moral and life-style issues, and on issues relating to national defense, they are not more conservative on most other issues (Lipset and Raab 1981). In the third place, the evangelical community is divided on a host of issues ranging from theological beliefs to domestic economic policy. Black evangelicals are much more liberal on domestic economic issues than are white evangelicals who, in turn, are divided along a variety of lines reflecting both historical divisions and recent trends. For exam-ple, traditional peace churches such as the Mennonites have a very different outlook on national defense and military service than do Baptists, and tradition-minded Lutherans are much more reluctant to mix religion with politics than are evangelicals whose roots are in the Calvinist tradition (Shriver 1981). Moreover, even among white Baptists, perhaps the largest single component of the Moral Majority, there are sharp disagreements as to the wisdom of involvement in right-wing causes. Those who describe themselves as fundamentalists are the most likely to support such involvement (Guth 1983).

Another reason why the evangelical community is unlikely to be-come a major conservative political force is that many of its leading intellectuals are adopting liberal attitudes on a wide array of social issues. Evangelical publications like *Sojourners*, *The Other Side*, and *The Wittenberg Door* question conventional middle-class life-styles, attack militarism and American imperialism, and question traditional attitudes toward homosexuality and the role of women. Although such views are not yet widespread among the laity, they are often found among young college-educated evangelicals. Young evangeli-cals even tend to be a shade more liberal theologically than their elders, as is evident from Gallup's 1978 finding that strict evangelicals are older and less well educated than the population as a whole

(Hunter 1980). If present trends continue, traditional fundamentalist attitudes will become less common than they are today.

Public support has also been waning for many of the positions long favored by fundamentalists and other religious conservatives (e.g., intolerance of homosexuals, atheists, and communists, and support for traditional sex roles). This trend is of long standing and continued even through the 1970s despite the defeat of ERA and various gay-rights ordinances and despite some increased resistance among religious conservatives, particularly on the issue of abortion. During the 1970s the public did become somewhat more conservative on certain economic issues and on national defense—a major factor in Reagan's 1980 victory—but it did not become more conservative on the moral issues emphasized by Falwell and his associates (Davis 1975; Yinger and Cutler 1982; Mueller 1983; Smidt and Penning 1982). In fact, viewed in historical perspective, even the new evangelical militants are considerably more liberal on certain issues than many of their predecessors. They are rarely overtly racist, anti-Semitic, or anti-Catholic, and they do not advocate national prohibition. In 1980 they had no difficulty supporting for the presidency a divorced Hollywood actor who is known to take a drink. Their forebears of 40 years ago would have found this unthinkable.

The recent upsurge of political evangelicalism has all the earmarks of a "bear market rally" led by a cadre of latter-day fundamentalists whose constituency is less extensive or durable than they imagine. They have been prodded and assisted by veteran right-wingers of various religious stripes who have long been searching for allies to help them build a conservative party strong enough to put an end to the dominance of liberals and moderates in national political life. In 1980, inflation, recession, and the demoralization of the political and religious left enabled them to capture the Republican party and win the presidency. But their victory was a shallow one. Reagan won a bare 51 percent of the popular vote and failed to reverse the long-term trends toward lower voter-turnouts and the erosion of party loyalties. These trends, together with the political alienation of young adults, clearly indicate that the national political malaise which began in the mid-1960s has not been cured and that there is a potential market for new political agenda having little to do with either Reaganism or the old left.

In the mid-1980s sociologists know far more about the intertwining of religion and politics in America than they did in 1960. It is simply no longer possible to hold the opinions about their relationship that were common then. Thanks to numerous studies using a wide variety of methods, including powerful new statistical techniques, and thanks to the growing availability of national data sets, sociologists now have a good general grasp of the main political profiles and trends of America's religious communities. But important topics remain relatively uninvestigated or understood. There has been little effort to update the work on black religion and politics begun by Gary Marx in the 1960s. Not much is known about the political socialization of the clergy or the interaction networks linking political and religious elites. More exploration needs to be made of the political and religious sensibilities of that large number of young adults who have abandoned their original faith but have not found another. Surprisingly little attention has been paid to the Hispanics, the nation's most rapidly growing Catholic group, who in their cluster of communities are destined to have an increasingly important political impact. And the role which theological tenets may play in the formation of political consciousness is still not well understood.

Thanks in part to studies documenting the vitality of American religion, many sociologists no longer accept the simple secularization model so common twenty-five years ago. Peter Berger, for one, has had second thoughts on the subject (Berger, 1976). The trend toward religious indifference continues among intellectuals, and liberal Protestantism may well have reached the end of its spiritual line, but the nation's other religious communities, including some of its newest ones, show little sign of exhaustion or decline. Although the future, as always, is uncertain, it seems clear that religion will remain a major influence in American life for generations to come.

REFERENCES

Bellah, Robert N.
  1967   "Civil Religion in America," *Daedalus* 96 (Winter):1–21.
Berelson, Bernard, Paul Lazarsfeld, and William N. McPhee
  1954   *Voting*. Chicago: University of Chicago Press.
Berger, Peter L.
  1961   *The Noise of Solemn Assemblies*. Garden City, N.Y.: Doubleday.
  1976   "For a World with Windows." *In* Peter L. Berger and Richard John Neuhaus, *Against the World for the World*. New York: Seabury.
Bibby, Reginald W., and Merlin B. Brinkerhoff
  1983   "Circulation of the Saints Revisited: A Longitudinal Look at Conservative Church Growth," *Journal for the Scientific Study of Religion* 22 (Sept.):253–262.

Carroll, Jackson W., Douglas W. Johnson, and Martin E. Marty
  1979   *Religion in America: 1950 to the Present*. San Francisco: Harper and
          Row.
Clelland, Donald A., Thomas C. Hood, C. M. Lipsey, and Ronald Wimberley
  1974   "In the Company of the Converted: Characteristics of a Billy
          Graham Crusade Audience," *Sociological Analysis* 35 (Spring):
          45–56.
Cox, Harvey
  1965   *The Secular City*. New York: Macmillan.
Davis, James A.
  1975   "Communism, Conformity, Cohorts, and Categories: America's
          Tolerance in 1954 and 1963–73," *American Journal of Sociology* 81
          (Nov.):491–513.
Frazier, E. Franklin
  1964   "The Negro Church and Assimilation." In *The Negro Church in
          America*. New York: Schocken. Pp. 68–81.
Glock, Charles Y., and Rodney Stark
  1965   "The New Denominationalism." In *Religion and Society in Tension*.
          Chicago: Rand-McNally. Pp. 86–122.
Greeley, Andrew M.
  1969   "Continuities in Research on the 'Religious Factor,'" *American
          Journal of Sociology* 75 (Nov.):355–359.
  1977   "How Conservative Are American Catholics?" *Political Science
          Quarterly* 92 (Summer):199–218.
Guth, James L.
  1983   "Southern Baptist Clergy: Vanguard of the Christian Right?" In
          Robert C. Liebman and Robert Wuthnow, eds., *The Christian
          Right*. New York: Aldine. Pp. 118–130.
Hadden, Jeffrey K.
  1969   *The Gathering Storm in the Churches*. Garden City, N.Y.: Double-
          day.
Harrison, Michael I., and Bernard Lazerwitz
  1982   "Do Denominations Matter?" *American Journal of Sociology* 88
          (Sept.):356–377.
Henriot, Peter J.
  1966   "The Coincidence of Political and Religious Attitudes," *Review of
          Religious Research* 8 (Winter):50–58.
Herberg, Will
  1955   *Protestant Catholic Jew*. Garden City, N.Y.: Doubleday.
Hunt, Larry L., and Janet G. Hunt
  1977   "Black Religion as *Both* Opiate and Inspiration of Civil Rights
          Militance: Putting Marx's Data to the Test," *Social Forces* 56
          (Sept.):1–14.
Hunter, James Davison
  1980   "The New Class and the Young Evangelicals," *Review of Religious
          Research* 8 (Winter):50–58.

Johnson, Benton
1966   "Theology and Party Preference Among Protestant Clergymen,"
        American Sociological Review 31 (April):200–208.
1967   "Theology and the Position of Pastors on Public Issues," *American
        Sociological Review* 32 (June):433–442.
Johnson, Stephen D., and Joseph B. Tamney
1982   "The Christian Right and the 1980 Presidential Election," *Journal
        for the Scientific Study of Religion* 21 (June):123–131.
Lazarsfeld, Paul, Bernard Berelson, and Helen Gaudet
1948   *The People's Choice.* New York: Columbia University Press.
Lipset, Seymour Martin
1964   "Religion and Politics in the American Past and Present." *In*
        Robert Lee and Martin E. Marty, eds., *Religion and Social Conflict.*
        New York: Oxford. Pp. 69–126.
Lipset, Seymour Martin, and Earl Raab
1981   "The Election and the Evangelicals," *Commentary* 71 (March):25–
        31.
Marty, Martin
1975   "Tensions Within Contemporary Evangelicalism." *In* David F.
        Wells and John D. Woodbridge, eds., *The Evangelicals.* Nashville:
        Abingdon. Pp. 170–188.
Marx, Gary T.
1967   "Religion: Opiate or Inspiration of Civil Rights Militancy Among
        Negroes," *American Sociological Review* 32 (Feb.):64–72.
Mueller, Carol
1983   "In Search of a Constituency for the 'New Religious Right,'"
        Public Opinion Quarterly 47 (Summer):312–329.
Opinion Roundup.
1978   *Public Opinion* 1 (Nov.-Dec.):21–40.
Petersen, William
1962   "Religious Statistics in the United States," *Journal for the Scientific
        Study of Religion* 1 (Spring):165–178.
Quinley, Harold E.
1974   "The Protestant Clergy and the War in Vietnam," *Public Opinion
        Quarterly* 34 (Spring):43–52.
Shriver, Petty L.
1981   *The Bible Vote.* New York: Pilgrim.
Smidt, Corwin, and James M. Penning
1982   "Religious Commitment, Political Conservatism, and Political and
        Social Tolerance in the United States: A Longitudinal Analysis,"
        Sociological Analysis 43 (Fall):321–346.
Warner, R. Stephen
1979   "Theoretical Barriers to the Understanding of Evangelical Chris-
        tianity," *Sociological Analysis* 40 (Spring):1–9.
Wilson, Bryan
1966   *Religion in Secular Society.* London: Watts.

Wuthnow, Robert
  1981   "Political Aspects of the Quietistic Revival." *In* Thomas Robbins
          and Dick Anthony, eds., *In Gods We Trust*. New Brunswick, N.J.:
          Transaction. Pp. 229–243.
Wuthnow, Robert
  1983   "The Political Rebirth of American Evangelicals." *In* Robert C.
          Liebman and Robert Wuthnow, *The New Christian Right*. New
          York: Aldine. Pp. 168–185.
Yinger, J. Milton, and Stephen J. Cutler
  1982   "The Moral Majority Viewed Sociologically," *Sociological Focus* 15
          (Oct.):389–406.
Zwier, Robert
  1982   *Born Again Politics: The New Christian Right in America*. Downers
          Grove, Ill.: Inter-Varsity.

XX

Policy Formation in Religious Systems

Jackson W. Carroll

It is reported that certain theologians refused to look through Galileo's telescope for fear of seeing something that they could not believe. Although conflicts between science and religion still exist in some quarters, they do not generally occur when it comes to the use of social science research as an aid to policy formation in religious institutions. Religious leaders have come to make considerable use of policy research, and that use is the focus of this chapter. Although much of the research on religion done by social scientists is relevant to policy in religious systems, the interest here is primarily with (1) research commissioned by leaders of religious systems as an aid to shaping policy, and (2) research which, though not commissioned by religious leaders, nevertheless has as a primary concern providing religious systems with policy-relevant information. In what follows, I refer to both kinds of research, as well as to other types of applied research, as "policy" research in contrast to "basic," or "discipline," research. Space precludes a discussion of the differences between policy and discipline research.[1] Suffice it to note that the most obvious and important difference is in their intent. Whereas discipline research is primarily aimed at increasing understanding or advancing knowledge in a particular discipline, policy research is primarily aimed at providing information that will help people extend their control over the institutions and situations in which they participate.

My aim, in keeping with the overall theme of the volume, is to consider developments in policy research in religious systems and their relationship to the secularization model inherited from the classics. In the first section, I consider the application of policy research in religion as reflecting a kind of secularization, illustrating this with reference to two of the pioneer policy researchers in religious systems. Next, I describe briefly developments in policy research in religion over the last two decades. Finally, I discuss several characteristics of recent policy research in religious systems which represent either continuities or new developments. My focus throughout is on issues concerning the practice and utilization of policy research in religious systems rather than on a review of policy studies and their substantive findings.

THE DEVELOPMENT OF POLICY RESEARCH IN RELIGIOUS SYSTEMS AND THE SECULARIZATION PARADIGM

The use in religious systems of policy research grounded in social science theory and methods is hardly the fruit of a natural relationship between religion and sociology or one in which there has been an absence of significant tensions and conflict. As is well known, most of the "founding fathers" of sociology, particularly in Europe, viewed religious beliefs, practices, and institutions as essentially anachronistic in the developing modern society. Although the situation differed to some extent in the United States, where there was considerable affinity between early sociologists and some expressions of Christianity, especially the Social Gospel movement,[2] American sociology also soon developed a strongly positivistic orientation and did not consider religion—especially religiously relevant policy research—as a part of its mainstream. It is not my purpose to review this history. With reference to the United States, that has already been done (Fukuyama 1963; Schroeder 1971). Rather, I want to draw on aspects of this history as illustrative in relation to the secularization paradigm.

A difficulty of this task, however, is determining which secularization paradigm is meant. As Shiner (1967) and others have made clear, there are multiple understandings of secularization. I argue nevertheless that the use of policy research in religious systems is itself an indicator that secularization of a sort has occurred. I do not make any assumptions, however, that this reflects a linear, or evolutionary, process or that it *necessarily* implies the weakening or decline of religion. Let me rather indicate two aspects of the secularization of religious life which have facilitated the development of policy research in religious systems despite the historic tension/conflict between sociology and religion.

The first is best illustrated with reference to the United States. It is the process of social differentiation—especially the separation of church and state—which left American churches as voluntary associations essentially dependent on their own resources for survival, in competition with other churches for members and resources, and, therefore, also highly vulnerable to changes in their environment. As a consequence, and in correspondence with the general American ethos, Protestantism developed a highly pragmatic, instrumental stance which was relatively open to innovation and experimentation in the interest of institutional growth or, in some cases, to survival. Many policy research studies in religion have reflected a response to the organizational vulnerability and pragmatic ethos of American religious organizations, promising assistance either in institutional expansion or in turning around or cutting losses in declining situations.

A second, separable but related development in religious life, true not only of the United States, has been the willingness to view religious institutions (or some parts of them) as human creations, amenable to analysis by empirical methods and to planned change efforts. To the extent that this has occurred—and there are variations as to what and how much in the church's life is viewed as humanly created—it is an expression of the kind of secularization that Weber (1946:139) preferred to call the "disenchantment of the world" or "rationalization." In this case, it involves the "disenchantment" of religious institutions and a concern to make them, in varying degrees, more calculable and efficient. I refer to this concern, as it is reflected in policy research, as "technical" rationality, to some extent begging the question whether it is primarily what Weber (1968:24–26) meant by "instrumental" or, in contrast, "value" rationality.[3]

Both of these aspects of religious life played a considerable role in creating a climate in which aspects of ecclesiastical institutions and practices became "fair game" for empirical research and in which leading church leaders looked to the social sciences for help in policy formation. Let me illustrate this by reference to the work and perspectives of two pioneer sociologists who engaged in religiously relevant policy research—one in the United States, the other in France.

The most important of the early policy researchers in the United States were H. Paul Douglass and his colleagues at the Institute for

Social and Religious Research who, in the thirteen years of the Institute's existence from 1921 to 1934, undertook over fifty research studies of American church life and published more than ninety volumes.[4] Douglass's work illustrates both themes of secularization in American religious life referred to above. His studies of rural and urban churches were concerned with the impact on them of a changing social environment. Not only was he interested in their survival, he was deeply committed to the practice of what he called "scientific churchmanship" (Douglass 1926:v), by which he meant the application of rational, scientific principles to the church, or at least to that visible, socially institutionalized part of it that stands in relation to "the spiritual order and [bears] the marks of [its] source" (Douglass and Brunner 1935:3). "The question for most of the churches," he wrote, "is simply whether they have intelligence and determination enough to adopt scientifically determined standards growing out of the actual evolutionary tendencies demonstrably at work within them" (Douglass 1926:39).[5] Expressive of both his pragmatism and rationalized view of the church as a social institution was his hope that "Institutionalized religion may conceivably be made to serve the interests of modern society, and no less the ends apprehended and professed by religious insight" (Douglass and Brunner 1935:13).

Roman Catholicism, prior to Vatican II, was much less open to the use of empirical research as an aid to policy formation; however, in addition to the important pre–Vatican II work of Joseph Fichter (see, for example, Fichter 1954) in the United States, the French religious sociologists can be cited as an important exception. The French case is, for example, particularly illustrative of a cautious but significant application of empirical research in the service of religion. Although the situation of Catholicism, especially in France, differed significantly from that of U.S. Protestantism, there was nevertheless a limited acceptance of research in the Church's efforts to reach segments of the French working class, who were perceived as having become "dechristianized"; that is, secularized. The French Church's caution in this connection is illustrated by its use of the designation "religious sociology" rather than the "sociology of religion" to describe its more limited concern with social aspects of religion rather than with religion itself as a social phenomenon. In particular, these social aspects, amenable to policy research, included:

. . . (a) the influence of the milieu, that is to say, the social group and its environment, on religious practice and behaviour; (b) the influence of religious life on the milieu; (c) the greater effectiveness of the Church's mission. (Boulard 1960:xxvi)

Boulard's maps of religious practice in various regions of France, accompanied by historical and contemporary analyses of the milieus of these regions, constitute important contributions both to church policy and to the sociology of religion, but the former were the primary focus of the research. Boulard (1960:xxvi) describes the "missionary purpose" of religious sociology as "determining the best methods of communicating the Christian gospel to collective groups," especially to various segments of the working class.

For both Douglass and his colleagues at the Institute, and the Roman Catholic religious sociologists, the principal reason for conducting research was that it provided a pragmatic service to the church, at least some aspects of which were viewed as amenable to study by empirical methods of the social sciences. Although Douglass went much further than Boulard in viewing the church itself as a social or humanly created phenomenon, neither made belief or religious experience a focus of their research. One suspects that Boulard avoided these and other areas of church life out of a conviction that they were "out of bounds" for religious sociology, but Douglass did so more because they were not readily amenable to objective analysis.[6] In spite of these limits which they placed on the scope of their research, and their acknowledgment of transcendent dimensions of the church's life, neither was without critics who opposed the use of sociological methods to study any aspects of religion.[7]

POLICY RESEARCH IN RELIGION SINCE DOUGLASS AND BOULARD

The role of policy research in religion greatly expanded—in quantity, though not, unfortunately, always in quality—especially among U.S. Protestants during the post-World War II movement of millions of Americans to the suburbs and the so-called religious revival of the 1950s. (In this section, I limit the discussion to the United States and do not pretend to include the full range of topics on which policy research has been done.) Estimates put the number of research and planning personnel employed by Protestant denominations and state and regional councils of churches between two hundred and four hundred (Hadden 1974). By far the majority was engaged in church extension research—that is, in planning where to locate new congregations. For Roman Catholics, major developments in policy-oriented research followed Vatican II, as theological changes in the understanding of the church, a greater appreciation of the potential contribution of empirical research to church policy, and organization changes fostered by the Council led to the establishment of such organizations as the Center for Applied Research in the Apostolate (CARA) in 1965 (Gannon 1967).

As Roman Catholic research was developing and expanding in the 1960s and 1970s (not only through the work of CARA but also of others, including Andrew Greeley and those associated with him at the National Opinion Research Center, the Boys Town Research Center at Catholic University, and the Glenmary Research Center), the Protestant research establishment went into something of a tailspin. The large research and planning staffs were reduced sharply, perhaps reflecting a low estimate of the usefulness of some of the work, but more likely reflecting a major shift in priorities in most denominations from church extension to issues of social justice, especially black civil rights and the antiwar movement of the late 1960s and early 1970s (Carroll 1979:40–41). Much of the policy research commissioned by the churches during that time, and especially that not commissioned by the churches but nonetheless aimed at influencing church policy, reflected these concerns—for example, Gibson Winter's *The Suburban Captivity of the Churches* (1961). It, and others like it, were both strongly critical of churches for failures in commitment to social justice and proposed strategies for confronting social justice issues. In a somewhat similar vein, Glock and Stark's research on anti-Semitism, especially their influential book on *Christian Beliefs and Anti-Semitism* (1966), was also carried out during this time and funded by the Anti-Defamation League of B'nai B'rith. Ministry studies constituted another active area of policy-oriented research during this period and reflected continuing concern with theological education, the quality of professional ministry, the adequacy of ministerial support, the development of specialized ministries in the denominations (especially campus ministries), and attrition in the ministry among Protestants and Catholics.

By the mid-1970s, issues fostering policy research in the U.S. churches had begun to shift again. While concerns among Roman Catholics over priestly vocations continued, the "new" issues capturing the church's imagination were those of church growth and decline, small-membership churches, whether rural or urban, and congregational research more generally. Additionally, the large-scale entry of women into the Protestant ministry, and an oversupply of clergy in several Protestant denominations were subjects of policy research. And one of the most costly and technically sophisticated policy-oriented projects undertaken under religious auspices was carried out for the Association for Theological Schools to develop instruments to test the "readiness for ministry" of seminary students (Schuller et al. 1980). Most of these policy studies were carried out, not by denominational research staffs—though several excellent ones remained—but by various independent and university- or seminary-related research centers.

In addition to these themes of policy research, mention should be made of the "discovery" by the churches in the early 1970s of organizational development and its incorporation as a perspective into policy research and planning in religious systems. In particular, emphasis was put on management by objectives and thus on the need for data for planning. Religious organizations came to be viewed as open systems.[8] To a considerable extent this signaled a shift away from the more demographic and contextual studies of H. Paul Douglass toward a focus on the internal functioning of religious organizations. It also reflected the more general decline of emphasis in the churches on social action and issues of social justice.

THE CURRENT STATE OF POLICY RESEARCH IN RELIGION—SOME CONCLUDING OBSERVATIONS

This all too inadequate overview of aspects of policy-oriented research in religion in the past two decades nevertheless reveals that such research has continued and expanded since Douglass and Boulard. I want to suggest here characteristics of present-day policy research and issues that persist for its practitioners and users.

Policy research in religion, including much of that cited, continues to reflect the two aspects of secularization that gave rise to it in the first instance. There has been no reversal of the social differentiation that made American churches voluntary associations and thus contributed to the pragmatic, instrumental orientation of American religion. This orientation continues to be widespread, although, as I will note, it does not go unchallenged.

As for the second aspect of secularization—that is, of the willingness to view aspects of religious institutions as human creations and amenable to empirical analysis and technical rationality—there has been a considerable broadening, as evidenced in the more recent policy research, of what is viewed as open to scientific scrutiny. From religious beliefs to religious experience to questions of how faith is developed, there is very little that is not now considered amenable to policy-oriented studies, if not to make religious life and institutions more efficient or effective, at least to increase understanding.

Several factors account for these continuities. One has simply been the increase in the last two decades in the number of social scientists involved in research on religion, much of which has been relevant to policy. Also, there has been the variety of pressing, pragmatic problems facing church leaders noted in the previous section. But beyond these factors, I would also cite the impact of the theological climate during this time. I refer to the impact first of neo-orthodox theology, subsequently of theologies of secularization and, more recently, of liberation theology. In neo-orthodoxy, for example, the emphasis was so strongly placed on the transcendence of God that all institutions came to be viewed as relative, provisional, and reflecting various degrees of corruption. Similarly, all aspects of religious institutions came to be viewed as *human* responses to God's revelation. Secular and liberation theologies, with important differences that cannot concern us here, likewise have tended to desacralize all institutions, including religious ones. While one effect of these theologies was to devalue any concern, including sociological, with the church as a human institution,[9] they have also helped to create a climate in which empirical analysis of more and more aspects of religious life and institutions is taking place. An example of this changed climate—and especially the fruit of the theology of secularization—was a World Council of Churches-sponsored project aimed at a search for "new missionary structures of the church" appropriate to the new urban reality of the late twentieth century. The project, which involved a number of social scientists, generated some important experimental urban ministries; however, funding difficulties and the power of more traditional institutional patterns brought an end to much of the work.[10] The spread of this climate of openness to Roman Catholicism came with the new theological and ecclesiological emphases of Vatican II and reflected a similar broadening of concern, though not perhaps as much as in Protestantism.

Although there are these continuities and further developments, policy research in religion also continues to encounter problems of resistance and underutilization (at least from the perspective of the researchers). There are many reasons for such problems, some of which lie with the researchers themselves and others with the client systems. Three in particular will be noted, but the third bears a special relationship to the issue of secularization.

First, there is the combination of traditionalism and inertia that often surrounds long-standing policies or procedures. Although this is true of all organizations as they become institutionalized—that is, "infused with value" (Selznick 1957:19)—it is particularly true of religious systems. The practices are often viewed not only as traditional but as sacredly so, and they are difficult to change, even when the appeal of the new is not simply on functional grounds but has a theological basis as well. Commenting on the considerable resistance generated in the Church of England to the report, *The Deployment and Payment of Clergy*, the author, Leslie Paul (1972), attributes it in large part to the inertia inherent in a traditional institution. An Anglican bishop more colorfully suggested that the character of the Church of England—"a mixture of ceremony, laziness and peasant simplicity"— renders it impervious to sociological techniques (cited in Gill 1975:17).

A second and related source of resistance and underutilization is the political arena in which policy research occurs. It is rare when changes in policies suggested by a particular policy study do not encounter opposition from one or more places within an organization, either as vested interests are challenged or, as is often the case, when multiple goals of the organization come into conflict. Robert Wilson and I (Carroll and Wilson 1980) found this to be the case in our analysis of the clergy job market. The relative autonomy and conflicting goals of various subsystems that form the clergy job market— denominational deployment structures, theological seminaries, and local congregations and other employers of clergy—made it difficult to suggest policy responses that did not encounter opposition from one or more of the subsystems involved. From a Roman Catholic perspective, McCready (1981) cites numerous instances of conflict between what he refers to as "bricks, mortar, and plumbing" issues and policy implications of research done for the Catholic Church by the Pluralism Center of the National Opinion Research Center.

Although each of these problems (and related ones space precludes mentioning) are difficult and frustrating for users and doers of policy research, they can be ameliorated if not overcome entirely. A growing body of literature on factors affecting the diffusion and adoption of innovations provides important insights into such issues and suggests strategies for dealing with them constructively (e.g., Zaltman 1973). A report (FAICA 1981) of a recent Catholic-sponsored symposium focuses entirely on issues of improving the utilization of policy research in religion. The essay in the report by Strommen (74–85) is especially insightful.

There is, however, a third source of resistance to policy research which is not easily overcome, and it is particularly relevant to the secularization paradigm. I refer to a recent and growing challenge by some to the assumption that a high degree of relationality and efficiency are necessarily desirable in religious systems. Instead, there is an assertion that the heart of religion is precisely its *nonrational* character as encounter with the sacred, and that this makes the application of technical rationality in religion of questionable value, if not reductionist and fundamentally subversive. In a similar vein, there is an appeal to other nonrational aspects of religious organizations—communal and affectional dimensions—that may be contrary to technical rationality.

These challenges have been aimed not so much at policy research—at least not yet—as at what is referred to negatively as the "professional" model of ministry (e.g., Holmes 1971) as well as at the uncritical use in churches of organizational development strategies, especially rational planning or management by objectives (e.g., Anderson and Hahn 1980, and Dudley 1977). To use the categories of Victor Turner (1969), religious institutions are understood at their best to reflect "communitas" in contrast to "structure." Therefore, efforts to treat them as structure, whether in terms of a professional model of leadership or an instrumentally oriented, associational model, are not only reductionist but also fundamentally subversive of their true character and should be resisted. Presumably this also applies to policy research on religious systems which does not honor, appreciate, and reflect the distinctive, nonrational character of religion.[11]

It is too soon to know what the implications of this emphasis will be for policy research in religion. If it represents a new version of the refusal to look through Galileo's telescope, then I believe it will be a step backward for religious systems. In spite of the sometimes poor quality of policy research or the research that has overextended itself in the direction of "scientific churchmanship," there have been many important contributions of policy research in religious systems—contributions that such systems can ill afford to lose. In this sense, secularization has functioned positively in so far as it has opened the way for the use of acceptance of policy research. I do not believe, however, that these critics are essentially opposed to all policy research in religious systems. Indeed, research by historians of religion, and anthropologists in particular, is used to promote understanding and appreciation of the distinctive, nonrational character of religion.

There is special appreciation for ethnographic approaches to the study of religious systems.[12]

Whatever the ultimate implications of this third source of resistance to technical rationality, and whether or not one agrees fully with the critique, it serves to remind the researcher and user of policy research alike that religious systems are both like other social systems and different from them. With other systems they share a number of structural, cultural, and social psychological characteristics. At the same time, they have a distinctive character, which sets them off. They grow out of an encounter with the sacred, and they involve communal and affectional experiences which may seem inimical to a concern with efficiency or "scientific churchmanship." Furthermore, for Jewish and Christian institutions, there is a sense of living toward a coming Kingdom of God. These and other characteristics make them, at least in principle, different from economic, educational, or political systems. By emphasizing this dual character of religious systems, I am not making the old distinction between a visible and an invisible church, nor am I urging a return to the caution of the religious sociologists which caused them to exclude some aspects of religious systems from the purview of policy research. Rather, I suggest two implications which I believe can help policy researchers to counter the resistance to an overemphasis on technical rationality in religious systems.

First, there is the need for attempting to build into one's research design a focus, not only on those characteristics religious systems share with other social systems but also, in so far as they are empirically available, on those distinctively religious dimensions of the system. Related to this is the need to be sensitive to the ways in which one's measures may limit or distort the particular religious dimension one is analyzing.

Second, there is needed the awareness that not everything research reveals to be pragmatically possible or efficiency-promoting for the religious system is necessarily faithful to its core commitments or mission. It is not clear, for example, that the achievement of "scientific churchmanship," to use Douglass's phrase, is always in the best interest of the system. Although the interpretation of research findings and theological reflection on the findings are separate tasks, they are nevertheless complementary. Other things being equal, the realization of that complementarity is, I believe, a key to effective policy research.[13] In this sense, it reflects the melding of technical rationality with what Weber (1968:24–26) called "value rationality."

In conclusion, the thrust of most recent policy research has been in considerable continuity with earlier efforts. It has reflected the continuing pragmatic orientation of religious systems stemming in large part from their socially differentiated, voluntary associational character. It has also reflected a continuation and extension of the application of technical rationality to almost all aspects of religious systems. In these two senses, the secularization paradigm has not been superseded, and I take this to be an essentially positive development as far as religious systems are concerned. However, in the case of what I referred to as an emphasis by some on the nonrational core of religion there is, perhaps, an effort to move beyond the secularization paradigm to a rediscovery and a renewed appreciation of the sacred and of communal and affectional aspects of religion.[14] Whatever the outcome of this emphasis may be, it at least suggests how important it is for policy researcher and user of research alike to keep in focus the distinctive character and mission of religious institutions.

NOTES

1. Coleman (1972) helpfully distinguishes between policy and discipline research, taking into consideration their differing functions, differences in the social context in which each is set, and differences in results and, thereby, in design and methodology.

2. In a recent article, however, Swatos (1983) has questioned the too easy assumption of an affinity between the interests of early sociologists and those of the Social Gospel movement.

3. It is perhaps just as well to beg the question since, as Weber (1968:26) pointed out, the two types are sometimes interrelated when, in the application of instrumental rationality, "choices between alternative and conflicting ends and results [are] determined in a value-rational manner." I suspect that most, though not necessarily all, policy research in religion has this dual character.

4. For assessments of Douglass and his colleagues' work, see Brunner (1959), Fukuyama (1963), and Hadden (1980).

5. Douglass (1935:287 ff.) does cite a number of belief and attitudinal studies conducted by others, including some of his colleagues, in a discussion of the religious climate in the United States in the early 1930s, but these do not seem to have played a major role in his research.

6. Douglass discussed at some length the opposition he experienced (Douglass and Brunner 1935:1–18), whereas Boulard (1960:73–92) gives only hints of some of the criticism.

7. One of the most extensive summaries of research using an open-

systems approach to religious organizations is found in Beckford (1973); also, see Scherer (1980).

8. James Gustafson (1961) calls attention to this tendency in neo-orthodox theology, but also to the opposite possibility of opening the church constructively to social scientific analysis.

9. For a summary of some of the work, see Wieser (1966). For an assessment, see Webber (1981).

10. Fr. Avery Dulles (1974) deals with various models of the church, Roman Catholic and Protestant, and considers particularly some convergences of post-Conciliar Catholic and Protestant ecclesiology. Also, see Howes (1972:6) for a discussion of continuing issues of tension in Roman Catholicism between what is appropriate and inappropriate for policy research.

11. Although Dudley does not use the "communal-associational" distinction, he places heavy emphasis on the essentially nonrational and affectional character of churches (especially small-membership ones) where relationships, spaces, and shared memories are vehicles of the sacred.

12. Examples of this approach and citations of additional anthropological studies of religious systems are included in several chapters of Dudley (1983).

13. A helpful method for bringing together theological and social scientific insights, while maintaining the integrity of each, is found in a recent book by James D. and Evelyn Eaton Whitehead (1982).

14. It can be argued that the renewed emphasis on the sacred is in actuality an expression of secularization. That is, it reflects a relocation and consequent shrinking of the arena of the sacred from the world more generally to special sacred places, observances, and persons (see Martin 1978:278 ff).

REFERENCES

Anderson, James D., and Celia Allison Hahn
   1980   "Communal and Associational Churches," *Alban Institute Action Information* September: 1–5.
Beckford, James
   1973   *Religious Organization: A Trend Report and Bibliography.* The Hague: Mouton.
Boulard, F.
   1960   *An Introduction to Religious Sociology.* M. J. Jackson, trans. London: Darton, Longman and Todd.
Brunner, Edmund deS.
   1959   "Harlan Paul Douglass: Pioneer Researcher in the Sociology of Religion," *Review of Religious Research* Spring-Fall:3–16, 63–75.
Carroll, Jackson W.
   1979   "Continuity and Change: The Shape of Religious Life in the

United States, 1950 to the Present." *In* Jackson W. Carroll, Douglass W. Johnson, and Martin E. Marty, *Religion in America 1950 to the Present*. New York: Harper and Row. Pp. 4–45.

Carroll, Jackson W., and Robert L. Wilson
1978   "Studying Clergy Supply and Demand—an Open Systems Perspective." Unpublished paper presented at the meeting of the Religious Research Association, Chicago.

Coleman, James S.
1972   *Policy Research in the Social Sciences*. Morristown. N.J.: General Learning Press.

Douglass, H. Paul
1926   *The Springfield Survey*. New York: George H. Doran Co.
1927   *The Church in the Changing City*. New York: George H. Doran Co.

Douglass, H. Paul, and Edmund deS. Brunner
1935   *The Protestant Church as a Social Institution*. New York: Russell and Russell.

Dudley, Carl S.
1977   *Making the Small Church Effective*. Nashville: Abingdon.
1983   *Building Effective Ministry, Theory and Practice in the Local Church*. New York: Harper and Row.

Dulles, Avery
1974   *Models of the Church*. Garden City, N.Y.: Doubleday Anchor Books.

FADICA (Foundations and Donors Interested in Catholic Activities)
1981   *Toward More Effective Research in the Church*. FADICA.

Fichter, Joseph
1954   *Social Relations in the Urban Parish*. Chicago: University of Chicago Press.

Fukuyama, Yoshio
1963   "The Uses of Sociology: By Religious Bodies," *Journal of the Scientific Study of Religion* 12:195–203.

Gannon, Francis X.
1967   "Briding the Research Gap: CARA, Response to Vatican II," *Review of Religious Research* 9:3–10.

Gill, Robin
1975   *The Social Context of Theology*. London: Mowbrays.

Glock, Charles, and Rodney Stark
1966   *Christian Beliefs and Anti-Semitism*. New York: Harper and Row.

Gustafson, James M.
1961   *Treasure in Earthern Vessels*. New York: Harper and Brothers.

Hadden, Jeffrey
1974   "A Brief Social History of the Religious Research Association," *Review of Religious Research* 15:128–136.
1980   "H. Paul Douglass: His Perspective and His Work," *Review of Religious Research* 22:66–68.

Holms, Urban T.
1971   *The Future Shape of Ministry.* New York: Seabury Press.
Howes, Robert G.
1972   "Research and Religion: A Practitioner's Viewpoint," *Review of Religious Research* 14:3–14.
Martin, David
1978   *A General Theory of Secularization.* New York: Harper Colophon Books.
McCready, William C.
1981   "Research in the Catholic Church, Undervalued, Underused, and Underfunded—the Researcher's Perspective." In *Toward More Effective Research in the Church.* Washington, D.C.: FADICA. Pp. 20–29.
Paul, Leslie
1972   "The Role of the Clergy Today—an Organizational Approach: Problems of Deployment." *In* C. L. Mitton, ed., *The Social Sciences and the Churches.* Edinburgh: T. & T. Clark. Pp. 163–180.
Scherer, Ross P., ed.
1980   *American Denominational Organization, a Sociological View.* Pasadena, Calif.: William Carey Library.
Schroeder, W. Widick
1971   "The Development of Religious Research in the United States: Retrospect and Prospect," *Review of Religious Research* 13:2–12.
Schuller, David S., Merton P. Strommen, and Milo L. Brekke, eds.
1980   *Ministry in America.* New York: Harper and Row.
Selznick, Philip
1957   *Leadership in Administration.* New York: Harper and Row.
Shiner, Larry
1967   "The Concept of Secularization in Empirical Research," *Journal for the Scientific Study of Religion* 6:207–220.
Strommen, Merton P.
1981   "Moving the Results of Applied Research into Systems: Principles Derived from Secular Studies." *Toward More Effective Research in the Church.* Washington D.C.: FADICA. Pp. 74–83.
Swatos, William H., Jr.
1983   "The Faith of the Fathers: On the Christianity of Early American Sociology," *Sociological Analysis* 44:33–52.
Turner, Victor W.
1969   *The Ritual Process.* Chicago: Aldine.
Webber, George W.
1981   "The Struggle for Integrity," *Review of Religious Research* 23:3–21.
Weber, Max
1946   "Science As a Vocation." In H. H. Gerth and C. Wright Mills, eds., *From Max Weber: Essays in Sociology.* New York: Oxford University Press. Pp. 129–156.

1968   *Economy and Society*. 3 vols. Guenther Roth and Claus Wittich, eds. New York: Bedminster Press.

Whitehead, James D., and Evelyn Eaton Whitehead
1981   *Method in Ministry*. New York: Seabury Press.

Wieser, Thomas, ed.
1966   *Planning for Mission*. New York: U.S. Conference for the World Council of Churches.

Winter, Gibson
1961   *The Suburban Captivity of the Churches*. Garden City, N.Y.: Doubleday.

Zaltman, Gerald, ed.
1973   *Processes and Phenomena of Social Change*. New York: Wiley.

XXI

Social Justice and the Sacred

Sister Marie Augusta Neal

Even though social justice has been a major factor in many religious groups over the past twenty years, it was not necessary for the 20-Year Index 1961–1981 of The Society for the Scientific Study of Religion to include the concept of "social justice" in its categories. Why this is so will be the subject matter of this chapter. After a definition of terms and a review of the literature, I will try to demonstrate why there is an acceleration of action for social justice on the part of the established churches in the late twentieth century, and then why this phenomenon has not received the same attention that has been given to the study of other new religious movements since 1960.

SOCIAL JUSTICE DEFINED

Social justice is based on the notion that people have rights to the goods and services they need to stay alive and develop their human potential. Action for social justice initiates and carries out what needs to be done to achieve these rights. Full recognition that peoples have such rights attained the status of law only with the promulgation of the human rights covenants of the United Nations in 1976 (United Nations 1978:1). Without going into detail about the origin and development of the United Nations' Declaration on Human Rights and its division into two covenants, one affirming political and civil rights, the other, economic, social, and cultural rights (Neal 1980:3), suffice it to say here that neither covenant in its original form considered "the right of peoples to self-determination and to enjoy and utilize fully and freely their natural wealth and resources." The addition of this newly understood right was made to both covenants in 1966 (United Nations 1978:2). It is this right that is embodied in the concept of social justice.

A REVIEW OF THE LITERATURE

The initial volume of the *Journal for the Scientific Study of Religion* laid a foundation for studying social justice with Kolb's examination of the images of man (*sic*) in sociology of religion and with O'Dea's analysis of the five dilemmas of institutionalization of religion, one of which is social responsibility (1961). Several articles since have addressed issues of social justice: a report on the black church and political power (Banks 1968); Hadden's study of religion and political affiliation (1962); the religious content of prejudice (Allport 1965); the active ecumenical role of church leaders in a workers' town (Wolcott 1983). Each of these articles suggests an awareness of the justice issue, but does not use it directly as a concept to explain, or to be explained with reference to, the sacred. William Garrett's examination of politicized clergy, the relationship of religious preference and political ideology, and the advent of social reform movements again touch on the domain of social justice (1973); the examination of ideas about God as transcendent and immanent and the relationship of such ideas to attention to social action comes close to the agenda of social justice (Wuthnow 1981), as does Max Stackhouse's essay on the religious roots of modern ideas on human rights (1983). Finally, the discussion of civil religion, begun by Robert Bellah and developed through more than a decade of discourse, refines ideas useful for the analysis of social justice within a national framework, but still it is without any specific recognition of this concept (Gehrig 1981, and Bellah and Hammond 1980).

ACCELERATION OF CHURCH ACTION ON
SOCIAL JUSTICE SINCE 1960

In the foundation year of the *Journal* (1961) the civil rights movement was at its height in the United States. The churches had been ambivalently involved in the struggle to define and change those violations of justice exhibited in the denial of the rights of black Americans to vote, to an education, hospital care, control of property, and to other human needs (Pettigrew and Campbell 1959). In the larger world scene, in that year, Pope John XXIII published *Mater et Magistra*, in which he called the Latin American Catholic Church to account for its close alignment with the wealthy and the powerful, and its relative neglect of the poor. Two years later, he followed this denouncement with the encyclical *Pacem in Terris*, a proposal for Christian social action claiming that peace, poverty, and human rights are the central concerns of the committed Christian (1963).[1] At this time African nations were demanding release from colonial control, rooting their claims in a new awareness of their human rights. The momentum was now right for the initiation of the second Vatican Council, the Council that would, in 1965, reaffirm the long-expressed but seldom-used claim of Saint Thomas Aquinas writing in the thirteenth century that, when the poor reach out to take what they need from those who are rich, they commit no sin but only do what they should do, since, when human need is the issue, all goods are held in common (*Gaudium et Spes*, No. 69: *Summa Theol.*, Q66, A 7, in Flannery 1975:975). A series of decrees from the Council followed in quick succession, bringing almost a century of social justice action to a climax in a clearly specified social justice agenda. Pope Paul VI's "The Development of Peoples" encyclical of 1967 proclaimed that the liberation of the dispossessed is the modern way to do justice work in the world; and his "Call to Action" letter of 1971 invited the laity to move into political action to transform structures of society to bring them into line with the demands of social justice without waiting passively for orders (Paul VI, 1971, No. 48, in O'Brien and Shannon 1977:380). In that same year, the World Synod of Catholic Bishops in their proceedings entitled "Justice in the World," declared that:

Action on behalf of justice and participation in the transformation of the world fully appear to us as a constitutive dimension of the preaching of the Gospel or, in other words, of the Church's mission for the redemption of the human race and its liberation from every oppressive situation. (World Synod of Catholic Bishops, No. 5)

With this document in hand, Catholic bishops around the world were mandated to set up offices of justice and peace. These offices provide an international network for action to address problems of world poverty and migration, and peace work. They have become centers for action for the realization of human rights that go well beyond the civil rights established by law in many countries.

The Uppsala meeting of the World Council of Churches in 1968 upheld similar principles about the just demands of the poor and, on the basis of these principles, established an agenda favorable to the development of Third World nations (SODEPAX 1978, 1979; Santa Ana 1979; Appiah-Kubi and Torres 1979). Although similar principles had been expressed since 1948, when the World Council of Churches gathered for its meeting in Vancouver in 1983, the organization was characterized in television and other news media commentary as becoming communist or at least too influenced by that ideology because of its involvement with social action for justice in Africa.[2]

On the organizational side, Church-associated publishing houses reflecting this justice focus rose up quickly in many First and Third World countries, and an ecumenical social justice reading public soon developed. Orbis Press has been outstanding in developing a collection of books on social justice, issues, and activities. Seabury, John Knox, Westminster Press and Fortress Press are other examples. National and international as well as regional and local organizations under various denominational auspices provide literature, slide shows, films, and other media forms for documentaries on justice work. These consciousness-raising devices came into existence in the 1970s, rapidly turning this new church focus into programs of social action for the realization of a social justice agenda taught in biblical perspective. Catholic, Protestant, and Jewish groups worked on this common agenda out of a shared biblical perspective.[3]

This ecumenical action for social justice touched both rural and urban areas of the United States, as seen in the collaboration of the churches following the publication of the Appalachian bishops' pastoral "This Land Is Home to Me," on land use in Appalachia in 1974, and the Episcopal bishops' pastoral on the city (Urban Bishops Coalition 1978). Collaboration, however, was particularly evident among missionaries in Africa and Latin America.[4]

With the collaboration among church missionary societies beginning in the late sixties came a new body of cross-denominational Liberation Theology (see Alves 1969; Gutierrez 1973; Miques-Bonino 1975; Ruether 1973; Soelle 1974; Schillebeeckx 1980; Sobrino 1978; Tamez 1976). With this theology came a common form of local organization called Basic Christian Communities (LADOC 1976) and a common method of biblical reflection called "Conscientization" (Freire 1970:19). Basic Christian Communities multiplied so rapidly that by 1980 there were more than 80,000 such communities in Brazil alone, though the phenomenon appeared in most Latin American countries, and spread from there to Africa through the work particularly of the World Council of Churches (Santa Ana 1979; Appiah-Kubi and Torres 1977).

Other forms of justice work were operating simultaneously. Amnesty International and the South Africa Defense and Aid Fund reported on individual political prisoners. Centers for the sharing of news about revolutionary struggle, such as the Washington Office on Latin America, Washington Office on Africa, New York Circus, Coalition for a New Foreign and Military Policy, Center of Concern, Network, and Sojourners, not only sprang up but established connections with one another in their common social justice efforts.

This collaborative action, among Christian groups particularly, was not limited to the United States. One example of an international collaboration is a complex international network entitled International Study Days: A Society Overcoming Domination. It was initiated by the Brazilian Catholic bishops, channeled through a communication office in Paris, and staffed by a Franciscan sister with an office at the National Council of Churches building in New York City before moving to the West Coast. It attempted to link Basic Christian Communities around the world with each other directly, thus eliminating the necessity of engaging intermediary experts and expensive consulting costs (see International Study Days 1978).

The funeral of Archbishop Romero in El Salvador, murdered at the altar in the spring of 1980 after he had formally proclaimed the right of the people to lay claim to the land they worked, was attended by major staff members of these several organizations similarly committed to land reform efforts (Erdozian 1981). When four Catholic women involved in the same struggle for justice were murdered in December of the same year, justice workers from the several Christian churches joined in public witness to this violation of human rights of struggling peoples. A similar demonstration took place in 1973 with the fall of Allende in Chile.[5]

The social justice agenda has not only accelerated the desire for ecumenism in the past twenty years but has also provided the main motive for collaboration among the churches (Brown 1978; Herzog 1980). Liberation Theology, a Latin American development, initiated a North American response in the form of the Theology in the Americas group, which had its first meeting in Detroit in 1975 and, after dividing into separate black, women's, Chicano, and white theological study groups, developed a relatively permanent source of theological reflectors on the world struggle for freedom from oppres-

sive social structures (Torres and Eagleton 1976). Catholic congregations of religious sisters, in the revision of their constitutions mandated by the Second Vatican Council, made social justice a main
element in their statements of mission.[6]

This action for justice on the part of religiously committed people
is no less characteristic of the religious scene than are the new
religious movements, the charismatic renewal, New Religious Right,
and the focus on Eastern meditation in the West. Still, these latter
movements are addressed more frequently in the scientific study of
religion, even though social justice participants clearly recognize common beliefs, practices, and behaviors and can quickly develop a network of religious groups around a commonly recognized agenda,
behavior we usually associate with religious movements and examine
as such. And yet social justice movements are treated segmentally,
often examined as secular or political behavior, not as stemming
specifically from deep religious commitment. Why is this so? There
appear to be several interrelated, historically grounded reasons for
this segmentation. I will discuss each one separately and then attempt
to integrate them into a theoretical framework.

THE ACT OF SOCIAL JUSTICE

Historically, justice has been defined as rights within law or even
reduced to rules of fair play (Rawls 1971). Only in the twentieth
century do we have the beginnings of a generally accepted literature
that recognizes organized evil as the object of systematic criticism
(Ferree 1951; Niebuhr 1940; Rawls 1971). Even as late as the 1930s,
sociologists were calling the study of social problems, "disorganiza-
tion," leaving the student with the assumption that what is organized
is good since what is disorganized is defined as a "social problem."
Yet social analysis reveals that much evil is highly organized. Apartheid is a striking example of organized injustice (Mbeke 1964;
Mzimela 1983). Since it is an institution of a nation state, one has to
ask whence will come effective action to judge it unjust and then to
change it? The development of the United Nations initiated that
possibility, and the conversion of the Declaration on Human Rights
to the International Covenants on Human Rights moved that moral
statement to the status of law (1976). We have yet to invent effective
sanctions on injustices, however, because historically sanctions have
ultimately rested with the power to take life violently, and even with
the establishment of the United Nations covenants, that power still

remains in the nation states; the force of moral suasion resting with religious institutions is still relatively uninstitutionalized.

SOCIAL JUSTICE AND THE NATION STATE

Religions have been linked with families (ancient Greece); with tribes (primitive religions); with nations (biblical peoples); with empires (feudal periods); and with states (early modern times). Religions can thus be examined as institutional elements of political units. In this context, early assumptions of tribal gods, who cared only for their own peoples, have been retained in popular cultures; or justice for nonmembers may be limited to temporary hospitality, as Scriptures prescribe. Currently, with the discovery of a human capacity for rapid literacy (Freire 1970), of responsible group decision-making, and of effective organization to claim rights as human beings, interpretations of ancient Scriptures take on new meanings with reference to peoples other than one's genetic progeny (Neal 1982). Church-affiliated organizations, trying to support the right of peoples to migrate, challenge the tribal limitations of membership by calling to the attention of church members the global character of the human community. Often this local church/global church distinction divides religious communities and calls for political and social analysis on the part of the ministers of religion before effective action can be taken. A case in point is that of the American congregations giving asylum to El Salvadorians in 1983.

This expanded understanding of human rights stands over the law. It acts as more than a moral force because it is now adopted as law by some of the United Nations. It is no longer possible to privatize a god to a specific people and expect effective moral action. Old religions are recognizing again their obligation to stand against unjust laws. Oscar Romero was a symbol of this obligation for many Christians, cutting across denominational and national lines though acting within the tradition.

SOCIAL JUSTICE AND ATHEISM

In recent history, the agenda of social justice is associated with atheism because Marx, the aggressive protagonist for the rights of the industrial worker, observed that the God Christians worshipped was a class-linked deity who acted in the interests of capitalism. When

Marx looked back, he saw that same God portrayed as espousing the cause of the feudal lord, and he concluded that the only possibility of achieving worker rights was through a formal rejection of all dominating gods, placing all ritual energy into a faith in people organized to take what is rightfully theirs. This action of taking what is rightfully the common heritage came in the twentieth century to be defined as the agenda of communism. Since communism was atheistic and politically potent, scholarship that researched the ongoing movements for social justice were perceived by university staff, funding sources, scholars and students alike, as a political act against the interests of the capitalist West. Such research thus appeared partisan, lacking the objectivity required of the scientist. Furthermore, since justice calls for action to change situations discovered to be unjust, scholars shied away from research in this area on the grounds that science is value-free and cannot be objectively conducted if the informed researcher by reason of his or her research findings is called from the laboratory into political action.

JUSTICE OUTSIDE OF LAW

Social justice action is often reaction to structured evil, that is, to a situation in which people suffer not because law is violated but because it is adhered to. The socialists of the nineteenth century challenged this anomaly, pointing out that people were suffering from lack of food, clothing, and shelter, from illness and ignorance, despite the fulfillment of the law. After the Industrial Revolution had come to full expression in the countries of western Europe, the Catholic Church, first in *Rerum Novarum*, 1891, expressed recognition of this criticism by formally supporting the principle that the working person has a right to a wage sufficient to live in simple dignity (Leo XIII). In *Quadregesimo Anno*, forty years later, Pope Pius XI declared that workers have a right to the strike and boycott as means to achieve some control over the allocation of the profits of industry. This understanding of human rights is, on the part of the Catholic Church, extended later in *Mater et Magistra*, in 1961, wherein Pope John XXIII called the Latin American Church to account for siding with the rich and powerful to the disadvantage of the poor, describing this affiliation as a violation of Christian commitment. In 1971, Pope Paul VI called the Catholic laity to move into political action to transform the structures of society into systems characterized by social justice. The occasion of this letter, entitled "A Call to Action," was the eightieth anniversary of the *Rerum Novarum* letter. On the ninetieth anniversary in 1981, Pope John Paul II taught that work entitles one to ownership in the means of production (John Paul II 1981; Baum 1982), thus providing a religious guideline to the struggle of the worker to control the means of production, even as the papal letters of the sixties had affirmed the rights of all peoples to the resources of the land for food, clothing, and shelter. It indicates the influence of the socialist revolution on the biblical reflection of church administrators and members, and the consequences of gospel reflection on the development of peoples. Where these reflections run counter to political policy, the churches today experience both new conflict and influence on states.

All these decrees on social justice are novel in the twentieth century. As the historical research of William Ferree, published as the Act of Social Justice (1950), reveals, Church handling of justice was limited to individual justice or justice under the law until the social encyclicals of the late nineteenth and early twentieth century were promulgated. This twentieth-century development of human rights, with churches assisting the United Nations to reach a consensus on a declaration in 1948 and a covenant in 1967, needs an an explanation.

RELIGION AND A NEW INTERNATIONAL ECONOMIC ORDER

The new reality of a world system for a political economy has introduced the student of religion to the need to review the moral qualities of existing political economies (Parsons 1971; McGinnis 1979). Critical analysis of both capitalism and communism in their current forms has been put on the agenda for theologians and other religious role players (Cassidy 1979; Baum 1980; Schiblin 1983; Holland and Henriot 1983). The new public focus in the expression of religion suggests that the privatization of religion (already evident in Hegel's analysis of God, the state, and the local community) was politically effective at legitimating secularization in the interests of the development of capitalism (Hegel 1953). It would seem that what discussions of civil religion (Bellah and Hammond 1980) and public theology (Mead 1975) are striving to explain at the national level are elements of a larger religious phenomenon which the concept of social justice addresses at the global level. This global phenomenon includes ideas about God which, far from declining at the present time, are effectively analyzed not with the secular-sacred dichotomy but rather with the concepts of immanence and transcendence. These concepts refer to the place where one seeks for and experiences God, rather than—like the secular-sacred dichotomy—assume an absence or presence of God, thus begging the question of religious commitment in the struggle for social justice (Suhard 1948; Garrett 1973; Neal, 1977).

Such examination of religious phenomena at the global level involves power and authority on the one hand, and commitment to altruism on the other (Neal, 1972, 1982). We must therefore agree on conceptual tools independent of the political and economic interests that are entrenched in the geographical units in which we live and do our work (Neal 1965) but, once past that hurdle, analysis of social justice and the sacred can proceed. We are just beginning.

NOTES

1. Encyclicals are circular letters addressed by the Pope to the Catholic community, and sometimes, as with *Pacem in Terris*, to all Christians. They are usually researched by a group of scholars and theologians and published under the name of the current Pope. They deal with questions of social moment and explore their biblical and theological bases and implications.

2. See "Delegates Defy Rightists by Affirming Human Rights" by Walter Mead (the *Guardian*, September 14, 1983, p. 14). The Religion and Democracy Institute in Washington, D.C., and a "60 Minutes" national television special called the World Council of Churches to account for giving funds to African liberation groups assisting SWAPO and activities of the African National Congress. The accusation implied communist cooperation.

3. Some of these Church-affiliated social justice groups include Clergy and Laity Concerned; Episcopal Peace Fellowship; Interreligious Task Force on El Salvador and Central America; New Jewish Agenda; Presbyterian Peacemaking Program of the Presbyterian Church, U.S.A.; Board of Global Ministries of the United Methodist Church; Baptist Peacemakers of the Southern Baptist Church; and others.

4. At a meeting of American missionaries in Ventnor, New Jersey, May 7, 1982, Jorge Lara-Brand, director of the Council on Theology and Culture of the Presbyterian Church in the United States, stated that "The center of gravity in world Christianity has shifted to Africa and Latin America," and, at the same meeting, Sister Barbara Hendricks, a Maryknoll sister who had worked in Bolivia, said that "The modern missionary believes that work for social justice is an essential part of the gospel" (*New York Times*, May 10, 1982, p. B6).

5. A documentary produced by Maryknoll, entitled *Roses in December*, details this participation and support of a violation of justice.

6. The research I have been doing on the changing structures of congregations of Catholic sisters provides evidence that over 80 percent of the Catholic sisterhoods have made the doing of justice and peace work the main factor in their revised statements of mission since the Second Vatican Council. This research is being completed at the present time and prepared for publication.

REFERENCES

Allport, Gordon W.
  1965   "The Religious Context of Prejudice," *Journal for the Scientific Study of Religion* 5:447.
Alves, Ruben
  1969   *A Theology of Human Hope.* New York: Corpus Books.
Appalachian Bishops' Pastoral
  1977   "This Land Is Home to Me." *In* O'Brien and Shannon, *Renewing the Earth.* Pp. 468–515.
Appiah-Kubi, Kofi, and Sergio Torres, eds.
  1979   *African Theology en Route: Papers from the Pan-African Conference of Third World Theologians. Accra, Ghana, 1977.* Maryknoll. N.Y.: Orbis Books.
Banks, Walter R.
  1968   "Two Impossible Revolutions? Black Power and Church Power," *Journal for the Scientific Study of Religion* 8:263.
Baum, Gregory
  1980   *Catholics and Canadian Socialism: Political Thought in the Thirties and Forties.* Toronto: Lorimer.
  1982   *The Priority of Labor.* New York: Paulist Press.
Bellah, Robert N.
  1970   *Beyond Belief: Essays on Religion in a Post-Traditional World.* New York: Harper and Row.
Bellah, Robert N. and Phillip E. Hammond
  1980   *Varieties of Civil Religion.* San Francisco: Harper and Row.
Brown, Robert McAlfee
  1978   *Theology in a New Key: Responding to Liberation Themes.* Philadelphia: Westminster Press.
Cassidy, Richard
  1979   *Catholic Teaching Regarding Capitalism and Socialism.* Detroit: Office of Justice and Peace, Archdiocese of Detroit.
Erdozian, Placido
  1981   *Archbishop Romero: Martyr of Salvador.* Maryknoll, N.Y.: Orbis Books.
Ferree, William
  1951   *The Act of Social Justice.* Dayton, Ohio: Marianist Publications.

Flannery, Austin, ed.
  1975   *Vatican Council II: The Conciliar and Post-Conciliar Documents.*
          Northport, N.Y.: Costello Publishing Company.
Freire, Paulo
  1970   *The Pedagogy of the Oppressed.* New York: Seabury Press.
Garrett, William R.
  1973   "Politicized Clergy: A Sociological Interpretation of the 'New
          Breed,'" *Journal for the Scientific Study of Religion* 12:385.
Gehrig, Gail
  1981   "The American Civil Religion Debate: A Source for Theory Con-
          struction," *Journal for the Scientific Study of Religion* 20:51.
Gutierrez, Gustavo
  1973   *Theology of Liberation: History, Politics and Salvation.* Maryknoll,
          N.Y.: Orbis Books.
Hadden, Jeffrey K.
  1962   "An Analysis of Some Factors Associated with Religion and Polit-
          ical Affiliation," *Journal for the Scientific Study of Religion* 2:209.
Hegel, G. W. F.
  1953   *Reason in History.* New York: Bobbs-Merrill.
Herzog, Frederick
  1980   *Justice Church: The New Function of the Church in North American
          Christianity.* Maryknoll, N.Y.: Orbis Books.
Holland, Joe, and Peter Henriot, S.J.
  1983   *Social Analysis: Linking Faith and Justice.* Rev. ed. Maryknoll, N.Y.:
          Orbis Books.
International Study Days
  1978   *For a Society Overcoming Domination,* vol. 1. Deposit, N.Y. Valley
          Offset.
John Paul II, Pope
  1981   *On Human Work (Laborem Exercens).* Boston: St. Paul's edition.
Kolb, William L.
          "Images of Man and the Sociology of Religion," *Journal for the
          Scientific Study of Religion* 1:5.
LADOC
  1976   *Basic Christian Communities.* Washington, D.C.: LADOC Keyhole
          Series, No. 14.
Leo XIII, Pope
  1942   *The Condition of Labor (Rerum Novarum, 1891).* Washington, D.C.:
          National Catholic Welfare Conference.
Mbeke, Govan
  1964   *South Africa: The Peasants' Revolt.* Baltimore: Penguin.
McGinnis, James B.
  1979   *Bread and Roses: Toward a New International Economic Order.* New
          York: Paulist Press.
Mead, Sidney
  1975   *The Nation with the Soul of a Church.* New York: Harper and Row.

Miquez-Bonino, Jose
  1975   *Doing Theology in a Revolutionary Situation*. Philadelphia: Fortress
            Press.
Moore, Basil
  1973   *The Challenge of Black Theology in South Africa*. Atlanta: John Knox
            Press.
Mzimela, Sipo E.
  1983   *Apartheid: South African Naziism*. New York: Vantage Press.
Neal, Marie Augusta
  1965   *Values and Interests in Social Change*. Englewood Cliffs, N.J. Pren-
            tice Hall.
  1972   "How Prophecy Lives," *Sociological Analysis* 33 (3):125–141.
  1977   *A Sociotheology of Letting Go*. New York: Paulist Press.
  1982   "Commitment to Altruism in Sociological Analysis," *Sociological
            Analysis* 43, (1):1–22.
Niebuhr, Reinhold
  1940   *Christianity and Power Politics*. New York: Charles Scribner's Sons.
O'Brien, David J., and Thomas A. Shannon
  1977   *Renewing the Earth: Catholic Documents on Peace, Justice and Libera-
            tion*. Garden City, N.Y.: Image Books.
O'Dea, Thomas
            "Five Dilemmas in the Institutionalization of Religion," *Journal for
            the Scientific Study of Religion* 18:260.
Parsons, Talcott
  1971   *System of Modern Society*. Englewood Cliffs. N.J.: Prentice-Hall.
Pettigrew, Thomas, and Ernest Campbell
  1959   *Christians in Racial Crisis*. Washington, D.C.: Public Affairs Press.
Pius XI, Pope
  1942   *On Reconstructing the Social Order (Quadregesimo Anno)*. Washing-
            ton, D.C.: National Catholic Welfare Conference.
Rawls, John A.
  1971   *A Theory of Justice*. Cambridge, Mass.: Belknap Press, Harvard
            University.
Ruether, Rosemary
  1973   *Liberation Theology*. New York: Paulist Press.
Santa Ana, Julio de
  1979   *Toward a Church of the Poor: The Work of an Ecumenical Group on the
            Church and the Poor*. Maryknoll, N.Y.: Orbis Books.
Schiblin, Richard
  1983   *The Bible, the Church, and Social Justice*. Liguori, Mo.: Liguori Pub-
            lications.
Schillebeeckx, Edward
  1980   "Liberation Theology between Medellin and Puebla," *Theology
            Digest* 28, 1 (Spring):3–7.
Sobrino, Jon, S. J.
  1978   *Christology at the Crossroads*. Maryknoll, N.Y.: Orbis Books.

SODEPAX
  1977,   *"Rocca di Papa Coloquium* on the Social Thinking of the Churches,"
  1978   Parts 1, 2, 3, and 4, *Church Alert,* Nos. 17–20. Geneva: Ecumenical
            Center.
Soelle, Dorothee
  1974   *Political Theology.* Philadelphia: Fortress Press.
Stackhouse, Max L.
  1983   "Some Intellectual and Social Roots of Modern Human Rights
            Ideas," *Journal for the Scientific Study of Religion* 20:301.
Suhard, Emmanuel Cardinal
  1948   *Growth or Deline: The Church Today.* South Bend, Ind.: Fides Pub-
            lishers.
Tamez, Elsa
  1976   *Bible of the Oppressed.* Maryknoll, N.Y.: Orbis Books.
Torres, Sergio, and John Eagleton
  1976   *Theology in the Americas.* Maryknoll, N.Y.: Orbis Books.
United Nations
  1978   *The International Bill of Human Rights.* New York: United Nations.
Urban Bishops Coalition
  1978   *To Hear and to Heed: The Episcopal Church Listens and Acts in the
            City.* Cincinnati: Forward Movement Publications.
Weber, Max
  1963   *Sociology of Religion.* Boston: Beacon Press.
Wolcott, Roger T.
  1983   "Church and Social Action: Steelworkers and Bishops in
            Youngstown," *Journal for the Scientific Study of Religion* 21:71.
World Synod of Catholic Bishops
  1971   No. 5.
Wuthnow, Robert
  1976   *The Consciousness Reformation.* Berkeley, Los Angeles, London:
            University of California Press.

XXII

The Sacred and the World System

Roland Robertson

I

The theme of the sacred and the world system necessitates an approach that is rather different from most others in this volume; there are two major reasons for this. First, social-scientific analysis of religion in a global, as opposed to a comparative, perspective is only in its infancy. Second, that school of social-scientific thought which has thematized "the world system" in recent years has promoted a negative view of religion and, for the most part, has implicitly adhered to a strong version of the secularization thesis.

Why, then, address the topic at all unless one is convinced (which I am not) that the arguments of world-system theorists are persuasive? My answer to that question falls into three parts. First, I think it can be shown that the world-systems perspective has something *interesting* to say about religion and the sacred, and that modifications which have been wrought by world-system theorists in their own programs are instructive vis-à-vis analytical problems concerning "the sacred." Second, the world-systems perspective does not, in spite of its recent prominence, have a monopoly on discussion of sociocultural and related matters in global perspective. Third, I believe the global perspective throws the work of a number of the classical social-scientific theorists into a new light and considerably complicates the argument that those men of the second half of the nineteenth century and early part of the twentieth century simply bequeathed to us a straightforward secularization model.

The notion of "the world" has traditionally been used by students of religion to refer to the domain of the secular or mundane—hence the idea, of which Max Weber was the major proponent, of degrees

347

and forms of "worldliness" as an approach to the sacred-secular theme. In fact that usage overlaps the other major sense in which the term has been used in academic contexts—namely, the world as a *place* in the cosmos—to the extent that the second usage has been predicated upon the idea of the secularity of the relationships centered upon that place. In other words, even though the actual referents have been dissimilar—the world as the mundane aspect of human existence for some, for others the world as a place whose systemicity is expressed in a highly "material" way—"the world" has connoted the absence of the sacred. Sociologists have tended to comply with the first convention, whereas "the dismal" social scientists—specialists in international relations and students of international or global economics—have largely adhered to the second.

It is my argument that the modern *confluence* of these two senses of "the world" in reference to what I call the process of *globalization* constitutes a major—perhaps *the* major—site for the contemporary generation of concern with the sacred (Robertson 1982*a*, 1983; Robertson and Chirico 1984). The concept of globalization refers to the processes by which the world becomes a single place, both with respect to recognition of a very high degree of interdependence between spheres and locales of social activity across the entire globe *and* to the growth of consciousness pertaining to the globe as such.[1] The first aspect has been recognized in such terms as *the global economy*, while we see the emergence of the second not merely in academic interest in, for example, the theme of *world theology* (Smith 1981) but also in the very recent proliferation of such terms as *global citizen*—not to speak of religious and quasi-religious concern with the fate of the global *community*.

II

That which currently goes by the name of "world-system theory" has taken a strong version of the secularization thesis for granted. Indeed, it may well be the case that mainstream world-systems theory in the form provided by its leading proponents represents the absolute high point of the secularization thesis. For it has implicitly claimed to see the thorough secularization of the entire world. The making of the modern world-system has, in that perspective, consisted, in a five-hundred-year process, of the stripping away of the autonomous significance of cultural ideas in the face of the onward march, on an increasingly worldwide basis, of capitalistic forms of economic organization (Hopkins 1982). There can in this sense be no other more crucial site for the evaluation of the secularization thesis than world-system theory.

Thus if we use the concept of "world system" in anything resembling fidelity to the convention of founders of world-system theory we thereby accept the secularization thesis, and the most that can be done by a social-scientist of religion is to show in precise detail how religion has, indeed, retreated across recent centuries and performed its "ideological functions" (e.g., Wuthnow 1980).[2] In fact in what constitutes the most important of the founding documents of world-system theory, Wallerstein (1974) provided the embryo of such a research program, in the sense that his book says quite a lot about the allegedly epiphenomenal status of religion in the founding of the modern system of nation states, which itself is regarded as largely an outcome of the crystallization of transnational capitalism. The core of that outlook is to be found in Wallerstein's claim that in the very early stages of the formation of the European world-economy (which was the basis for the eventual formation of the world-economy) there were two major "transnational" forces in Europe. Those were, on the one hand, the Church and, on the other, "an equally transnational economic system" (Wallerstein 1974:156). Prior to the sixteenth century there was simply a late-medieval Christian civilization, but during the sixteenth century the transnational economic system gained in strength in a kind of zero-sum game. That game took the concrete form of the economic system finding its political strength in the creation of strong state apparati in certain societies, while the Church was constrained to become "the opposition of modernity." According to Wallerstein (1974:156), the church played that role so successfully that "its very success in the peripheral countries . . . ensured the long-run success of the European world-economy." Thus Protestantism functioned as the ideology of the core countries in the European world-economy while Catholicism was ideologically significant in the consolidation of the periphery.

The peace of Westphalia in 1648, marking the termination of the thirty years of "religious" wars and, more generally, the passions stirred during the Reformation, resulted not from exhaustion and stalemate "but rather because the geographical division of Europe after 1648 . . . was the natural fulfillment of the underlying thrusts of the world-economy" (Wallerstein 1974:156). It may, then, be concluded that the peace of Westphalia constituted, from a world-systemic perspective, the termination of the significance of "the sacred" in world history (and it had been sharply on the downswing for the previous two hundred years or so). For as the European world-economy gained momentum—as it obtained autonomy (although partly in political form) in relation to the medieval Christian synthesis that constituted the historical matrix from which (for reasons not specified) it had sprung—it extended itself to the entire global circumstance and became what it is today: the hub of a truly *world* social-system. Note that in this theoretical depiction nothing is actually said to the effect that "the economic factor" (even in its political translation) has *always* been the motor force of history. Note too that there is no explicit claim that, as the "contradictions" which are said to inhere in the world-capitalist formation—principally the "contradiction" between the global-unifying thrust of capitalistic appropriation and exploitation, on the one hand, and the political-state form in which appropriation almost inevitably concretely occurs, on the other—multiply and spell its eventual collapse, there will *then* ensue a thoroughly secular global circumstance. The collapse of the truly global world-economy is supposed to result in the shift to a world *socialist* system. Thus in the most abstract terms it is *possible* to conclude that from a world-system perspective the period between about 1500 and—let us say, for the sake of argument—2000 is to be regarded as a kind of interregnum. In that regard one *can* interpret "the world" of the mainstream world-system theorist as conforming to the essential spirit of Max Weber's famous prognosis that *until* the last ton of fossilized coal is burnt we will live in "the iron cage" (Weber 1958:181). In other words, just as Weber cast an image of a bureaucratic world that on one hand had become increasingly centered on what he called the monetary economy but which, on the other hand, would not last forever, so too can we regard Wallerstein, Hopkins, and their closest collaborators as saying only that for a long duration—marked at its beginning and its end by virtually ontological ruptures—does "the economic factor" prevail. We know that prior to that long duration the sacred and the profane "co-existed," and it is even possible that a new or "higher" form of co-existence will prevail in the period following the collapse of the global world-economy (or, in Weberian terms, the "post-fossilic" era).

It must be emphasized that this is a very free interpretation of world-systems theory and one to which few, if any, self-proclaimed proponents of that theory would subscribe. I nevertheless maintain that it is a reasonable one. This theme—concerning the interregnum status of the autonomous world-economy—may be brought into sharper focus via two further considerations. The first of these has to do with the old Marxian problem of the transition to socialism, and the second centers on a specific manifestation in recent world-systems theory of what I will describe as the secularist's impasse vis-à-vis the idea of a purely secular world.

What relevance does the Marxian problem of the transition to socialism have to a discussion of the sacred and the secular in the modern global circumstance? The simplest response to the question is that—for better or for worse—it is a particular brand of Marxist who has been more prominent than any other kind of social analyst in giving thematic flesh to the global circumstance. In turn, we must note that any recognizably Marxist argument is forever going to run into the problem of the relationship between an economistic account of the existing world and the image of a noneconomistic world of the future. This indeed was a paradox of late nineteenth-century socialism noted by Durkheim and Weber. The paradox has two major ramifications. First, emphasis on the purely economic (and its political expressions) makes it exceedingly difficult to deal with the continuation of a particular state of affairs which in terms of purely economic "laws" ought not to continue. (In fact much of Western Marxism has become more concerned with the phenomenon of the continuation of capitalism and thus, for many, the problem of the relative autonomy of ideas and values.) In turn, the problem of the transition to socialism increasingly is treated in terms of its being a normative-ideational problem as much as an economic-political one. The newest—or at least nearly the newest—member of the family of Marxist paradigms has run into these problems very quickly. For within about ten years of its "takeoff," we now find its founder (Wallerstein 1983:25) arguing that analysis of "the metaphysical presuppositions" of "the capitalist world-economy" is an essential piece of intellectual business, and we must accept the injunction that science should be conceived as a form of re-enchantment, rather than disenchantment, of the world. The Heisenberg Uncertainty Principle (concerning the interpenetration of the analyst and that-which-is-analyzed) applies to macroscopic—not only microscopic—phenomena; and thus the social scientist of the global circumstance has grave responsibilities with respect to how the world operates and changes (Wallerstein 1983:32–36). This is, to say the least, a striking concession to the significance of ideas in world history and—presumably unintentionally—creates "a space for the sacred."

At this point, mention should be made of "revisionist tendencies" within the general school of world-system theorists—a label that may be applied to those who have resisted the total emphasis given by the Wallersteinians—at least until very recently—to the economic factor. In that regard the most immediately relevant argument is that which has been advanced concerning the crystallization in the modern period of a world *polity* in partial response to, and standing in an embryonically regulative role vis-à-vis, the global economy. The most significant general thesis of that approach—as developed, in particular, by Meyer (1980) and Boli-Bennett (1979)—is that modern nation-states have become increasingly subject to the constraints of "the cultural content" of an emergent world polity. The latter is not intended to denote a definite form of world government but rather the set of rules defining the global legitimacy of the nation-state itself and the terms in which it is supposed to operate. Specifically, the notion of a world polity helps us to explain why it is that there has been such a remarkable similarity in the appurtenances—for example, the formal constitutions—of recently founded states. But with reference to the theme of the sacred at the global level, a more important point arises from Meyer's (1980:132) argument that "with the increased legitimation of the world polity, and the decreased legitimation of the world exchange economy [presumably in large part because that economy is now globalized], come alterations in *"the broader depictions of reality."* (Emphasis added.) Because "legitimation of the world polity" entails a sense of collective selfhood across the human race, there is a big expansion of "the cultural labors of the elites of the world polity," depicting the external-natural world as "infused with meanings that impose or require limitations on human society" (Meyer 1980:132). In Meyer's (1980:133) view these activities, in turn, consolidate the world polity and its social controlling functions in such a way as to elaborate new types of "justification for world-level rules." The relevant elaborations include world views concerning the moral and natural universe which confronts human beings as a collectivity. Meyer insists that these are *secular* and certainly not spiritual. Thus whether we are talking about "world-systemic reenchantment" (that is, re-enchantment of the world by world-systems *theorists*) or about Meyer's "cultural laborers," one finds no concession to the idea of "the sacred" in its sociology-of-religion connotations.

Nevertheless, it is clear that world-system theory has arrived at a critical point in its development which has considerable relevance to the theme of the global significance of religion. In one sense we may regard world-system theory as one among a number of movements which are currently competing with each other in *defining the global situation*; and, in terms of the stakes involved it is—*contra* Meyer—almost inconceivable that religion would *not* be revitalized in response to what I have called globalization. There is an important question involved here as to whether globalization, world-systematization, or whatever, could have occurred without "assistance" from global mythologies or modes of discourse concerning the world-as-a-whole—besides which, as we will shortly see *via* some thoughts of Dumont and Parsons, respectively, we have to entertain the idea (which is certainly not unique to the modern era) that the world is *now* only comprehensible in terms of a world history which has occurred within global constraints that take on a sacred character by virtue of their deep-structural "secretness" (see Fenn 1978). More to the immediate point, if we are now—as a sheer consequence of globalization—at the point where nothing less confronts us than the nature of the human condition itself (Robertson 1983) one would expect and indeed one finds the modern crystallization of *overtly* religious movements that address that theme in the specific sense of the *global-human condition*—by which I mean the concrete, worldwide circumstances of humanity, as opposed to the more abstract ways in which that term has been used in the past by philosophers and theologians. (Almost needless to say, the modern awareness of and attitudes toward the possibility of species death is profoundly implicated in this new circumstance.)

A number of matters to which world-system theorists have drawn attention assist in the comprehension of religious themes in the modern world, then, in spite of the basic secularity of that school of thought. Among the more striking developments in the modern world from the standpoint of the sociologist of religion are: the almost worldwide resurgence of fundamentalist movements, notably those which claim to speak for and infuse religious meaning into particular societies or civilizations; the related occurrence—again on an almost globewide basis—of tensions between church and state; and the coming into prominence of religious movements that claim to interpret the modern global circumstance as a whole (Robertson 1981). The first two of these developments must surely be related significantly to the worldwide strengthening of the modern state (which is, as Meyer and Boli-Bennett have shown, primarily an outcome of a global political culture). Insofar as the expansion of the state stirs up a host of moral and religious issues, it "invites" religious response, whereas in a situation of great global interdependence, the question of the identities of societies and the relationship between the individual and his/her society of membership is also significantly enhanced. The first phenomenon increases the likelihood of church/state tensions and the thematization of the relationship between the sacred and the secular, whereas the second increases the likelihood of movements arising which claim to know what the "real" identities of particular societies are.

Although fundamentalist movements that are particularly concerned with the identity of the society in which they develop frequently *also* issue mythological constructions of the global scene, it is in the more international or transnational religious movements that one obviously finds the most elaborate concern with the global-human condition per se. What appears to be a revitalization of Catholicism as a whole, for example, may well have been facilitated by globalization (precisely because it is the most global of churches), whereas the particular form of Catholicism known as Liberation Theology has clearly been facilitated by what Meyer calls the decreased legitimation of the world exchange economy. For Liberation Theology addresses, inter alia, the inequalities in the world system of stratification; much of "the space" for Liberation Theology has been created by the global interest in radical international inequality. Finally, mention should be made of the Unification Church, which addresses its doctrinal message directly to the global-human circumstance and in fact involves itself in activity directed at nothing less than the concrete unification of the entire world. It is likely that there will be a proliferation of such movements—some of them overtly religious—engaged in defining the global-human situation or proffering *global* civil-religious doctrines.

III

The sociological secularization thesis was essentially based upon the analysis of *societies*. It was the attenuation of religiously grounded values and beliefs and of religiously oriented institutions and roles which was given special attention in the 1950s and 1960s. (Of course since the 1960s, increasing doubt has been expressed about the extent to which there had ever been the kind of "religious society" which proponents of the secularization theses had used as their benchmark, but that is not a critical consideration at this juncture.) And in that view, the secularization thesis was seen to stand in direct succession to the major ideas of classical sociologists. For notwithstanding some difficulties in rendering Durkheim as having subscribed to that thesis (largely premised on the—by now, highly suspect—categorization of *The Elementary Forms of the Religious Life* as a piece of anthropology which was irrelevant to Durkheim's account of the modern world), there can be little doubt that the general *Gemeinschaft-to-Gesellschaft* perspective of classical sociology itself hinged largely on the idea of the secularity of modern societies.

The most recent, forceful and explicit expression of that standpoint is Wilson (1982), who specifically defines the shift from *Gemeinschaft* to *Gesellschaft* as a process of *societalization,* involving the rejection of religion, which is largely defined as "the ideology" of the communal social formation (*Gemeinschaft*). In that scenario, society—as opposed to community—is bereft of other than peripheral religiosity. Since the modern global circumstance is largely regarded in this perspective as having been constituted by extensive societalization, it follows that the world as a whole stands on the threshold of complete secularization. For not merely has there been a globewide *series* of processes of societalization, the global circumstance *itself* hinges increasingly upon "agglomerations" of states, the relationships *among them* being characterized by the societal principles of "rationality" (Wilson 1982:158). In other words, societalization has begotten a form of suprasocietalization such that the world itself is now based upon the principles of instrumental rationality, both intrasocietally and intersocietally.

And yet Wilson comes close to conceding that the societal and global circumstances which he depicts as being governed by entirely instrumental-rational norms are not permanent. It may yet be discovered, he suggests, that "the virtues nurtured essentially in local communities in religious contexts [will] in the long run be shown to be as indispensable to the society of the future as they were to the communities of the past" (Wilson 1982:52). A critical question, however, arises in connection with the "communality" on the horizon. For, as I have hinted, it is at the *global-human* level that one would expect to find *the problematic* of community in the future. One finds, indeed, very strong suggestions to that effect toward the end of *The Elementary Forms of the Religious Life* (Durkheim 1961:452–496), as well as in the general Durkheimian idea that we shall soon have nothing in common—societally or individually—but our common humanity (which Durkheim saw as a new source of sacredness). In that connection it may well be that a number of sociologists of the classical period, while willing to subscribe to the idea that societalization per se involves secularization, were also conscious of trends which, so to speak, took the individual out of society and produced transsocietal forms of consciousness. At least they expressed concern with what I have called the global-human condition (Robertson and Chirico 1984). In turn, however—as I have tried here to show—"globality" itself is likely to produce religiously cast definitions of societies.

One of the themes I have been developing is that the "baring" of a particular aspect of the "world" is likely to produce attempts to infuse it with meaning—if you will, to enchant it. In that regard Parsons (1979) attempted to show that the Industrial Revolution involved both the baring of the economic factor *and* the symbolic religious and quasi-religious responses to it (of which Marxism was one, and the romantic ideology of the religious community another). In one sense all I am saying in this regard is that particular forms of secularization—in Parsons's case, economic secularization—produce, by way of meaningful reaction, "sacred" interpretations. I would suggest we are now in another phase of secularization concerning the thematization of global interdependence, which is being reacted to in a variety of ways along symbolic-interpretive lines. If one takes the general view—as, inter alia, Durkheim, Parsons, Troeltsch (1969) and Weber (at least in his historical work) did—that religion is in significant part *about* the patterning and provision of meaning to the basic means of the production and reproduction of life—namely, economic and sexual activity—then it follows that each stage of a particular baring and thematization of life will bring forth religious and quasi-religious responses. Now, as I have said, we face nothing less than the baring of life itself in the sense of awareness of the global-human condition.

Dumont (1980) is one of the exceedingly few social scientists who have clearly raised the question of the theoretical terms in which one can envisage the world as a whole. In the general sweep of his work Dumont has argued—in a refashioning of Toennies' *Gemeinschaft-Gesellschaft* theme—that there have been two basic "ideological" interpretations of the human society: the Western, centered on the salience of the relationship between man and things, and the Eastern, centered on the relationships between men (in the generic sense). Now, in our time, however, there is the problem of the relationship between these two "ideologies," and also of the fact that we tend at one and the same time to think on the one hand of all humans being the same and, on the other hand, of all societies being different. How, then, is the modern world *possible*? According to Dumont it may well be that in producing an analytical synthesis to resolve these apparent contradictions in the world as a whole we then find the global Whole logically needs "a superior entity from which to derive its own value. . . . Clearly religions have a place here [*mytho*logically], and one could even try to deduce what the Beyond should be like in order to be final" (Dumont 1980:223).

On that Durkheimian note I close. There seems no doubt at all that the phenomenon of "globality" is raising all kinds of interests in the sacred.

NOTES

1. Independently, McCoy (1980) has used the term *globalization* rather differently, but in reference to some of the same concerns of the present essay.

2. I concentrate here exclusively on one central form of Marxist world analysis. Other schools do not, however, raise issues of relevance to sacredness. For an approach markedly different from the Marxist ones, see Nettl and Robertson (1968).

REFERENCES

Boli-Bennett, John
 1979 "The Ideology of Expanding State Authority in National Constitutions, 1870–1970." *In* J. W. Meyer and M. T. Hannan, eds., *National Development and the World System*. Chicago: Chicago University Press.
Dumont, Louis
 1980 "On Value," *Proceedings of the British Academy*. Oxford: Oxford University Press.
Durkheim, Emile
 1961 *The Elementary Forms of the Religious Life*. New York: Collier Books.
Fenn, Richard
 1978 *Toward a Theory of Secularization*. Society for the Scientific Study of Religion, Monograph no. 1.
Hopkins, Terence K.
 1982 "The Study of the Capitalist World Economy." *In* T. Hopkins, I. Wallerstein, and Associates, *World-System Analysis*. Beverly Hills, Calif.: Sage.
McCoy, Charles S.
 1980 *When Gods Change*. Nashville: Abingdon Press.
Meyer, John W.
 1980 "The World Polity and the Authority of the Nation-State." *In* A. Bergesen, ed., *Studies of the Modern World-System*. New York: Academic Press.
Nettl, J. P., and Roland Robertson
 1968 *International Systems and the Modernization of Societies*. New York: Basic Books.

Parsons, Talcott
  1979   "Religious and Economic Symbolism in the Western World,"
            Sociological Inquiry 49:1–48.
Robertson, Roland
  1981   "Considerations from Within the American Context on the Sig-
            nificance of Church-State Tension," *Sociological Analysis* 42 (Fall):
            193–208.
  1982*a*   "Societies, Individuals and Sociology: Intra-Civilizational
            Themes," *Theory, Culture and Society* 1 (September):6–17.
  1982*b*   "Parsons on the Evolutionary Significance of American Religion,"
            Sociological Analysis 4 (Winter):307–326.
  1983   "Religion, Global Complexity, and the Human Condition." In *The
            Search for Absolute Values and the Creation of the New World*. New
            York: International Cultural Foundation.
Robertson, Roland, and JoAnn Chirico
  1984   "Humanity, Globalization and Worldwide Religious Resurgence:
            A Theoretical Exploration," *Sociological Analysis* (in press).
Smith, Wilfred Cantwell
  1981   *Towards a World Theology*. Philadelphia: Westminster Press.
Troeltsch, Ernst
  1969   "Religion, Economy and Society." *In* N. Birnbaum and G. Lenzer,
            eds., *Sociology and Religion*. Englewood Cliffs, N.J.: Prentice-Hall.
Wallerstein, Immanuel
  1974   *The Modern World-System*. New York: Academic Press.
  1983   "Crisis: The World-Economy, the Movements, and the Ideolo-
            gies." *In* A. Bergesen, ed., *Crises in the World System*. Beverly
            Hills, Calif.: Sage.
Weber, Max
  1958   *The Protestant Ethic and the Spirit of Capitalism*. New York: Charles
            Schribner's Sons.
Wilson, Bryan
  1982   *Religion in Sociological Perspective*. New York: Oxford University
            Press.
Wuthnow, Robert
  1980   "World Order and Religious Movements." *In* A. Bergesen, ed.,
            Studies of the Modern World-System. New York: Academic Press.

About the Contributors

William Sims Bainbridge, Associate Professor of Sociology at Harvard University, is the author of *Satan's Power* and co-author of *The Future of Religion* (1984). He has written extensively on sects and cults of both the past and the present.

Dr. Eileen Barker, a member of the Department of Sociology, is currently the Dean of Undergraduate Studies at The London School of Economics. Her research interests are the relationship between science and religion in contemporary society, and the new religious movements. She has written over fifty articles, is the editor of *Of Gods and Men* (1984) and *New Religious Movements in the West* (1982), and the author of *The Making of a Moonie* (1984).

James A. Beckford, Senior Lecturer in Sociology at the University of Durham, Durham, England, is the author of *The Trumpet of Prophecy* (1975) and *Religious Organization* (1975). His recent research on public responses to new religious movements is presented in *Cult Controversies* (forthcoming). He is Editor of *Current Sociology*, official journal of the International Sociological Association, and President of the association's Research Committee for the Sociology of Religion.

David G. Bromley, Professor and Chairman of the Department of Sociology and Anthropology at Virginia Commonwealth University, has written extensively on both cults and anti-cults. He is co-editor of the recently published *New Christian Politics* and of the forthcoming *The Future of New Religious Movements*.

Donald Capps is Professor of Pastoral Theology at Princeton Theological Seminary. He is the author of five books in pastoral theology, including *Life Cycle Theory and Pastoral Care* (1983) and *Hermeneutics and Pastoral Care* (1984). He is co-editor of *Psychology of Religion* (1976), an annotated bibliography, and of two books on religious biography. He is current editor of the *Journal for the Scientific Study of Religion*.

Jackson W. Carroll is Director of the Center for Social and Religious Research at Hartford Seminary and author, co-author, or editor of several publications on American religion, including *Small Churches are Beautiful, Too Many Pastors?, Religion in America: 1959 to the Present,* and *The Varieties of Religious Presence.* He has served as president of the Religious Research Association and as Council Member of the Society for the Scientific Study of Religion.

Phillip E. Hammond is Professor of Religious Studies and Sociology, and chairs the Department of Religious Studies, at the University of California, Santa Barbara. He is the author most recently of *The Role of Ideology in Church Participation,* co-author of *Varieties of Civil Religion,* and co-editor of the forthcoming *The Future of New Religious Movements.*

Barbara W. Hargrove is Professor of Sociology of Religion at Iliff School of Theology, Denver. She has written on new religious movements, on family and gender, and is the author of the recent text, *The Sociology of Religion.*

Ralph W. Hood, Jr., is Professor of Psychology, University of Tennessee. A member of the Council of the Society for the Scientific Study of Religion, he is a frequent contributor to the journals specializing in religion and psychology.

James Davison Hunter is Assistant Professor of Sociology at the University of Virginia. He is author of *American Evangelicalism: Conservative Religion and the Quandary of Modernity* (1983) and co-author (with Robert Wuthnow et al.) of *Cultural Analysis: The World of Peter L. Berger, Mary Douglas, Michel Foucault and Jurgen Habermas* (1984).

Benton Johnson, Professor of Sociology at the University of Oregon, is a former Editor of the *Journal for the Scientific Study of Religion* and a former President of SSSR. He is a frequent contributor of articles on religion and politics and on the sociopolitical meaning of cultic phenomena.

Bennetta Jules-Rosette is a Professor of Sociology and Chairperson of the Department of Sociology at the University of California, San Diego. Her major research focuses on the new African religions, religion and state control, the sociology of art, urban migration in Africa, and women in development. Since 1979, she has conducted a series of field studies on Zaire, Zambia, the Ivory Coast, and Kenya sponsored by the National Science Foundation, the National Endowment for the Humanities, and the Wenner-Gren Foundation. Her major books include: *African Apostles* (1975), *A Paradigm for Looking* (1977), *The New Religions of Africa* (1979), *Symbols of Change* (1981), and *The Messages of Tourist Art* (1984). She is currently working on a book on the adaptation of new technologies and computerization in Africa.

Meredith B. McGuire is Professor of Sociology at Montclair State College, Upper Montclair, New Jersey. Her books include *Religion: The Social Context* (1981) and *Pentecostal Catholics* (1982), as well as a forthcoming (1985) volume on non-medical healing beliefs and practices among middle-class suburbanites. She has served as President of the Association for the Sociology of Religion and on the Executive Committees of the Society for the Scientific Study of Religion, Association for the Sociology of Religion, Religious Research Association, and Research Committee for Sociology of Religion of the International Sociological Association. Her research interests include alternative healing systems, new religious movements, and social and religious change in rural Ireland.

Edgar W. Mills, in addition to continuing work in the sociology of religion, studies and writes about the sociology of the life course and aging. Lately he has been trying to explain adult development with a dialectical or inconsistency-based theory in which post-childhood development changes emerge from the interaction of dissonant forces of history, biology, role and intention. He also corresponds with others working on similar problems. He is Associate Professor of Sociology at the University of Texas.

Hans Mol is Professor of Religious Studies at McMaster University, Hamilton, Ontario, Canada. He is author of many books dealing with religion and identity, most recently *The Fixed and the Fickle*, *The Firm and the Formless*, and the forthcoming *Faith and Fragility*.

Sister Marie Augusta Neal (Ph.D., Harvard University) is Professor of Sociology, Emmanuel College, Boston, Massachusetts, and author of *A Sociotheology of Letting Go* (1977) and *Catholic Sisters in Transition from the 1960s to the 1980s* (1984). She is past president of the Society for the Scientific Study of Religion and the Association for the Sociology of Religion. She was also Research Associate in Women's Studies in Religion, Harvard Divinity School, 1982–83.

Paul W. Pruyser, Ph.D., is a clinical psychologist, and Henry March Pfeiffer Professor of Research and Education in Psychiatry, the Menninger Foundation, Topeka, Kansas. He is a past President, Society for the Scientific Study of Religion, and the author of *A Dynamic Psychology of Religion* (1968), *Between Belief and Unbelief* (1974), *The Psychological Examination* (1979), and *The Play of the Imagination: Toward a Psychoanalysis of Culture* (1983).

James T. Richardson is Professor of Sociology at the University of Nevada. He has published numerous articles in the area of sociology of religion, particularly studies of new religions. He has authored or edited three books in the area of new religions, including most recently *The Brainwashing/Deprogramming Controversy* (with David Bromley).

Roland Robertson is Professor of Sociology and Religious Studies, Department of Sociology, University of Pittsburgh. His books include *The Sociological Interpretation of Religion, International Systems and the Modernization of Societies, Identity and Authority,* and *Meaning and Change.* Forthcoming are books on Talcott Parsons and on contemporary sociological theory. His research interests include religion and revolution, the global system and religion, and religion and economic structures.

Wade Clark Roof is Professor of Sociology at the University of Massachusetts at Amherst. He served as Executive Secretary for the Society for the Scientific Study of Religion from 1978 to 1983. Currently he is engaged in research on liberal Protestantism in the United States, and is at work on a book on American denominationalism.

Anson Shupe is Associate Professor of Sociology at the University of Texas at Arlington, where in 1982 he received that institution's Outstanding Research Award. He is co-editor of *New Christian Politics,* and the author of a number of books dealing with new religious movements.

Rodney Stark is Professor of Sociology at the University of Washington. Author of many books on religion, Stark is co-author of *The Future of Religion* (1984) and the forthcoming *A Theory of Religion.*

Bryan Wilson is Reader in Sociology, University of Oxford, and Fellow of All Souls College, Oxford. He was Harkness Commonwealth Fund Fellow, 1957–58; Fellow of the American Council of Learned Societies, 1966–67; President of the Conference internationale de Sociologie religieuse, 1971–75; and joint editor, *Annual Review of the Social Sciences of Religion,* 1977–82. His books include *Sects and Society, Religious Sects, Magic and the Millennium, The Noble Savage,* and *Religion in Sociological Perspective.*

Robert Wuthnow is Professor of Sociology at Princeton University and past director of Princeton's Science in Human Affairs Program. He is the author of *The Consciousness Reformation* and *Experimentation in American Religion,* co-author of *Adolescent Prejudice* and *Cultural Analysis,* and editor of *The Religious Dimension* and *The New Christian Right.* He has been an active member of the Society for the Scientific Study of Religion for a number of years and has served on its Executive Council.

Index

Religion · sacred · secular : these are social rather than sociological categories (following Dobb's comments on public/private). As such, what requires explanation is the fact that certain orgs/individuals/actions are labelled religious or based in religion is a social fact. Raises the question: is action/org that is understood as religious by participants (+ observers) in anyway different that action similar except for this self-understanding. This bypasses the definitional morass but perhaps in a productive way — the religious label is occasionally adopted by activists & orgs — why? What difference does it make? It creates certain problems (alienation of secular allies) & and has certain advantages (tax exemption). Those legitimately (by this I mean accepted more or less w/o contention by participants + observers + opponents — not conforming to some "objective" sociological def.) religious orgs — whose religious identity is not at issue — those can still be usefully studied · but what consequences does this collective identity have on action · strategy · organization?

The sociological definition of religious action, then, is action oriented toward values, goals, principles that the participants understand as religious. Religious orgs are those whose collective identity is understood by both insiders and outsiders as religious. "Religion" is an identity that a self-understanding — that is often contended. It is a social fact of some import that this identity is occasionally granted w/o serious contention. There are the orgs & want to study: those for whom the legitimacy of the label is not a serious issue. There are the orgs for which religious identity can be expected to be institutionalized to a degree that, if there are effects, we should see them. No other sociological definition isolates the orgs in the same way.

Arguing about whether X "really is a religious org doesn't get us anywhere. This approach does. Can now ask: how are these orgs different from others (if they are)?

Perhaps is a continuum from orgs whose claims to religious identity are completely uncontested to orgs whose claims to religious identity would be accepted by no-one

This approach is Weberian in 2 senses.
① takes self-understanding as factors in decision
② refrains from a sociological definition other than
that ~~offered~~ which depends on self-understanding.

Perhaps "what is religion" is a question better left
to theologians than to sociologists.

Perhaps sociology of rel. org can be grouped according
to what parts of orgs are studied. Lack of attention to
religious social action ~~and its org~~ maybe due to its perception
as "governed by secular concerns."

Of the greater is ~~there~~ "what is distinctive about rel. orgs?"
can only address it if have rel. v. non-rel. orgs that are
otherwise similar. If define rel. too broadly, ~~then~~
~~orgs not non-religion, if define~~ or it too narrowly, then ~~don't~~
~~have anything to~~ nothing to compare rel. orgs too - in
former case because nothing is outside circle of rel. orgs
except orgs different in too many other way; if in latter case
cause rel. orgs too isolated. ~~the~~ Attempts to draw a circle
around rel. orgs makes it impossible to ~~see~~ study effect
of religion unless ~~there are a the~~ the circle excludes groups
similar to rel. orgs in every other way believed to be
relevant. Both substantive and functional defs of
religion have the feature that nothing outside the circle
will be similar in every relevant way except religion.
(This is too strong.) Problem is that they cross-cut the
social category of religion in controversial ways - substantive
defs exclude groups of rel. self-understanding while functional
defs include groups of secular - even anti-religion - self-
understanding. These impose a sociological abstraction on
a social reality that is uncooperative. This leads to
endless definitional disputes. I propose a soc. def. that
more closely correspond to the
social category. Variation in this
social category could also be studied.

Designer: UC Press Staff
Compositor: Prestige Typography
Printer: Vail-Ballou
Binder: Vail-Ballou
Text: 10/12 Palatino
Display: Palatino